The Rolling Stone Book of Rock Video

The Rolling Stone Book of Rock Video

MICHAEL SHORE

QUILL NEW YORK
A ROLLING STONE PRESS BOOK

Library of Congress Cataloging in Publication Data

Shore, Michael.
   The Rolling stone book of rock video.

   "A Rolling Stone Press book."
   1. Rock music—History and criticism.   2. Television
and music.   I. Rolling stone.   II. Title.
ML3534.S5 1984   784.5′4′009   84-8426
ISBN 0-688-03916-2 (pbk.)

Printed in the United States of America

First Quill Edition

1 2 3 4 5 6 7 8 9 10

BOOK DESIGN BY RICHARD ORIOLO

Song Lyric Credits

"Ashes to Ashes" by David Bowie. Copyright © 1980 Bewlay Bros. and Fleur Music, Ltd.
"Beautiful World" by Mark Mothersbaugh and Gerald Casale. Copyright © 1981 Devo
     Music/Nymph Music, Inc.
"Boob Tube" by Eva Everything. Copyright © 1984 Soundsabound Publishing.
"Der Kommissar" by R. Ponger and Falco. Copyright © 1982 Chappell Music.
"Do You Wanna Hold Me" by Matthew Ashman, Dave Barbarossa, Annabella Lwin,
     Leroy Gorman. Copyright © 1983 April Music.
"Fashion" by David Bowie. Copyright © 1980 Bewlay Bros. Music and Fleur Music, Ltd.
"Freedom of Choice" by Mark Mothersbaugh and Gerald Casale. Copyright © 1980 Devo
     Music/Nymph Music, Inc.
"Girls Just Wanna Have Fun" by Robert Hazard. Copyright © 1983 Heroic Music.
"Hate and War" by Joe Strummer and Mick Jones. Copyright © 1977, 1978, 1979 CBS
     Records.
"Ice Cream for Crow" by Don Van Vliet. Copyright © 1982 Don Van Vliet/Singing Ink
     Music.
"New Frontier" by Donald Fagen. Copyright © 1982 Freejunket Music.
"Once in a Lifetime" by David Byrne, Brian Eno and Talking Heads. Copyright © 1980
     Index Music/Bleu Disque Music.
"Shock the Monkey" by Peter Gabriel. Copyright © 1982 Cliofone Ltd.
"Sound and Vision" by David Bowie. Copyright © 1977 Fleur Music, Ltd. and Jones
     Music America.
"Turning Japanese" by David Fenton. Copyright © 1980 Glenwood Music Corp.

Photo Credits

p. 20. From the United Artists release *The Jazz Singer* copyright 1927 Warner Bros. Pictures Inc., renewed 1955 Warner Bros. Picture Inc.

p. 25. Fischinger Archive.

p. 34. Copyright © 1968 Raybert Productions Inc./BBS. Photo courtesy of the Museum of Modern Art/Film Stills Archive.

p. 38. Epic Records.

p. 42. From the MGM release *Blackboard Jungle.* Copyright © 1955 Loew's Incorporated. Copyright renewed 1983 MGM/UA Entertainment Co. Photo courtesy of the Museum of Modern Art/Film Stills Archive.

p. 45. From the MGM release *Jailhouse Rock.* Copyright © 1957 Loew's Incorporated and Avon Productions Inc. Photo courtesy of the Museum of Modern Art/Film Stills Archive.

p. 47. From the film *Help!* Copyright © 1965. Courtesy of Walter Shenson. Photo courtesy of the Museum of Modern Art/Film Stills Archive.

p. 49. Courtesy of Boyd's Co. and Virgin Films. Photo courtesy of the Museum of Modern Art/Film Stills Archive.

p. 63. Photo courtesy of the Museum of Modern Art/Film Stills Archive.

p. 66. Courtesy Ralph Records/The Cryptic Corp.

p. 70. Photo by Video Transcripts. "Making Plans for Nigel" from the Virgin Records album *Drums and Wires.*

p. 75. Photo by Video Transcripts. "Boys Keep Swinging" from the RCA Records album *Lodger.*

p. 79. Photo by Video Transcripts. "Fade to Gray" from the Polygram Records album *Visage.*

p. 83. Photo by Video Transcripts. "Mickey" from the Chrysalis Records album *Word of Mouth.*

p. 85. Warner-Amex/MTV.

p. 89. Photo by Video Transcripts. "Girls on Film" from the Capitol/Harvest album *Duran Duran.*

p. 96. Photo by Video Transcripts. "Since I Met You, Baby" from the Warner Brothers Records album *The Nashville Seasons.*

p. 100. Photo by Video Transcripts. "Every Breath You Take" from the IRS Records album *Synchronicity.*

p. 102. From the MGM release *Pink Floyd: The Wall.* Copyright © 1982 MGM/UA Entertainment Co. Photo courtesy of the Museum of Modern Art/Film Stills Archive.

p. 107. Photo by Video Transcripts. "Gimme All Your Lovin' " from the Warner Brothers Records album *Eliminator.*

p. 112. Photo by Video Transcripts. "Cum on Feel the Noize" from the Pasha/CBS Associated Records album *Metal Health.*

p. 116. Photo by Video Transcripts. "Pressure" from the CBS Records album *The Nylon Curtain.*

p. 120. Photograph © Robert Ellis. Courtesy JettLag Management.

p. 123. Photo by Video Transcripts. "Shock the Monkey" from the Geffen Records album *Security.*

p. 128. Photo by Video Transcripts. "You Can't Stop Rock 'n' Roll" from the Atlantic Records album *You Can't Stop Rock 'n' Roll.*

p. 132. Photo by Video Transcripts. "Genius of Love" from the Sire Records album *Tom Tom Club.*

p. 139. Photo by Video Transcripts. "Say Say Say" from the CBS Records album *Pipes of Peace.*

p. 151. Rail Roadtrack by Joe Dea. Courtesy Joe Dea/Video Caroline.

p. 155. CBS Records.

ACKNOWLEDGMENTS

I wrote and researched this book myself. But that is not to say that a lot of people didn't give me a lot of invaluable assistance along the way.

I would first like to thank the staff of Rolling Stone Press: Janis Bultman, Elisa Petrini, Larry Wilson, and Carrie Schneider.

I would also like to thank the many record company, television, club, management and production people who gave so generously of their time, energy, and knowledge: Doreen Lauer, Pam Lewis, and Roy Trakin of Warner-Amex/MTV; Cynthia Friedland, Stuart Shapiro, and Geoff Patack of ATI Video/*Night Flight;* John McGhan and Pearl Lieberman of NBC/*Friday Night Videos;* Scott Sassa of WTBS/*Night Tracks;* Cathy Rozell of Atlanta's Video Music Channel; Steve Sukman and Candace Brown of Revolver; Dick Clark and Kari Clark; Bill Gerber and Sharon Barosene of Lookout Management; Karen Schlossberg and Ellen Goldin of the Howard Bloom Agency; Jeffi Powell of JetLag Management; Bob Hart of Picture Music International; Lisa Blewett of A&M Records; Melanie Rogers of Arista Records; Gila Lewis of Atlantic Records; Jill Christiansen of Bearsville Records; Michelle Peacock and Mark Rodriguez of Capitol Records; Gary Lucas of CBS Records; Rhonda Shore of Chrysalis Records; Robin

Sloane of Elektra Records; Clay Baxter of EMI Records; Allasonne Lewis and Bob Currie of EMI Records U.K.; Susan Blond and Vivian Piazza of Epic Records; Betsy Alexander of IRS Records; Ellen Smith and Kris Puskiewicz of Island Records; Len Epand, France Harper, Sherry Ring, and Rhonda Markowitz of Polygram Records and Polygram Music-Video; Homer Flynn of Ralph Records; Barbara Pepe of RCA Records; Ted Cohen, Sally Piper, and Pat Smith of Warner Brothers Records; Robin Walker of MGMM; Siobhan Barron and Simon Fields of Limelight; Marcello Epstein, Don Orlando, Mark Rezyka and Michael Heldman of Pendulum Productions; Gordon Lewis of GLO; Annabelle Jankel and Andy Morahan of Cucumber Studios; John Weaver of Keefco; Lenny Kalikow of *New on the Charts;* Randy Hock of Randy Hock Promotions; Daniel Pearl; Joe Dea; Juanita of Video Caroline; Alan Hecht; Ron Fermanek and James Karnbach; Rob Patterson; Andrew Halmay of Halmay Productions; Mary Quarterone of CIRPA; Eva Everything of Great Shakes Productions; Dr. William Moritz of the Visual Music Alliance; Elfrieda Fischinger of the Fischinger Archive.

For service above and beyond the call of duty, special thanks to Ed Steinberg of RockAmerica; Jo Bergman of Warner Brothers Records; Barry Yuzik and Jerry Katz of Video Transcripts; Laura Foti of *Billboard;* Ken Walz, Dave Wolff, and Cyndi Lauper; and Gerald V. Casale of Devo.

Extra-special thanks to my wife, Susan, and to my parents, Joyce and Lester Shore.

I would also like to thank my editor at William Morrow, Jim Landis; and, at Rolling Stone Press, my editor, Patricia Romanowski, and Sarah Lazin, Jonathan Wells, and Jann S. Wenner.

—MICHAEL SHORE

CONTENTS

To my father,
Lester Shore

The Rolling Stone Book of Rock Video

INTRODUCTION

The rock-video revolution is fully upon us. Rock videos (also known as promo clips, pop promos, music video, or picture music), those eye-catching, three- to four-minute filmlets that accompany rock—and other—songs, are everywhere. And they're changing the way music is made, perceived, marketed, and consumed.

Between national and local broadcasts, cable, syndicated, UHF, and low-power TV, there are some five hundred outlets around the country playing rock videos. Warner-Amex's twenty-four-hour cable network, MTV—Music Television—a nationwide visual radio station, has over eighteen million viewers. Add up all the potential viewers for all TV's rock-video outlets, and a band with a video clip can conceivably gain instant exposure to more than a hundred million potential record buyers and concertgoers. In addition to TV, there are over three hundred clubs with video installations and hundreds of college campuses showing rock videos. Soon, every place that has a jukebox will have a video jukebox.

Nowhere has the power of rock video been so apparent as in the record industry. There are dozens of top bands, including Duran Duran, Men at Work, the Stray Cats, Quiet Riot, and Def Leppard, whose enormous success, measured in multimillion-selling albums and sold-out tours, is the result in large part of video exposure. In a soft economy—and hot on the heels of a record-sales slump in the late seventies—record companies are pouring hundreds of thousands of dollars a month, millions per year, into the production and distribution of rock videos. And in 1983, record sales increased dramatically. Everyone gave the credit to rock video. As former Arista Records Vice-President of Marketing Randy Hock put it, "Rock video is the silver bullet that knocked the doldrums out of the record industry." Next, rock video evolved from a promotional device to a bona fide consumer item with Sony's Video 45s, compilations of two or three video clips that retailed for under twenty dollars.

During all this, the media were giving rock video a very close examination. At first, the industry and the public were skeptical. After all, people had been listening to rock video for over thirty years; it was the sound that mattered most. Besides, the common wisdom suggested, one could listen to a record played countless times, but watch it over and over? As recently as 1980, the very idea of someone watching rock video was still considered a somewhat bizarre concept. Then came video-equipped clubs, and people began to see things they had never seen before. There were also scattered TV outlets. But then, in 1981, came MTV, followed quickly by a deluge of press.

By 1982 it seemed hard to imagine the world without rock video. That January, *Time* magazine's "Best of '82" for television gushed, "MTV's imaginative use of video tapes illustrating rock recordings expands TV's generally unadventurous vocabulary." A few weeks later, the *New York Times* sampled MTV and concluded, "Television has never had this impact before, and television will never be the same again." (Thus echoing MTV's own slogan, "You may never look at music the same way again.") By August, it was impossible to open a copy of a major magazine or a metropolitan daily that did not contain a spread on MTV or rock video.

In September 1983, the science-fiction comics magazine *Heavy Metal* named the winners of its first annual "Clips" awards for rock videos, and the music trade *Billboard* announced that in November it would give *its* first annual video-music awards. In August, *Film Comment* devoted a seventeen-page midsection to rock video, and *Billboard* carried a thirty-page salute to MTV on its second anniversary. The section was full of positive testimonials to the revolutionary power of MTV in exposing and selling music and musicians.

Then there was mainstream network TV. In April 1983, Johnny

Carson incorporated an MTV joke in his opening monologue: "In Southern California, they kind of update the school math books. For example, it says, 'Sally's mother gets five hundred dollars a week in alimony, but spends two hundred dollars a week on an analyst. Will there be enough money for Sally to get her MTV?'" Rock video was suddenly a part of everyday American life.

In June, the first annual American Video Awards were broadcast. The host was veteran AM radio DJ Casey Casem, whose half-hour weekly broadcast, *American Top Ten,* was the first American TV show —in 1979—to regularly play rock videos. Its AVA nominees, in pop, soul, and country categories, were limited to video clips for songs that had made the *Billboard* Top Ten, and the program was only syndicated to scattered areas around the country. But it was a start. Casem opened the program with a speech in which he described rock video as "the most exciting new art form in the world today."

Later that month, anchor man Ted Koppel opened ABC-TV's late-night news program *Nightline*'s rock-video report thus: "It has done wonders for a sagging record industry. It has made overnight stars of rock groups whose records had been gathering dust. It uses some of the most creative visual and editing techniques seen on television. Yet, if you don't have cable TV, you may not have even seen it yet—musical video tapes, with popular and frequently not-yet-popular songs set to slick, sometimes bizarre, choreography. It's a bonanza for singers, dancers, musicians, and the record industry." Then, by July, you didn't necessarily need to have cable to see rock video, as NBC-TV's *Friday Night Videos* hit the air.

In July, the syndicated *Wall Street Journal Report* joined in: "Rock video, as in MTV, is largely responsible for the recent recovery of the record business. CBS Records reports that MTV exposure of Michael Jackson's "Beat It" and "Billie Jean" video clips helped sell eight million copies of . . . *Thriller.* . . . CBS also reports that its second-quarter profits for 1983 are up a staggering one hundred and one percent over figures for this time last year." By December 1983, *Thriller* had sold more copies than any other record in Columbia's history.

In September, MTV was running a local New York commercial for a music-video production house, with a pretty blond sexily cooing, "When you make a music video, make it right—because you're investing in *your future* [emphasis added]." That same month, soap-opera star Darnell Williams was a guest VJ—video disc jockey—on *N.Y. Hot Tracks,* WABC-TV's showcase for black-music video clips. Asked by host VJ Carlos de Jesus to introduce the video for Billy Joel's "Tell Her about It," Williams raved, "Yeah, man, it's a hot song—I saw it the other day. . . ."

Meanwhile, the motion-picture industry, from which rock videos plundered much of their style and technique, was aping rock videos and their non-narrative cut-to-the-beat montages. The runaway box-office smash *Flashdance* was the paramount example. And while rock-video directors like Russell Mulcahy, Steve Barron, and Brian Grant were landing feature film deals, experienced motion-picture directors were turning around and making rock videos: Tobe Hooper (*Texas Chainsaw Massacre, Poltergeist*) directed Billy Idol's "Dancing with Myself" video, and John Landis (*Animal House, An American Werewolf in London, Trading Places*) directed Michael Jackson's thirteen-minute "Thriller" clip on a budget of roughly $1 million. And, finally, the TV commercials from which rock videos also borrowed were looking more and more like rock videos.

Take a few moments to digest all that. Then consider this. ABC's *Nightline* closed its rock-video report with veteran TV newsman Hughes Rudd on location at a video-game arcade where a prototype video jukebox was installed. Before the video jukebox, which Rudd described as "Where it's at, heaven help us," danced a few dozen happy teens and preteens. Rudd stuck his microphone in the face of one dancing, prepubescent girl to ask what all the fuss was about.

"You have to have the video to have fun," giggled the girl.

"But," complained Rudd, "my generation never needed video to be able to dance to a jukebox."

"Well," the girl blithely replied, "this is the eighties, not the forties, and we're havin' video!"

Now consider what modern classical composer Carlos Chavez once said: "Any advance in science and technology produces a corresponding change in music and the arts."

It's the eighties, and we're having the video, and it is surely wreaking profound changes in the music and in other arts as well. But how? Why? Where did it all come from? And where is it all going? These are some of the questions this book will try to answer, from the points of view of musicians, rock-video directors and producers, consumers, and the music and television industry executives. Much was revealed in the media blitz of 1983, but not the whole story.

Rock Video History, Part I

TEST PATTERNS—TV

To discuss the history of rock video, one must take into account the history of music-visual combinations. It's a long one, with roots stretching at least as far back as opera and musical theater, and is the subject of dozens of other tomes.

The history of modern-era matings of music with technological entertainment media begins in *fin-de-siècle* France, where music was first played from 1895 onward as accompaniment to the earliest silent films of the Lumière Brothers and Georges Méliès. Soon after, movie companies released cue sheets classifying popular tunes like "O Sole Mio" and "Ragtime Cowboy Joe" according to appropriate dramatic situations. In 1915, the first feature film for which music was specifically composed, D. W. Griffith's epochal *The Birth of a Nation,* premièred on Broadway, complete with a full orchestra and a crew of special effects personnel behind the screen. One of the earliest talkies, *The Jazz Singer,* starred Al Jolson and was the first movie to have music and singing as well as sound. A few years later, film technology advanced to the point that the soundtracks for films were added to the celluloid filmstrips themselves. Highly sophisticated Hollywood movie musicals followed.

But what we're concerned with here are rock visuals, and specifically,

Al Jolson inaugurates the new era of musical-visual synergy in the "first talkie"—actually a silent movie with sound for some musical sequences—*The Jazz Singer* (1927).

rock visuals on television. Remember, video is really just a fancy term for television.

Rock videos as we now know them represent a break with the long history of music and visuals. Generally speaking, until recently, music for opera, musical theater, movie musicals, and film soundtracks, was created *after,* or at best concurrently with, the story and visuals. It was not until rock "concept" videos came along that the story and visuals were created after, and as a complement to, the music. There were, however, a few exceptions.

First there was Oskar Fischinger, a remarkable pioneer who, in 1921 in his native Germany, began making animated abstract films that were tightly synchronized to jazz and classical music. In the mid-twenties, many of Fischinger's films played European, Japanese, and American theaters. Fischinger's protean work—which was not music video, but musical films; let's call it "visual music"—was promotional shorts, as each film was shown to advertise the record to which it was synchronized. By 1933, Fischinger was making his first color films. In 1936, he gained so much popular and critical acclaim that Paramount brought him over to Hollywood; in 1938, he went to work for Disney and contributed the outstanding animation to the opening sequence of the 1940 Disney masterpiece *Fantasia* (a pioneering example of visual-music synergy itself). Eventually, though, due to language problems and Fischinger's own decidedly independent temperament, he ended up getting fewer and fewer jobs; his last years (he died in 1967, just months before his sixty-seventh birthday) saw him vainly pursuing such never realized projects as three-dimensional films and the Lumigraph, a color-organ light-show instrument he invented but could never get distributed.

One really has to see Fischinger's 1934 shorts like *Composition in Blue* to appreciate just how ahead of his time he really was. His use of rhythmic patterns of abstract geometric forms and color swirls still dazzles, and has been eclipsed only in terms of high budgets and high technology by latter-day computer-graphic animation. At times, Fischinger went beyond abstract animation, as in the 1935 promotional short entitled "Muratti Gets into the Act," where to the tune of Bayer's "Doll Fairy," row upon row of pixilated (real, three-dimensional figures animated through stop-action photography) Muratti cigarettes march, dance, and figure skate in formation, all of it shot from dramatic low-frontal and high-overhead angles.

Disney's *Fantasia* is a similar exception to the music-and-visuals rule. As in Fischinger's work, the animation was created after and synchronized with preexisting music, in this case, well-known classical pieces. After seeing Fischinger's work, it seems clear that his contribution to *Fantasia* came in the film's most effective and least-cloying sequence—the opening abstract waves, notes, and staffs sailing through space to Bach's "Toccata and Fugue."

In the late forties, the first visual jukebox, the Panoram Soundie, was introduced. It stood taller than regular jukeboxes, had a diagonal screen on top that measured approximately twenty-inches, used a rear-projection film system, weighed about two tons, and played a song (and its accompanying black-and-white filmlet) or two for some change. Panoram Soundies were installed in bars, restaurants, and other locations where one would expect to find a jukebox. For reasons that are now unclear—the early years of music visuals are very poorly documented —the Panoram Soundie enjoyed but a brief vogue until the early fifties, when it was taken out of circulation and quickly forgotten.

One of the few people who knows anything about the Panoram Soundie, and about the early years of music visuals and rock video, is film and video archivist Ron Fermanek. "For a while," says Fermanek, "*everyone* made 'soundies.' White singers and black singers, pop and jazz, even some rhythm & blues performers. In addition to being shown on the Panoram machine, soundies were also used as trailers for feature films, along with cartoons, newsreels, and coming attractions. Some of the soundies were actually just excerpted from movie musicals. Most of them were pretty obvious and corny, like Bing Crosby singing while strolling through a park or along a beach, or the Andrews Sisters singing 'Don't Sit under the Apple Tree,' set, of course, under an apple tree. They used some primitive special effects at times, too—say, super-imposing dancing feet over a big band horn section."

So why did the Panoram Soundie die out? "It's hard to say," says Fermanek, "but it was probably just too far ahead of its time and too unwieldy." The music and film industries probably weren't really ready to devote the proper attention to adequately servicing it with program-ming. Maybe the screen itself was too small. At any rate, the final blow to the Soundies' potential popularity came with the concurrent intro-duction, and far faster spreading popularity, of home television sets. Greater convenience won out, as it usually does.

At any rate, Fermanek's descriptions of typical soundies reveal that much of the subsequent pattern of music-visual conceptualization was already set: take a popular performer with a popular song, and place them in a setting either literally suggested by the song's lyrics or one that mirrored the escapist pleasantries common to movie musicals. With but a few exceptions, this would be the basic formula for rock visuals, and music visuals in general, until recently.

Concurrent with the Panoram Soundie, there came broadcast televi-sion. From the very beginning, popular music was a staple of television, mainly in variety shows based on tried-and-true vaudeville and radio formats. Nearly without exception, television has always presented singers and bands straightforwardly performing, no doubt a direct holdover from the format of radio shows on which many early televi-sion programs were based. At best, the setting might be a fanciful theatrical set. Occasionally, a performer was too busy to actually appear on the show in person, and—provided the performer had sufficient stature—he would make a film or video tape that was presented on the show instead. Invariably these were in the soundie mold of light, sweet, movie-musical-style fantasy evocations; occasionally, where appropriate, a touch of cute comedy would be added. Speaking of comedy, the only person in those days to stretch the bounds of TV visuals the way rock videos do today was the anarchic comic visionary Ernie Kovacs.

Among the better-known popular music shows in TV's golden age were: *Paul Whiteman's TV Teen Club* (1949–1954), *Face the Music* (1948–1949), *Your Hit Parade* (1950–1959), *The Peter Potter Show* (1953–1954), *Upbeat* (1955), and *The Big Record* (1957–1958). *Upbeat* and *Face the Music* both ran a mere fifteen minutes and presented their own in-house singers doing renditions of the day's hits, a format that would be most successfully exploited by the long-running *Your Hit Parade.* The very presence of someone like Paul Whiteman as host of a show with a name like *Teen Club* was indicative of broadcast TV's attempts to domesticate wild adolescent impulses; Whiteman was by then an elderly gent who, in his glory years in the Roaring Twenties, was the leader of the biggest, plushest middle-of-the-road swing band in the land.

The Big Record was the first such show to start in the wake of the rock & roll explosion; yet mainstream star Patti Page ("The Singin' Rage," as she was known) was its host, and it generally featured only the tamest, adult-groomed-and-approved teen idols as nods to the rock audience. In 1959 NBC made an abortive stab at prime-time pop-rock programming with *The Music Shop,* with mainstream orchestral arranger Buddy Bregman (who, again, had nothing whatsoever to do with rock & roll) as host. Its première episode featured such bona fide rock acts as rockabilly stars the Collins Kids, Latin rocker Ritchie Valens, the Champs, and the Teddy Bears (who included the eighteen-year-old Phil Spector). But the show constantly offset its rock talent with Hollywood luminaries like George Burns, Jim Backus, and Steve Allen, and before the show's two-month run was over, it had veered even closer to the middle of the road.

For the most part, music on television has remained steadfastly in the video-musical-theater groove, straightforward unselfconscious entertainment. In fact, the early days, when everything was live, are still considered television's golden era. Certainly live performances—even when broadcast over television—have an immediacy and spontaneity impossible to capture on film. It wasn't until later that lip-synching—

whereby a singer mimes the lyrics of his song to the record—became the standard. Miming to a prerecorded and preperfected backing track ensured that the singer on TV would sound exactly as he or she did on records, and in live situations, for better or worse, many rock performers couldn't have matched the sound of their recorded performances if their lives depended on it. While most rock-on-TV shows have relied as much on lip-synching as traditional TV-variety shows, the only TV music programs to rely consistently on *live* rather than lip-synced performance have been concert shows (e.g., *Don Kirshner's Rock Concert* in the mid-seventies, PBS's *Soundstage,* and the more recent *Rock & Roll Tonight*). And that's only fitting: rock was and is supposed to be a revolt against the kind of establishment conventions lip-synching represents. Rock is supposed to violate the staid, predictable decorum lip-synching emblematizes. Of course, that's an idealistic view that only occasionally holds up in the face of show-biz realities. But that's something that's been almost completely forgotten as rock has evolved through the years from a genuinely revolutionary force to an established entertainment institution.

Still, when rock & roll first exploded in 1954—a few years after the introduction of television and the passing of the Panoram Soundie—it presented some big problems to the establishment authorities, in the entertainment world as elsewhere. Rock & roll was for the most part considered dangerous and undesirable—yet it was *popular.* With money to be made, the movie and television industries faced two options: either present rock & roll straightforwardly or exploit it and tame it with show-biz convention.

The first big nova in the rock & roll explosion was, of course, Elvis Presley. In 1956, the year he broke it all wide open, there was, in a sense, the birth of rock video. Elvis's crucial appearances on the Dorsey Brothers' *Stage Show,* and Milton Berle's, Steve Allen's and Ed Sullivan's variety shows were early examples of the impact of rock music with visuals. These were, for the most part, straight live performances rather than tricked-up concept pieces. And by this time, Presley's records had been country & western and R&B hits. In 1956 alone, Presley had five number-one records: "Heartbreak Hotel," "I Want You, I Need You, I Love You," "Don't Be Cruel," "Hound Dog," and "Love Me Tender" (the title theme from his first movie). Certainly Presley was a star, and his TV spots fulfilled much the same purpose that rock videos do now: they gave millions of people—most of whom would never have gone to see him live—an opportunity, in a few fell swoops, to experience the sight as well as the sound of Elvis. These appearances

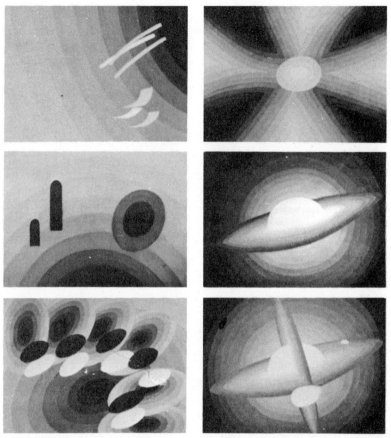

Excerpts from a dance of geometric patterns typical of the pioneering visual-music work of innovative German filmmaker Oskar Fischinger

not only served as a great promotion for Elvis's career (not to mention the ratings of the programs on which he appeared), but also provided fodder for the legions of critics who turned Presley's very existence into an ongoing public debate. In this way, television was as much a part of early rock as the electric guitar, the pompadour or swiveling hips. Conceptualization in the form of condescension marked Elvis's July 1956 appearance on Steve Allen's show. Allen, long a critic of rock & roll culture, had Elvis—in white tie and tails—sing "Hound Dog" to a basset hound seated on a pedestal.

Ironically, that old middle-of-the-road standby *Your Hit Parade* was a pathfinder in the conceptualization of music video. The weekly show had its own cast of wholesome-looking singers who performed renditions of current hits. Frequently, little dramas and set pieces were worked up to complement the songs and provide added visual diversion. One eye-opening example was shown in kinescope form on a summer 1983 installment of ABC's *20/20* that covered rock video. "It's an idea whose time has come," intoned host-anchor Hugh Downs about rock video, "but like all good ideas, it isn't exactly new." Well put, for there onscreen was *Your Hit Parade*'s "concept video" for the Rays' 1957 doo-wop hit "Silhouettes" (later a 1965 hit for Herman's Hermits). A man and woman sat on a couch in what appeared to be a suburban living room; on a table next to the couch was a lamp. *Your Hit Parade*'s string-laden version of the song came up, and suddenly the face of the show's own Gisele MacKenzie, who sang the song, appeared superimposed on the lampshade. In a delightfully naturalistic comic touch, the man abruptly rose from the couch in apparent disbelief at the proceedings, before his companion gently tugged him back to the couch; then the two seated figures became silhouettes, as did MacKenzie's face on the lampshade, while the seated figures watched MacKenzie's performance.

These days that may seem rather quaint. Not so. While most rock visualizations of that day *were* naive—matching the tone of the times and the spirit of the music—in many ways today's rock videos have not come all that far from "Silhouettes." Here was a playful use of visuals as a literal complement to the song's lyrics, a fragment of dramatic narrative actually based on the song's lyrics, and, in a matter of seconds, a complex set of allusions involving silhouettes and actors in the scene (performers, if you will) *watching* another performance in the overall performance. Every one of these ideas has been used over and over in even the newest rock videos. Two examples of the performance-within-the-performance concept are Roxy Music's "More than This" (1982), in which Bryan Ferry croons before a movie screen showing his image (a similar image graces the back cover of Ferry's 1979 solo LP *The Bride Stripped Bare*), and the Rolling Stones' version of Smokey Robinson and the Miracles' "Going to a Go-Go" (1982), in which Mick Jagger is seen entering an orgiastic house party where he sees himself performing on TV. The same approach is used with humorous results in Krokus's "Screaming in the Night" (1983). All that has really changed since the early days is the level of sophistication, the tone and content of the imagery, and the budgets.

By the early fifties, television had another, slightly more subtle form of adult-sanctioned rock music, *American Bandstand,* debuted locally as *Bandstand* in Philadelphia on WFIL in 1952 as a youth-oriented variant of *Your Hit Parade*. In 1956, Dick Clark became the show's host, and in 1957, ABC picked it up. It is one of the longest-running programs in television history, and, along with Clark, has become an American institution. (Indeed, in 1981, Clark donated the original podium he used on the show to the Smithsonian Institution.) The show's format has hardly varied in over thirty years: a studio full of youths dance to and rate the records of the day's most popular performers, while two performers per show appear to lip-synch their hits. Thanks in large part to Clark's smooth, friendly presence, *American Bandstand* made rock & roll safe for America, and instantly became a wildly popular show. It may never have been much of an example of rock video as we now think of rock video, but as a seminal instance of rock and television coming together to spawn an important cultural phenomenon, *American Bandstand* is virtually unrivaled, even by MTV (after all, let's wait and see if MTV lasts thirty-five years unchanged). Ironically enough, however, *Bandstand* had begun as a "music video" show of sorts in 1952, with original host Bob Horn hosting a series of "Snaders"—straightforward, made-for-TV musical shorts in the vein of the Soundies from the film library of one George Snader. As Dick Clark recalls, "The 'Snaders' were considered a bore, certain death, so within a few weeks, they changed the show to something that seemed much more interesting—having real live kids in the studio dancing to the latest pop hits."

American Bandstand has since inspired many programs with the same format—with such disc jockeys as Clay Cole and Lloyd Thaxton as hosts—but while some of them were actually far more exciting and off-the-wall than *Bandstand,* only *Bandstand* has survived. Of late, there have been more *Bandstand* variants, like the new-wave-oriented *MV3,* based in Los Angeles and now widely syndicated; it makes greater use of in-studio lip-synchs and rock videos. More on it later.

As the fifties became the sixties and rock & roll's first golden age drew to a close, the French introduced the Scopitone. It weighed about half a ton, used sixteen-millimeter rear-projection films projected onto a top-mounted twenty-inch screen, and contained well over two hundred moving parts. The biggest differences between the Scopitones and the Panoram Soundies were, in Ron Fermanek's words, "The Scopitone films were in glorious Technicolor, they were more conceptually ambitious, and they usually featured French or European pop stars, like Johnny Halliday and Sylvie Vartan. About the only British or American singers who made Scopitones were the ones big enough to sell internationally. Petula Clark made some. Dionne Warwick made one

for 'Walk on By' that started with her lip-synching while walking down
the street, then shifted to her singing while lying in bed. The best one
I ever saw was for Neil Sedaka's 'Calendar Girl.' It was surprisingly
elaborate for its day: for every month of the year, the scene changed,
and Sedaka was in a different suit. For instance, for July there was a
night-sky backdrop with fireworks going off. And there were a dozen
calendar girls . . ."

Since the Scopitone and the bulk of the performers it showcased were
European, most Scopitone films were made in Europe, especially in
France. Such future filmmakers as Claude Lelouch (director of *A Man
and a Woman, Cat and Mouse,* and other French romantic comedies)
honed their styles by churning out gaudy, action-packed Scopitone
"minimovies"—in much the same way that today's rock-video scene
has proved a spawning ground for a new generation of feature-film
directors. But the Scopitone never caught on in the United States
because of its unwieldiness and the cost of supplying it with programming.

Back in America, imaginative rock or pop conceptualizations were
still sporadic, and generally more naive and understated than Scopitone's frequently overdone spectaculars. One such came in 1963 on a
TV special called *It's Happening, Baby!,* whose host was New York DJ
and "Fifth Beatle" Murray "the K" Kaufman. The show featured
numerous quick snippets of big-name rock and pop acts crooning their
hits in various New York City street locales. For instance, the Ronettes
sang their classic "Be My Baby" to a blithely unconcerned, hot-dog
munching young man whom they trailed down Fifth Avenue. A guy
ignoring the lovely Ronettes, pleadingly cooing "Be my baby," in favor
of a hot dog? Talk about an incredible concept!

Rock & roll and youth-oriented pop music were making headway on
television in an even more peculiar fashion. Teen-aged characters in
prime-time family series were having hits with songs that gained their
primary exposure from the stars' TV shows: Shelley Fabares and Paul
Petersen of *The Donna Reed Show* had, respectively, "Johnny Angel"
and "My Dad" and Patty Duke of *The Patty Duke Show* (which also
sported one of the more memorable theme songs of the day) had
"Please Don't Just Stand There."

In early 1964, rock was ready to enter another golden era with the
British Invasion. Once again, as in 1956, history repeated itself, and a
TV variety show documented and magnified it all with a straight in-
studio live performance. The program was *The Ed Sullivan Show,* and
the performers were the Beatles. It is entirely possible that none of the

many, many acts Sullivan showcased on his long-running variety show proved more memorable to several generations of TV viewers than the Fab Four. Certainly no one who saw the Beatles on Sullivan's show has forgotten the experience, and indeed, countless latter-day rock stars cited that experience as an inspiration for their ambitions.

At roughly the same time that Sullivan was virtually creating, as well as intensifying, Beatlemania in America, Britain had already gotten its own rock TV shows off the ground. As of the late fifties, Britain had had its own answers to *American Bandstand* (*Juke Box Jury*) and *Your Hit Parade* (*Top of the Pops,* which based its programming on whatever songs happened to be in the Top Thirty of Britain's ever-changing pop charts, restricted its performances to staid in-studio lip-synchs with backing from a house orchestra). But in the summer of 1963, with Merseybeat fever running high in Liverpool and London, a young British producer named Jack Good formulated the idea for an alternative rock TV showcase for Britain's rapidly expanding population of rock fans. On Friday, August 9, 1963, his creation, *Ready Steady Go!*, debuted on the BBC. Though rather quaint by today's standards, *RSG!* was far wilder and woollier than *TOTP,* and the acts it featured were nearly always up-and-coming young rockers who usually performed live, without lip-synchs.

It took about a year for American television to catch up. In the wake of the Beatles' spectacular showing on *Sullivan,* Jack Good approached all three U.S. networks with an idea for a *Ready Steady Go!* spin-off. Finally ABC struck a deal with him to produce a half-hour, prime-time, black-and-white pop-rock show. *Shindig!*—the name came from a slang term for a harmlessly high-spirited teen party—debuted on September 16, 1964, and featured Sam Cooke, the Everly Brothers, and regulars Bobby Sherman and the Righteous Brothers. *Shindig!* was a happy, hoppy medium between the old variety-show straight-performance approach and *American Bandstand*'s house-party atmosphere: a steady stream of British and American rockers lip-synched their hits, amid a slightly stylized, multilevel rec-room-style set. *Shindig!* was looser and higher in energy than *Bandstand,* and its host, West Coast DJ Jimmy O'Neill, at least looked and acted younger and hipper than Dick Clark. Jack Good himself became a familiar figure to viewers of the show through frequent Hitchcockian signature appearances in his trademark dark topcoat and black derby.

Working on *Shindig!* were two people who would go on to become seminal rock-video *auteurs* in the late seventies and early eighties. With him from Britain, Jack Good brought David Mallet as *Shindig!* director. Mallet, then in his early twenties, had already worked as assistant director on *Juke Box Jury* and *Top of the Pops,* to which he would return as director after *Shindig!* He would also go on to collaborate on all of David Bowie's rock videos and direct scores of others for a wide variety of performers. And assisting *Shindig!* choreographer David Winter was seventeen-year-old Antonia Christina Basilotta, who—after further work on the great mid-sixties rock-performance film *The T.A.M.I. Show,* a supporting role in the film *Five Easy Pieces,* and choreographing David Bowie's extravagant 1974 *Diamond Dogs* tour—found fame as recording artist Toni Basil. She would also become the first rock performer to sign a recording contract as a music *and visuals* artist, and in 1981 and 1982 would become one of the first and best examples of an artist whose hit (in this case "Mickey") became a chart-topper almost entirely because of video exposure.

Shindig! was so great a success that by the end of the year, ABC extended it to one hour and for a while ran it twice a week. In January 1965, NBC responded with its own hour-long, full-color *Hullabaloo* (from an antiquated slang term for disturbing the peace), the brainchild of Lester Gottlieb, who produced the ABC weekly variety show *The Hollywood Palace.* Despite the implications of the show's title and the presence of a bevy of go-go girls frugging and twisting with abandon in suspended cages over a predominately bright stylized pop art set, *Hullabaloo* was actually far more sedate and family oriented than its competitor, as middle-of-the-road guest hosts like Sammy Davis, Jr., and Jack Jones confirm. *Hullabaloo* also kept its fan-hysteria level beneath that of *Shindig!* by limiting the number of teenagers allowed into the studio audience.

Still, *Hullabaloo* represented a distinct advance over *Shindig!* in terms of conceptualizing its in-studio lip-synchs. For instance, the Beatles performed "Day Tripper" in a mock railroad car (no doubt a reminder of some scenes in *A Hard Day's Night*). Even better, a band called the Astronauts mimed their version of "Roll Over Beethoven" amid plaster busts of classical composers, potted palms, and a string quartet composed of mod-attired fashion models!

With three much-seen shows on the air in the U.S. (oh yes, there was also the Saturday morning Beatles cartoon series) and the U.K., and with rock bands touring more than ever, bands began making promotional films to be sent to the TV shows whenever they were too busy or too far from the studio to make a personal appearance. American TV, more rooted in the straight performance idea, rarely, if ever, showed them. British and European rock shows did.

"It seems like 1965 or 1966 were the years when promo films really started being made in significant numbers," says Fermanek. "A lot more bands, both British and American, made them than most people think. It's just that Americans never saw them. This whole era is totally undocumented. Nobody knows who directed these things, how much they cost, how long they took to shoot. You can only make an educated guess, based on how they look and on how schedules and budgets still run for rock videos these days, that they were shot very quickly and on shoestring budgets."

Jo Bergman, current vice-president for video at Warner Brothers Records, where she started their video department in 1977, worked as a publicist with the Beatles from 1963 to 1965, and with the Rolling Stones from 1965 to 1969. She recalls, "Making promo films was no big deal. The bands just did them as they came along. They were fun, a novelty. The Beatles would rent out Shepperton or Pinewood Studios in London for a day and slap something together. In most cases, nobody knows who directed them—but then, a lot of them are hardly what you'd call 'directed' anyway.

"I remember the Beatles made some for 'We Can Work It Out' and 'Paperback Writer' that looked very Richard Lester-ish—lots of kooky, sped-up action and crazy-cut scenes. The Stones made some interesting ones, too, some of them directed by Michael Lindsay-Hogg, who also directed *Ready Steady Go!* (and who would go on to direct the Beatles' documentary *Let It Be* as well as numerous TV rock concerts).

"The Stones did one for 'Have You Seen Your Mother Baby, Standing in the Shadow?' that caused a bit of a stir, because it included footage taken from that photo session they did for that song's single sleeve, where they dressed in women's drag. But the rest of it was straight performance. They did one later for 'Jumping Jack Flash' that was performance mixed with shots of Mick Jagger putting on makeup. They did some *very* strange films with Lindsay-Hogg for the album *Their Satanic Majesties Request.* There was one that was known as 'Charlie Is My Darling'—referring to Charlie Watts, of course—but it was really 'We Love You' with a trial-of-Oscar-Wilde scenario; Marianne Faithfull was in it. [Jagger was Wilde and Richards the Marquis of Queensbury.] And there was one for 'Child of the Moon,' which had the band as highway brigands, with a little girl, a teen-aged girl, and an old lady coming across them. That was a really weird one; I don't know what was on Michael Lindsay-Hogg's mind the day they shot that one."

Here we can already see the roots of current rock-video productions:

a young but experienced TV director, playing off a band's well-known visual image—in this case the Stones' legendary outrageous bad-boy reputation, and the sexual androgyny in which they were dabbling at the time—and coming up with something serviceable, quickly and cheaply.

Other examples of early rock videos from this era that stand up remarkably well in comparison with today's more expensive and ambitious conceptual rock videos include:

The Kinks' "Dead End Street" (circa 1966): importantly, the band is *never* seen playing instruments here, and only bothers to lip-sync the shouts of "Hey!" on the choruses. The clip is a black-humored scenario that literally complements *and* imaginatively and dramatically fleshes out the song's sardonic working-class-desperation lyrics. In it, the band members are undertakers, attired in long coats and stovepipe hats, wheeling a coffin through London's most Dickensian streets. Either lead singer Ray Davies, or his brother, guitarist Dave Davies (it's hard to tell who, since the scenes flash by so quickly and the two brothers look so much alike), dons housewife's drag to play the widow into whose home the coffin is wheeled. It all winds up with a morbid slapstick finale: the band members are sitting dejectedly atop the closed coffin in a bleak alleyway when suddenly, the "dead" man opens the coffin lid from within, dislodging the Kinks. The man runs away, and the Kinks give chase, Keystone Kops-style. Nobody knows who directed this one, but it's fitting that one of the best early rock videos was done by the Kinks, who have recently maintained a consistently high level of quality in their rock videos. Kinks singer/songwriter Ray Davies would go on to score the film *Virgin Soldiers* in 1967, and the BBC-TV special *Arthur (or the Decline and Fall of the British Empire)* (the soundtrack later successfully released as a Kinks album in 1969), further solidifying his status as a pioneer music-visual artist.

The Who's "Happy Jack" (circa 1966): Not only do the band members never play guitars, they never once lip-sync, either. Instead, they play bumbling burglars trying to break a safe, in a Chaplinesque silent-film-style caper. Again, nobody seems to know who directed this, and that's a shame, because the Who look very comfortable indeed on camera, and the clip moves along smartly. It is included in *The Kids Are Alright,* as is a later clip for "Call Me Lightning." In the latter, the Who's Pete Townshend, Roger Daltrey, and John Entwistle find a huge, Union Jack-covered box lurching around an abandoned lot and then discover that the box contains maniacal Who drummer Keith Moon, who wears a homemade space helmet on his head. For some reason, the film's soundtrack is dubbed over with the Who instrumental "Cobwebs and Strange."

However, promo production dropped off following the cancellation of these main outlets (*Shindig!* in January 1966, *Hullabaloo* in August 1966, and *Ready Steady Go!* in December 1966). Up until then, of course, promos followed in the tried-and-true funny-antics vein, or in the equally time-honored setting of the performer in a park, on a beach, wherever.

But before the demise of *Shindig!* and *Hullabaloo,* two other shows came on American TV that somewhat picked up the rock-video slack. Dick Clark's daytime afternoon show, *Where the Action Is,* which debuted in July 1965 and ran through April 1967, took *American Bandstand* outdoors and on location around the country. It pioneered the use of exotic locations shoots for performance settings, though often that amounted to little more than, say, the Turtles performing "Happy Together" on a beach surrounded by bikini-clad go-go girls in scuba gear, or Paul Revere and the Raiders dressed as cavemen to perform "Alley Oop." A year or two before, the mammothly successful Clark had gotten his own eponymous *Saturday Night Show* on the ABC network, and though the show was basically a live, onstage cavalcade of stars, it occasionally used modest set pieces to dramatize tunes—such as having the members of the Royal Teens, for their hit "Short Shorts," follow and "sing" (they were, of course, lip-synching) to a girl in short shorts slinking up the balcony stairs of the theater where the show was shot. Before long, *Where the Action Is* was being imitated, and expanded upon, by *Malibu U.,* which was most interesting for placing rock performances in a teen-fantasy context—a fun "school" (an idea pioneered earlier by *American Bandstand* rival Lloyd Thaxton's *Discotech*) in the form of a California beach perpetually populated by even more bikini-clad go-go girls (the "Malibeauties"). (The theme-song lyrics claimed, "You could earn a degree riding surfboards.") The "dean" (read host) of *Malibu U.* was none other than Ricky Nelson, who in 1957 had become a teen singing idol partially because of exposure on his parent's family TV series *The Adventures of Ozzie and Harriet.*

Then there was *The Monkees,* a half-hour weekly rock sitcom that debuted on NBC in September 1966. Despite its standing as a blatant, prefabricated capitalization on the Beatles and their lovable *Hard Day's Night* wackiness—producer Don Kirshner (who of course turns up later in the history of rock on TV) recruited "band" members Davy Jones, Mike Nesmith, Peter Tork, and Mickey Dolenz purely on their

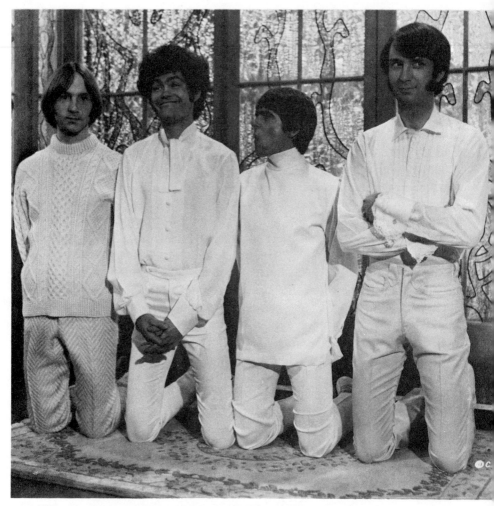

The Monkees—(left to right) Peter Tork, Mickey Dolenz, Davey Jones, and future rock-video pioneer Mike Nesmith—take a rare moment's pause from the surreal shenanigans of *Head.*

telegenic rather than musical abilities (Stephen Stills was among the thousands who failed the screen tests); they didn't play their own instruments (session musicians did); they didn't write their own songs (Neil Diamond and the Tommy Boyce-Bobby Hart team did)—the show actually remained truer to its Lesterian roots than many rock purists would admit.

Directed by Bob Rafelson, *The Monkees* was easily the most energetically surreal thing on TV in its time (just as *A Hard Day's Night* was the most energetically surreal popular cinema of *its* time, two years earlier), way ahead of *Laugh-In*'s similar zip-zap-zoom pop-surrealist antics. Aside from Rafelson's furious Lesterisms and quixotic ingenuity, *The Monkees* is also important in the history of rock video because the band itself was first formed by TV executives with the TV show in mind *before* the music, and one member of the Monkees, Mike Nesmith, would go on to become a leading rock-video pioneer in the late seventies. A feature film, *Head* (which proved to be the group's own version of *A Hard Day's Night*-meets-*8½*), was spun off the show in 1968, but by that time, the popularity of the band and the show had declined, and few people saw the film, which took the show's Lesterisms to perhaps too-frenetic heights. Still, *Head*'s crazy-quilt surrealism and emphasis on action and montage over plot did anticipate rock video (and *Head*'s sequence of the band members trekking through Victor Mature's hair must stand as some sort of rock-cinema highlight).

In August 1983, Rafelson directed a rock video for Lionel Richie's "All Night Long." Mike Nesmith, whose Pacific Arts firm is one of America's first and longest-lived music-video concerns, produced it. Says the fifty-one-year-old Rafelson, "Almost all the effects you see in videos today, the psychedelic solarizations, the quick cutting, are things we were doing years ago. It's really hard to imagine that video directors who are using these special . . . effects really think they're doing anything new."

As the sixties progressed, rock began to change radically. The birth and growth of psychedelic rock, album-oriented FM radio, and the youth movement in 1966 and 1967 emphasized the "organic" honesty of in-person concerts and rendered TV "uncool." Hollywood, of course, was ready, willing and able to rerun its fifties exploitations and sixties beach-blanket gambits by co-opting psychedelia's souped-up, double-exposed, solarized trappings. Production of rock promo films and videos, however, fell off somewhat, as there were no regularly scheduled television shows either in America or Britain that would show them. However, such European performance showcases as the Dutch *Beat Club* frequently used solarization, layered multiple imagery, and psychedelically decorated backdrops to enhance its in-studio lip-synchs (excerpted reruns of the show were aired in 1983 on USA Cable Network's *Night Flight* and *Radio 1990*).

As in the past, what rock promo films *were* made were hardly seen in America. The Rolling Stones made clips of "Charlie Is My Darling" and "Child of the Moon" at this time, as well as their aborted, never-shown BBC rock-variety special *The Great Rock & Roll Circus* (one scene, featuring the Who, is preserved in *The Kids Are Alright*). About the only rock videos seen on American TV at this time were made by a band big enough to merit American TV exposure no matter what the context: the Beatles.

In 1967, the Beatles were big enough to cease touring and remain hugely popular worldwide. Furthermore, with their 1967 landmark album, *Sgt. Pepper's Lonely Hearts Club Band,* their recordings had taken a quantum leap in terms of the use of studio technology, leading the band members to justifiably fear that the recorded music could never be reproduced faithfully live. So they again anticipated rock video's function by teaming with Swedish avant-garde filmmaker Peter Goldmann to make films for their two new singles of the time, "Penny Lane" and "Strawberry Fields Forever," and shipped them out to whatever TV stations in whatever countries would show them. In America, they were shown on *The Hollywood Palace* (I can still remember host Van Johnson shaking his head and clucking, "What was *that* all about?" after showing them) and *American Bandstand* (after showing them in an atmosphere of hushed reverence, Dick Clark polled his teen audience for their generally mystified reactions to the two clips). "Penny Lane" was a more or less literal visualization of the song's cheerily offhand pop surrealism. But "Strawberry Fields" was something else again: Richard Lester meets Kenneth Anger in the Twilight Zone, with surreal settings (mainly a cobwebbed upright piano in a meadow), chiaroscuro lighting, slow-and-backward motion, multiple overlapped images, and ominously slow dissolves to enigmatic closeups of the Beatles' faces. None of it made any sort of conventional sense; it was a nonliteral extrapolation of the song's disquieting *mood.*

The Beatles did it again a year later with a tape for their smash "Hey Jude," which was seen in the U.S. on *The Music Scene* and *The Smothers Brothers Comedy Hour.* The clip showed the Beatles performing the song in what appeared to be the audience-seating part of a studio, with large plywood boxes of varying heights in place of chairs; as the song progressed, first a few and then dozens of people gathered round the band, harmonizing with them on that long, long fade-out.

At roughly the same time in 1968 and 1969, ABC unveiled what rock pundits of the day considered the hippest rock-performance showcase ever to hit TV, *The Music Scene,* a forty-five-minute show (which segued into the teens-of-the-future serial *The New People,* also forty-five minutes long) with host David Steinberg, Canada's answer to Dick Cavett. *The Music Scene* featured the widest and most adventurous assortment of rock and rock-related acts of its era, covering everyone from the Beatles to Joe Cocker to James Brown and Sly and the Family Stone. It lasted a few months and was canceled because of inconsistent ratings, which were no doubt largely due to its forty-five-minute length.

In 1970, there was another stab at rock video. It came from Captain Beefheart (*né* Don Van Vliet), an unreconstructed American native-surrealist whose musical blend of free jazz and rural blues all but the most die-hard cultists find impossibly *outré*. Still, somehow, Beefheart's record label, Warner Brothers (he was actually signed to his old school chum Frank Zappa's Straight label, a Warner's subsidiary) let him make a sixty-second black-and-white TV commercial for his album *Lick My Decals Off, Baby*. Like Beefheart's music, the clip was a totally original, uniquely idiosyncratic, surrealist document. It mixed extreme closeups of a woven basket, over which a wonderfully straight-sounding announcer intoned Californian cities and the fanciful names of the members of Beefheart's Magic Band (e.g., "In Encino, it's Zoot Horn Rollo . . . ") with snatches of a Beefheart song playing on the sound-track; more extreme closeups of Beefheart's fingers flicking a smoking cigarette butt against a wall, the butt making a hugely amplified thud; static shots of hooded band members walking sideways across the screen against a darkened background, working flour-sifters and egg-beaters; a frontal medium-shot of Beefheart executing his "hand-and-foot endorsement" (waving an arm while simultaneously wiggling a foot parallel to the arm); and a closeup of Beefheart's foot tipping over a bowl of thick white batter, the batter oozing over the white dividing line of a highway. It closed by fading in on the *Decals* album cover as the announcer, sounding as though he were touting a new brand of luggage, boomed, "New, on Reprise, it's *Lick My Decals Off . . . Baby!*" Though no TV station would play the *outré Decals* spot in 1970 (it was inevitably too strange, and some stations found the album title obscene), in 1982, New York's Museum of Modern Art, as part of its ongoing Video Collection, accepted Beefheart's *Decals* commercial as well as his 1982 rock video for "Ice Cream for Crow."

Through most of the seventies, things moved along in fits and starts. In some instances, greater strides were made in the concert arena. In the wake of psychedelic "happenings," some bands—especially British progressive rock bands, such as Genesis—refined and made extensive use of light shows, slide and film accompaniments, and costume changes in their stage shows. The grandest prerock video example was Pink Floyd's 1974 world tour, during which still-frame and moving film images, carefully synched to the music, were projected onto a giant round screen high above the stage. As in many Pink Floyd album

Captain Beefheart (second from right, in hat and moustache) and his Magic Band kick up a dust storm in the Mojave Desert during the filming of the "Ice Cream for Crow" video (1982), which, along with Beefheart's 1970 *Lick My Decals Off* television commercial, is included in the Museum of Modern Art's permanent music-video installation.

covers and their film *The Wall,* most of the visuals were surreal, semiabstract graphics, luridly enigmatic representational images only intermittently providing explicit, literal visuals for the lyrics. Aside from performance clips, rock videos were rarely made and rarely shown on American TV. We got *Don Kirshner's Rock Concert* and *Midnight Special,* and precious little else.

Both of those shows had their bland aspects—middle-of-the-road formats, less-than-ideal hosts (*Rock Concert*'s underwhelming, industry-oriented Don Kirshner, *Midnight Special*'s overbearing Wolfman Jack), and *Midnight Special*'s stilted atmosphere, in which the screams of the studio audiences often drowned out the lip-synching acts—yet they did serve the same function rock videos fulfill today, that of vicarious substitute for concerts. Rock fans who were too young or too far from major cities to see stars perform live, could see them on such TV shows. A highly visual-conscious performer like Alice Cooper may not have been discovered through rock TV shows, but his career certainly was aided considerably by televised exposure of his *Grand Guignol* extravaganzas. Other forms of incipient rock-visual creativity were occasionally on display on *Rock Concert* and *Midnight Special* as well: Cat Stevens with his *Teaser and the Firecat* cartoons, and such pioneering promotional videos as Queen's "Bohemian Rhapsody" and the Rolling Stones's "Dancin' with Mr. D."

But there was other activity going on, activity that would foreshadow much subsequent rock-video production, and that involved some future rock-video producers and directors.

One such is Ken Walz, a forty-two-year-old New York rock-video producer/director who has made video clips for Blue Angel ("I Had a Love" and "Late" in 1980), Pat Travers ("I La La Love You" and "I'd Rather See You Dead" in 1981), Dr. Hook ("Baby Makes Her Blue Jeans Talk" in 1982), Zebra ("Who's behind the Door?," an MTV favorite in 1983) and ex-Blue Angel singer Cyndi Lauper ("Girls Just Wanna Have Fun" in 1983). According to Walz, much of the current impetus and technique for today's rock videos came from extended demonstration tapes that record companies made for in-house marketing meetings, company-wide conventions, etc. From 1972 to 1974, Walz produced and directed many such films for CBS Records.

"I started out in advertising," Walz recalls, "with Ogilvy & Mather. One day a guy came into my office who wanted to have my clients, like, say, Dr. Pepper, promote live concerts. Eventually I had to change jobs to do it, but I liked the idea and I eventually got companies like Harley-Davidson, Miller Beer, and Arrow Shirts to sponsor concerts by people like Melanie, the Grateful Dead, and Mountain, mostly at college campuses in the Northeast.

"After that I hooked up with a young director named Steven Verona, who went on to make the movie *Lords of Flatbush,* and we made a TV concert documentary on Roberta Flack and Donny Hathaway in 1971. Laszlo Kovacs, who shot *Easy Rider* and a lot of other movies, agreed to photograph it for two hundred and fifty dollars, because he felt like it. So we had a great time doing it, we shot at a UCLA concert, and we ended up with a really nice half-hour concert film. So I naively took it to all three networks, and they all said, 'Hey, real good job and all, but you know, rock music just doesn't work on television.' "

That conventional industry wisdom—"rock just doesn't work on

TV"—did hold true, in general, until the last half of the seventies, when cable technology slowly began opening things up. So Walz turned elsewhere to find rock-visual work:

"I began working freelance for CBS, doing these company convention films for them. I could be wrong, but I consider those the beginnings of rock video. The company needed a film to show their regional staff, who'd fly in for these huge conventions. I had to film between thirty and fifty acts who were going to be releasing records in the next few months, so people within the company could get an idea of who was doing what. Of course they always had one or two big names perform or appear at the conventions in person, but there was no way to showcase them all there live. The films were sixty to ninety minutes long, and had pretty substantial budgets—between three hundred thousand dollars and four hundred thousand dollars.

"So my crew and I had to fly all over the place to shoot Johnny Winter in Houston, then Johnny Cash in Nashville, then Boz Scaggs in San Francisco, Chi Coltrane in Los Angeles, Liza Minnelli in New York. . . . But frequently the time limits on us were such that the bands were unavailable, or we simply couldn't get to them in time. So we had to go out and shoot *something* to go with the music. Usually it would be something pretty simple, gliders riding around, or pretty scenery, waves on the beach, or we'd animate things or treat them with special effects. Sometimes, even if we did have footage of the band performing, we thought it got too static, so we'd cut in some other footage. We tried to make the added footage appropriate to the songs—like for a Bruce Springsteen song, show kids on the street or the Asbury Park boardwalk or something—but it just wasn't possible all the time.

"I also did some half-hour concert specials for CBS with acts like Loggins and Messina, Chicago, Herbie Mann, the Staple Singers. Then I did some concert shoots for Atlantic Records, mainly in-house stuff, though I'm sure they must have farmed some of it out for European and maybe even American telecasts. Then I went into industrial films, in-house corporate product packages, things like that. In the late seventies, I got my own production company back into music video, and it was still going kind of slow, until MTV came along, and now we're busier than ever." Walz's comments form an accurate picture of rock-video history, at least up through the mid-seventies.

Still, as far as rock was concerned, television was there mainly to document its existence from time to time, with the exception of the inevitable sporadic outbursts of creative experimentation.

Not coincidentally, the same holds true for much of the history of rock in the movies. Rock films featuring or exploiting the music and its stars began to appear at roughly the same time that TV took the plunge from mainstream adult pop towards wilder adolescent waters. Richard Brooks's *Blackboard Jungle* in 1955 was arguably the first rock movie, insofar as making crucial use of the music itself; the typically potboiling "teen problem" saga opened and closed with Bill Haley and the Comets' seminal, chart-topping rock & roll hit "Rock around the Clock." This musical bracketing of the plot—in which prerock high-school hoodlums are fans of (believe it or not) Perry Como—was more than enough to implicitly seal the connection between rock & roll and teen rebellion that had been fermenting under the starched collar of gray-flannel-suited America. From coast to coast, and in England as well, *Blackboard Jungle* provoked riots among full-house throngs of teenagers—thus making those rock-rebellion connections explicit.

Blackboard Jungle also highlighted the fact that rock, as a popular music, sold movies. Thus, in the wake of *Jungle*'s success, Hollywood began churning out an endless stream of contrived, "jukebox musical" quickies: *Rock around the Clock, Don't Knock the Rock, Let's Rock, Mr. Rock & Roll, Rock, Rock, Rock,* and on and on. More and more genuine rock acts—Chuck Berry, Little Richard, Fats Domino, Frankie Lymon and the Teenagers—were featured in such films, enlivening hackneyed, tissue-thin "plots" (i.e., young band on its way to the top, cavalcades of rock stars saving the local high school hop, parents being won over by rock by tapping their feet while chaperoning record hops, capering music-biz satires, and on and on) with frequently riveting performances. For instance, Frank Tashlin's witty *The Girl Can't Help It* (1959) and Jack Arnold's luridly sensationalistic *High School Confidential* (1958) each opened stunningly with flaming versions of the title songs, performed respectively by Little Richard and Jerry Lee Lewis.

But a few years before there was rock & roll music, there were movies that anticipated the rock & roll explosion with prototypes of rock characters, attitudes, and images. In 1953, there was Laslo Benedek's *The Wild One,* with Marlon Brando as a tough, latently existentialized motorcycle gang leader whose torn white T-shirt and black leather jacket would become *de rigueur* rock & roll apparel. Despite its contrived happy ending, *The Wild One* staked its claim to rock-ethos history admirably with this unforgettable exchange: a girl asks Brando, "What are you rebelling against?" Brando, with casual insolence, replies, "Whattaya got?" As rock critic Greil Marcus has written, "the identification teenagers made between Brando's bitter lone-wolf biker

Vic Morrow as a young punk in a record-breaking pose from Richard Brooks's *Blackboard Jungle* (1955) that would later be repeated in Brian Grant's 1979 video for M's "Pop Muzik."

and the Elvis Presley of two years later was not only automatic, it was correct." Two years later—and prior to the release of *Blackboard Jungle*—Nicholas Ray's *Rebel without a Cause* presented James Dean as the idealized mirror image of the rock & roll *audience*—young and pretty, instantly iconographic in his leather, tight jeans, and pompadour, alienated from and driven against uncomprehending adult authority by inarticulate but profound urges (hence the film's title). In both *Rebel without a Cause* and *East of Eden* (also released in 1955, in which Dean, as the "bad" son, was again cast as a confused but well-meaning young outsider), Dean became a role model for an ethos aborning. His untimely death shortly thereafter in an auto accident, combined with his screen persona and real-life image as a driven, sensitive, misunderstood soul, all combined to make him an eternal rock-culture hero, whose praises have continued to be sung by rock performers to the present day.

Not long after the run of jukebox musicals of 1955 and 1956, and his own epochal television appearances, Elvis Presley went Hollywood. Just about all of Presley's films are not only a genre unto themselves, but represent the pinnacle of show-biz exploitation, the adulteration of rock rebellion. In fact, most of them had no implicit or explicit relationship to rock at all; they were simply Elvis Movies, and as such were inevitable box-office successes, even though many of his fans could not bear to sit through them. Fittingly, the few Elvis movies that presented him as a rock & roller, or at least as a performer, were easily his best —*Jailhouse Rock* (1957, directed by Richard Thorpe) and *King Creole* (1958, directed by Michael Curtiz).

Jailhouse Rock, in fact, is the first rock movie to have any aesthetic influence on the rock videos we see today—mainly in its classic dance number for the title tune (it also felicitously had Presley portray a tough young rockabilly singer). However, ironically or not, most rock movies bear little or no relation to most rock videos, which plunder *all* of film history—and only occasionally intersect with rock-film genres. The dynamic dance sequences and stylized urban sets of a classic movie musical like, say, *West Side Story*—not a rock musical, though it did have a rock-related sensibility—have been alluded to far more often in rock videos (i.e., Michael Jackson's "Beat It," Toto's "Rosanna") than has any single rock film. In fact, much of the history of rock movies —from the fifties jukebox musicals through the beach-blanket epics of the mid-sixties, to the wild-hippies-in-the-streets paranoid scenarios of the late sixties—has been one of tawdry, exploitative banalities and camp. Most rock-video directors set their sights a bit higher when raiding the vault of cinematic imagery, perhaps seeking the classier imprimatur of a reference to a more "legitimate," more highly produced, and more widely shown bit of filmic lore.

The rock-film genre did mature somewhat over the years, and there are some examples of rock movies that *are* relevant to rock videos:

Kenneth Anger's *Scorpio Rising* (1963): in which the brilliant avant-gardist set fifties and sixties jukebox standards with ironic felicity (and without plot trappings) to fetishistic montages of teen-punk bikers (i.e., a young tough carefully grooming himself to the tune of Bobby Vinton's "Blue Velvet") and their iconic heroes (Brando and Dean). Though Anger's decidedly underground reputation and the film's blatant homoerotic overtones ensured its undeserved obscurity for many years, *Scorpio Rising* was the first, and remains one of the finest, examples of rock music commenting on visual action. In the film's high point, Anger's nervy aestheticism neatly encapsulates the antiinstitutional audacity of the best rock music: in a scene taken from Cecil B.

DeMille's 1927 *King of Kings,* we see Jesus Christ riding an ass; we hear the Crystals singing "He's a rebel and he'll never be any good/He's a rebel and he'll never be understood. . . ."

Richard Lester's *A Hard Day's Night* (1964): The first truly great popular rock movie. Merging handheld *cinéma vérité,* vertiginous montage, cheeky wit, wonderful performances by the Beatles and everyone else (everyone appearing to *be themselves,* in itself revolutionary), madcap *mis-en-scène,* and techniques borrowed from the avant-garde—the jump cuts from Jean-Luc Godard's epochal 1960 new-wave film *Breathless,* the quick-cut static compositions giving the illusion of movement (first used by Lester in his 1952 jukebox musical *It's Trad, Dad*)—this was a celebration and sendup of pop stars and their stardom. It was also the first rock film to transcend previous genre limitations, the first to possess a genuine, organic, artistic truth to its subject, and hence, to its audience. Very significantly, because of the pop-idol status of the subjects, *A Hard Day's Night* was able to bring those avant-garde techniques into the mainstream—in much the same way that today's conceptual rock videos do. When film critic Andrew Sarris called *A Hard Day's Night* "the *Citizen Kane* of jukebox musicals," he wasn't kidding. Though Lester's second and last Beatle film, *Help!,* in 1965, was a bit too contrived, formulaic, and predictably unpredictable for comfort, Lester holds a hallowed place in the history of rock visuals, and to this day many a rock video echoes his innovations.

The Beatles' *Magical Mystery Tour* (1967): Actually made for British television and never aired on American TV, probably because of its wayward, hazy, self-conscious surrealism. It doesn't really hold up that well to close inspection, but it was still an important pioneering effort and remains one of the very few films made *by* as well as about a rock band. The Beatles' direction, however sloppy, owes as much to Richard Lester as to surrealists like Luis Buñuel or Jean Cocteau.

Stephen Binder's *The T.A.M.I. Show* (1965): The first great concert "rockumentary," and a perfect time capsule of that lost age of innocence when black and white acts were freely presented as equals and everyone was happy just to dance, dance, dance to the music. And what music: James Brown, the Rolling Stones, the Beach Boys, the Supremes, Chuck Berry, Smokey Robinson and the Miracles, Marvin Gaye, Gerry and the Pacemakers, Billy J. Kramer and the Dakotas, Lesley Gore, Jan and Dean and more, all in *Shindig!*-style high-energy straightforward performance, shot on video tape (making this a TV show in a movie). The title acronym stood for Teen-Age Music International, and it meant it; the movie opens up with Jan and Dean skate-

Elvis Presley and cohorts in the immortal dance sequence from the
1957 *Jailhouse Rock*

boarding at the camera, crooning, "They're comin' from all over the
world," and they did. Truly the Wide World of Rock, and performances like Brown's and the Stones' especially transcend camp nostalgia. Director Binder would later apply his talents to another landmark
rock-visual event, Elvis Presley's 1968 "comeback" TV special.

Mike Nichols's *The Graduate* (1967) and Dennis Hopper's *Easy
Rider* (1969): Both legitimized the use of pop (*The Graduate*'s middle-
of-the-road Simon and Garfunkel ditties) and rock (*Easy Rider*'s formi-
dable collection of songs like Steppenwolf's "Born to Be Wild" and The
Band's "The Weight") songs to comment seriously on the action. *Easy
Rider* went further, of course: Its soundtrack at times actually *replaced*
narrative and character in moving the action forward.

Michelangelo Antonioni's *Zabriskie Point* (1969): Many consider Antonioni's 1966 *Blow Up* a protean rock movie, because of its enigmatic evocation of amoral "Swinging London" and its great set piece with the Yardbirds recreating the Who's destructo stage act (though its soundtrack, by Herbie Hancock, is jazz). But *Zabriskie Point* hits closer to home: its cryptic exploration of the hippie *Zeitgeist* was accompanied by both original (by Pink Floyd) and found (by the Rolling Stones, Grateful Dead, and others) rock music; it often superseded narrative in favor of pure, mysterious-yet-provocative imagery, stunningly composed and photographed. The emphasis on painterly image over literate narrative, and the appositeness of the rock soundtrack (especially the grand finale, in which a house explodes in slow motion to the tune of Pink Floyd's space-surfing epic "Come in Number 51, Your Time Is Up") foreshadowed conceptual rock-video technique and aesthetic.

Michael Wadleigh's *Woodstock* (1970) and Adrian Maben's *Pink Floyd at Pompeii* (1971): *Woodstock,* of course, was a signal event in itself. But both of these films were equally unprecedented as rock movies in their expansiveness of scope, intensity of focus, and production values. *Woodstock* pioneered the use of split screens, but *Pink Floyd* is far more protean and fascinating in regard to rock video: It took the crystal-clear, super-real, clinical techno awe of Kubrick's *2001* (a considerable influence on rock-video aesthetics itself) and lavished it, for the first time, on a rock band in performance. And who more deserving than Pink Floyd of such treatment?

Donald Cammell and Nicolas Roeg's *Performance* (1970): Living up to its title, this was, after *A Hard Day's Night, the* first great triumph of rocker-as-actor (Elvis, in *Jailhouse Rock,* the possible exception)— in the person of Rolling Stone Mick Jagger, perfectly cast as an amoral androgynous *agent provocateur* in a decadent modern-day environment. The motif of identity loss and the cryptically chic milieu, as well as Roeg's luridly lush cinematography, foreshadowed much of what we see in rock videos today.

George Lucas's *American Graffiti* (1973): A great movie on any level, but especially relevant here for its brilliant and heartfelt use of a classic sixties rock soundtrack to anticipate, parallel, and follow up the action.

Ken Russell's *Tommy* (1975): Russell, with his vulgar, orgiastic wallowing in gratuitous visual excess, is probably *the* granddaddy of conceptual rock-video aesthetics. In this case, he applies himself with usual over-the-top gusto to an actual rock-related subject. Certain scenes and images actually do work—especially Tina Turner's bawdily terrifying "Acid Queen" number, with Roger Daltrey of the Who as deaf-dumb-and-blind messiah Tommy, encased in a hypodermic-

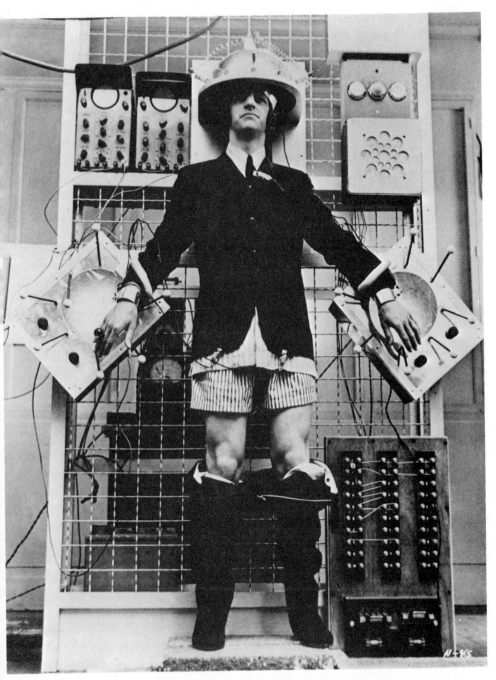

Ringo Starr in Richard Lester's 1965 *Help!* A nearly identical sci-fi-horror image appears in the "Acid Queen" sequence of Ken Russell's *Tommy* (1975).

Martin Scorsese's *The Last Waltz* (1978): Scorsese had already made wonderful use of rock music to comment on the action in such films as 1968's *Who's That Knocking on My Door?* and 1973's *Mean Streets.* Here he had a Genuine Rock Event to work with: the Band's last-ever concert, featuring a host of rock, blues, and soul luminaries as guest stars. With the likes of Bob Dylan, Eric Clapton, Van Morrison, Neil Young, Muddy Waters, Paul Butterfield, the Staple Singers, and more, *The Last Waltz* really couldn't miss. But what sets it apart from all other concert rockumentaries is the fact that Scorsese meticulously choreographed and made storyboards of the entire film in advance, down to redecorating San Francisco's Winterland to turn it into an elegant make-believe ballroom set.

Peter Clifton's *Led Zeppelin: The Song Remains the Same* (1976): From its opening dream-sequence gangland raid to the rainbow trails rotoscoped around Led Zep's Jimmy Page at the climax of "Stairway to Heaven," a true pre-MTV rock-video-as-extended feature: Its post-psychedelic comic-book flourishes, which were aesthetically quite apt for a heavy-metal/art-rock band like Zeppelin, had no higher aspiration than to make its audience go "Oh, *wow!*" And, like many promo clips, did just that. Appropriately, Clifton had made some early rock promos (i.e., Procol Harum's "Whiter Shade of Pale") in the sixties and seventies.

Francis Ford Coppola's *Apocalypse Now* (1979): Mainly for its stunning opening montage of Vietnam War horror and insanity set perfectly to the tune of the Doors' apocalyptic "The End." As a sequence on its own it is unforgettable—and better than most rock videos. The film's use of other found rock material, especially the Rolling Stones' "Satisfaction," is also wonderfully apt.

Julian Temple's *The Great Rock & Roll Swindle* (1980): A scathingly brilliant mock-rockumentary on the history of British punk-rock bad boys the Sex Pistols, told as a series of object lessons in fomenting stylish, subversive sensation by the band's situationist manager, Malcolm McLaren. It was originally to be a more traditional mock-jukebox musical, titled *Who Killed Bambi?* and directed by exploitation master and all-time breast-fetishist Russ Meyer (whose 1969 *Beyond the Valley of the Dolls* is another candidate for greatest rock film of all time, though hardly relevant to rock video). But Pistols lead singer, Johnny Rotten (né Lydon), fed up by then with McLaren's Machiavellian manipulations, blatantly tried to sabotage the whole thing. At the last minute, film student Temple, who'd been the band's unofficial film archivist since 1976, came in to perform a miraculous job of salvage

Sex Pistol Sid Vicious concludes his singular version of "My Way" *his* way, in Julian Temple's brilliant mock-rockumentary *The Great Rock 'n' Roll Swindle* (1980).

(this film was his graduate thesis!). Concert footage, animation, set pieces (especially Sid Vicious's pistol-in-hand "My Way" and Tenpole Tudor's hysterical "Who Killed Bambi?"), and diabolically knowing wit coalesce into perhaps the most honest rock film ever. How does it relate to rock video? Well, Temple went on to become one of rock video's most accomplished *auteurs;* the film was very loosely structured and used lots of abrupt montages; and possibly, in its honesty, it stands as an antithetical remedy to rock video's worst excesses. Unfortunately, it was never released in the U.S. because of legal wrangles in the wake of the band's breakup; the existence of U.K. video-cassette versions leaves hope for American home-video release.

Alan Parker's *Pink Floyd: The Wall* (1982): Personally, I found this what-a-drag-stardom-is opus unendurable, but it is certainly a pioneering example of a feature-length rock video: there's no plot, no character, encrusted coffin. But the image that is most appropriate to rock video is that of Ann-Margret as Tommy's mother submerged in a river of baked beans that have exploded out of her TV set—the exploding TV set being a staple rock-video motif.

no dialogue, only a constant barrage of unsettling imagery—created *after,* and as a visual complement to, the aural album *The Wall.* Also noteworthy is Gerald Scarfe's hideous animation, which often contains much the same kind of blatant misogyny (i.e., blood-engorged vulvate flowers devouring phallic buds) that finds its way into rock videos.

Adrian Lynne's *Flashdance* (1983): Basically a streamlined update of John Badham's similar, and similarly successful, *Saturday Night Fever* (1977)—a trite and insubstantial populist plot serving as a thin premise for the real matter at hand, the music-and-dance set pieces. The crucial and relevant differences between *Flashdance* and *Fever* are Lynne's cutting-to-the-beat of the very loud and prominent music, and the story's implicit emphasis on the heroine as a solitary figure disconnected from *Fever*'s images of community. Lynne has freely admitted that he took *Flashdance*'s look and style—image, montage, and visual energy substituting for plot and character—from MTV. But the film's underlying post-Me-Generation solipsism is another rock-video hallmark as well.

All of these films are exceptions to the general rule of rock on film. They stand as a legacy that has foreshadowed and influenced the style and content of rock videos—but all of film and TV history is freely plundered in rock videos. This is a phenomenon that will be covered in greater detail later in the chapter on Aesthetics and *Auteurs.*

Rock Video History, Part II

PIONEERS ON THE
NEW FRONTIER

By 1975, rock was first and foremost a big entertainment business. There would be the occasional insurrectionary movement like punk rock, but by now rock culture and rock aesthetics had so completely infiltrated society through clothing, hairstyles and imagery that were co-opted by advertising media that it could hardly be anything but entertainment. Still, rock did not really have a place on television, at least, not in America.

But rock had been around for twenty years. Several generations had grown up with it. Many of them were not rockers themselves, but talented creative and technical people who would have loved to inject rock aesthetics into their work—if only there was an outlet for it. The only nationally broadcast outlets for rock on American TV were Don Kirshner and *Midnight Special.* The rock videos being made were cheap, unambitious performance clips shipped overseas, to such shows as Britain's *Top of the Pops* (which by this time, out of necessity, had had to suspend its anticlip union rules from time to time to showcase European or American artists in Britain's Top Thirty, or even on occasion British acts who were too busy touring abroad to appear in person), *Top Pop* in the Netherlands, and *Countdown* in Australia, the first country to develop a high degree of rock-video consciousness, if only because of the difficulty many bands have in touring there. It has long been the case that, without a video, a band simply will not have a hit record in Australia.

Still, in their homes and in their schools, some of the children of the rock generation were tinkering, experimenting. One example is Daniel Pearl, who is now an experienced cinematographer, having worked on some twenty-five feature films (the most famous of which is Tobe Hooper's low-budget cult horror classic *Texas Chainsaw Massacre*) and hundreds of rock videos. In 1969, then a film student, Pearl made a conceptualized short based on the Byrds' song "So You Want to Be a Rock & Roll Star" using a friend of his to portray a would-be rock star. It was later shown on WNET, the New York Public Broadcasting Station.

Another is Joe Dea, who in the mid-seventies was in high school in North Plainfield, New Jersey, studying filmmaking and working a light show for school rock concerts. Eventually he added his Super-8 films to the lights. "People would *always* come up to me at the light board and say, 'Wow, man, you made those movies just for those songs?' " Dea recalls. "Of course I didn't, but *they* didn't have to know that."

Both Pearl and Dea went on to work extensively in rock video in the eighties. Dea directed Greg Kihn's "Jeopardy" and Krokus's "Screaming in the Night." The comments Dea's work elicited from people at his high-school dances indicate just how ready at least part of the rock audience was to watch visuals as they listened to the music—after all, that generation had grown up with TV and with rock music. Paradoxically, the generation that grew up with rock and TV didn't watch much television. Rock music was their entertainment of choice; TV represented establishment entertainment, and despite rock music's lack of serious political impact, it was still a talisman, a cultural badge to its audience—it was *their own,* and TV was not. In-concert shows were okay; rock movies were okay, mainly because movies were a separate thing from television—movies were spectacles, events that perhaps somehow legitimized the music.

So, in 1975, rock and TV still didn't go together, and all the incipient rock-video pioneers could do was dream. Jo Bergman of Warner Brothers remembers: "When I came to Warner's in 1973, I said, 'You know those little promotional films we make for the International Department? Wouldn't it be interesting to try to get them on television here?' Most people either shrugged or laughed. So I did some research around the country. And of course everyone's attitude at all the networks was, 'You know rock doesn't play on TV.' Nobody was ready to be even slightly interested. It was just an idea—not even a *good* idea. Just a crazy idea."

Soon, though, it wouldn't seem so crazy. In 1975, Sony introduced the Betamax home-video tape recorder, and the first reports of the coming of the video disc were publicized. Concurrent with the introduction of futuristic home-video technology, cable TV began to spring up around the country. Still, it would be several more years until rock video would explode, and most of the initial tremors would come from England. Why?

As to the first question, there was the residual mistrust of rock on TV by both TV programmers and the rock audience. Television flattened rock dynamics into two dimensions; at least when movies did that, it was on a big screen, which lent more spectacular impact. A very simple fact of television life, one which hasn't changed until very recently, also played an important role in slowing the progress of rock video: the tinny sound of tiny television speakers, which in the eyes of rock fans with ever more expensive stereo systems only further denigrated the music to the level of another game show, soap opera, or movie of the week. On the other hand, television programmers had extensive demographic research indicating that during the big-money prime-time hours, the rock audience was not watching TV. They were —as teenagers responding to parental queries of where they've been all night have always put it—"out." So the problems of rock on TV became a self-fulfilling prophecy.

As to the second question, an answer is provided by Simon Fields, twenty-eight-year-old production chief of Limelight U.S., one of the world's biggest and busiest rock-video production houses. "Most rock video came from England first," explains Fields, "because of Britain's cultural milieu. Britain's very small and *tight,* everyone is very, very conscious of what everyone else is doing. Culturally, Britain is very elastic and explosive, much more so than America, because it's so much smaller. Things change all the time, the charts are a real pepper pot. And because there isn't much in the way of rock radio—instead there's TV, clubs, and the press—Britain has a very heightened visual consciousness. For some time now, visual style has been crucial to success in Britain. In the punk era, those bands not only looked and acted outrageously onstage, they lived that way on the streets. There was no gap between art and life. That still holds true. The result of it all is that bands naturally have been inculcated with this consciousness of how to visualize what they're all about. And that naturally extends to rock video."

In Britain, the landmark event of 1975 was the appearance of Queen's "Bohemian Rhapsody" video clip, directed by Bruce Gowers, produced by Lexi Godfrey for Jon Roseman Productions. Bruce Gowers had been directing network variety shows for London Weekend television. In 1974, Queen's management company asked him to shoot a concert documentary on the band. It was later shown theatrically in Britain.

" 'Bohemian Rhapsody' wasn't, as a lot of people seem to suppose, a case where the song was released and was going nowhere, and we cooked up this video to help push it," Gowers recalls. "I met with the band, with whom I already had a good rapport, and they played me the tune. I instantly flashed on how visual it could be; it was such a sprawling, big, dramatic thing. And the boys in the band agreed with me. The actual idea for the look of the video came from an earlier album cover of theirs, *Queen II,* where the four band members had their faces on the cover in a sort of foursquare formation, against a black background. So we used that setup as the basis for the piece. And I kept getting all these ideas from hearing the track. When there was echo thrown on the vocals, we'd throw 'echo' on the visuals by trailing multiple images of their faces, and so on. For big chorus effects, we'd come up with some sort of visual equivalent. It was mainly a mix between live performance and special effects, and in those days, there weren't any fancy visual effects; we did it all by wiping and trailing imagery with these prisms and things, very primitive. So we managed to get this 'Queen choir' thing in there, which seemed to be what everyone who saw it reacted to the most."

The shooting itself took four hours; the final version of the video—with effects—was completed by the following evening. The total budget: about $7,000.

"At that time, most of the preproduced clips on *Top of the Pops,* and they were rare anyway, were by American bands who simply couldn't get over to appear in person," says Gowers. "And most of those were either just the band performing, or people walking along a beach or through a meadow—real classic, naive rock visuals. Now when the song itself was released, it entered the charts at number thirty, I believe, which was *Top of the Pops*'s cutoff point. They were loath to play the clip because of their union rules. But the song was on the chart, so they didn't have much choice. After one airing, the song shot up to the top five in the charts, and they had to play it again, and the week after that it was, 'Yes, it's number one, it's top of the pops!' And then the thing stayed on top of the charts for something like twelve or thirteen weeks in a row, and they were forced to play it every week. Eventually they'd run maybe thirty seconds of it or something, you know, like, 'Yes, it's still up there. . . .' "

"Bohemian Rhapsody" was an early example of a song skyrocketing up the charts almost purely on the strength of its video. The response from American record labels was quick. Gowers says, "All of a sudden I was getting these calls from Los Angeles. The 'Rhapsody' video had gone on *Midnight Special,* and that had spurred a lot of sales the week after it was on. I was getting all these calls from the labels, saying 'Can you do one of those for us?' So I came to America later in 1975 and shot a few. I did 'Hot Legs' for Rod Stewart. I did some promo things for the Bee Gees and Rush as well. All of them were shot in one or two days, the entire production would always be wrapped well inside a week. The budgets were in the ten- to fifteen-thousand-dollar range, and they were invariably made for bands who sold well enough that they could easily absorb any loss on the production of the video.

"The thing that really made it difficult in those days was that the labels were still using the clips mainly for European TV, and so they kept insisting on showing the band performing and nothing else, I guess because the bands didn't get over to Europe much and the labels just wanted to remind people of who was who and who did what in the band. That's a reasonable consideration, I guess, but the reason the Queen clip did so well in England is because it was something *other* than that, which we'd all seen a hundred times before. Anyway, it was a constant running battle to get the labels to let us show anything more than the band playing guitars. When we did use other things, they were my own ideas, although I did work pretty closely with the bands themselves. They weren't especially excited about doing the videos or anything, but they usually did take some sort of interest in them, if only because they knew that a lot of people would be seeing them."

Gowers directed another important early-concept video—"Robbery, Assault and Battery" by Genesis, one of three 1976 clips the group made with Lexi Godfrey again producing, for a lump sum of under $10,000. " 'Robbery, Assault and Battery' is the one I remember best," Godfrey recalls, "there was no lip-synching and no miming with guitars in it. It was all story, which involved Phil Collins, the drummer and singer, playing a bank robber and getting into trouble. We shot it on the *Oliver* lot at Shepperton Studios in London, which was kind of funny, because Phil had first made a name for himself as a child actor, and his biggest role was as the Artful Dodger in *Oliver.* Anyway, that video did quite well for Genesis here, and it got shown on American TV as well."

In another part of London, another seminal rock-video director was gearing up: Keith McMillan, who with producer John Weaver formed Keefco Productions in 1975. Since then Keefco has made roughly six hundred rock videos. John Weaver describes what happened:

"Keith had actually formed Keefco as a sort of one-man company in 1970, doing album covers for people like Rod Stewart (*Gasoline Alley*), Black Sabbath, all sorts of artists. That was a way of visually interpreting or complementing the music and the band, so in a way that paved the way for doing videos. In 1975, Keith called me up and said, 'I've just read about this thing called the video disc, and they're just bringing out these things called Betamaxes that are home-video-tape recorders.' I had no idea what he was talking about, but he kept raving on to me about it, saying that the future was in rock videos and all. I thought about it: maybe he had a point. So we formed Keefco Productions right away, and dove into video."

Among Keefco's six hundred-odd rock videos are Paul McCartney and Stevie Wonder's "Ebony and Ivory," Blondie's "Denis," Uriah Heep's "That's the Way It Is," Haircut One Hundred's "Love Plus One," Kate Bush's "Wuthering Heights" and "Babushka," Pat Benatar's "Precious Time," Nina Hagen's "African Reggae," New Edition's "Candy Girl," and concert productions featuring Tina Turner, Billy Squier, Santana, the *Rock for Kampuchea* concerts, and Paul McCartney's video album *Back to the Egg.*

"The first promo clip we did was for a long-defunct British pop band called Kenny, and it cost about one thousand, seven hundred dollars," Weaver says. "Then we did one for Gary Glitter, who was very big in England with the kids but who never really made it in America except for one hit, 'Rock & Roll Part 2.' The clip we did for him—I can't remember the name of the song—had Gary in his silver glitter suit, swinging in a silver hammock strung between two silver palm trees. It was just delightfully over the top. That one cost about two thousand dollars.

"In those days, we didn't do any postproduction at all, we'd just go into a studio, use their backup studios for cheaper rates, and shoot as we went along with an Editek system, where you set the camera on record, then hit pause, set up your shot, then shoot it, and if it doesn't come out right, you rewind and set it up again. It's really not a bad system, but things have moved way beyond that level now. Back then we'd set up in the morning, get the band in just after noon so we didn't have to feed them, shoot for a few hours, and at the end of the day, their manager would walk out with a completed two-inch master tape.

"These things started paying dividends immediately. If we started in 1975, then by 1976 or 1977 *Top of the Pops* was playing them pretty regularly, even though they didn't like to, simply because so many people were making them. And of course they'd go out to European and Australian shows, and the international departments at all the labels were wild over them. It was great, cost-effective promotion for them. We weren't making a lot of money at it, but in a little while, we were turning out three of them a week and having loads of fun, we were loving it and growing with it all along.

"In February of 1978, Keefco was set up in a room at the Hyatt Sunset hotel in L.A., that was our U.S. production office. By that time we'd done well over two hundred videos in the U.K. I had this enormous show reel I was very proud of, and I naively and excitedly went to all these record companies with it. Because of my sincere enthusiasm I got through a lot of doors—people would roll their eyes and look at me and say, 'You came all the way from *London* to show us this? Well, okay . . . '—but I could never get the executives to understand what they were looking at. But I could understand that in a way: pop promos just weren't a current reality to them.

"The ones that really turned it around for us in America were a pair of clips we did of Blondie in 1978, of 'Denis' and 'Detroit 442.' Those clips went to this big international record convention, the MIDEM, and started a whole buzz on the band in Europe, primed the Continent for their tour, and after that the band returned to the States as conquering heroes, sort of, and they started getting big here as well. [Blondie's label] Chrysalis was actually the first American label to cite videos as having broken their bands."

Videos took another bold step forward in England with *The Kenny Everett Video Show,* which debuted late in the year. The show featured both video clips and in-studio performances by rock bands, comedy skits, and the saucy gyrations of the Hot Gossip dance troupe flash-dancing to popular rock songs. But the show was dominated by Everett himself, an elfin, irreverently loony presence, and by the "video-eyezed" direction of David Mallet, who had been involved in rock video way back in the mid-sixties as an assistant director of *Shindig!,* and as director of such British pop music shows as *Juke Box Jury* and *Top of the Pops.* By this time, Mallet was also a veteran director of British TV commercials, churning out action-packed, quick-cut little spots in which he worked out many of the trademark stylistic touches of his rock videos (e.g., the fluttering triple-strobe repeat quick cut, as in David Bowie's "D.J.," when Bowie hurls a spray-paint cannister at a mirrored wall).

Everett was, in effect, the first-ever rock-video jockey, and he was a great one: never a mere talking head, always ready to mock rock stars with Monty Python-style banter. Mallet's direction employed an avalanche of special effects, with multiple Everetts arguing with each other or all confronting one befuddled rock star (one-time British teen idol and latter-day born-again Christian Cliff Richard was the running butt of most of Everett's pranks, though Richard himself participated good-naturedly in the jests). In one episode, Mallet managed to place Everett inside a facsimile of Elvis Costello's brain (this show was a true heir to Ernie Kovacs's video pranksterism). In another episode, Everett walked off the set onto the roof of his studio, where he found David Bowie posing, still as a statue, with a violin. Everett tweaked and tickled Bowie until the latter cracked up laughing and ran away, to be pursued over the roofs of London by the merrily cackling Everett. *The Kenny Everett Video Show* was syndicated in America for a few years in the late seventies and early eighties—but always in those early A.M. weekend spots.

In America in 1975, we had *Saturday Night Live,* the first televised product of the generation that grew up with rock and TV. *SNL* always featured hot rock and pop acts, but since the show billed itself as live, there were never any video clips of bands. Rock-video pioneer Toni Basil, however, did manage to collaborate with resident *SNL* filmmaker Gary Weiss on a few preproduced music and dance video pieces featuring the Lockers, a Los Angeles street-dance troupe who, thanks in large part to Basil's promotion, were able to pioneer a protean form of what has since come to be known as "break dancing" and "electro-boogie." But *Saturday Night Live* did not show what preproduced rock videos there may have been.

In fact, one day during the show's second season, *SNL*'s Dan Aykroyd (as he admitted in a 1982 *Penthouse* interview) received in the mail a video tape from a band in Akron, Ohio. The band was called Devo (short for De-Evolution Band). The ten-minute video tape was titled "In the Beginning Was the End: the Truth about De-Evolution." It contained conceptualized video presentations (actually shot on sixteen-millimeter film) of two songs, "Jocko Homo" and "Secret Agent Man," as well as a brief montage of perverse, freak-show images from old medical textbooks on strange phenomena. Aykroyd threw the tape in the wastebasket.

Devo (who ended up appearing live on *SNL* in 1978) was a totally new kind of rock unit. Bands and artists had made "concept albums" in the past. But Devo was a self-contained concept band. They created their own music, their own costumes, their own packaging and marketing formulas, and their own very unique and cynical world view. Devo was actually a futuristic protest band, whose target was nothing less than humanity itself. They were the group with the scoop, the band with a plan. The scoop was de-evolution, the concept that humanity was going backwards, not progressing as everyone thought but regressing through ever more decadent and perverse stages of decline. Their plan was to both embody and illustrate that perception through a total multimedia conceptual presentation. They wrote and played songs that merged classic rock guitar riffs with an electronic edge that was several years ahead of the new-wave electropop synthesizer sounds of the early eighties. They dressed in baggy reactor-room antiradiation jump suits, 3-D sunglasses, elbow and kneepads and hockey helmets (all of it implying that they had a dirty and dangerous job to do, and implicitly equating play, as in music, with work and sport). They designed their own advertisements and record sleeves, making slyly ironic use of fifties pop-culture artifacts (again, way before anyone else did). They released their records themselves. And they made stunning films for their songs that they always screened before and during their stage shows, and that they tried to get played anywhere else they could.

"From the very beginning," says Devo bassist, singer, songwriter, and head conceptualizer Gerald Casale, "Devo was into the idea of making films, or videos, or whatever you want to call them. Not as some promotional afterthought, but as an integral part of our overall artistic and marketing approach. To us, it was a very quaint, obsolete, hold-over-sixties-utopian idea to keep the music and the marketing separate. This is the music business, and its business is music. You can't separate the two; they're parts of the same whole. Right from the start we called ourselves Devo, Inc., and said, 'Are we not men? We are Devo.' And video was integral to our artistic and marketing plan.

"We'd all sort of grown up together, me and the rest of the band [Mark and Bob Mothersbaugh, Gerald's brother Bob Casale, and Alan Meyers] and we all went to Kent State together. We just came up with the Devo idea one day, sitting around as kids eating creamed corn and Spaghetti-O's on white bread, you know, and it just hit us. So anyway, we got the band together around 1970 or so, and we worked and we worked and nobody seemed to take much notice for a long time. Meanwhile, at school I met Chuck Statler, who was studying filmmaking. We shared a lot of the same ideas, so we agreed that sometime we'd try to get together and make some Devo films somehow."

Statler, who, aside from directing most of Devo's rock videos, has made clips for Elvis Costello, the Waitresses, Donnie Iris, the Michael Stanley Band, Nick Lowe and the J. Geils Band, recalls, "Gerry and I became friends, we shared the same ideas, the same imagery. After we graduated, I moved up to Minneapolis and worked in industrials and all sorts of other films, just to get experience, and got a little production team together. Meanwhile, I kept in touch with Gerry and the band.

"Around early 1975, on a holiday trip . . . I ran into Gerry. He told me about how the band was getting really tired and disgusted, they were thinking of calling it quits, but before that happened, Gerry wanted to make a film. So we corresponded and mapped the project out by mail and on the phone. I financed half of it, and they financed the other half. The first thing we made was 'The Truth about De-Evolution.' The total budget for that was maybe five thousand dollars. We actually finished it in 1976. They had the concept for it basically all worked out. I was there mainly to point the camera and make sure that everything went properly. I was more a technical director than anything else, although since they didn't know much about the actual process of filmmaking, I had more input in those early days than on the later ones."

Casale picks up the story: "We shot 'Jocko Homo' in the Kent State student government chambers, and 'Secret Agent Man' in a factory warehouse sort of a place. We were very consciously trying to make them both as disturbing and as entertaining as we could. I thought they came out pretty well, considering the budgets and the fact that we shot them pretty quickly. But since we weren't signed to any label, we had lots of time to fine-tune them."

"Secret Agent Man" was mainly straight-performance footage, but calling it "straight performance" is somehow inappropriate. The band played a sardonic, robotic mutation of the mid-sixties classic, wearing transparent plastic masks over their faces, and moving like spastic automatons. Intercut with the performance were cryptic, unsettling images of people wearing grotesque mutant-chimp masks and pig heads, holding medical calipers, and the like. And in the performance sequences, lead singer Mark Mothersbaugh wore his "Booji Boy" mask, a sort of grotesque infant head (Booji Boy represents the infantile spirit of de-evolution).

A man, tormented by lust, pulling the weight of Western Civilization—priests, pianos, donkey carcasses—in Luis Buñuel and Salvador Dali's 1928 surrealist classic *Un Chien Andalou*. The film has been frequently plundered for *outré* imagery by rock videos; Devo, at least, have been able to apply a Buñuelian aesthetic to rock video with some integrity and originality.

"Jocko Homo" was even better. The music was a queasy mock-march lurch, a perfect crystallization in sound of Devo's own self-descriptive slogan, The sound of things falling apart. In the film, Mark Mothersbaugh, in lab coat and safety goggles, executed a herky-jerky marionette dance while lecturing an amphitheater full of attentive science students with the song's lyrics, which bluntly spelled out the Devo philosophy: "They tell us that we lost our tails / Evolving up from little snails / I say it's all just wind in sails / Are we not men? We are Devo! . . ." Strewn about the amphitheater were bound, body-stockinged human forms, spasmodically writhing on dissecting tables.

The magic of this film lay partly in the fact that it looked like nothing else anyone had ever made, at least in rock video. Also, it effectively summed up exactly what Devo was all about: they were the avenging chem-lab nerds, gleefully formulating parodistic pop atrocities. Finally, while it *was* a totally original rock-visual production, it also strongly evoked the cinematic *auteurs* Casale and Statler cite as favorites and influences: Casale mentions Stanley Kubrick, "for his strong sense of irony and classical form," and Federico Fellini, "for his unparalleled ability to capture grotesque, surreal images"; Statler mentions Russ Meyer and master surrealist Luis Buñuel. Though many observers have compared Devo's work to Richard Lester's, probably because of Devo's antic humor, Buñuel's influence is most apparent. Like Buñuel, Devo presented extremely strong, disturbingly perverse imagery in a flat, unostentatious, almost antistylish way. There were no attention-grabbing special effects, no razzle-dazzle camera moves or showy edits, yet there was an incredible sophistication of expression, an iconoclastic and sharply defined world view.

Devo, once signed by Warner Brothers Records, would go on to make more superb protean rock videos: "Satisfaction" (their first hit, a spastic-robot-disco version of the Rolling Stones classic), "Come Back Jonee," "The Day My Baby Gave Me a Surprize," "Whip It," "Beautiful World," "Thru Being Cool," and others. Devo has been virtually unexcelled, in terms of creativity and assuredness of expression, in the admittedly rather brief history of rock video.

But back in the mid-seventies, they had a hard time of it. "The world just wasn't ready for it, I guess," muses Casale. "When we contacted record companies to try to show them our films, they thought we were *nuts,* wasting our money. But then 'The Truth about De-Evolution' won an award at the 1977 Ann Arbor Film Festival, and that renewed our hopes a bit. So we sent a tape of it to a friend of mine in Los Angeles, and he showed it to an A&M Records executive, who loved it. That guy showed it at a party for *Slash* magazine [a now defunct L.A. punk monthly that gave birth to a successful independent record label of the same name], and then *Slash* printed stills from the film, which led to our getting a showcase at the Starwood club in L.A. The A&M exec saw us there, and afterwards he said, 'Sorry, you guys are just *too* bizarre for us. But keep making those great films.' So we kept at it anyway, and a year later we played in San Francisco and Neil Young saw us, and he convinced his management company and Warner Brothers to sign us."

Since then, Devo have become at least as well known for their rock videos, and their overall visual presentation, as for their music. In 1978 they released the very first long-form feature-length conceptual rock-video program, *Devovision: the Men Who Make the Music,* which compiled all their early videos and interwove them around Devo propaganda and record-biz satire. It still stands as one of the best long-form rock videos.

Also in 1975, in San Francisco, a mysterious quartet of avant-rockers who'd come to the West Coast from Louisiana were out-Devoing Devo. The group had been working since 1972 on an operatic feature film to be called *Vileness Fats;* though it would never be completed, a three-minute clip from it survives today. The "band" sent that clip to record labels as a music-video demo tape. The clip showed four maniacs in neo-Ku Klux Klan hoods and robes made out of newspapers, banging on trash cans and oil drums in sped-up motion, in a futuristic-tribal, trash compacter mutation of the sixties rock classic "Land of 1,000 Dances." Of course, the tape was rejected by every label that got it. When the quartet received one rejected demo addressed to "Residents" at their address, they took that as their name. To date, the Residents —operating on their "Theory of Obscurity" (they call their production company the Cryptic Corp.)—have never revealed their true identities; they rarely, if ever, perform onstage, and if they do, it's only with masks and costumes and behind screens. But their "Land of 1,000 Dances" clip, with its utterly *outré* antics and stunning German Expressionist sets and lighting, remains one of rock video's most invigoratingly original classics. In 1975, it began to be seen occasionally on cable outlets, and in college campus film festivals.

Also in 1975, when cable TV was still a hazily defined fringe format, New Yorkers Pat Ivers and Emily Armstrong began filming New York's punk-rock scene. Their work was somewhat crude and unadorned; they used handheld Sony Portapaks—and thus its visual fidelity to its subject matter was perfect. They soon got a late-night cable show in Manhattan and titled it *Nightclubbing*—"because," says Armstrong, "it was all about the idea of just bopping around to all these clubs where all this new music was happening. Staying out late, partying, getting crazy . . . it was all there. We purposely kept the production values low because we couldn't afford to make them much better anyway, and because we thought it better reflected what it was really like in those days. Pat and I had been working at Manhattan Cable, and at night we'd always be out at the punk-rock clubs, so one day we figured, why not put our two obsessions together? *Nightclubbing* was the result." Ivers and Armstrong subsequently programmed the "video lounge" at the first version of the New York rock club Danceteria in 1980 and 1981, but much of their collection was lost after the club was closed by police for liquor-license violations. Among their surviving gems is a tape of the acoustic, three-piece Talking Heads performing the garage-rock classic "96 Tears" at New York punk haven CBGB in 1975.

Invasion of the Mutant Shopping-Cart-Tanks: the mysterioso Residents in a scene from the pixilated opening of their seminal "Land of 1,000 Dances" filmlet (1975)

In their wake came more cable rock programs, as the new medium began living up to its promise of alternative entertainment. As the seventies progressed, another New York rock-video concert documentarian, Paul Tschinkel, got his own show on Manhattan Cable TV. In San Francisco, Joe Rees's Target Video began setting montages of found, topical newsreel footage and televised war reports to the songs of local punk-rock bands. Those, too, were shown on local cable outlets.

In 1977, former Monkee Mike Nesmith formed his own music-video production company, Pacific Arts Video Records. He began releasing his own records and making his own video clips. His first production was "Rio," in 1977, and for a first production, it, like Devo's early work, is remarkably sophisticated and holds up extremely well against subsequent bigger-budget rock-video productions. But unlike Devo, Nesmith's was obviously influenced by classic Hollywood tradition, especially Busby Berkeley song-and-dance musicals. There is a fanciful sweetness about "Rio," which is basically a visualization of a Walter Mitty-style fantasy. In it, Nesmith literally flies to Rio, via well-executed video matte effects, by holding out his arms like a little boy imitating an airplane. In this fantasy, Nesmith soars against a starry, night sky background, accompanied by exotic-looking women in Carmen Miranda-style costumes. Concurrently, Nesmith released the song as an audio single. Though it failed to sell well in America, it made the Top Tens in much of Europe and in Australia—*after* the video had gotten heavy television exposure. Nesmith would go on, with his director, Bill Dear (who has also made some fine rock videos like Cheap Trick's "She's Tight," Juice Newton's "Love's Been a Little Bit Hard on Me," and Rosanne Cash's "I Wonder"), to repeat the trick with 1979's "Cruisin' (Lucy, Ramona and Sunset Sam)," a kinetic street-scene travelogue that showed more of Nesmith's wry humor and again was very smoothly produced. While setting new standards for music-video production, Nesmith also found that with "Cruisin'," international demand for the video itself far outpaced demand for the audio record alone.

Meanwhile, in Australia, a young cinematic renegade named Russell Mulcahy was getting his rock-video act together. Born in Melbourne in 1955 and raised in the coal-mining town of Woolongong, forty miles south of Sydney, Mulcahy was making Super-8 films when he was fourteen. Three years later he moved to Sydney, where he worked as film editor with Channel 7 News in Sydney. "With the access I had to all the editing machines," he recalls, "and some financing I'd rounded up, I made a couple of one-hour experimental films, *Contrived Mind-flashes* and *Delicious Dreams to Survive Depression,* which were both very offbeat narratives, mainly me playing with imagery to tell a story, experimenting with pictorial compositions with movement, that sort of thing."

Mulcahy has since become one of rock video's most sensational,

prolific, and visible *auteurs,* given to lush, sweeping, technically over-
whelming works that are literally "minimovies." Some would argue
that a title like *Contrived Mindflashes* unwittingly reflects the tone of
Mulcahy's insolently sexy work, with its constant references to cinema
chic and modern fashion photography. Mulcahy himself chuckles at the
suggestion.

"Yeah, I guess you could say that title did sort of predict a lot of my
subsequent work," he says, "and in fact a lot of the images and techniques I used in rock videos turned up in those films, like using inks
on bodies in Duran Duran's 'Rio.' Anyway, both those films won first
place at the Sydney Film Festival in 1972 and 1973. I got some money
out of the prize as well, and some notoriety, which was lucky for me
because none of the film schools wanted to know from me, and the
government wouldn't give me any grant money. I guess I was too
strange for them."

"Graham Webb, who was host of a two-hour Australian rock-video
show, rang me up and said, 'Shouldn't Australian bands have their own
pop promos?' At that time a lot of music videos were being seen in
Australia, but they were all by American and British bands who
couldn't afford to tour Australia. In that sense Australia's always been
more into music video than most places. But it was true that few, if any,
native bands had their own music videos. So I began making cheap
promos for Graham—me and a partner who manned the camera. I'd
direct and edit, it was a two-man band, driving around Australia in a
clapped-out old car with a camera in the back. The first one I did was
for a band called Stylus, a cover of that Seals and Crofts tune 'Summer
Breeze,' and that cost about eighty dollars!

"We carried on until 1975 or so, making promos for Australian
bands. They were mostly lightly conceptualized, and I wrote them
myself. We'd shoot them in a day, edit them that night, and that was
it. They were all pretty cheap, too. Then in 1976 I was invited to
England to shoot some punk band whose name I can't remember, and
we did these very silly little concepts with the band and all these other
punky types hanging off scaffolds in a shack in the countryside, and
outside the shack were these zombie types rising out of the ground.
That cost about three thousand dollars.

"I was only supposed to be in England for a few weeks. It was my
first trip there. I'd left the milk in the fridge and my two cats in the flat
back home. Then Richard Branson of Virgin Records called me and
wanted me to make a promo film of Peter Cook and Dudley Moore
making one of their 'Derek and Clive' albums. It was only supposed to

take a few more weeks, but we had mountains of film to edit. So I ended up staying there for six months. And while I was there, Bruce Gowers's 'Bohemian Rhapsody' and Mike Nesmith's 'Rio' came out and caught my eye, made big impressions on me. Then I met Bruce, and Lexi Godfrey, and Jon Roseman, and it all just sort of fell into place.

"Virgin was signing new bands left, right and center, and I was making at least a promo clip a week for all of them: Orchestral Manoeuvres in the Dark, XTC, the Members, Human League, even the Sex Pistols and Public Image Ltd. I was still writing all the concepts, pretty much. Most bands didn't have any input at all, they'd just turn up for the shoot and say 'Right, what do you want us to do, then?' It was only occasionally that a band like XTC would take a real strong interest in the concept."

Back in the States, in 1977, Jo Bergman started the Warner Brothers Records video department. "At the time," she remembers, "we'd just started Warner Cable, it wasn't Warner-Amex yet. I was booking acts for TV appearances, mainly live or lip-sync things. Very gradually we began to creep into the concept of maybe using these promo films domestically. I suggested using them in record stores. People said, 'That's a *terrible* idea.' Of course they were starting to do that in Europe already. Then I thought, 'Why not try colleges?' But that didn't work out either. So it moved along very very slowly here, although more and more awareness of promo clips was growing around the edges of the industry."

On one of those edges was Ed Steinberg, who in 1980 founded and still runs RockAmerica, the country's largest video pool servicing video-equipped rock clubs. In 1974, Steinberg founded his own production company, Soft Focus. "I began taping New York punk-rock acts —Patti Smith, the Ramones, etc.—for local cable outlets. I also taped middle-of-the-road acts, like Buddy Rich, for network and cable TV. At that time there were hardly any clubs with video installed. If they had it, it was a big screen for showing sports or *Saturday Night Live.* Then in 1978 I began working for *Billboard,* in a division they had called Starstream, which was basically a forerunner of RockAmerica: we serviced people with promo clips. Occasionally bars or clubs with video would ask for them, but mainly it was for trade shows and conventions like NARM [National Association of Record Merchandisers], for companies to make their buyers aware of acts and things.

"In those days, there were more videos being made than people think. But there were no real outlets for them here, except maybe occasionally on cable, but mostly it was going out to European TV.

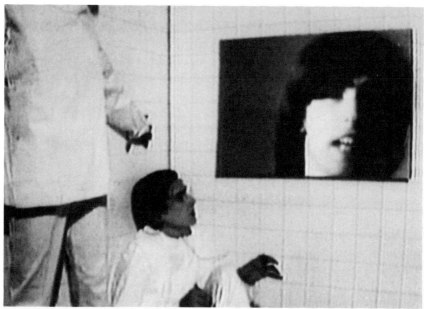

In XTC's "Making Plans for Nigel" (1979), band member Colin Moulding sings through a chroma-key "window" while the asylum-inmate title character looks on. This was one of the earlier directorial efforts by master rock-video *auteur* Russell Mulcahy, who chuckles, "Yeah, the asylum motif is always popular."

RockAmerica came into existence simply because I saw a gaping hole there in the industry's overall attitude toward videos. I knew things were going to change, that there would be more rock video. So I quit Starstream in 1979 and started RockAmerica in September 1980. At that time we operated basically the way we do today: we'd compile a reel of fifteen to twenty clips, from major and smaller labels, from unsigned bands, whatever looked and sounded interesting. In the beginning, I'd say we had subscriptions from just about every single new-wave club in America that had video equipment—that would have been about ten clubs."

Today RockAmerica serves over four hundred rock-video clubs around the country (Soft Focus itself has produced dozens of video clips) and it has competition from about a dozen other major national pools and dozens more smaller localized pools across the country.

But what caused things to change, to escalate so dramatically? Why did Steinberg know in 1978 that there soon would be a greater emphasis on rock video? Why, in 1979, did veteran pop-rocker Todd Rundgren declare rock video to be "the wave of the future" and begin construction of the two-million-dollar, digital-effects-equipped Utopia Video Studios in his Woodstock, New York home, and upon its completion in early 1980 set about lavishing huge sums of money on both conceptual promo clips and long-form rock-video programs? There are several reasons that astute observers noted at the time, and that, in retrospect, set the stage for the rock-video explosion.

Mainly, it was because FM radio—which had started the seventies as a wide-open, "free form" underground alternative to sterile AM radio—had become a demographically researched, narrowly formatted, self-fulfilling musical-marketing prophecy. In the mid-seventies, radio consultants (the most famous being the Burkhart-Abrams firm) entered the picture, polling listeners, not to find out what they'd like to hear but what they *wouldn't* like to hear—what would make them turn the dial. This is known as "passive programming," and what the research turned up was that people wouldn't turn their dials if they heard heavy metal, hard rock, British classical-influenced "progressive rock," or Los Angeles-style slick studio rock. Consultants went for the biggest, most homogeneous audience, which was white youth. What they wanted to hear was music based on the above-mentioned styles, so a new genre of blandly derivative and predictable music took hold across the FM dials around the country. Album Oriented Rock and Album Oriented Radio (both AOR) were rooted in what originally had distinguished FM programming from AM programming—that the former played *album* cuts rather than singles. But with the AOR format taking hold, bands simply began making album cuts as they would have made singles earlier: to fit into a preexisting market format. Thus, the term "AOR" may be used interchangeably for this kind of radio, and for the kinds of songs that are played on this kind of radio. Thus, the self-fulfilling prophecy. So certain bands—Foreigner, Kansas, Styx, Rush, Journey, REO Speedwagon—sold albums in platinum quantities (that is, one million copies sold) by refashioning what consultant research had determined were acceptable sounds. Such bands fused the power chords and hard-hitting medium-to-slow tempos of heavy metal with the pompous neosymphonic orchestrations and high-harmony vocals of British classical rock, and so on. As a result, while certain acts were guaranteed success through radio, a medium that record companies traditionally relied on very heavily for promotion, many other acts could not break through AOR's stultifying format. An alternative was needed, and in video, it came.

A few years after AOR began to take hold, and despite the platinum sales of successful groups, the record industry entered a mammoth economic depression. It partly reflected America's hard times overall, and it partly was due to the corner the industry had painted itself into with AOR, with spendthrift promotions, lavish press parties, and contracts based on the outdated economics of the sixties. Finally, the record industry was simply too massive to respond quickly enough to sudden changes in the demographic base for popular music, which was shifting from age-concentrated younger rock fans to a wider scope of young adults with more catholic tastes. There may have been more people out there to buy records, but there were also more *different* kinds of people, and more different kinds of groups, and the resulting audience fragmentation meant that it was harder for any single band to sell quantities of records that would match the terms of their sixties-economy-based contracts. What it all meant was that touring, especially, became less an obvious and natural promotion route and more something to be selectively applied to bands whose success seemed guaranteed. Again, video and the concurrent growth of cable TV, presented the obvious and logical alternative: whether as an adjunct or as a substitute for touring, a video *could* give a band effective and cost-efficient exposure to millions of potential consumers.

THE ROCK-VIDEO EXPLOSION

By 1980, both the Tubes from San Francisco and Toronto's avant-feminist-rock-cabaret troupe the Hummer Sisters had made intriguing use of live and prerecorded video in their multimedia stage extravaganzas, raising the fringe consciousness of music video. And though both acts would remain fringe curiosities—the Hummers would anyway; the Tubes would finally hit the winning AOR formula in 1982 with "Talk to Ya Later"—the rock-video impetus began spreading to all strata of the rock establishment.

In January 1980, Blondie's *Eat to the Beat* full-length video disc was premièred at the New York new-wave rock disco Hurrah. A month later, the Kinks' full-length video rockumentary *One for the Road* was unveiled at New York rock-pop cabaret the Bottom Line. It seemed as though rock video was making it to the here and now. The Kinks program was a rockumentary video tape; Blondie's, being a conceptualized video disc, made more waves and was subjected to closer scrutiny. It was immediately declared a disaster by the critics, and commercially it didn't do too well, either, mainly because problems between film crew and musicians' unions prevented it from actually being released as a video disc for a year and a half. Still, the mere fact that a rock club like

Hurrah could be fully outfitted to show a rock video, and that that video was *album-length,* served notice that rock video had arrived. Hurrah was the first rock club in New York to install a video system: in this case, a half-dozen nineteen-inch color monitors suspended from the ceiling over the bar and near the banquettes at the back of the club. Soon after, the legendary (and, like Hurrah, now defunct) Max's Kansas City installed two TV sets around its bar. Later that year, the Ritz, a huge rock ballroom, opened in New York; its video screen was a huge, fifty-foot-square rear-projection job. Simultaneously, as more and more young Americans rejected AOR pomp-rock, England and America supplied a steady stream of up-and-coming young new-wave post-punks. Their records and videos were played in dance-rock clubs like Hurrah and the Ritz, where the bands also made live appearances. An underground circuit was developing, and rock video was a part of it. How vital a part is open to debate: in those days, before rock video had become a widespread subject of discussion, videos were often played while club DJs spun completely different tunes by different bands. Thus, video clips were often reduced to found, silent, abstracted background imagery, a latter-day psychedelic light show—something compounded by many clubs' tendency to play effects-generated abstract images and animation as often as promo clips.

Even then, people would stop dancing and talking to crowd around the video monitors whenever a Devo or David Bowie video came on the screens. The involvement of someone like David Bowie in rock video was at least as great a benediction as Blondie's video disc. Bowie was a long-established star; unlike all those new British bands (for whom Bowie was an artistic godfather in many cases), he didn't *need* rock-video exposure. Indeed, Bowie's first videos—for the title cut of his 1977 *Heroes,* and "Boys Keep Swinging," "Look Back in Anger," and "DJ" from his 1979 *Lodger*—weren't really seen in America until a year after they were made. That's partly an indication of how far rock video still had to go before it was considered crucial to promotion, and partly an indication of the artistic and budgetary license Bowie's stature granted him.

Though ostensibly a singer, songwriter, guitarist, and saxophonist, Bowie's main instrument had always been his image, his personae, his peculiar aptitude for about-face image shifts that were seemingly always one step ahead of the next big trend. Bowie had always been a very *visual* artist: he'd studied with British mime Lindsay Kemp before becoming a rock star; in 1974, Bowie's "1980 Floor Show" (based on his *Diamond Dogs* album, originally intended as a rock version of

David Bowie in drag at the conclusion of his "Boys Keep Swinging" video (1979), codirected with David Mallet, smearing his lipstick in the trademark gesture he repeated at the end of his "China Girl" video in 1983

Orwell's *1984*), in which he sported an outrageous costume with plaster female hands clenched around his torso, had enlivened *Midnight Special*'s typical straight concert lip-synchs with its protorock-video conceptualized set pieces; in 1976, he'd embarked on a distinguished stage-and-screen acting career in Nicolas Roeg's film *The Man Who Fell to Earth.* Bowie's involvement in rock video seemed the logical fulfillment of artistic and technological destiny, incipient evidence of the inevitability of rock video. And with all the other image-conscious British bands coming out with videos as fast and furious as independent singles, one had to wonder not how far it might go, but where it would all end.

As it happened, those first Bowie videos, especially "Boys Keep Swinging" and "Look Back in Anger," contained motifs of multiple identity and ego loss that have since become staples of rock video. Other typical motifs were apparent in the videos being seen in those days: the colorful, flash-cut asylum dementia of XTC's "Making Plans for Nigel" (1980) and Alice Cooper's "How You Gonna See Me Now" (1980), both directed by Russell Mulcahy for Jon Roseman; and the inspired performer elevating a mere performance, as in Iggy Pop's "I'm Bored" and "Five Foot One" (both 1980).

At the time, Bowie began making statements about rock video: "I see it as an artistic extension; I can visualize the day when the interface of music and video will create an entirely new kind of artist." Still, up to that time, the only group seeming to embody that new artistic synergy was Devo. In 1980, Devo attained new rock-video heights with clips for "Freedom of Choice" (casting Devo as sci-fi aliens warning us of the hypocrisy of consumerist democracy) and their big hit, "Whip It" (a sardonic, beautifully choreographed sendup of western-style Americana, with S&M down on the farm). But, significantly, Devo finally began to be challenged in 1980 both in the aesthetic felicity of the rock-video synergy and in sheer, strikingly bizarre imagery. The Residents's stunning, seriocomic "Land of 1,000 Dances" began to be seen in video-equipped rock clubs. From New York came "Frankie Teardrop," a mesmerizingly haunting and surreal (and sadly under-viewed) visual complement to an epic opus of urban dissolution by New York's protopunk future-shock electronic duo Suicide, created by local underground filmmaker Edit DeAk and part-time Manhattan Cable TV video editor Paul Daugherty.

At this point, rock video was making further progress towards MTV-style programming. From Carmel, California, home of Mike Nesmith's Pacific Arts operation, came *Popclips,* a year's worth of weekly half-hour shows, made in conjunction with Warner Cable and shown through most of 1981 on Warner Cable's youth-oriented Nickelodeon channel. *Popclips* director and Nesmith collaborator Bill Dear describes the show: "*Popclips* was basically MTV before there *was* MTV. Our VJ was Howie Mandel, who at the time was a loony L.A. stand-up comic, and who has since become a star of the NBC series *St. Elsewhere*. We had Howie acting maniacal in this high-tech set with all these video-tape and video-disc machines and monitors, and there was a video-switching control console, so you'd actually see him sit there and say, 'Okay, now here's a clip by so-and-so,' and 'cue it up,' and then the clip would come on. We wanted the VJ segments to be as crazy as the clips we were showing.

"Anyway, Warner Cable wanted to buy the name and the idea of the show from us and develop it into what has now become MTV. When Mike Nesmith and I heard what they wanted to do with it, we nearly had heart attacks, from disgust and laughter. So they just watered down the idea and came up with MTV. Still, in a way, I'm glad they did it, because MTV certainly has validated the form."

But this was still long before MTV worked its magic. From England, came more groundbreaking rock videos. In late 1979 there had been

David Mallet's "I Don't Like Mondays" for the Boomtown Rats—one of the first concept clips actually to work multiple sets and characterizations into a lucid, compelling narrative. The Mallet-directed Blondie *Eat to the Beat* broke further ground in some ways, even though it was a contrived visual eyesore. And in 1980 there came another clip made in England in late 1979, Russell Mulcahy's "Video Killed the Radio Star" for the Buggles. With a title like that, lyrics like "We can't rewind, we've gone too far/ Put the blame on VTR" (as in Video Tape Recording), and shots of TV sets erupting up through a floor to displace a pile of old thirties-style radios, the clip and especially the song became anthems among rock-video prognosticators—of whom there were still comparatively few. But in August 1981, "Video Killed the Radio Star" would become the first video clip MTV ever played.

By 1980, Mulcahy had moved to London and was turning out a clip a week for MGM Productions, an independent production company he formed with David Mallet and producer Lexi Godfrey. They did a lot of contract work for producer Jon Roseman, who'd overseen the Blondie *Eat to the Beat* video disc. It's ironic that news of the coming of the video disc in 1975 provided a spark for pioneering rock-video efforts, and yet this first rock-video disc proved such a bust. To date the video disc still trails far behind video cassettes in terms of hardware and software distribution. At any rate, in the wake of *Eat to the Beat,* Roseman had returned to London. Always interested in big-budget rock-video productions, Roseman was rock video's first David O. Selznick—he was just too far ahead of his time. However, since then his London operation has kept near the forefront; among its more recent eyecatchers was Eurythmics's "Sweet Dreams (Are Made of This)" (1983).

By 1980 the five-year-old U.K. rock-video production firm Keefco was concentrating as much of its attention on the American scene as on the British. MGM's main competition came from another team that frequently contracted with Roseman—Millaney-Grant, composed of producer Scott Millaney and director Brian Grant. Millaney had been overseeing Island Records' video operations in London when the two met. Grant had become an assistant cameraman with Lord Lew Grade's ATV in 1970, and had since worked on countless shows, including Tom Jones specials; Sammy Davis, Jr.'s talk show *Sammy and Company;* and *The Muppets.*

"I'd always been as much into music as into cameras and TV and film," says Grant, now thirty-two. "I was a Motown freak as a kid, and I played drums in all sorts of amateur bands. So when the pop promo things started happening in the mid-seventies, I took note of that and thought that when I was less busy with other things, I'd check them out. I was moonlighting on a video shoot in the north of England and I met Scott Millaney. We hit it off right away and found we had the same attitudes about pop promos. One day after work, we both sat in a bar and hatched the idea to form Millaney-Grant. We hocked everything we had and, in 1979, set up shop in Scott's front room. We had one telephone and we rang up *everybody* all day long—hassle, hassle, hassle. And to show you what it was like in those days, we had a tape of people typing and talking, phones ringing, that sort of thing. Whenever anyone called us back, or when we called someone, we'd always have that tape playing in the background so they'd think we were in this super-busy office!

"In early 1980, this friend of Scott's comes in and says, 'I have this act, M'—M was actually this one-man synthesizer band, Robin Scott —'and this song, "Pop Muzik," and we'd like to make a video for it.' We shot the thing in one afternoon on Editek for three thousand dollars. A few days later, M's manager took the clip to the *Kenny Everett* show, and David Mallet saw it and loved it, and a week later it went out on the BBC. And since then, the phone hasn't stopped ringing."

There were many other people in London who became leading rock-video *auteurs,* among them Kevin Godley and Lol Creme, former member of ultraclever British art-rock band 10cc, which, in 1980, made three rock videos that still rank among the genre's finest: Visage's "We Fade to Gray" and "Mind of a Toy," and Duran Duran's "Girls on Film."

"Getting into video was natural for us," says Godley. "I first met Lol back when we were in art school together—and there's a tip-off right there, art school: I mean, where do you think the English got all this video stuff?—when I was shooting a Super-8 version of *Dracula.* I was casting for a hunchback; I met Lol, and guess who got the part? Since then, we've obviously devoted most of our time to music. But we always had very visual leanings: we designed our album sleeves, and we always wrote very visual, imagistic, film-script-type lyrics anyway. So the potential was always there to exploit.

"I think what really happened was, two guys who were supposed to make films ended up training by making music, and in 1976 found themselves in a position where they wanted to leave their band and do other things. Which we did. We went out as a duo, and one of the first things we did was make a film for a song of ours called 'An Englishman

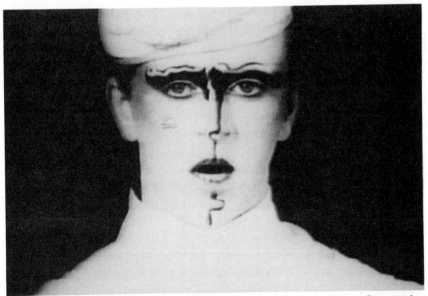

The performer as a work of art (pre-Boy George, yet): Steve Strange's decorated visage in Visage's "Fade to Gray" (1980), one of the earliest directorial successes for ex-musicians-turned-rock-video *auteurs* Godley and Creme

in New York,' around 1978. Then we made another one, for 'Reds in My Bed.' They were shown on *Top of the Pops* and such, and Steve Strange of Visage saw them. He approached us to make some promo films for his band. After that, Duran Duran happened, and we've just been into it since then. We found ourselves immediately stimulated by it, as if we'd suddenly found ourselves on the right side of the camera. We've stuck with it, almost to the exclusion of other projects, because we enjoy it so much. Believe me, there isn't much money in it. Our pockets are *very* thinly lined."

Elsewhere in London, another future rock-video production biggie was getting started—Limelight Film and Video, whose prolific stable of directors includes Steve Barron, Don Letts, Pete Sinclair, Chris Gabrin, and Arthur Ellis, and used to include Julian Temple (as of mid-1983 on his own with Midnight Films). Limelight was formed in 1979 by Steve Barron and his producer-sister Siobhan. Their parents are both film-industry veterans: father Ron as a soundman in British films; mother Zelda (who directed Culture Club's 1983 video "I'll Tumble 4 Ya," and who as of this writing was slated to direct her own first feature film, *Secret Places*) as script supervisor and continuity woman on such films as *Reds* and *Yentl.* Both Barron children were already familiar with the film industry before founding Limelight. Steve, who'd started tinkering with cameras in his midteens, later met British cinematographer Geoffrey Unsworth and worked with him as assistant cameraman on *A Bridge Too Far* and *Superman,* as well as with Ridley Scott on *The Duelists;* Siobhan was wardrobe mistress and production assistant on *Superman.*

"When rock videos started happening," explains Steve Barron, "I was immediately interested: I'd always been into rock music as well as filmmaking, and on features, you're out there months and months at a time. I wanted to get into shooting myself, with something that was quicker, more immediate. Rock promos seemed a logical place to go. So Siobhan and I formed a company out of our front room in late 1978."

"Our first project," says Siobhan Barron, "was a sort of conceptual rockumentary on the 1978 Reading Rock Fest in England. Steve wrote this little story line for it to mix in with the performance footage; it had to do with a little kid—who was actually the son of Lemmy from the heavy-metal band Motorhead—wandering through the festival, imagining himself as a rock star. So we'd cut from him to the bands. But halfway through the shoot our financing dropped out. I'll never forget it: the crew agreed to stay on and shoot even though we couldn't pay them for it, simply because they were having so much fun. I cried, I couldn't believe it. But it's been that way ever since—there isn't much money in this, not yet, and everyone's in it for the love and fun of it."

Steve Barron continues: "Our first actual project, the first one that really came off, was a twenty-minute rockumentary on this British band, Barclay James Harvest, in 1978. Later that year, I directed my first promo, 'Strange Town,' by the Jam. To show you what it was like back then, I had wanted the clip to be half performance and half street scenes to go with the title and lyrics. But on the day we'd scheduled to shoot on the street, it rained, and the band wouldn't go out to shoot in the rain. And that was that. So it's a performance clip. Siobhan and I, meanwhile, kept going round to all the labels, and they'd always say, 'No, we *won't* spend five thousand dollars on a promo film.' They *were* making them, but their own way. I guess they didn't want to know from anyone else. We needed to make our own break. It finally came late in the year when I did 'Antmusic' with Adam and the Ants. We got lots of calls after that. Then our next break came with Human League's 'Don't You Want Me,' which I consider my first really successful concept clip, though today I can hardly look at it. But the song became a huge hit, everyone saw the video, and then MTV happened, and everything just exploded."

Meanwhile, back in Los Angeles, cameraman Daniel Pearl had begun shooting rock videos in 1979. His recollections further focus just how different pre-MTV attitudes were from today's: "In the days before MTV, making videos was seen by the bands as a hassle. They'd show up and do a few takes, but after that they couldn't be bothered. If anyone complained, they'd say, 'Hey man, we're *rock* stars, not *film* stars.' " This is not to indicate that all rock stars felt that way before MTV came along; according to Steve Barron, an image-conscious British rock star like Adam Ant "was actually very concerned, had a lot of input, into his video, at least on the level of making creative suggestions and wanting to know exactly what was happening and how it would all look."

But consider Daniel Pearl's conclusion, in relation to perhaps less image-conscious American artists outside the visually oriented British milieu: "I guess to the bands back then, videos were just something that some bunch of foreigners were going to see somewhere," says Pearl, "probably because there just wasn't anything as massive as MTV here yet. The bands just couldn't relate to it on that kind of level. You can't really blame them."

By 1981, Mike Nesmith had released his full-length video album *Elephant Parts.* Ed Steinberg's RockAmerica was now servicing some seventy subscribing clubs with rock videos. Toni Basil, who in 1979 had signed a music-and-video recording deal with British-based Radial-choice Records, released her *Word of Mouth* audio and video albums simultaneously. More-established artists like Paul McCartney and even veteran country-blues-rocker Commander Cody (for whom Joe Dea directed the comic "Two Triple Cheese, Side Order of Fries" video in 1981, for $250) were making rock videos. Elvis Costello had made two in 1979 for his *Armed Forces* album; in 1980 he made three for *Get Happy!!* The clips, directed in Richard Lester-style by Devo collaborator Chuck Statler, countered Costello's arrogant-young-man image with lighthearted, self-mocking frolics. In 1979, British new-wave mystery girl Lene Lovich made antic, enhanced-performance videos for her hits "Lucky Number" and "Say When" that proved very popular on the new-wave rock-disco circuit; in 1980, she followed them up with a lush, studiously Hitchcockian concept clip for "Bird Song."

In late 1980, David Bowie and Mallet upped the aesthetic ante with two superb clips for Bowie's *Scary Monsters* album, "Ashes to Ashes" and "Fashion."

There were more and more clips being made, of both British and American bands. There were more and more outlets for them in clubs and on cable TV. This was the time that the gears really began to shift. Entertainment megaconglomerate Warner Communications (which owns Warner Brothers Records, Warner Brothers Films, Warner Books, what used to be Warner Cable, Warner Home Video, and more) began plotting a new venture, a massive merger with American Express to form Warner-Amex Satellite Entertainment Corp. (WASEC). As Bill Dear indicated, Pacific Arts' *Popclips* had aroused the interest of Warner Cable. Says former WASEC executive vice-president John Lack, "The radio stations weren't playing new artists, so the companies needed new ways to promote records. Cable television offered us the possibility of promoting music in stereo on television."

Thus was born the idea for MTV. Feelers were put out, contacts made, programming and promotional executives recruited from all strata of the music and television industries. Concepts and formats were proposed, researched, tested, fine-tuned. Literally thousands of people tried out to be MTV video jockeys, with bleary-eyed channel executives viewing demo tape after demo tape, waiting for that special magic. What video clips existed were rounded up from record companies, viewed by MTV programming panels, and selected for the channel's library and programming rotation according to MTV's music-mix format. By August 1, 1981, MTV was launched: a twenty-four-hour, nationwide, visual radio station. Record companies adopted an alert, watch-and-wait attitude at first: after all, this was a completely new concept for American TV, and besides, MTV started with only about four million cable homes subscribing. In March 1981, USA Cable Network, with about twelve million subscribers, had premièred *Night Flight,* produced by New York's ATI Video. But *Night Flight* was, as producer Cynthia Friedland puts it, "a *cultural* service, a *program,* not just a string of promo clips." *Night Flight* showed, and still shows, a highly eclectic mix of feature-length music video as well as rock-generation cult movies, video art, and various locally produced programs from around the country. As Friedland says, "We're an alternative, a complement to MTV."

Before MTV even came on the cable, and while *Popclips* was still running on Nickelodeon, and just as *Night Flight* debuted, NBC's Canadian-based late-night conceptual comedy show *SCTV* introduced Rick Moranis (himself a former Canadian radio DJ) as Gerry Todd, "the all-night video DJ." Todd wore a leisure suit, horn-rims, and an aging hipster's goatee, sat at a video-switching console and gave forth

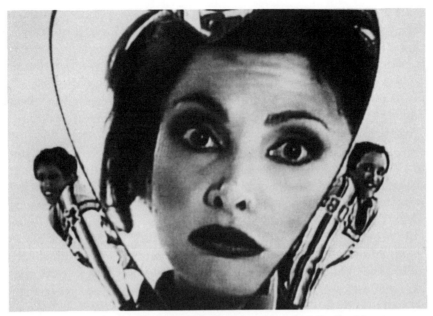

Toni Basil, framed in a special-effects valentine and flanked by two
Dorsey High (Cal.) cheerleaders, in her classic video "Mickey" (1982),
one of the first songs to become a smash hit almost totally due to
MTV exposure

with a nonstop stream of drive-time patter: "We got news, sports and
weather for ya at the top of the hour, but first here's some fine video
from Tom Monroe's latest, *On a New Wavelength,* a little tune called
'Turning Japanese.' " There appeared Moranis again, this time as
polyester-clad lounge crooner Tom Monroe, sashaying coolly through
a hysterical easy-listening parody of British band the Vapors' current
new-wave rock hit, "Turning Japanese." In the video, Monroe alter-
nately grinned and looked earnest as he strode through what appeared
to be an Oriental theme park—complete with little bridges, little
brooks, and kimono-clad women between whom Monroe peeked while
lip-synching *"Hey,* I'm turning Japanese, yeah I really think
so-o-o-o-o. . . ."

Moranis had neither seen nor heard of *Popclips.* "It was just an idea
I had," he says, "based on my radio experience, where I'd see these guys
just like Gerry Todd, who could sit there and fill dead air forever. I
thought, 'What if a guy like that was on *TV?*' The 'Turning Japanese'
thing was inspired by Scopitones I used to see in Canada."

Several months later, MTV debuted. MTV didn't come to New York until a year later; WASEC execs and staff drove to Fort Lee, New Jersey, the nearest city to Manhattan with MTV, to watch its opening night. But a few days before August 1, 1981, MTV threw a press party at which a bank of TV sets played tapes of what MTV's four million households would soon be seeing: an endless avalanche of essentially the same corporate pomp-rock acts that AOR radio had always been playing (and which rock video was supposed to supplant), like REO Speedwagon and Rush, and nary a Devo or Bowie in sight; loads of eyecatching MTV in-house promos; and, sandwiched in between, the MTV VJs, the ones who'd had that "magic" that enabled them to make the grade ahead of thousands of competitors in the earlier tryouts. They were blond all-American preppie Alan Hunter; dark, curly-haired Mark Goodman; jolly, rotund black man J. J. Jackson; sweet, plain-Jane brunette Martha Quinn; and blond California girl Nina Blackwood. Hunter and Blackwood had acting experience; the rest had been radio DJs. While none of them were facsimiles for Gerry Todd, they *were* mainstream: in fact, the "magic" MTV executives saw in them seemed to consist of little more than ready smiles, and the fact that each appeared to have marched, made-to-order, out of a demographic test tube; together, they seemed to cover nearly all the possible audience bases.

MTV, started up at a cost of over twenty million dollars, has always been a promotion-minded enterprise. Its programming consists of promotional video clips; it receives the clips free from record companies seeking the channel's unparalleled capacities for exposure; it runs Chyron-generated captions naming the band, song, album, and label at the start and finish of every clip. After some initial recalcitrance about giving away their promo clips, most labels quickly capitulated; the only holdout was Polygram, which changed its tune within months. Though MTV was initially seen in only about four million homes, its barrage of in-house promos and especially its contests—like "One Night Stands," in which the winner and some friends are flown via private Lear jet to a free concert and night on the town with a big-name rock act (Journey and Fleetwood Mac were among MTV's first "One Night Stands") at MTV's expense—kept viewers tuned in and created a lot of word-of-mouth publicity. Though media and advertisers were slow to pick up on MTV's the-future-is-now promise, others reacted quickly. Within months of MTV's debut, Fred Silverman, former programmer at all three major broadcast networks, pronounced it "the most interesting and exciting new thing to happen to television yet."

And record labels began to increase their production of video clips.

Rock video's preeminent camp counselors, the MTV VJs: (left to right) Alan Hunter, Mark Goodman, Martha Quinn, J. J. Jackson, and Nina Blackwood

For the first time, they began to send their clips unsolicited to Ed Steinberg at RockAmerica, which was then servicing over one hundred video-equipped clubs around the country. Some clubs had already begun "video only" nights, charging lower admission prices to fill the house. At the Ritz in New York, a handheld camera was often taken through the dance floor, beaming images of customers onto the huge screen over the stage.

Now, rock-club patrons had yet another diversion added to live bands, DJs spinning dance records, drinking, and picking up patrons. And, with generations having been weaned on TV, whenever something came on a club's video monitor, people *watched*. Reports began cropping up all over the country, bemusedly noting that when rock videos came on in clubs, people stopped dancing with their partners and stood dancing with themselves while watching the screens. But not everyone was all that excited about it. A club VJ like Joe Verange of the Metro in Boston claims, "Just like that Billy Idol song, people were dancing with themselves. But the thing is that while video *was* becoming a draw in itself, when you're dealing with the hard realities of running a club, you want people to drink and all, and when they're just *glued* to the video screens, they don't drink."

More and more often these days, bands make two different versions of a video: one for MTV and other more mainstream televised outlets, and one for more adult cable and club outlets. Godley and Creme directed the "Girls on Film" video; Kevin Godley says, "People are always accusing that tape of sexism, and of course they're right. Look, we just did our job: we were very explicitly told by Duran Duran's management to make a very sensational, erotic piece that would be for clubs, where it could get shown uncensored, just to make people take notice and talk about it."

Meanwhile, the video-only club was becoming a phenomenon in itself. Back in late 1979, San Francisco rock entrepreneur Richard Kawecki and cinematographer Steve Katz had started holding "video only" nights at the San Francisco rock club Midnight Sun. By August 1982, they'd moved to Los Angeles, and with VJ Steve Sukman, opened the video-only bar Revolver (which, as of this writing, was slated to open a New York branch in the winter of 1983). In the autumn of 1981, Larry "Zee" Zimberg had begun a similar service in such Los Angeles clubs as the Atomic Cafe, the Veil, and the Sunspot, calling his movable rock-video feast the Scat Club. Most recently, he's been working at Hollywood's male-stripper club, Chippendale's.

Also in late 1981, the RockWorld video pool had begun servicing college campuses with rock videos, operating along RockAmerica's lines: subscribing colleges pay a monthly rate to receive a cassette compilation of twenty or so of the latest rock videos. RockWorld started with about fifty colleges; it now services several hundred.

In August 1981, "club video" moved from a burgeoning cottage industry to news headlines, as Public Image Ltd., the band ex-Sex Pistol Johnny "Rotten" Lydon had formed, provoked a riot at the Ritz in New York by using the club's video screen during a hastily organized, erroneously advertised, sold-out concert. Recalls ex-Public Image guitarist Keith Levene, who orchestrated the concert, "It *was* hastily organized, and the Ritz couldn't advertise the show the way it should have been, as 'Public Image Live Video Concert,' or something. I'd been aware of video at the time, it wasn't a real big deal yet, but it was very apparent that it was the wave of the future. I wanted to do something different with it, and came up with the 'live video' idea: have the band onstage *behind* the club's screen, and beam live simulcast images of us behind the screen and other footage we'd already shot onto the screen. The idea was that the Ritz's screen would be like a giant TV screen, with the band in the back of the set. When the Ritz approached us to play there, I demanded that we get to use the video or else we wouldn't play. I did *not* intend to provoke a riot, but aside from the unfortunate violence, I think the whole thing was a more than partial success just in terms of impact. It *was* the event of the season."

Indeed it was. Here's what happened: Bow Wow Wow had canceled their scheduled Ritz show at the last minute; Public Image was booked as the replacement, and the ads for the show simply read "Public Image Ltd.," mentioning nothing about the video. The show started with a pretaped, farcical interview between Manhattan new-wave scenemaker and gossip Lisa Yapp and Levene. When the band's silhouettes were seen behind the screen, and the band was heard tuning up, the packed house got restless. When Public Image broke into one abortive number, and the screen still didn't rise, the crowd began throwing bottles at the screen. The ever-ready Lydon promptly teased the crowd, leering, "Next time throw *full* bottles!" The band shambled through several songs, never completing a one; the video screen showed a chaotic mix of footage shot earlier that day on New York City streets and of the band playing behind the screen. Meanwhile, those fans near the stage were being pelted with the bottles hurled at the screen from the rear and balcony of the club. In twenty minutes it was all over: chairs as well as bottles had been thrown at the screen, which had finally been torn down by the throng; the stage parapet had been pulled into the crowd, and the instruments on it were destroyed. Public Image Ltd. fled, and by the time police arrived to clear the crowd out, several patrons and Ritz security personnel had suffered injuries.

We may never know exactly what was to blame for the unusually violent crowd reaction (which, indeed, went against the prevalent grain of acceptance of rock video): at the least, it appears to have been a combination of shoddy technical execution due to hasty, last-minute planning, and the frustrated expectations of a misinformed weekend audience that was looking for fun and entertainment not avant-garde *agit prop*. Yet, despite moral compunctions about the gratuitous violence Public Image Ltd. provoked that night, the show does still stand as an unparalleled event in rock-video history: the first and so-far only (thank God) rock-video riot.

At any rate, rock video was manifesting itself in all these different forms—not to mention satellite-simulcast concerts, which Home Box Office began in early 1981, and which Oak/ON-TV, in conjunction with Campus Entertainment Network, would undertake with at least partial success in 1982 with the Rolling Stones, Devo, and the Who. But the record labels were training their eyes mostly on MTV in 1981. They were waiting to see how long it would take before the twenty-four-hour music-video channel would actually pay off in record sales. It didn't take long. As Buzz Brindle, an MTV executive who oversees acquisitions of tapes to be added to the playlist, says, "When we started, we didn't have this enormous library of thousands and thousands of tapes like we do now. Most of what we had was from new-wave British groups, who were already very conscious of video's power. They had already cultivated a 'look,' and the British directors had already cultivated a 'style,' one that still dominates rock videos to this day. Back then, the British videos just looked better—they were instantly recognizable against the American ones."

By the end of 1981, many labels had noticed that MTV was programming bands radio was not playing—and that those artists had then gotten radio play, which only further increased the record sales MTV had already sparked. One of the first and best examples was Duran Duran, graduates of the early eighties, fashion-conscious British "new romantic" movement. Their debut eponymous album on Capitol/EMI Records had failed to yield a hit single despite dogged touring and lots of teen-mag press, and the album had never risen higher than number 150 in the charts since its midsummer 1981 release.

Michelle Peacock, who oversees EMI's production and distribution of promotional videos, remembers what happened then: "MTV wasn't on yet in New York or L.A., so most label executives just didn't fully understand the concept, the potential of it. Those two cities, aside from being media centers, are also the centers of the recording industry. I'd been working in the field in the South and the Southwest, where they did have MTV in markets like Dallas and Tulsa. And almost instantly after MTV came on there, something funny began to happen. Duran Duran's album, with *no* radio play, and with a band who were already *huge* in England and Europe and who'd been touring and touring here to no apparent gain, was selling like hotcakes wherever they had MTV. We checked into it, and sure enough, the band had a video or two on MTV, and our accounts at retail were calling us with these wild stories

An Oriental woman flips a sumo wrestler—illustrating the typical rock-video equation of women and sex with fear, pain, and humiliation —in Duran Duran's "Girls on Film," the sensationally sexploitative clip directed by Godley and Creme (1980).

about kids who'd come into the stores saying, 'I saw this band on MTV. . . .' And they were buying the record. That was all I needed to know. It so happened that a couple of months later I was transferred to the L.A. office. The first thing I did was tell everyone what MTV had done for Duran Duran in the field. At that time the record was just inching up the charts a bit. People were still slow on the uptake.

"I was running around raving to people: 'Don't you understand? This is going to be the greatest thing!' I remember when MTV sent Bob Pittman and John Sykes, their two head execs, out here to introduce us to MTV. I was the only person who'd talk to them, and they were sort of meekly pleading with me to try and get as many people as I could to this luncheon in their hotel where they were going to show some tapes of MTV. I remember *two* people showed up, me and someone else. Of course *now* it's a whole different story, everyone calls MTV their best buddies. . . ."

It was around August 1981, concurrent with MTV's debut, that EMI decided to invest over $200,000—then an unprecedented sum for rock videos—to send Duran Duran to Sri Lanka to shoot three exotic promo clips with director Russell Mulcahy. One of them, "Hungry like the

Wolf," became an instant MTV favorite. (The other videos shot there were "Save a Prayer" and "Lonely in Your Nightmare.") EMI's financing of the Sri Lanka shoots was not quite the visionary gamble it might seem in retrospect; as EMI executive Michelle Peacock puts it, "Duran Duran got that financing mainly because they'd already done so well in Britain and Europe. We hoped it would work for MTV, and of course it did." Less than two months after the two-week shoot, "Hungry like the Wolf" was not only in "heavy rotation" on MTV (that is, their videos were being shown three or four times a day), but was also getting heavy radio play, and Duran Duran's album was bulleting into the upper reaches of the album chart. Both "Hungry like the Wolf" and "Rio" went Top Ten in the U.S.

By mid-1982, many other labels had seen the same sort of payoff from MTV exposure. Randy Hock, former Arista Records director of promotion and one of the industry's biggest rock-video boosters, recalls, "When Bob Pittman came to me with his idea for MTV, I thought it was fascinating. Then, naturally, being in this business, I immediately wondered about the dollars to be spent on these videos, and more important, about the money we could get back indirectly through promotional value. And with MTV willing to play all these new British bands that AOR radio was *not* playing, MTV began to look like a really viable alternative.

"At the time, we had these two new British bands who we thought were very unique and exciting and deserved to be played on AOR radio —Haircut 100 and a Flock of Seagulls. But radio didn't feel the way we did about them. By that time we knew that with AOR, we'd created this monster that was tyrannizing *us*. They told us, 'Take them to *college* radio, maybe they'll play them.' MTV seemed even more viable.

"It helped us formulate a new strategy for success in this country: clubs, college radio, retail, touring, AOR, *plus* MTV. That's meant success not just for us, but for CBS with Men at Work and Tommy Tutone; for Polygram with ABC, Golden Earring, and Def Leppard; for Epic with Culture Club, Adam Ant, and Eddy Grant; for Capitol/ EMI with Stray Cats, Duran Duran, and Kajagoogoo. And on and on."

Susan Blond of Epic Records tells a similar tale, but one on a different level: "With Adam Ant and Culture Club you had classic examples— very visual new bands that radio wasn't playing until *after* MTV had made them successful; then radio came along to further it. But the best example I can think of to illustrate the power of MTV is Cheap Trick. This is an established American band with a solid following, not a strange new band from somewhere else. In 1982 they released an album, *One on One,* that did its usual strong initial sale with their regular audience, and then didn't move beyond that level. Radio simply wasn't playing the singles, 'If You Want My Love' and 'She's Tight.' The album was dying on the vine, dropping right off the charts. *Then* we made videos for 'If You Want My Love' and 'She's Tight,' and MTV put them into top rotation, and *then* radio play and sales shot right back up. It really opened our eyes."

At that time, MTV still actually reached only eight to ten million cable homes (roughly one third of America's total cable population). Again displaying its promotional savvy, the channel embarked on its now legendary series of promotions in which big-name rock stars—Pete Townshend of the Who, Mick Jagger of the Rolling Stones, Pat Benatar, and others—were seen in commercials on broadcast and advertiser-supported cable outlets, screaming, "I want my MTV. . . . Pick up your phone, call your local cable operator, and *demand* your MTV." The stars made the ads for free: if they could help spread MTV's gospel, they too would benefit from the channel's exposure of their videos. The ads worked: Warner-Amex reported an average of one million new subscribers signing up each month.

In August 1982, New York's Museum of Modern Art sought agreements to add these clips to its video collection: Captain Beefheart's 1970 *Lick My Decals Off, Baby* commercial and his just-completed video for "Ice Cream for Crow"; Laurie Anderson's "O Superman"; Toni Basil's "Mickey"; and Talking Heads' "Once in a Lifetime."

In addition, rock video was no longer simply an adjunct to the record. It was creating true video stars. Toni Basil (who directed the Talking Heads clip) is perhaps the first video star, someone who *needed* video to become a success. "I ended up with a number-one record with 'Mickey,' " she says, "and that was a record no radio station would play till long after MTV had the video in heavy rotation. In fact, I never played a live show in support of that record. Not that I'm proud of that fact; I'd love to do live shows. But I can't. How could I afford to take the twenty or thirty dancers and the multiple sets I use in the videos on the road? It'd cost a fortune. The video made it easy for me to do exactly what I wanted, and for it to be seen all over the place. It was efficient and effective. It sure worked for me."

On September 1, 1982, the crucial final step was taken: MTV came on cable in New York and Los Angeles. As when it first debuted a year earlier, it signed on in New York and L.A. with the appropriate Buggles video for "Video Killed the Radio Star." MTV's subscriber total was now about fourteen million. As Jo Bergman of Warner Brothers says, "There's the world of rock video before and after MTV, but more important, there's the world before MTV hit New York and L.A. and the world after that. *That's* when the comprehension and sophistication of rock video began to escalate at an incredibly fast rate."

Indeed. A little over a year before, Mike Nesmith had won the first video Grammy Award. His acceptance speech went like this: "Thank you. The music-only phenomenon is now history."

Now—with MTV in the big media and industry centers, and seemingly being seen everywhere else, and with Olivia Newton-John's *Physical* video disc having more recently won the second video Grammy—Nesmith's prediction seemed to be coming true. Record labels reported that *every* new band they signed specified contractual provisions for a certain number of videos per year; record labels started their own video departments (EMI started EMI Music Video, now known as Picture Music International, in 1981; Polygram started its own Polygram Music Video in late 1982); rock video was included in overall marketing and promotional strategies as a matter of course. Video production companies sprouted up all over America, from New York to Minneapolis to New Orleans to Los Angeles to San Francisco. In England, there were already over one hundred such firms. RockAmerica was now servicing roughly three hundred video clubs and was competing with over a half-dozen other video pools that had recently sprung up. Some video jukeboxes appeared in Europe, Australia, and Canada, and prototypes were unveiled in selected American locations. The Devo and Who concert simulcasts took place within months of each other in late 1982.

In January 1983, Sony took rock video to the next logical step—from promotional tool to self-contained consumer item—by marketing its first batch of video 45s, video cassettes priced under twenty dollars and containing two or three of a band's clips. Though Sony will not quote sales figures, Sony Software Division vice-president John O'Donnell says of Sony's first three video 45s (Mike Nesmith's "Rio" and "Cruisin'," Duran Duran's "Hungry like the Wolf" and the uncensored "Girls on Film," and Scottish video artist Jesse Rae's "Rusha" and "D.E.S.I.R.E."), "They sold out their first pressing in a few weeks, and we had to rush to fill reorders all over the country."

Then, with rock-video-clip budgets escalating steadily to the point where the average expenditure rose from the fifteen-thousand-dollar to twenty-five-thousand-dollar range to the thirty-five-thousand-dollar to fifty-thousand-dollar range, and some clips (like Michael Jackson's

"Beat It," a breakthrough video in other ways that will be discussed in the next chapter) breaking the hundred-thousand-dollar budget mark, came the summer of 1983. There was the media barrage on rock video, when one could not turn on the TV or open a magazine or newspaper without running into a splashy feature on rock video—and more often than not one that *equated* rock video with MTV. There was the plethora of other rock-video shows on cable and then broadcast TV. There were feature films that looked like rock videos, to complement rock videos that already were being called minimovies and microoperas; rock-video directors were landing feature-film deals, and feature-film directors were making rock videos; there were commercials that looked like rock videos (again, to complement rock videos that were, in effect, three-minute commercials for bands and songs, and which accordingly used commercial techniques); movies like *Flashdance,* and *The Hunger,* and Jim McBride's remake of *Breathless,* and Sylvester Stallone's *Stayin' Alive,* and *Dr. Detroit* were cut down into rock-video-length trailers that ran on MTV; rock publications, from heavy-metal fan-mag *Hit Parader* to *Rolling Stone* sister publication *The Record,* started regular music-video columns.

By the end of the summer, there was an ad being seen on MTV and other broadcast and cable outlets for a K-Tel-style compilation-of-hits album in which a fast-talking announcer blared, "Don't just *watch* the music—*own* it! Here's an amazing new breakthrough: music you don't have to watch, on good old-fashioned records and cassettes!" Ironically, concurrent with that, EMI's Picture Music International announced that it would be releasing what marketing VP Bob Hart called "a K-Tel-style compilation of EMI music video on cassette and video disc," featuring the likes of Duran Duran, Kim Carnes, the Stray Cats, and Kajagoogoo, to be titled *Picture Music.*

Meanwhile, the concept of the "video tour" was expanding beyond that of the satellite-transmitted simulcast. In January 1983, Devo again broke new ground with the world's first "video synchronized tour," during which the band performed live before a giant rear-projection video screen; the screen showed characters, scenes, animation, and computer graphics that fleshed out songs from the band's latest album, *Oh No, It's Devo!,* and the band interacted with the characters in the video. The whole thing was choreographed with a sequencer pulse electronically encoded into the video's soundtrack. During the summer of 1983, Duran Duran, in conjunction with Sony, which was promoting its own Video 45s as well as Duran Duran's long-form video cassette, went on a video tour of major clubs across America: the compilation cassette, which of course included the two songs on Sony's Duran Duran Video 45, was shown on big-screen systems in the clubs. Each date on the video tour sold out, and in every city the video tour hit, Duran Duran's records sold out within days. Previous to this, most record companies viewed consumer-owned rock video as potential competition for the record buyers' dollar. But Sony's John O'Donnell says, "Our research shows that music is an owner-oriented medium rather than a rental medium like movies. With music video, the key is the music—people want to experience that music over and over again, and if they want to watch the video over and over, it's there as well."

Rock-video consumerism has already been promoted by such technical advances as Sony's introduction of Beta Hi-Fi in mid-1983, as well as the inevitable lowering of prices and heavier penetration of home-video hardware that will come with time.

Meanwhile, the summer of 1983 saw another video tour, by Swiss new-wave electronic band Yello, in which clubs all across the Midwest were packed with people watching the band's three-concept clips ("Pinball Cha-Cha," "The Evening's Young," and "I Love You") for bargain admission prices. The Yello video tour was coordinated by Second Vision, first of what is sure to be a wave of independent video promotion firms offering their coordinating services to record labels that, understaffed in the wake of previous soft-market financial crises and overworked by the demands from both their own bands and the ever-proliferating TV and club-video outlets, sorely need advice and manpower. Second Vision was founded by Bruce Kirkland, formerly head of independent British label Stiff's American operation. The press kit he wrote for Second Vision neatly encapsulated just how far rock video had come in the eyes of the music industry: "Your video represents your single biggest investment behind a record. You want guaranteed results and greater utilization. . . . The one-song promotional video used to be an extravagance in the real business of selling records. These days the promotional video *is* the real business of selling records. It's a high stakes investment that could deliver a Men at Work or a Stray Cats."

At roughly the same time as Second Vision's Yello video tour, over in England the Kinks were enjoying their first big hit in a dozen years with "Come Dancing." Already a hit in the U.S., thanks in large part to MTV play of the song's Julian Temple-directed video, "Come Dancing" had been released in the U.K. in the spring of 1983 and had gone nowhere. In late August, Britain's *Top of the Pops* did a rundown of the American charts, and with "Come Dancing" in the U.S. Top Forty, played the video. The next day, "Come Dancing" sold out of British record stores. Arista Records, the Kinks' label, had to rerelease the single to keep up with the demand. Further proof of the power of rock video.

Another demonstration of that status was the trend over the summer of record company press releases gushing forth with the latest rock-video details. A CBS Records press release dated August 31, 1983, on Loverboy termed "Queen of the Broken Hearts" "Loverboy's *new video (and single)*" [emphasis added], and went on to note that "the decision to clad the band in the desert garb of mercenary warriors for the video proved so electrifying that the band and their managers decided not only to revamp the band's physical appearance onstage during their current tour, but also the entire stage setting itself." Thus, video could create, as well as mirror, a band's visual image. Even a tiny independent label like Los Angeles' Slash Records (affiliated now with Warner Brothers, but still . . .) got into the act: a June 30, 1983, Slash press release on the signing of two L.A. bands, Los Lobos and Red on Green, noted that "both records are slated for mid-September release. Plans for videos of both bands are under way."

Late in the summer, Slash Records artists the Violent Femmes, whose all-acoustic music fused folk sounds with punk-rock energy and attitude, were quoted in the *Village Voice:* "Yeah, we sold out to MTV, but it's okay—we made a horrible video." Never mind that the video, for "Gone Daddy Gone," was actually quite good. What's important is that MTV had already gained enough stature to be seen by a band like the Violent Femmes as the kind of establishment institution it's always been rock's sworn duty to combat.

During that same summer, MTV "presented" the sold-out U.S. tour by IRS Records supergroup the Police in a co-op promotional deal. MTV's VJs introduced each show; the onstage action was broadcast in larger-than-life detail to the furthest reaches of the mammoth arenas the band played, by an enormous "Diamond Vision" video screen (which had been similarly used earlier in the summer at the US Festival in California); and reels of MTV videos were shown between the live acts. The *Chicago Tribune* reported that at the all-day Police concert extravaganza there in mid-August, only the headliners themselves received more applause than the MTV videos—and the warm-up acts at that show included such popular rock acts (and MTV video stars) as Joan Jett and Flock of Seagulls.

Basically, rock video was *everywhere.* At the beginning of September 1983—one year after MTV had made its crucial move into New York

Dean Martin "inadvertently" knocks a row of new-wave models into a
swimming pool in "Since I Met You Baby," the hilarious "parody"
video directed by his son Ricci in 1983.

and L.A.—Jo Bergman of Warner Brothers reflected, "It's awesome
how quickly everything has escalated since MTV came to New York
and L.A.: Last week Dean Martin made an MTV-style video. It's for
'Since I Met You Baby,' a typical Dino crooner ballad. His son Ricci,
who's in his mid-twenties, directed it, and Ricci told me he just got the
idea to do it after seeing all that MTV. So the clip is a sort of parody
of all the cliché images you see on MTV. It's a *surreal golfing* video,
if you can believe that: there's Dino, cool as ever in his golf sweater,
out on the links, but it's all solarized, so the sky is pink and Dino is
blasting out of blue sand traps . . . and there are all these new-wave
models with Devo sunglasses standing around all over the golf course.
. . . It's absolutely hysterical. I think I'll put it in an unmarked cassette
and send it to MTV's acquisitions committee. Hopefully they'll see it
by mistake and laugh so hard they'll put it into rotation. Can you
imagine?"

Indeed I could. One had only to think back a couple of years to *SCTV*
and Gerry Todd and Tom Monroe and wonder just how far it had all
really come.

CONTRIVED MINDFLASHES, MEDIA DREAMS, AND PUZZLING EVIDENCE: ROCK-VIDEO AESTHETICS AND AUTEURS

If anything, rock video is a director's medium. Yes, some artists *do* contribute to the conceptualization and execution of their clips, and many more will do so as time goes by, with greater and greater input. But for now, the directors most often are responsible for the concepts, the vision, the imagery, and the editing rhythm that coalesce into a look that keeps people watching. Labels now go to certain rock-video directors to get a particular look—*the* look—that will guarantee an eye-catching, and hence an actively promotional, video.

But where do they get their ideas, their imagery, their styles? What about the aesthetics of rock video? Are rock videos really minimovies —or just maxicommercials? Or do they fall somewhere in between? Are rock videos artistically a brave new world of liberated expression, or just compacted collections of cops from other modern media? Are they just "contrived mindflashes," to borrow the seemingly prophetic title of Russell Mulcahy's early experimental film?

Well. First a few relevant quotes.

"On its face, postmodernist art is noisy with seduction, affect, and meaning. Yet peel away the surface surge of impact, and one finds little underneath. One finds instead a generation ambivalent, unsure of what they believe in or what the future holds. A generation that, in place of passion or commitment, settles for intoxicating, low-risk incursions into 'evil,' the decadent, the absurd." —Carey Lovelace, *Harper's,* Summer 1983.

"The decor of our lives is taken from advertising, such as cars or movie posters . . . I am a modernist. I don't have respect for things— I have love." —Jean-Jacques Beineix, director of *Diva* and *The Moon in the Gutter,* interviewed in *Film Comment,* August 1983.

"Videos attempt to reinforce product familiarity with shtick, be it narrative mini-melodrama or the worst clichés of pop surrealism (album art come to turgid life). In either case, the video aesthetic is closely related to that of the television commercial. But, encouraged by greater relative length, video tends more towards Dionysian self-indulgence than Apollonian mind-control. Last winter's Bonjour jeans commercial offers less flaccid entertainment than almost everything on MTV." —J. Hoberman, *Film Comment,* August 1983.

"[In] the spectacularly shoddy value system espoused by rock video, [the] central message is that sexual desirability is the be-all and end-all in life, and that sex is a mean game one strives to win." —Kristine McKenna, *Los Angeles Times,* August 1983.

"In music video, cliché has already become a too-frequent substitute for creativity. British Surrealism and American Vaudvideo have spawned a circus of Russell Mulcahy clones who seem more concerned with copying images than with finding original visual metaphors. Like AOR music, the whole process of making a rock video is quickly being reduced to formula. The most abused shot in rock video is a guitar smashing through glass. But there's more, much more. If after ten minutes with MTV you find yourself asking, 'Didn't I just see this?,' you've been victimized by one too many rock video clichés." —Alan Hecht, *The Record,* August 1983.

"Please add the following rock video clichés to your preliminary listing: water splashing in slow-motion close-ups; things breaking in slow-motion close-ups; *film noir* lighting; motorcycles and their accessories; circus performers; white voids; black voids; eyes with tears; animals (particularly cats and horses); stars and/or crosses; strange headgear; wet streets; and *anything* pastel." —A letter to *The Record,* September 1983.

Now, add it all up: recycled styles . . . surface without substance . . . simulated experience . . . information overload . . . image and style scavengers . . . ambivalence . . . decadence . . . immediate gratification . . . vanity and the moment . . . image assaults and outré folks . . . the

death of content . . . anaesthetization of violence through chic . . .
adolescent male fantasies . . . speed, power, girls, and wealth . . . album
art come to turgid life . . . classic storytelling motifs . . . soft-core
pornography . . . clichéd imagery . . . that's rock-video aesthetics in a
nutshell or three. Right?

Rock videos, like much postmodern art and most mass-media entertainment, *do* plunder all sorts of preexisting, received imagery from
both popular and esoteric culture. Like TV commercials, rock videos
are manipulative packages that entertain and sell simultaneously (or so
their makers and backers hope). They are a bastard offspring of art and
commerce, falling somewhere between the minimovie and the maxi-
commercial. There is much that is boring, indulgent, disquieting, and
specious at the least.

But to dismiss rock video is to bury one's head in the sand. As
Richard Corliss pointed out in *Film Comment,* MTV—and by extension, rock video—does mirror and extend pop-culture trends. And, as
he wrote, if you are put off by rock video, it "doesn't matter, it's here."
Or, as the Clash once sang in "Hate and War": "We have to deal with
it/ It is the currency."

By now we know the many ways in which a rock video can work.
There are straight lip-synched performance clips, some of them crash-
ing bores, some of them wonderful if you just want to see a well-shot
band performing. There are high-concept clips, full of image overload
and deliberately ambiguous narrative tangents that only occasionally
resolve to constitute the semblance of a plot. In between, there are
various hybrids of the two polarities—clips that mix performance with
conceptualized plot (say, Kajagoogoo's "Too Shy," in which the band's
performance at a club is played off against the time-traveling fantasies
of a club waitress who may or may not be living through a post-WWII
the-boys-are-back memory), or performance with flashes of associative
imagery (say, Def Leppard's "Photograph," with cryptic snapshots of
Marilyn Monroe and caged amazons vying for attention with the band's
athletic stage show). There are computer graphics, animation, pixilation (stop-motion animation with plastic or clay figures), stop action,
superfast action, superslow motion, eye-popping special effects, solarizations, split screens, and on and on and on. But if it is all stuff that
we've seen somewhere else before—at least in *other* rock videos—then
it's important to remember an old cliché that still holds true, especially
now: "Everything old is new again."

What's most important about rock video's image-assault aesthetics
is not how different they appear to be from all that has come before,

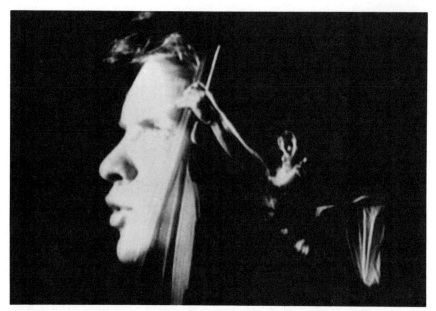

Overlapping imagery in a slow-dissolve shot from the exceptional
performance video "Every Breath You Take," directed by Godley and
Creme for the Police (1983)

but rather how much rock video symbolizes an *extension* of twentieth-
century cultural attitudes, of the impulses at the heart of what we think
of as twentieth-century art, or modern art, or whatever. The dominant
tendency of most modern art has been to react *against* that which came
before. From the futurists and dadaists and surrealists, through James
Joyce and Picasso and e.e. cummings, to John Cage and Jackson Pol-
lack and "free jazz" and the "free cinema" underground to punk rock,
modern art and culture have been about remaking, circumventing—or
destroying—established traditions and conventions of narrative logic
and pictorial representation. In a sense, rock video—with its emphasis
on image and montage over narrative and character, on sensation and
attitude over genuine emotion—just may represent the ultimate triumph (or debasement, depending on your perspective) of this modern
artistic impulse, or at least of the assimilation of that impulse. Rock
video is a popular medium, not an esoteric one. It has brought avant-
garde attitudes and techniques into the mainstream.

In the summer of 1983, Paul Schrader—director of such stylish-
looking "cinema chic" films as *American Gigolo* and *Cat People*—
called rock video "technically the most refreshing new thing happening

right now, a wonderful place for directors to hone their visual senses."
Then check out Pauline Kael's review of Schrader's *Cat People* in the
New Yorker: "Each shot looks like an album cover for records you
don't ever want to play." Kael's reference to album-cover art is no
accident. The similarities in style between *American Gigolo* and *Cat
People* and the comparable eye-catching eroticism and use of brilliantly
lit color in rock video is no accident.

Consider that *Flashdance* director Adrian Lyne is but one of a bevy
of British filmmakers who graduated from making eye-catching British
TV commercials, full of the quick cuts and eye-grabbing superreal
hard-lit colors and teasing sexual innuendo common in rock videos.
Others of this school include Ridley Scott, his brother Tony (most
famous in America for his splashy, sexy commercials for Diet Pepsi),
and Alan Parker. Ridley Scott's most famous and successful feature
film is *Bladerunner* (which appropriately has taken on a second life as
a home-video cassette)—a triumph of art design and set decoration
over shallow characters and ham-fisted plot. Tony Scott's first feature
film, *The Hunger,* balances stunning photography of the lush sets and
nonsensical characters with a flimsy plot. The film starts with by far its
best sequence, what amounts to a rock video featuring British band
Bauhaus. Consider Alan Parker's *Fame,* where brassy, sassy, constant-
action song-and-dance production numbers ride roughshod over a thin
plot. And consider his *Pink Floyd: The Wall,* which—no dialogue, no
plot, just music and visuals—predated *Flashdance* as a feature-length
music video.

The sadomasochistic festishism of fashion photographer Helmut
Newton also finds its way into so many rock videos. When in doubt of
holding a viewer's attention, directors seem to resort to the rock-video
cliché image of having a cadaverously made-up new-wave model do
nothing more than wet her lips or just scowl at the camera and "give
attitude" (which is what fashion models are always instructed to do just
before stepping out onto *haute couture* runways). Then there are all
those rock-video clichés of things shattering or falling in superslow
motion, strobe-lit to superreal brilliance, and the way so much modern
photography captures similar images of implied violence. Consider
Russell Mulcahy's recurrent water imagery—the glasses always spilling
or smashing, the liquid splashing over a woman's thighs, always in
strobe-lit slow motion—and Julian Temple's comment on Mulcahy's
style: "He obviously just flips through some art-photo book or a copy
of *Zoom* magazine and picks out several bizarre, provocative images to
use in a video." And Mulcahy blithely admits to doing precisely that.

A scene from Alan Parker's *Pink Floyd: The Wall* (1982), which predated *Flashdance* as an extended rock video in feature-film disguise

videos, and remember Andy Warhol's famous quote, "If it moves, they'll watch it." Consider that both Paul Schrader's recent films and most rock videos have been dismissed by most film critics as shallow exercises in surface flash (so it figures that Schrader would relate to rock video). And consider that most of the recent feature films to embody the rock-video connection, like *Flashdance* and *The Hunger,* were made by commercial-trained Englishmen, predicting and then mirroring rock video (Jim McBride's comparable remake of *Breathless,* which seemed to have been shot to go with its rock soundtrack rather than vice-versa, is the chief American exception). Whether rock video partakes of bastardized avant-garde techniques by default, by design, or by dint of sheer necessity and expediency, they *do* grow from this entire modern cultural continuum, a continuum brought full circle when such movies as *Flashdance* and *The Hunger,* which look and function like videos, are cut down into three-minute trailers that run as video clips.

Now consider rock video's constant and oft-cited allusions to and plunderings of surrealism, whether it be from Dali and Magritte paintings, or film classics like Buñuel's *Un Chien Andalou,* or Cocteau's *Blood of a Poet,* or, as more than one critic has noted, "the worst excesses of pop surrealism." Then consider the speed of the typical rock-video creative process, the free-association of instinctual, subconscious imagery in a director's conceptualizing of a song. Rock video is actually a true form of surrealism; it's automatic filmmaking. The exception to the rule of classic surrealism, though, is that rock-video directors get most of their imagery not from private fantasies but from an attic full of half-remembered media images, plundering not just surrealistic films but all of film history as well as painting and photography, and even television shows (as in Billy Joel's Ed Sullivan spoof, "Tell Her about It," or Mick Fleetwood's "I Want You Back," which echoes a *Twilight Zone* devil-in-disguise episode when Fleetwood is seen physically changing as he walks from pillar to pillar in a room).

However, keep in mind that, for all the criticisms—many of them valid—that are leveled at rock videos, many are examples of exciting, experimental, innovative filmmaking. Rock video *is* one of the most unusual and intriguing things one can see on TV. And for all rock video's mindless traipses through the image bank, there always seem to be enough that somehow *do* work, and *just* often enough, there are those that manage to transcend the genre's limitations and take scintillating steps towards, yes, art.

Also keep in mind that rock videos arise from, and perhaps exacerbate, another crucial twentieth-century sociocultural phenomenon: the continued diminution of attention spans and literacy rates in tandem with the seemingly constant acceleration of the pace of life itself. In this sense, rock videos might embody the most daring and colorful paintings on the walls of the global village's cave.

Before considering the *auteurs* responsible for rock video's aesthetics, let's discuss a few more important aspects and elements of those aesthetics.

Video Art: Video art has not proved much of a source for, or influence on, rock video. Video art started with Korean conceptual artist Nam June Paik in the early sixties (though, truth to tell, none other than Ernie Kovacs was probably there first), and has since become a bona fide manifestation of the avant-garde. Video art generally comments on Now. Consider the perpetual motion of most constant-cut rock

TV itself, often by using masses of TV sets as show-within-a-show sculptures (as in Paik's "installations") as well as by electronically doctoring picture tubes, using solarizations and other effects. Video art is a conscious revolt against TV's entertainment obsession, and that's where video art and rock video part ways. Video art may delve into neopsychedelia with time-lapse image assaults that resemble supersonic channel-switching, but more often than not, video art makes its anti-TV comments by being purposefully boring. Video artists like Vito Acconci often make long tapes of themselves doing nothing in particular, as a threefold statement: it's nihilistic; it elevates the banal into art (or so the artist hopes); and it implicitly challenges and/or besmirches popularly held notions of telegenic entertainment. Although rock video has occasionally resonated with video art (most often through video effects and those time-lapse image assaults, which also have a source in the avant-garde films of Bruce Conner)—it is, after all, inevitable, what with rock video's insatiable appetite for plundering—and though *Night Flight* has taken the bold step of trying to make video art mainstream by constantly presenting it, and though a few video artists have made rock videos (John Sanborn, Laurie Anderson, Merrill Aldighieri and Joe Tripician), there's something too self-consciously esoteric and academic about video art that prevents most rock videos from even caring to plunder it. Video art is basically conceptual art on video tape, and while rock videos are often "conceptual," they don't function like conceptual art. Conceptual art is inevitably too radical and anti-entertainment to be seen by the mainstream audience to which rock video plays as anything more than arrant pretension, camp, or some combination of both.

Rock video most often intersects with video art in the work of club VJs, who spontaneously mix found footage, animation, effects, and the like to new-wave dance tunes. Not surprisingly, both John Sanborn and the Aldighieri-Tripician team have worked video installations at rock clubs (New York's Danceteria and Hurrah, respectively). Otherwise, the main similarity between rock video and video art is that both share an obsession with image and image overload.

MTV: The importance of MTV in casting a suggestive shadow over the creation of rock videos cannot be overestimated. Getting a video clip aired on MTV is always foremost in the minds of the people creating the video. Even a club-video maven like RockAmerica's Ed Steinberg, who also produces and directs clips (i.e., Ebn-Ozn's "AEIOU" and Randy Fredrix's "The Hunter") for his own Soft Focus Productions, has to admit it: "Whenever a band comes to me to make a clip, they always agree how nice it is that RockAmerica can get it out to nine million people through the clubs. But the big question always is: what can we do to make sure it gets onto *MTV?*" "There are three ways to guarantee MTV rotation," continues Steinberg, "no black faces, pretty women, and athletic guitar solos. If a band comes to me with a song, and they want to make a video out of it, I always tell them to add a guitar solo to the middle of it—the more notes and the faster it's played the better."

Then there is the loyalty many bands feel towards MTV as the first and largest forum for rock-video promotion. With more and more competition for MTV springing up, such bands and artists make sure MTV still has first dibs on their videos. Explains Joan Jett's manager, Kenny Laguna, "We have a relationship with MTV because they were there first, they helped break us through video with 'I Love Rock & Roll.' When that video first came out, the song had already been number one for four weeks, and MTV wanted and needed it. To this day, MTV is the only place we license that video to. Nobody else can show it."

And finally there is MTV's status as the ultimate rock video forum. If each rock video is a nonstop image assault, then MTV is a nonstop series of nonstop image assaults. Seeing videos end-to-end without letup on MTV reveals a second nature to the aesthetics of rock video, a subtext that seems to declare that, truly, the medium is the message. On MTV, one gets the impression that rock-video imagery is not there to stay in the viewer's mind, but to draw the viewer's attention and hold it until the next image comes along. Watching rock videos on MTV is unlike seeing them anywhere else. If MTV is an Eternal Now of rock-video-image onslaught, then each rock video is a moment in time from that eternal now, a grain of eye-catching, "wow"—inducing sand in the hourglass of media dreams. Visuals become as abstractly functional as musical hooks and riffs, and come from the same sort of pool of modern collective unconscious, fulfilling the same function as musical phrases that spark recognition by harkening to something familiar and half-remembered. Rock video is no less incestuous than pop music itself. Serious narrative momentum within rock videos is the exception to the rule, just as serious revolutionary content is the exception to the rock-song rule, because in either case, something that deep would disrupt the abstract flow that is the overriding point of the proceedings.

Misogyny: By now it's no secret that rock video has taken the degradation of women as sexual objects to new heights (or depths). There are all the aforementioned images of rock-video women as *femmes fatales,* punk Lolitas, tempting sirens, virginal princesses, arrogant amazons, ad nauseam. And, of course, there are rock videos that take the cake: Rod Stewart's "Tonight I'm Yours" (directed by Russell Mulcahy), in which a bevy of bikini-clad beauties scratch and crawl all over one another for the privilege of crawling over Rod's thighs while he lip-syncs at poolside atop L.A.'s Sunset Marquee Hotel; Duran Duran's "Girls on Film," which plays out such classic male wish-fulfillment and sadomasochistic fantasies as having gorgeous, scantily clad women pillow-fighting on a whipped-cream-covered phallus, flipping sumo wrestlers, and appearing to kiss a man so aggressively that he drowns in a wading pool; Tony Carey's "I Won't Be Home Tonight," in which three different women, ostensibly in search of Carey, are first shown haughtily making up (getting ready to move in for the kill), then are ridiculed by being kicked out of bars and barred from backstage doorways, while the camera cuts to Carey smirkingly crooning; and the all-time prize winner, Joe Salvo's "I Don't Wanna Hear It." In this, a winner of the June 1983 MTV *Basement Tapes* competition, Salvo takes the generalized rock-rebel sentiments of the title and applies them to pretty women, all of whom he utterly loathes. Lows of this gem include shots of Salvo lip-synching in a meat locker while models sit prettily atop meat-weighing scales and hang from meat hooks. There are also shots of Salvo righteously shaking his fists at women standing arrogantly with hands on hips and feet splayed, and the "special effect" of Salvo waving *Star Wars* light sabers, which are reflected in his mirrored sunglasses.

Then there are rock videos that exploit sexist female stereotypes, but do so with such obviousness and humor directed at pathetic male fantasies that the inherent sexism may be excused. The Tubes's "She's a Beauty" (directed by Kenny Ortega) presents a young boy's indoctrination into fear of women and dread of sex via a leather-clad dominatrix who takes the boy on a hellishly tantalizing carnival ride through a Tunnel of Love. Tubes singer Fee Waybill plays the carny huckster who suckers the boy in for the lesson of a lifetime. The punch line comes at the end of the clip, when the young boy rides out of the tunnel, still gripped in a half-nelson by the dominatrix, wearing a mask of an old man's head. ZZ Top's "Gimme All Your Lovin'" (and, to a lesser extent, "Sharp Dressed Man") presents women as strutting, predatory sexpots—the first thing one of the three female principals does is lift the hem of her high-slit dress and pull a wad of bills out of her garter belt that she waves at a gas-station attendant while making eyes at him; he

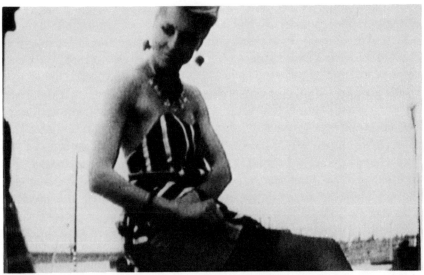

A somewhat more knowing and witty exploitation of sexism than usual
for a rock video, from ZZ Top's "Gimme All Your Lovin' " (1983),
directed by Tim Newman: one of three strutting *femmes fatales* hikes
her skirt and prepares to proffer a wad of bills to an innocent grease
monkey, while flashing a wicked come-hither look.

reacts with the typical mixture of befuddlement, fear, and yearning—
but also as obvious embodiments of adolescent male fantasies.

When asked about all this, most rock-video *auteurs* have a stock
answer that makes for a pretty valid rationale: for one thing, these are
promotional videos, and as we all know, sex sells; rock music has always
had its inherent misogyny. Furthermore, there is something inherent in
the macho mystique of much of the hard rock (or, as it used to be
known, "cock rock") that gets onto MTV that seems to mean that
whenever a rocker who cherishes his mike stand or guitar as an orna-
mental phallic extension desires a woman, the vulnerability inherent in
that desire results in an instant objectification, resentment, fear, and
loathing of the woman desired. Beyond all that, one has to worry: it's
one thing for an adolescent rock consumer to hear these songs; it's
another when he sees, several times a day for weeks on end, these songs
literally fleshing out male fantasies with sexist imagery. This has led
some parents to rethink their attitudes towards video. Should an eight-
year-old child see women hung on meathooks?

Jennifer Brown, executive director of the National Organization for
Women, comments, "These images are very destructive, especially in

such a new genre as this, and we're very distressed to see a new avenue of exploitation opening up. But we can't advocate censorship. There's a First Amendment issue there, for one thing. For another, cable may show exploitative rock videos, but it also lets us produce phone-in shows on feminist issues."

For its part, MTV has censored some videos: "Girls on Film" was allowed on the channel only after close-ups of full-frontal female nudity and ice cubes being rubbed on bare nipples were excised; no less a star than David Bowie had to cut the "China Girl" video to get it on MTV; Van Halen's "Pretty Woman" clip was actually removed from MTV rotation in 1982 when the channel received scores of complaints about the clip's alleged exploitation of women, transvestitism, and dwarfs. The clip itself was actually an apparently self-mocking, adventure-burlesque in which the woman the heroes were trying to save ended up removing her wig to reveal a short-haired androgyne—whether male or female was left unclear. And yes, it had dwarfs in it—but then, so do many videos MTV plays, such as Peter Gabriel's "Shock the Monkey."

"We have a very open relationship with the record industry," says MTV programming executive John Sykes, "and they know we have certain guidelines and limitations. We won't show anything we consider to be gratuitous sex or violence. But censorship is a gray area—it's art, and the artist's mind can wander in a number of directions. That's the artist's decision. We're only the gallery. And we are talking about rock music here, not Mister Rogers. At any rate, record companies understand that by now, and they never send us anything we have to censor."

Sykes's comments about gratuitous sex and violence explain a lot about why rock videos always show *implied* sex or violence in the form of meaningful stares and glances and ominous or provocative movements, edited to titillate without ever showing the actual payoff. The self-censorship he mentions is a further indication of MTV's status. And censorship has been the mother of rock-video invention in other areas. As Russell Mulcahy himself says, "Before MTV, the BBC or wherever else pop promos were shown would always censor certain things—you couldn't show people smoking or drinking alcohol, whatever. Eventually we figured, if they're gonna keep ruining our narratives with arbitrary cuts, why bother with narrative at all? So we just started making them more abstract."

But all of that does not explain why so much of what MTV and other outlets let pass is so much more offensive and potentially dangerous than a nude human body could ostensibly be.

To date, there have been only two alternatives to the typical rock-video woman: Donna Summer's "She Works Hard for the Money"

(directed by Brian Grant), epochal not just in combating female stereotypes, but in actually making a cogent, valid statement about what it's
like to be a woman these days; and, ironically enough, heavy-metal
band Helix's "Heavy Metal Love" (directed by Rob Quartley), a sincere
paean to a musclebound female body builder. While some might argue
that there is an inherent sexism in female body building—if you believe
women seek to remake their bodies in the images of masculine power
—at least the woman in this clip is being seen positively rather than
being scorned or abused. And in the midst of rock video's often morally
bankrupt sensibilities, that is some kind of progress.

Puzzling Evidence: This is the term coined by Devo's Gerald Casale
for the genre's clichéd images and their possible significance. Casale
explains: "In the seventies, record producers had a certain sound or
texture they got that labels all sought in order to guarantee sales. Now
video directors work the same way; they're creative mercenaries hired
out by all these bands who need video all of a sudden but never really
thought about it before. It's stamp-out time, just like with Tin Pan
Alley and disco. The video directors are hired out to apply their aesthetics to the band, so *the video clothes wear the band*—instead of the other
way around, which is how it should be. Now, some of these videos are,
in terms of production value and craft, obviously very good. In terms
of content, they're obviously totally vacuous. But they have to be
vacuous. Just like Hollywood movies or TV shows, there's a formula,
a shell, and it's all-too-rarely ever filled with any guts or meaning or
content or insight or information.

"However, televised imagery is powerful, and even if it is gratuitous,
as in most rock videos, it always means *something*. At the very least,
rock videos reveal more about the bands than the bands themselves ever
imagine, just by documenting the kind of imagery they want to associate with themselves. You can notice all these different motifs in these
videos, which I put under the bracket of 'puzzling evidence.' There are
the motifs of constantly breaking glass, breaking furniture, the guitars
smashing through walls and TV sets, lockets dropping onto art-deco
checkerboard floors and smashing in slow motion, shot with strobe
decay . . . and it's always followed by *the hostile look,* usually in slow
motion or extreme close-up on the eyes, nose and mouth. It's that tired
old visual arrogance completely derived from fashion photography."

The Medium as the Message: One reason TV has never, until very
recently, had a prosperous relationship with rock music is that rock
music has always been, or was supposed to have been, an *active,* energetic, involving, direct, and immediate medium. TV is a *passive,* de-
tached, distancing, intermediary medium. Rock is hot, TV is cool. You

might go so far as to conclude that rock is not meant for TV. The music that once inspired generations to gather in revolt against establishment oppressors can now only get people to turn on their TVs and watch. But the purist forgets that by the late seventies, rock had mutated subtly from anarchistic impulse to calculated, anaesthetic product. Yet rock has always been able to retain just enough of its original rebellious spark through decades of assimilation to keep purists holding out hope and belief in the form. And rock video, being the most unusual and intriguing thing on TV, still has the potential—and occasionally realizes that potential—to make serious waves.

Abstract Song vs. Concrete Imagery: This is one of rock video's longest-standing ideological debates—doesn't making an abstract song concrete ruin people's ability to imagine their own visuals? Others say that such complainers simply have unduly paltry imaginations. Many rock-video directors are aware of this potential problem and consciously make rock videos that are as ambiguous as possible, with just enough narrative or suggestive concept to draw a viewer in, but never so much that one can easily come to a conclusion and digest the clip in one or two viewings. This is also the reason for much of rock video's image overload and constant fast-cutting. As Russell Mulcahy puts it, "You try to pack as much into a clip as possible with editing and imagery, so that people can see the clip over and over and still be noticing things they haven't caught before." Mulcahy speaks for the majority of rock-video *auteurs* when he adds, "I always prefer to stay away from a literal approach to a song and take it to another level, where people can take it wherever they want. That's how most musicians feel about their music, too, so in that sense, a rock video can be 'visual music.' You build that abstract, noncommittal quality in there to give it a more universal appeal, and because if people can figure it out, then they get bored with it. You want to keep them intrigued."

Performance Clip vs. Concept Clip: Another longstanding rock-video issue: Which is better and truer to the rock medium? Can a rock video really capture the feel of a live onstage performance—and if so, is that necessarily a good thing? Kenny Laguna isn't so sure: "Rock video's an incredible art form. But rock & roll *lives* in the clubs and concert halls, onstage, person to person. With video, you can't really capture that. But video can capture enough of the look and sound of a band performing that if a kid sees a video of a band performing 'live' several times a day over a few weeks, he might not want to shell out fifteen dollars to actually go through the hassle of seeing the band play live at his local arena."

Back when MTV first started, most of its videos were straight performance clips of those typical AOR and hard-rock bands; they had it easy. Critics noted how boring such performance clips were, and artistically inclined rock-video *auteurs* complained that having to show bands lip-synching and playing guitars that weren't plugged in was an insult to their intelligence. But after one year of operation, an MTV audience survey indicated that the channel's audience overwhelmingly preferred performance videos to concept clips. However, by mid-1983, MTV's audience response had shifted radically towards concept clips. Why? Because in the beginning, performance clips typically documented the bands MTV's audience loved most; within two years, though, MTV's rotation of more British acts in concept clips, combined with TV's insidiously seductive power, had conquered much of MTV's audience's resistance to both the foreign concept clips and the music.

Meanwhile, two other important facts remain. One, a good performance clip—like Prince's oft-cited "1999" and "Little Red Corvette"—can come as a real breath of fresh air in the wake of all the imagistic contrivance of concept clips. Two, there is the fact that lip-synching itself is a lie, and a necessary one from the industry's point of view: the video is promoting a record, so the artist has to mime to a preperfected track that is being promoted in another medium. So, if lip-synching is a lie, then which is worse, to compound the lie by trying to present it as a "performance" video, or just to go ahead and put the lip-synching performer in some far-flung concept? Artist and director juries are still out on that question, although most directors seem to feel that in light of the above, one *should* abandon all inhibitions and go for the concept. One possible answer may come in the future, when rock videos become artistic and commercial entities in themselves rather than promotional afterthoughts; then, we may see the creation of "live" videos, where the artist actually sings and plays for the video's soundtrack.

The one rock genre that maintains the integrity of the performers to its benefit in both straight performance clips and concept clips is heavy metal. Such bands tend to be overdone comic-book heroes, and the music itself embodies adolescent-male macho fantasies. Thus heavy metal's typical trappings—the leather-and-studded costumes, the allusions to Gothic imagery—are of the same sort of ancient-futuristic mythic continuum into which something like *Star Wars* tapped more benevolently. Heavy-metal performers and their fans delight in going "over the top," and both transcend the pose. The result, on video, is a peculiar kind of organic sincerity and vitality, in its own

A classic image of heavy-metal teenage-male fantasy-fulfillment from Quiet Riot's hugely successful clip "Cum on Feel the Noize" (1983), directed by Mark Rezyka for Pendulum Productions: the regular-kid hero (actually a soundman who volunteered to star in the clip) rolls out of bed to see his bedroom open out into a stage on which Quiet Riot perform the metal anthem.

way not that far from the artistic truth with which Richard Lester served the Beatles in their movies, and which provides a refreshing break from the studious self-consciousness of many more fashion-conscious bands.

There are plenty of lame heavy-metal videos, but the genre has also provided such great moments as: Twisted Sister's "You Can't Stop Rock & Roll" (directed by Arthur Ellis), in which the band blows out the protective headphones of the Taste Squad that pursues them; Rose Tatoo's "Branded" (directed by the Albert Brothers), in which stout, skinheaded singer Angry Anderson actually bashes his chrome dome through the roof of a car to sing to the car's bewildered occupants; Joan Jett's ultrastark "I Love Rock 'n' Roll" (directed by Arnold Levine—not strictly heavy-metal, but . . .); the perfectly appropriate use of special effects in Aldo Nova's "Fantasy" (directed by Richard Casey), in which Nova, as some sort of commando in league with his band, blows open the door to a warehouse by firing a laser beam from his guitar; and the equally appropriate, literal visualization of a "guitar duel" in Buck Dharma's "Born to Rock" (also by Casey). In these and many other instances, heavy metal seems right at home on video, and on MTV.

"Album Cover Art Come to Life": Many critics deride rock videos with this description. One wonders whether they realize how right they really are. Keef MacMillan is not the only cover-artist-turned-video-*auteur;* Storm Thorgeson, mastermind of Hipgnosis, creator of some of the most striking album covers of the past decade or so, has gone on to direct such classy, eyecatching clips as Planet P's "Static" and "Why Me?," Yes's "Owner of a Lonely Heart," and Robert Plant's "Burning down One Side," "Big Log," and "In the Mood." Since album covers serve as visually enticing promotion for their vinyl contents, it makes complete sense for rock videos to be "album cover art come to life." And in the hands of an able pro like Thorgeson, the results usually make for splendid viewing, at least on the sensory surface.

Directorial Credit: MTV has always run Chyron-generated readouts of the band, the song, the album from whence it comes, and the album's label at the beginning and end of every video. Even when an unsigned artist got a video onto MTV, such as Lenny Kaye's "I Got a Right," MTV still ran his name and the song's title without any label. But MTV has never run Chyrons listing directorial and production credits of rock videos. Most directors don't complain much about this; they admit that their job is to promote the bands, and that MTV has the same job, and is not there to promote them; they add that in most cases, their ultimate aim is to use promo video as steppingstone to feature filmmaking, and that within the relatively close confines of the still-burgeoning rock-video industry, their names get around to the right people anyway. Still, director Graeme Whifler (the Residents's "One Minute Movies," Sparks's "Cool Places," Translator's "Unalone") says, "I can understand that MTV is there to promote the bands and not the directors— to a point. Without us directing these clips, would there *be* an MTV? At least a little ego-gratification would be nice."

Finally, in October 1983, he got it. On *America's Top Ten,* Casey Casem began verbally crediting directors of rock videos; a few days later, MTV VJ Mark Goodman did the same thing. Explains an MTV source, "It was mainly a matter of the VJs always having been given the names of directors along with all the other informational tidbits to read on-camera. We all finally decided by late 1983, we could mention certain directors making new clips who had also made clips we'd shown before, so that the audience could hear their names and the clips they'd made and there'd be a recognition factor there. The VJs had been pulling for it for a long time."

Here are the readouts on rock-video's top directors:

RUSSELL MULCAHY

AGE: 29

PRODUCTION COMPANY: MGMM

BUDGET RANGE: $30,000 to $100,000

CLIPS INCLUDE: Duran Duran—"Hungry like the Wolf," "Rio," "Is There Something I Should Know?," "Save a Prayer," "Planet Earth"; the Motels—"Only the Lonely," "Take the 'L' Out of Lover"; Ultravox —"Vienna," "The Voice," "The Thin Wall"; Elton John—"Elton's Song," "I'm Still Standing"; Bonnie Tyler—"Total Eclipse of the Heart" (with Jim Steinman); Rod Stewart—"Young Turks"; Supertramp—"It's Raining Again"; Kim Carnes—"Bette Davis Eyes," "Voyeur"; Buggles—"Video Killed the Radio Star"; Billy Joel—"Pressure," "Allentown," "She's Right on Time"; Icehouse—"Hey Little Girl"; Spandau Ballet—"True."

Mulcahy is probably rock video's first great *auteur,* or at least the first nonperforming directorial star in the field. Master of countless cinematic and pictorial styles, Mulcahy's a consummate editor, able to elicit telling, connecting performances and to set rock stars perfectly within sprawling scenarios (i.e., Billy Joel as a sideline troubadour amid the American-prole protest and celebration of "Allentown"), able to tell stories within a three-minute promo clip. Mulcahy is also the prime source of most rock-video clichés—strobe-lit, slow-motion shots of objects shattering and water splashing, the back-lit elegant or decadent sets with wisps of blue smoke and diaphanous curtains or lady's garments blowing through, etc. He is one of rock video's busiest *auteurs.* Yet he has also been a much-copied innovator: it was Mulcahy who first cut off the top and bottom of the video image, bordering it in black, to make it look more like a Cinemascope screen ("I hate the square dimensions of the TV screen, I have trouble composing shots for it, so I figured, why not make it more like a movie screen?" he says) with Ultravox's "Vienna"; it was Mulcahy who began making as many references to film history in his clips as possible; it was he who first perfected the insolently provocative sex-surrogate flashing of "the look" that has become endemic to rock videos; it was he who first perfected extensive use of sequential split-screen and triple-screen edits, cutting both on and around and against the beat (since copied most notably by Michael Jackson's "Billie Jean," directed by Steve Barron).

Though he never really enjoyed huge budgets until very recently, it was Mulcahy who pioneered the rock-video impression of high production values through multiple sprawling sets, loads of extras, and other factors that add a sense of grandeur and stir memories of even grander Hollywood classics.

Mulcahy was also probably the first big-time rock-video *auteur* to land jobs because of his style. He says, "My job is to promote the band; I just happen to feel that a well-done concept can do that at least as well as a straight performance. I just put myself in the position of the audience and try to please myself; I hope that'll please everyone else, too. I just think, 'Do I want to be uplifted here, or mystified, or tantalized, or what?' Usually I come up with one image, one impression, and base everything else around that. The key image in 'Bette Davis Eyes,' for instance, is the people slapping each other; in 'Total Eclipse of the Heart' it's those big doors flying open; in 'Only the Lonely,' it's the sheet music blowing off the music stands while the string quartet keeps playing.

"But," he adds, "if people see my videos and say, 'Great video—now what was that song?,' then I've failed. Ideally, people should see the video and say, 'That was great'—meaning the video *and* the song. The video is supposed to draw you into the song." Still, the fact remains that, more than with any other rock-video *auteur,* a Russell Mulcahy video is a Russell Mulcahy Video, more his than any band's. His trademark imagery, lighting, sets, and editing keep recurring.

"I have two basic styles," says Mulcahy. "One is the sweeping, epic drama sort of thing with loads of extras and extravagant sets, which comes from just growing up at the movies, loving everything—romances, spectacular adventures, sci-fi, thrillers, horror movies, you name it—except, for some reason, westerns, which I could never stand. I've got all these movies rattling around my subconscious, and what with the frantic work schedules and the moment-to-moment inspiration that goes into a video, they can't help but pop out.

"My other style is very pictorial, very composed, and that comes from a long love of surrealist art and modern photography. I love the idea of a video consisting of beautifully composed pictures, but with movement. I studied surrealism for a few years in school, and my favorites were Dali and Magritte. You can see the Magritte thing in Duran's 'Is There Something I Should Know?' And modern photography is a wonderful source of imagery. Sure, I do flip through *Zoom* magazine for inspiration sometimes. I was looking at that stuff before I started making promos. I admit I get my imagery from all over, but I think just about everyone else does, too. It's what you *do* with it."

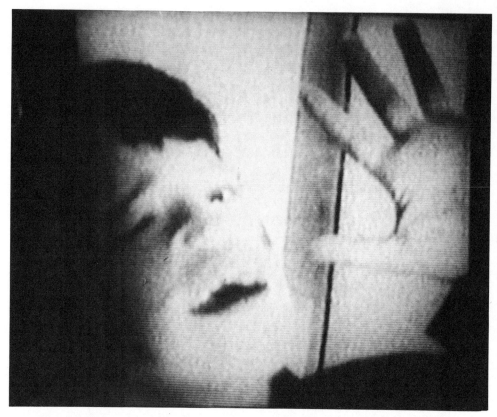

The boy trapped inside the TV screen in Billy Joel's "Pressure" (1983), directed by Russell Mulcahy—an homage to *Poltergeist,* and a typically Mulcahyesque-received psychodramatic image

What about that water-imagery fetish? "Oh, am I into water sports, is that it?" he laughs. "No, it's just, well, I grew up by the ocean, I was *in* water a lot and loved it, but mainly it's something I got from modern photography, and I think water flowing in slow motion is a very attractive, expressive, even poetic image, and it can connote any number of things, depending on what's going on around it. I did see *The Last Wave,* and I loved it, but I was making promos with water imagery before I saw it. The ambiguity of the aquatic imagery is important. I like building ambiguity in wherever possible, because then it won't be so easy for people to figure it out and get bored with it."

As of this writing, Mulcahy had just finished editing his first feature film, for Warner Brothers, called *Razorback.*

Though finally fulfilling his dream of making feature films, Mulcahy will not forsake rock video, or so he says. "Oh no, it's still the most creatively free and exciting area there is, and as long as it stays that way, I'll keep doing them." But will he go back to making as many as three clips a week, as he used to do? "Oh, I don't know about that," he says, "it can get very crazy. A funny thing happened when I was going to do Ultravox's 'Vienna.' I'd just been jetting here and there to exotic locations to shoot Duran Duran videos and such, and I was so jet-lagged and discombobulated that when I met with Ultravox, I said, 'Right, I see a concept having to do with all those Viennese canals and gondoliers. . . .' And the band had to remind me that it was *Vienna,* not Venice."

DAVID MALLET

AGE: 37

PRODUCTION COMPANY: MGMM

BUDGET RANGE: $30,000 to $100,000

CLIPS INCLUDE: David Bowie—"Boys Keep Swinging," "DJ," "Look Back in Anger," "Ashes to Ashes," "Fashion," "Let's Dance," "China Girl," "Heroes"; Boomtown Rats—"I Don't Like Mondays"; Joan Jett: "Crimson and Clover," "Do You Wanna Touch Me," "Bad Reputation," "Fake Friends," "The French Song"; Billy Idol—"White Wedding"; Def Leppard—"Photograph," "Rock of Ages"; Peter Gabriel—"Games without Frontiers."

With his experience on *Shindig!, Juke Box Jury, Top of the Pops,* and *The Kenny Everett Video Show,* Mallett goes back farther with rock on video than most. He's also been a very busy director of British TV commercials for many years, and still makes them. Many of his typical rock-video effects, lighting, camera angles, etc., were first perfected in his slam-bam commercials and in *The Kenny Everett Video Show*'s daffy, dizzy pop-surrealist format: in fact, the "exploding kitchen" set in Bowie's magnificent "Ashes to Ashes" is actually an old Everett set (and was reused in Billy Idol's "White Wedding"). His early seventies British TV commercials feature the same sorts of strobe-repeat edits as in Bowie's "DJ" (as when Bowie hurls a spray-paint canister at a mirror). Mallet's 1979 clip for the Boomtown Rats' "I Don't Like Mondays" was a seminal classic of workable narrative (no doubt helped by the song's topicality—the title was actually the explanation given by a California high-school sniper for her unprovoked assassination attempts), but he's most distinguished as one of the very few rock-video *auteurs* whose style has resolutely stuck closer to video than to film.

Long after most rock-video *auteurs* had moved on to more "tasteful" sixteen-millimeter film, Mallet was still glorying in the garishness of color and foreshortened perspectives attainable only through video stock and video matte and chroma-key effects. More recently Mallet, too, has moved into film with Bowie's "Let's Dance" and "China Girl" and Def Leppard's "Photograph" and "Rock of Ages," capturing a richer look—but at the same time, he was still churning out antic *video* videos for Joan Jett, like "Fake Friends" and "The French Song."

"I've always loved rock music," says Mallet, "and the way I approach each video, depending of course on the artist's own abilities and inclinations, is to act as more or less a technical director for their ideas. If they have no ideas, I'll come up with something for them to approve based on whatever ideas they may throw at me. With a Joan Jett, that's the way it happens, since she has ideas but doesn't know anything about filmmaking. But with a David Bowie, it's like, if we were making a commercial, he'd be the ad agency scriptwriter and art director. He draws all his own story boards, he comes up with the concepts, and I'm just there to execute them properly. I'm a conduit, a translator. I'm there to satisfy my clients. So what satisfaction do I get out of it? In satisfying my clients, I do get to exercise a lot of creative freedom, more so than in commercials—though there's less money—and I have loads of fun.

"I don't think I have a particular style. I try to be as flexible as possible for every different project. If I have worked out an identifiable style, it's probably because I tend to work with artists many times over, and it's really *their* style coming through me that you see. The 'video style' thing I can see, and that's because I've never looked at film as being inherently superior to video like a lot of other people do. I think each medium has its own value. I wouldn't *mind* making a feature film someday, but I'm also quite content to go on making TV commercials and rock promos."

BRIAN GRANT

AGE: 31
PRODUCTION COMPANY: MGMM
BUDGET RANGE: $30,000 to $75,000
CLIPS INCLUDE: Olivia Newton-John—all clips, including "Physical" and *Physical* video album; Donna Summer—"She Works Hard for the Money"; ABC—"The Look of Love"; Peter Gabriel—"Shock the Monkey"; Asia—"Don't Cry," "The Smile Has Left Your Eyes"; Hair-

cut 100—"Favorite Shirts," "Love Plus One"; Squeeze—"Black Coffee in Bed"; The Fixx—"Saved by Zero"; Kim Wilde—"Kids in America"; Landscape—"My Name Is Norman Bates," "Einstein a Go Go"; M—"Pop Muzik."

In a field where versatility is a key, Grant—as a quick survey of the above résumé indicates—is Mr. Versatility, equally adept at enhanced-performance, *noir* mystery, televaudeville comedy, enigmatic psychodrama, cinematic spectacle, and arrogant punk chic. With a background including work on literally a thousand different TV shows for Lord Lew Grade's ATV, that figures.

"I've taken a long time to work out a style I really like. Early on, I'd been working with TV, so I always shot on video. Now I have a deal to make a feature film, so I've been working more with film. Basically, I approach each video individually, and generally get ideas more from the song itself than from what the artist's image is. I always approach a project with a completely open mind, which is usually more than you can say for the artists or their labels. With Olivia's 'Physical' it was quite funny, because when I came up with ideas of replacing the sex that was obviously alluded to in the lyrics with guys working out, and to make it fat guys working out in a health spa so it would be funny, this whole room full of people all sucked in their breath and there was this awful pregnant pause, followed by 'This *is* Olivia, you know. . . .' But she herself was just fabulous about it; she'd been scared about releasing that track at all, what with her image, and she saw that humor would be a good way of taking the sting out of it all.

"Sometimes bands make suggestions, but usually it's never enough to sustain a whole three- or four-minute clip. If there isn't enough going on, three minutes can seem like an eternity. It's not as easy as it might seem. Personally, I really love *noir*ish, ultra-complicated mystery thrillers, like *Marathon Man* or *Three Days of the Condor* or my favorite, Orson Welles's *Touch of Evil.*

"Basically, you just plow through, and through mad dialogue, brute force, and sheer ignorance, you hope you come up with something that'll work. Don't ask me what it means to 'work'! It just does, that's all. But it's getting harder and harder to get something to work, what with MTV. Watching MTV for an hour, it seems like everyone's ripping everyone else off, like rock video peaked in 1982 or something, and now it's just regurgitation time, really no better than *Flashdance.* I hope rock video can go to another level." As of this writing, Grant was about to enter preproduction on his first feature, a complicated thriller tentatively entitled *The Nighttime Guy,* and he was set to start working with

Pioneering rock-video director David Mallet (right) gives pointers to Joan Jett (left) on the set of Jett's "Everyday People" video (1983).

MGMM scriptwriter Keith Williams on a new Olivia Newton-John project. He does not plan to give up rock videos.

JULIAN TEMPLE

AGE: 30

PRODUCTION COMPANY: Midnight Films (formerly with Jon Roseman and Limelight)

BUDGET RANGE: $20,000 to $50,000

CLIPS INCLUDE: the Kinks—"Predictable," "Come Dancing," "State of Confusion," "Don't Forget to Dance"; Stray Cats—"Stray Cat Strut," "Rock This Town"; Mitch Ryder—"When You Were Mine"; ABC—"Poison Arrow"; Culture Club—"Do You Really Want to Hurt Me";

Dexy's Midnight Runners—"Come On, Eileen"; Judas Priest—"You Got Another Thing Comin' "; Rolling Stones—"Undercover," "She Was Hot."

After studying history at Cambridge, Temple went to film school; his graduation thesis was that great lost Sex Pistols movie, *The Great Rock & Roll Swindle.* His love of, and concern for, history is apparent in many of his fabulous Kinks videos, especially "Predictable," with its wry time traveling via subtitles, and the bittersweet nostalgia for bygone eras of "Come Dancing"—both truly exceptional in rock video.

Though versatile, Temple's work has constants: an emphasis on narrative content over flashy images is his dominant hallmark; there is also an ingenious use of color (especially in his two Stray Cats videos, which were crucial in solidifying the band's cartoon-rockabilly image), and a tendency to use rock stars in multiple roles within a video, and in roles that aren't necessarily flattering (i.e., Mitch Ryder as a singer and then a pimp in "When You Were Mine," Martin Fry as a pathetic bellboy, opera watcher, and stage star in "Poison Arrow," and Kink Ray Davies as himself, a sixties mod, a seventies hippie, and an eighties new-wave trendy in "Predictable").

"I think the rock-video form is hugely overrated," says Temple, "mainly because you're still being paid to flatter a pop star, so you always have to take an old prat like Rod Stewart and make him attractive because he's supposed to be some sex god or something. I have a real love-hate relationship with the medium. Promos are a great way to gain filmmaking experience, but they're also a good place to disguise sloppiness and lack of intelligence.

"I will only make a promo for a song if I have a definite angle on the song, if I feel I can come up with something substantial and exciting, not just a string of meaningless, random imagery. I like to build little riddles into narratives. I much prefer working with a pop star who can act, like Ray Davies, and who, like Ray, or Martin Fry, or Mitch Ryder, is not put off by the idea of playing an unflattering role. Ray never balked at playing an aging spiv [British slang for gangster or lounge lizard] in 'Come Dancing,' and he happens to be an extraordinary actor. That really helps. You can play with their ability, and their willingness to be malleable, and introduce multiple dark, ironic levels underneath the surface narrative.

"For rock video to progress, it'll have to get to where the movie musicals of the forties were, when directors and composers worked together to create a vital third entity from the music and visuals. It'll have to become more of a two-way street between directors and musicians. For now, I think any ten frames of a Vincente Minnelli movie musical are far superior to any rock promo, my own certainly included."

Temple has irons in many fires: though still busy making rock videos, as of this writing, he had just started work on his first feature film, *Absolute Beginners* (based on Colin MacInnes's black comic novel); he had another treatment for *Mandrake the Magician* being considered for feature production; and he had just shown a controversial TV film on the BBC, *It's All True: a Cautionary Tale for the Video Age,* which was "about two people trapped inside two TV sets, seeing the whole world broadcast through the eyes of the broadcast media. It was just a comment on all this British video mania and the way people implicitly believe whatever the electronic media show them."

Julian Temple just may be too deep a thinker to last very long with rock video. Let's hope not.

STEVE BARRON

AGE: 28
PRODUCTION COMPANY: Limelight
BUDGET RANGE: $30,000 to $70,000
CLIPS INCLUDE: Human League—"Don't You Want Me," "Mirror Man," "(Keep Feeling) Fascination"; Michael Jackson—"Billie Jean"; Toto—"Rosanna," "Africa"; Fleetwood Mac—"Hold Me"; Bryan Adams—"Cuts like a Knife," "This Time"; Joe Jackson—"Steppin' Out," "Real Men," "Breaking Us in Two"; Eddy Grant—"Electric Avenue," "I Don't Wanna Dance"; Rod Stewart—"Baby Jane"; Adam and the Ants—"Antmusic"; Hayzi Fantayzee—"John Wayne Is Big Leggy"; Madonna—"Burning Up"; Orchestral Manoeuvres in the Dark—"Maid of Orleans," "Genetic Engineering."

Scion of a film-industry family, child of the rock age, Barron was seemingly born to make rock videos. He made some waves with "Antmusic," memorable for the constant forward-motion of its frantic choreography and the shot of Adam Ant pulling a gigantic plug from a wall socket (to the lyric "Unplug the jukebox. . . ."). He broke through to the big time with Human League's "Don't You Want Me," the epitome of rock videos that feature extreme close-ups of people flashing that intent, supposedly soulful "look," and which also happened to be one of rock video's most sublime movie homages (in this case, Truffaut's *Day for Night*). Though he's never worked with huge budgets, Barron

Peter Gabriel in tribal-Kabuki makeup in the classic "Shock the
Monkey" video (1983), a powerful mini-epic of psychic dissolution
directed by Brian Grant, which won "Clip of the Year" in *Heavy Metal*
magazine's first annual music-video awards in 1983

always gets an expensive look onscreen and has a nice neo-Mulcahy
way with provocative ambiguity.

"I like to go halfway between the realistic and the abstract. If you
go too far in either of those directions, you're liable to lose people's
interest after a while. I like to set a mood for the song, so people can
get anything they like out of the visuals but are still left with a feeling
of the song that's not necessarily a literal parallel. I find that shooting

with film helps me do that better than video. Film has a richer texture; you can do more with depth and stuff. Whereas video's so flat, it either looks like TV news documentary or it's totally lurid and cartoony. That can work too, but for what I like to do, I usually prefer film. Film and video take effects differently.

"For instance the Hayzi Fantayzee clip 'John Wayne Is Big Leggy' is 'posterized' to get that psychedelic look. But Eddy Grant's 'Electric Avenue' and Rod Stewart's 'Baby Jane' are posterized as well, and they look completely different, because film takes the effect differently, more subtly. Posterized film is quite good for a 'dreamy,' slightly other-worldly effect.

"The concepts for the videos are inevitably mine. I can't remember the last time a band gave me a concept. I don't know where my ideas come from. Where do painters and writers get their ideas from? Wherever, right? You just hope it'll work, and if the band approves, you run with it. Though, coming up with my own concepts all the time, Siobhan [his sister, Limelight's production chief] has to keep reminding me that these are promotional films, not my own creative exercises. Actually, they're a bit of both, and that's what makes them exciting. The ultimate objective is definitely to promote the song and to make the artist look good. Since most musicians aren't actors, it's real easy to make them look bad on camera, but I think that serves as *demotion* rather than promotion. If people see my video and think, 'Great video,' and don't remember the song, then I haven't done my job."

As of this writing, Barron was busily preproducing his first feature film, *Electric Dreams;* he had previously been offered, and had turned down, an epic about mutant teens on the rampage, *Spider Hive.* "*Electric Dreams* is sort of a domesticated *WarGames,*" says Barron, "about a home computer that runs amok. I don't think it'll look like my rock videos, though that may be inevitable—promos and features are two totally different media."

DON LETTS

AGE: 27
PRODUCTION COMPANY: Limelight
BUDGET RANGE: $25,000 to $40,000
CLIPS INCLUDE: The Clash—"London Calling," "The Call-Up," "Rock the Casbah"; The Pretenders—"Back on the Chain Gang"; Musical Youth—"Pass the Dutchie," "Never Gonna Give You Up";

Elvis Costello—"Every Day I Write the Book"; Martin Briley—"Put Your Hands on the Screen."

While a DJ at London's punk hotbed the Roxy in 1976 and 1977, Letts began tinkering with a Super-8 camera, documenting "all these crazy white punk-rock kids," and ended up with *The Punk Rock Movie,* an appropriately grungy performance rockumentary that had a very limited American run. He then became close with the Clash, and after making several promos for them, Letts joined Limelight.

"I don't like to sell a band's face and make teenage girls wet their pants when they see them. The way rock videos are going now, it's like punk rock never even happened. I'll only work with a band or a song that I like, and that means they or the song have to be saying something, doing something honest and with quality. It's hard to find groups and songs like that these days, and it seems to get harder as time goes by, so I get less active. The whole promo video thing's getting too lopsided; it looks as if in the near future, if a band isn't pretty enough to make it on video, they won't make it, period. That's real scary. All my life I've been trying to associate with people who are trying to be constructive, to set a good example. You can pollute the airwaves just like you can pollute the air.

"When I work with a band, it's usually my concepts and my images, but I always work closely with them—because like I said, I work with them only if I like them and their music, so there's a mutual degree of trust. Sometimes I work up something with a band and then their label doesn't like it. That happened with Musical Youth. I made a clip for them of 'Youth of Today' showing them being chased by policemen. Then they got signed and their label trashed that clip and ordered them to come up with another one. So we did 'Pass the Dutchie,' which had them being chased by a schoolteacher. *That* was all right. That's the kind of politics you have to deal with.

"Speaking of black bands, I'd really love to work with more of them. I think I'm one of the last guys left who still believes that the best videos are the ones that simply do a good job documenting a good performance. I think black artists are generally better performers than whites. The thing is that at the end of the day, someone's gonna have to spend some money to get a black video to look comparable to most white videos. And nobody wants to spend the money on black videos because they know they won't get the airtime in the first place. It's that old ironic, self-fulfilling prophecy. I'd love to break that vicious circle. But I don't know if I'll be able to. I like to throw a spanner in the works. There seems to be less and less room for a guy like me in pop promos."

CHRIS GABRIN

AGE: 34

PRODUCTION COMPANY: Limelight

BUDGET RANGE: $25,000 to $40,000

CLIPS INCLUDE: Martin Briley—"Salt in My Tears"; Saga—"Wind Him Up"; Culture Club—"Time"; Captain Sensible—"Wot?"; Madness—"Grey Day," "It Must Be Love"; Heaven 17—"Temptation"; Yaz—"Don't Go"; John Cougar Mellencamp—"Crumblin' Down," "Pink Houses."

Gabrin started out as a still photographer doing rock album covers (Elvis Costello's *This Year's Model,* Nick Lowe's *Pure Pop for Now People*). Then he worked at a London rock club, where he met Hugh Cornwall of the Stranglers, whom he'd often encountered after the lights came up, sitting a few rows away at the same movies. When Cornwall decided to make a video for a solo record, he asked Gabrin to make it. "So I said sure," laughs Gabrin, "then I walked next door to a filmmaker friend of mine and said, 'Hey, how the hell do you go about making a film anyway?' So I did it, and that led to Stranglers videos, and that led to Stiff videos with Madness, then I came to Limelight."

Gabrin is an efficient filmmaker, an avid round-the-clock workaholic who usually outlasts his cohorts (and that's saying something). His style is malleable and subtle, never ostentatious, and in the best examples—"Salt in My Tears," "Wot?"—incorporates welcome doses of humor, both subtle and overt. "I'm a real media-obsessed person," he says. "I watch everything I can. My favorites are Buñuel and Kurosawa, but I hardly ever get to show that in a promo. Doing a promo, you have to remember, especially with a band's first video, not to go too over the top with the concept and obscure who the hell the band is. I'm still learning as I go along. Basically, the concepts are usually nominally mine, but they're inevitably suggested by the song's lyrics or whatever the band tells me. I usually do try to inject some humor if at all possible. There's nothing worse than a pop star who takes himself too seriously. If you can make people laugh, you really get across to them before they even know it. What I'd like to do in the future is to better coordinate the creative process of working with a band on a clip—sit in with them while they're mixing their album and discuss ideas more ahead of time. I've mentioned that to a few bands, and they liked the idea. It makes sense to me, and it'll mean saner work schedules, too."

ARTHUR ELLIS

AGE: 32
PRODUCTION COMPANY: Limelight
BUDGET RANGE: $20,000 to $40,000
CLIPS INCLUDE: Twisted Sister—"You Can't Stop Rock & Roll"; Jefferson Starship—"Planet Earth Rock & Roll Orchestra"; Ronnie James Dio—"Holy Diver," "Rainbow in the Dark"; Status Quo—"Dear John"; M—"Official Secrets"; Gary Moore—"Always Going to Love You"; Ian Gillian—"Long Gone," "Living for the City."

Possibly *the* ranking director of heavy-metal videos today, Ellis started out winning a local art-association script award in his native Yorkshire, and with the cash prize, he produced a film he describes, with his typically understated mordant humor, as "a pisstake of a psychotic horror film trailer, steeped in parody but mainly intended to make people *sweat.*" Since then, he's made short films for Paramount and has dabbled in rock videos. Like Julian Temple, Ellis is a stickler for narrative content and violently despises what he calls "the lack of direction in all these pretty, polite, toilet-roll rock videos where they just try to mystify the audience with so much imagery and editing and effects that the audience can't even think about the lack of substance anymore. . . . I mean, I watch a half-hour of MTV, and I retch. It's Godawful. My number-one priority is good-looking camera work, but I can't stand all these feature films that are like rock videos; they look lovely, but they have an awful script and pathetic direction and no plot sense or character development.

"I'll only work with bands I like. Usually they're very smart and receptive to my ideas; they pick up on my story lines and humor right off. It's only the others around them—the labels, management—who get in the way. Paul Kantner of Jefferson Starship and I worked on a great script for their video, which he was very happy with, but it had shotguns being used in it, and the label was afraid MTV would censor it, so we had to redo it four times."

Despite all that, Ellis has managed to craft some highly entertaining and aesthetically apt heavy-metal videos, full of strong plot lines and pointed humor, yet remaining true to heavy metal's punch-drunk *Grand Guignol* sensibilities. As of this writing, he was talking over a possible feature-film deal with *Halloween* producer Mustapha Akkad.

Despite covering his head with a trash-can lid for protection, Twisted Sister's music turns this member of the "Taste Squad" into a long-haired, heavy-metalhead in the classic heavy-metal clip "You Can't Stop Rock 'n' Roll" (1983), directed by Arthur Ellis for Limelight of Britain.

TIM POPE

AGE: 27

PRODUCTION COMPANY: GLO (Gordon Lewis Organization)
BUDGET RANGE $20,000 to $50,000
CLIPS INCLUDE: Men without Hats—"Safety Dance"; Neil Young— "Wonderin'," "Cry, Cry, Cry"; Psychedelic Furs—"Love My Way"; Bow Wow Wow—"Do You Wanna Hold Me," "Mario," "Baby Oh No"; Altered Images—"I Could Be Happy"; the Cure—"The Walk," "Let's Go to Bed"; Wham UK!—"Bad Boys"; Tygers of Pantang— "Love Potion #9"; Soft Cell—all clips, including "Tainted Love," "What?," "Say Hello, Wave Good Bye," "Sex Dwarf," "Seedy Films," and "Bedsitter"; Hall and Oates—"Adult Education."

Pope began tinkering with Super-8 cameras at age eight, studied at film school, filmed politicians for TV appearances, then hung out on London's punk-rock and new-wave scenes, where he befriended bands and applied his filmmaking experience to their videos.

"My experience with politicians actually helped as far as pop promos go," he says, "insofar as presenting people well. Basically, my style is to not have a style; I try to be as flexible as possible." Indeed, Pope has proved himself at home in a variety of media and styles: on the one hand, there's his intentionally cheap, poppy, high-energy video style, as in Bow Wow Wow's "Do You Wanna Hold Me" (actually a mix of film and video); on the other, there's his richly cinematic old English fair setting for Men without Hats' "Safety Dance" (shot on thirty-five-millimeter film).

"For the Men without Hats video, just from listening to the track, I got this sort of medieval feel, this sort of madrigal or Gregorian chant thing, or whatever you call it, and I just pictured medieval types dancing in a sort of Bruegel wide shot, which we actually used in the video, and everything just grew out of that—how do they get to the dance in the wide shot? We show the singer and his dwarf companion trekking through the highlands, and so forth. . . ."

Pope's favorite of his own clips is Neil Young's "Wonderin'," which he claims is "just about Neil living his life at a different place than everyone else. The way we got that exaggerated sort of step-framed look was, we filmed Neil at half-speed, lip-synching to half-speed playback, then doubled it again for the playback."

Pope conceptualizes by "becoming part of the band—which is not to say they contribute equally with me, but that I just get as close to them as possible. Bands don't usually have any real knowledge of filmmaking, they just have ideas of what they've seen and liked and want to go for. But I'm usually a very big fan of the bands I work with."

Though he started out shooting almost exclusively on video, and thus became a sort of neo-David Mallet, Pope has lately been working only in film, and says, "I seem to have lost the feel I originally got from video. Strange. But I'm making two or three promos a week now; it's great, I'm having a ball. All this work is pushing me to the brink of insanity, but it seems that the more insane I get, the better work I do!"

ANNABELLE JANKEL

AGE: 29
PRODUCTION COMPANY: Cucumber Studios
BUDGET RANGE: $30,000 to $50,000
CLIPS INCLUDE: Donald Fagen—"New Frontier"; Tom Tom Club—"Genius of Love"; Chaz Jankel—"Questionnaire"; Elvis Costello—"Accidents Will Happen."

Jankel, along with codirector Rocky Morton and producer Andy Morahan, is responsible for some of rock video's most enduringly beautiful creations. Cucumber is the kingpin of rock-video animation. It may be the only one doing it for now, but the quality of its work is consistently no less than awesome, whether pure abstract animation ("Questionnaire"), ever-metamorphosing cartoons ("Genius of Love"), computer-animation based on live footage ("Accidents Will Happen"), or a perfectly poised mix of animation and live action ("New Frontier").

Jankel and Morton both studied film and animation at West Surrey College of Art and Design in Britain and went on to make numerous award-winning animated commercials and short films before turning their talents to rock video with Elvis Costello's "Accidents Will Happen" (which bears a striking resemblance to Cucumber's computer-animation for NBC's *Friday Night Videos*—they're both based on the same technique).

"We use our own concepts," explains Jankel. "I guess because once people see our work and like it, they just want us to do whatever it is we do. So we'll listen to the song and then send them a storyboard of what we've come up with, and if they like it, we go on with it. We take six to eight weeks to do one promo, which is exceptionally long for promos, but that's the way it is with animation, it's very time-consuming. We have dozens of animators working round the clock on them.

"For us, animation is just a good way of communicating ideas and feelings, and if it can be done better by live action, then that's what people should do. But with animation it's easier to make the visuals sort of abstract, and that is easier to make work with the music."

Influences? "Definitely *not* Disney—those sort of white middle-class values are just what we're trying to break down. Bugs Bunny, on the other hand, is great. We really loved Devo's early stuff, and early experimental films like *Metropolis* and *Un Chien Andalou*. *Eraserhead* is a big fave around here. But influentially speaking, I guess we get most of our ideas from graphic design, advertising illustrations, that sort of thing."

Future plans? "We want to integrate more live action with animation; that worked out well in 'New Frontier,' which I understand they're blowing up to thirty-five-millimeter to show as a theatrical short. Inevitably, we want to make feature films. After struggling with the limitations of the three-minute promo, the subtleties of dialogue are fascinating."

CHUCK STATLER AND GERALD CASALE

AGES: 34 (Statler), 32 (Casale)

PRODUCTION COMPANIES: Location Services (Statler), DevoVision (Casale)

BUDGET RANGE: $15,000 to $40,000.

CLIPS INCLUDE: Statler: Devo—"Jocko Homo," "Secret Agent Man," "Satisfaction," "The Day My Baby Gave Me a Surprise," "Worried Man," "Freedom of Choice," "Girl U Want" (codirected with Casale); Elvis Costello—"Oliver's Army," "(What's So Funny 'bout) Peace Love and Understandin'," "I Can't Stand Up for Falling Down," "Love for Tender," "High Fidelity"; J. Geils Band—"Love Stinks"; the Cars—"Panorama," "Touch and Go" (codirected with Casale); Michael Stanley Band—"He Can't Love You"; Madness—"One Step Beyond," "Madness," "Baggy Trousers"; Graham Parker—"Local Girls"; Nick Lowe—"Cruel to Be Kind," "Ragin' Eyes"; Waitresses—"Go Make the Weather"; Donnie Iris—"Do You Compute?" Casale: Devo—"Whip It," "Beautiful World," "Thru Being Cool," "Love without Anger," "Peek-a-Boo," "That's Good," "Time Out for Fun," "Theme from *Dr. Detroit.* "

The deans of American rock-video *auteurs,* Statler and Casale merit a place in the pantheon if only for their Devo clips. As noted earlier, they both have their directorial favorites: Statler the antiflash, neoindustrial directness of Buñuel and Russ Meyer; Casale the black-humored classicism of Kubrick and the surreal grotesqueness of Fellini. As Statler says, "Buñuel especially had a peculiar way of capturing the most outrageous things in a totally everyday way. He never made a big deal about fancy style; he just wanted to capture strong imagery as directly as possible. That's what Devo's stuff is all about, too. Meyer, too—a master industrialist with a surreal touch, no camera moves, just montage and stuff, plus his wonderful gaudiness and crassness. It's hard to apply those kinds of aesthetics to a rock video, but what I do is just refuse to go for big sweeping Hollywood camera moves and showy edits and all that garbage. I like to keep things simple and to the point."

Naturally, with an outlook like that, Statler finds himself somewhat behind the times. Indeed, from his Minneapolis home, he says, "The rock-video business has moved to New York and L.A. It's like any other entertainment industry now. Meanwhile, I'm staying in Minneapolis, where I have a lifestyle I enjoy. Sometimes I guess I do feel kind of like the pioneer left in the wilderness with his musket and

Cucumber Studios' fanciful depiction of James Brown in Tom Tom Club's delightful animated video "Genius of Love" (1982), directed by Annabelle Jankel and Rocky Morton

coonskin cap. . . . It's not an image I particularly like, but I guess in a way I deserve it. I am sort of pigeonholed as a low-budget director. I guess my big shortcoming is that I just don't want to relocate to movieland and go through the old Hollywood shuffle."

Casale, meanwhile, has relocated to Hollywood with the rest of Devo (they made the move in 1979). But that's hardly dampened his unique imagistic creativity and appears to have only added to his excellent grasp of technical effects, which Casale never, ever uses merely for their own sake. The interaction of live characters with matte video images has always been a Devo video hallmark (going back at least to "The Day My Baby Gave Me a Surprise"), but it reached new heights with "Peek-a-Boo" and the *Dr. Detroit* clip. The latter is by far the best and most creative video clip as movie trailer as of this writing, as well as arguably the only Devo video to possess a remotely *sweet* sense of humor (along with a darker subtext about identity transference through high-tech gadgetry, and a mastery of playful video special effects that rivals anybody's).

As Casale puts it, "The synching of visuals to music is probably the single most powerful media phenomenon of this century. There's a power to that synergy—even when the music and/or visuals are insipid and shallow—that shouldn't be underestimated. Devo tries to respect that synergy, respect the medium. We believe in *imagery with integrity,* as opposed to the run of the mill on MTV, which just begins to look like chimps on parade after a while." Call Casale an insolent cynic if you like, but the fact remains that he means what he says, and his videos easily live up to his own high standards. Casale and Devo as a whole —with or without Statler—also have established themselves as far and away rock's most innovative video band. It seems safe to say that whatever you see Devo doing in a video, everyone else will be doing within six months to a year. Devo's rock-video firsts are almost too numerous to list here, but they include: first clips self-produced by a band; first long-form home-video program to go beyond concert footage (1979's *The Men Who Make the Music*); first use of extramusical noises on soundtrack (in "Whip It," where the beer can is shot with a resounding *"thunk"*); first use of the now familiar motif of multimedia character interaction (in "Surprize"); first use of posterization (in "Girl U Want"); and, in the 1979 "Worried Man" (included in Neil Young's 1983 antinuke musical feature *Human Highway* and in the *We're All Devo* long-form program), the pre-"Beat It" opening with rising warehouse doors.

JOE DEA

AGE: 28
PRODUCTION COMPANY: Video Caroline
BUDGET RANGE: $20,000 to $40,000
CLIPS INCLUDE: Greg Kihn—"Jeopardy," "Happy Man"; Krokus— "Screaming in the Night," "Eat the Rich"; Commander Cody—"Two Triple Cheese, Side Order of Fries"; David Johansen—"Animals Medley"; the Hits—"Backstabber."

Though some industry insiders remember Dea fondly for his pioneering, cheapo comedy classic for Commander Cody (a budget of $250 for a hilarious clip that's all too seldom seen these days), Dea didn't really get hot until "Jeopardy" and "Screaming in the Night" vividly demonstrated his peculiarly American knack for fusing macabre spectacle with comedy arising from purposefully overdone vulgarity. Though "Jeopardy" looks cheaper (it was shot on video tape), both clips cost about $25,000; both became MTV smashes.

Both clips also displayed an exceedingly strong grasp of plot development (also shown in Dea's earlier "Happy Man") unhindered by multileveled, self-referential scenarios. "I got the original idea for 'Jeopardy,' from the song's chorus and those 'ooo-woo' harmony vocals —it just sounded like ghosts or something, haunted-house music, and with those lyrics, 'Our love's in jeopardy,' the idea of something ominous or paranoid seemed obvious. But I didn't get a fix on it till me and my crew were sitting around brainstorming, and a guy named Richard Day said, 'How about zombies?' And it *clicked:* a wedding with zombies! So in about ten minutes, I had it all down, I was throwing out all these ideas, 'then this,' 'then *this,*' and the crew was cracking up.

" 'Screaming in the Night' was my concept. It's a takeoff on that Charlton Heston flick, *The Vikings,* only it's on land. You should see the uncensored version of that—in that scene where the guy stabs the girl, I originally had a shot of the guy licking the blood off the knife with this maniacal grin. It was intended to be real *Grand Guignol.* No serious statement or anything there. A lot of people complain that video is too gross and sexist or something. Gimme a break! Are you gonna make a tasteful video for a heavy-metal song like that? Hey folks, it was supposed to be gross."

GRAEME WHIFLER

AGE: 32
PRODUCTION COMPANY: Whifler/Nimmer
BUDGET RANGE: $20,000 to $30,000
CLIPS INCLUDE: the Residents—"One Minute Movies" ("Moisture," "Act of Being Polite," "Simple Song," "Perfect Love"), "Hello Skinny"; Sparks, with Jane Wiedlin—"Cool Places"; Translator—"Unalone"; Tuxedomoon—"Jinx"; Snakefinger—"Man in the Black Sedan"; Renaldo and the Loaf—"Songs for Swinging Larvae"; MX-80 Sound—"Why Are We Here?"

Whifler did *not* direct the Residents' stupendous "Land of 1,000 Dances" clip, but the "One Minute Movies" he did codirect with the Residents equal the earlier effort for sheer unadulterated, dreamy-nightmarish bizarreness. Whifler's clips for such other Ralph Records acts as Tuxedomoon (Todd Rundgren's "You Make Me Crazy" for

Utopia bears a striking resemblance to "Jinx"), Snakefinger, and Renaldo and the Loaf are similarly bizarre and disturbing, and technically overpowering. There's a very distinctive personality, a point of view to Whifler's mastery of camera work and color schemes and lighting. While "Cool Places" is far more mainstream—a fresh, bouncy sight gag with Go-Go Jane Wiedlin and band members dancing, chroma-keyed over constantly moving, video matte backdrops—Whifler's "Unalone" for Translator managed to work still more strange, dark touches into an ostensibly mainstream scenario of love lost and sought.

"I get most of my inspiration from TV commercials," says Whifler, "though *never* prime-time shows, which are so stupid and insulting. But I like TV imagery as opposed to the movie imagery everyone cops these days. I think TV imagery is more appropriate to rock videos. Movies grew out of a *narrative* tradition; that kind of thing just doesn't work in a three-minute promo video. TV's all about big images flashing by, no time to extend a thought very long. But with films like *Flashdance,* that clichéd rock-video style is infecting movies, which is bad.

"Most rock videos are garbage, I think. The production values are nice, but everything keeps getting tied down to the lowest common denominator. I hope rock video doesn't addle the minds of young people too much. But one encouraging thing I've noticed, in San Francisco, at least, is that a lot of kids, and I mean ten- and twelve-year-olds, see MTV and say, 'Oh, that's so boring.' That's great!

"Directing rock videos means you have to be a director, writer, producer, advertising executive, and psychiatrist all at once. Most bands are rather inarticulate with their concepts if they have any; once you get a concept out of them, or give them yours, then you have to deal with the fact that they're musicians who aren't used to acting for the camera. And they're likely to be on camera without instruments, which makes them feel naked. You have to give them constant reinforcement. To me, the funny thing about rock videos is that they're really like silent films—there's no dialogue, just the music and the visuals. It's like the film industry is starting all over again from ground zero."

MARCELLO EPSTEIN, DOMINIC ORLANDO, MARK REZYKA

AGES: 33 (Epstein), 32 (Orlando), 34 (Rezyka)
PRODUCTION COMPANY: Pendulum Productions
BUDGET RANGE: $20,000 to $60,000
CLIPS INCLUDE: Epstein: Berlin—"Sex (I'm a . . .)"; Wet Picnic—"He Believes"; Oxo—"Whirlygirl"; Hiroshima—"San Say."

ORLANDO: Kansas—"Fight Fire with Fire"; Berlin—"The Metro"; The Screamers—"Jazz Vampire"; Carly Simon—"You Know What to Do"; REZYKA; Quiet Riot—"Metal Health," "Cum on Feel the Noize"; Danny Spanos—"Excuse Me"; Cheap Trick—"I Can't Take It"; Lindsey Buckingham—"Holiday Road"; Heart—"How Can I Refuse."

When this reporter asked rock-video vet Simon Fields, Limelight's U.S. production chief, what American rock-video directors he liked, he immediately responded, "The Pendulum people," and could think of nobody else. That's understandable. For, aside from Bob Giraldi, no American rock-video *auteurs* have yet equaled Epstein, Orlando, and Rezyka for lush production values and imagery. From the graphic implications of sex in Berlin's clips to the stunningly wrought male-wish-fulfillment fantasies of "He Believes," to the product identification and aesthetically apt apocalyptic scenarios of Quiet Riot's clips, to the malaria nightmare of "Fight Fire with Fire," the Pendulum people have got it all down.

Epstein, born in Argentina, made commercials and dance films there before winning a Fulbright Scholarship and moving to the U.S. Orlando and Rezyka were veteran animators and effects people for such shows as *The Smurfs* and Hanna-Barbera cartoons as well as various film projects.

Epstein says: "For me, the music of a song relates to the look and pace of a clip the way the lyrics relate to the concept. The first thing I thought of when I listened to 'Sex' by Berlin was that it needed a lot of traveling shots, because that's what the rhythm and tempo suggested. Your imagery should flow with the feeling of the music."

Orlando: "Being an animator, I draw story boards for songs all the time, even if I have no chance of doing a clip or if the clip's already been done by someone else. I do it just for the fun of it. I try to come up with things that aren't literal to the song but associative, that will still complement the song and be eye-catching enough to hold up to repeated viewings. With the Kansas video, I thought of an analogue for fire and came up with fever. Then I thought, 'What can cause fever? Malaria.' And that was it, the whole concept came from there. I outbid five other directors for that one based on my concept. I guess it was the only concept the whole band loved."

Rezyka: "I like to go for darker scenarios, because rock music usually isn't about all sweetness and light; there's usually at least some sort of underlying aggression or something there, and with a band like Quiet Riot, it's real aggressive. But the 'Holiday Road' clip is a good example of that. Lindsey Buckingham wanted something divorced from the idea of holidays and vacations because that song was used as the theme for *National Lampoon's Vacation.* So I came up with a totally opposite, ironic thing; it's about a guy trapped at this desk in the office, wanting to get out on a holiday. It played off the song lyrics and the bouncy feel of the music. Lindsey loved the idea."

Yet there is a mouthwatering beauty to most Pendulum productions, and seeing any of them, one might easily mistake them for a Mulcahy or Steve Barron job. Which is meant as a complement to the Pendulum people. In fact, Orlando's "Fight Fire with Fire" was, as of this writing, one of the first rock videos (along with "Beat It" and "New Frontier") to be blown up to thirty-five-millimeter to be shown in movie theaters as a trailer. It shouldn't be long before at least one of these three moves into making those extended things that follow trailers in movie houses.

BOB GIRALDI

AGE: 45
PRODUCTION COMPANY: Gotham Entertainment/Giraldi Productions
BUDGET RANGE: $100,000 and up
CLIPS INCLUDE: Michael Jackson—"Beat It"; Diana Ross—"Pieces of Ice"; Pat Benatar—"Love Is a Battlefield"; Lionel Richie—"Running with the Night"; Paul McCartney and Michael Jackson—"Say, Say, Say"; Barry Manilow—"Read 'Em and Weep."

One of the most in-demand directors, Giraldi is responsible for those all-singing, all-dancing Dr. Pepper spots, the Miller Lite beer ads featuring sports stars, those late seventies razzle-dazzle ads for Broadway shows, and other familiarities on behalf of General Electric and McDonald's. He's also directed one feature film, the never released *National Lampoon Goes to the Movies.* Giraldi already had a well-established reputation as a creatively chameleonic advertising wizard before dipping his toes into rock video.

His entrance into the field with "Beat It" remains the most auspicious auteurial bow yet—a classic clip for a great song by a brilliant performer that rock critic Dave Marsh called "Only the greatest rock video ever made." It is superb musical and theatrical drama, is perfectly appropriate to the song, and injects strong social comment. Giraldi's next clip, "Pieces of Ice," is something of a disappointment—it starts with a far weaker song than "Beat It," is paced rather lethargically and ends up coming off stilted. Pat Benatar's "Love Is a Battlefield" has Giraldi once more fashioning dramatic rock-video innovations—it purports to be a socially conscious tale of teenage runaways, and though it ultimately fails to deliver on that promise, it is the first rock video to feature spoken dialogue that is not part of the original song.

"I have a tin ear and no rhythm, but to me you should only make a rock video for a great song," he says. "With a great song, you can have a tin ear and no rhythm and still sense what's great about it— that's what makes it great, that it transcends. I discuss ideas with the artists, then I write the concept, and from there it's all up to me. Making 'Beat It' was a real trip. I'd listened to *Thriller* and loved it and wanted to do 'Billie Jean,' but they got someone else to do it. Then they called me back and said they wanted to try someone different for 'Beat It.' So I'm there in Santo Domingo, vacationing with my wife, and the phone rings in the hotel, and she picks it up, and then she says to me, 'It's Michael Jackson.' He says to me that the song is just about turning the other cheek, but that he wanted to do something 'street' with it. That was all I needed. I went out on the beach with a cassette of the song and started writing the concept. I came up with the gangs and all that, and when we shot it, we had actual L.A. street gangs the police got for us. One of them was called the Crips—short for the Cripplers! These guys were very skeptical of me at first, but they saw Michael Peters (choreographer of "Beat It" and "Pieces of Ice") leading all these dancers, and they were impressed. I think the greatest directing experience of my life was seeing those gang members warming up to my direction. They found another kind of macho from the piece, which was the whole point of it; it was saying macho is bullshit, it was antiviolence.

"There's too much violence on TV anyway. And there's too much poorly portrayed, infantile violence on MTV. Maybe it's just that most rock songs aren't great—they can't be; you have to be selective.

"I still have this very weird ambivalence about working in the field myself: I think we professionals are liable to ruin MTV by making it one more lovely media form and taking that wildness out of it."

TIM NEWMAN

AGE: 41
PRODUCTION COMPANY: Dancing Buffalo Productions
BUDGET RANGE: $30,000 to $60,000
CLIPS INCLUDE: Randy Newman—"I Love L.A."; ZZ Top—"Gimme All Your Lovin'," "Sharp-Dressed Man"; Don Felder—"Bad Girls."

Another invader from the world of TV commercials, Newman is, in

Michael Jackson and Paul McCartney clown it up in "Say Say Say" (1983), directed by Bob Giraldi. The clip, an obvious take-off on *The Sting*'s lovable-con-men motif, was one of an increasing number of superstar videos with budgets in the hundreds of thousands of dollars.

his own words, "a comedy and dialogue man" making ads for companies like Coca-Cola, Texaco, Amaco, Bell Telephone, and Continental Airlines. His father was famed film scorer Alfred Newman; he made his first rock video for his cousin Randy Newman.

"The reason I got into rock video was, a friend of mine called me one day just to look at these videos she's been collecting. She showed me the early Devo stuff, which I loved because it was funny, and very uncinematic; it had a cheap pop-cartoon quality that was very different, and it had great imagery and actually made me like the band a lot more than just their music. Then she showed me the Duran Duran 'Girls on Film' clip, and I said, 'This looks like *fun*! People get *paid* to do this?' So one thing led to another, and what with my commercial commitments, I finally got round to doing Randy's clip, which was a lot of fun to do and people liked it. Then the ZZ Top thing came along. That became a huge success and led to the first rock-video sequel and all."

"I Love L.A.," which, according to Newman, "was suggested totally by the song itself, was easy to conceptualize" and demonstrated Newman's remarkable aptitude for rhythmic cutting and building a pure-visual momentum that pulls the viewer in, as well as touches of great humor. Newman's ZZ Top clips are discussed at great length elsewhere in this book, and will be dealt with again in the "Rock Video's Hot 100" chapter. Suffice it to say they are masterworks of the genre.

"I'm still not sure about rock video," he sighs. "It's very open creatively, much more so than advertising, but on the other hand, the money's not there, and the logistics are always completely nuts. And things will have to change legally. As of now, I'm a member of the Director's Guild, and working in rock videos is basically illegal in their eyes because nothing's been worked out with unions yet. The Guild could conceivably come after me for violating my union rules."

PAUL JUSTMAN

AGE: 34
PRODUCTION COMPANY: Paul Justman Productions
BUDGET RANGE: $20,000 to $35,000
CLIPS INCLUDE: J. Geils Band—"Centerfold," "Freeze-Frame," "Angel in Blue"; the Cars—"Since You're Gone," "Shake It Up"; Rick Springfield—"Don't Talk to Strangers," "What Kind of Fool Am I"; Tane Cain—"Holdin' On."

Justman, whose brother is J. Geils's keyboardist, Seth Justman, is a veteran of independent and low-budget features and documentaries. In the late sixties, he was coeditor of Robert Frank's controversial Rolling Stones rockumentary *Cocksucker Blues.* Given that background, it's logical for him to say "Kenneth Anger probably did the best rock videos ever. Anger's stuff—*Scorpio Rising* and *Invocation of My Demon Brother*—is artistically honest, not like the stuff that goes down now."

In "Centerfold" and "Since You're Gone," Justman demonstrates more than humor and entertainment with uniquely limpid pacing and a talent for making lust and romantic longing resonate through bitter-sweet whimsy. "Don't Talk to Strangers" inaugurated the now time-honored rock-video motif of having the singer play a cuckold who becomes a pathetic voyeur watching his ex-girl with another guy (a ploy repeated in, among others, Tommy Tutone's "Jenny"). As of this writing, he was completing a feature film, *Rock & Roll Hotel,* and planned to continue making rock videos.

JOHN SANBORN

AGE: 29

PRODUCTION COMPANY: VCA Teletronics

BUDGET RANGE: $5,000 to $20,000

CLIPS INCLUDE: King Crimson—"Heartbeat"; Adrian Belew—"Big Electric Cat," "I'm Down"; Jim Capaldi—"That's Love."

This is the New York avant-garde's most volubly outspoken video-art whiz-kid (formerly a partner of Kit Fitzgerald's; French film review *Cahiers du Cinéma* once called them "unparalleled masters of the video form"). Sanborn enjoys discussing concepts like "visual humming" and "imagic thinking," which describe people's abilities to internalize visual imagery the way they memorize song melodies and lyrics. One of the very few video artists to move into rock video, Sanborn is given to using effects for their own sake, as in "Big Electric Cat"—which is a brilliant example of digital-effects video animation and "visual humming." His trademarks are superfast edits in constant streams that make it impossible to digest all the imagery of a clip in one viewing, and subtitles racing across the bottom of the screen (as in "That's Love," in which Jim Capaldi actually took a preexisting piece of Sanborn-Fitzgerald video art and set his song to it).

"Pictures are the way I think," says Sanborn. "Music is the way I feel. I see music video as a logical extension of the musical-theatrical tradition, but most people don't seem to take music video seriously as an art form. MTV comes very close to being a viable outlet for a new art form, but it misses the mark—the imagery of MTV videos seems stunted and removed, a new Dark Ages of sorts. My faith in pictures, in visual humming and imagic thinking, is simple, growing out of an age-old tradition whereby the qualities of music have developed to the point of [being] supremely collective unconscious materializations of thought, emotion and idea. . . . We've had visualizations with music at least since opera, but rock video reinvents the equation—the music is at the core of expression and invention, and the imagery is allowed to form a picture of the artist to the public. But most of the images I see on MTV are insulting. MTV talks down to me."

Still, Sanborn's stunning "Heartbeat" clip for King Crimson did get on MTV for a little while in mid-1982. As of this writing, he and partner Dean Winkler were heavily into the most advanced digital video effects equipment, and were using it to craft overpowering neopsychedelic opuses like "Act III" for avant-garde minimalist composer Philip

Glass. Will he try to make more rock-video waves? "I'd like to," he says, "but seeing all the gratuitous, disconnected, shallow, provocation-and-titillation-oriented stuff, I don't know if I'm right for it. Unless things change, MTV videos will keep looking like *General Hospital* on acid or something. I want to go more for 'visual humming,' where the images are created and edited in such a way that they're visually analagous to the way good songs are created, as expressions of abstract concepts—something present, yet elusive at the same time."

MERRILL ALDIGHIERI AND JOE TRIPICIAN

AGES: 32 (Aldighieri), 30 (Tripician)
PRODUCTION COMPANY: Co-Directions
CLIPS INCLUDE: Sony "Danspak" Video 45, including Man Parrish—"Hip Hop BeBop"; Shox Lumania—"Pointy Headgear," "Falling"; Richard Bone—"Alien Girl"; Living—"Boat Talk"; Lenny Kaye—"I Got a Right"; *Live at Hurrah* rockumentary compilation cassette; Jim Carroll—"Sweet Jane."

Aldighieri and Tripician met while doing screen tests of potential Muppets for Jim Henson in the late seventies. Merrill went on to become the first woman VJ in the world, at New York's now-defunct Hurrah (their live rockumentary recordings of vintage new-wave bands —in stereo—are compiled on the *Live at Hurrah* cassette). Together they made such video-art and comedy pieces as "Love among the Mutants" (boy meets girl, girl is a vacuum cleaner at heart) as well as the above music videos. "Danspak" is far and away Sony's most daring and unusual Video 45 (only Jesse Rae's comes close). With John Sanborn, this team represents the most important intersection to date of video art and rock video.

"Being VJs at Hurrah," says Aldighieri, "we learned pretty fast about coordinating visuals with music and what kind of imagery and cutting and rhythm held a crowd's attention. We found that certain images are perfect for rock music, because they're expressive yet have any number of different meanings to different people—like, say, mushroom-cloud explosions or something. We also did a lot of animation, squiggly patterns scratched onto black tape stock. And my favorite thing was to show really lush, high-contrast color European commercials, especially French ones where they just have these intense close-ups on a woman's lips, so you can just relish the texture of the image. I like that idea a lot."

"And," adds Tripician, "we learned how to work *fast,* which helps in making music videos; at Hurrah, we never knew what the DJ was going to play, so we were never sure what we were going to play. We learned to be very spontaneous and flexible."

Like Sanborn's work, the Co-Directions team is given to onrushing time-lapse imagery, otherworldly video effects treatments and fast, polyrhythmic jump-cuts. "The important thing," says Aldighieri, "is to use imagery that doesn't *reveal* everything about itself at first. If it does that, I get bored with it pretty fast, and if that happens, I can't use it."

What follows is a partial list of other major rock video directors and their works to date.

KEITH MACMILLAN

KEEFCO: Paul McCartney and Stevie Wonder—"Ebony and Ivory"; Uriah Heep—"That's the Way It Is"; Scorpions—"No One like You"; Blondie—"Island of Lost Souls," "Denis," "Detroit 442"; Pat Benatar —"Precious Time"; Kate Bush—"Wuthering Heights," "Babushka"; Laura Branigan—"Solitaire"; Nina Hagen—"African Reggae"; Paul McCartney—"Coming Up," "Pipes of Peace," "So Bad."

THOMAS DOLBY

LIMELIGHT: Thomas Dolby—"She Blinded Me with Science," "Europa and the Pirate Twins," "Radio Silence," "Hyperactive!"

KEVIN GODLEY AND LOL CREME

GODLEY & CREME/MEDIA MAN: Duran Duran—"Girls on Film"; Visage—"We Fade to Grey," "Mind of a Toy"; the Police—"Every Breath You Take," "Wrapped around Your Finger," "Synchronicity II"; Herbie Hancock—"Rockit," "Autodrive"; Graham Parker—"Temporary Beauty"; Elton John—"Kiss the Bride"; Godley and Creme—"An Englishman in New York," "Reds in My Bed."

TONI BASIL

RADIALCHOICE/CHRYSALIS: Toni Basil—*Word of Mouth* video album (including "Mickey," "Nobody," "Little Red Book," "Shoppin' A to Z"); Talking Heads—"Once in a Lifetime," "Cross-Eyed and Painless."

ADAM FRIEDMAN

KEN WALZ PRODUCTIONS: Rolling Stones—"Emotional Rescue"; Hall and Oates—"X Static"; Zebra—"Who's Behind the Door"; Jean-Luc Ponty—"Far from the Beaten Paths"; Runner—"Lies"; Krisma—"Nothing to Do with a Dog."

MICK HAGGERTY AND C. D. TAYLOR

NEO-PLASTIC PRODUCTIONS: Hall and Oates—"Family Man," "Maneater"; Go-Gos—"Vacation"; Jefferson Starship—"Find Your Way Back"; Bill Wyman—"Come Back Suzanne"; B-52's—"Legal Tender," "Song to a Future Generation."

MARK ROBINSON

MODERN PRODUCTIONS: Eddie Money—"Think I'm in Love," "Shakin' "; George Thorogood—"Bad to the Bone"; Pretenders—"Brass in Pocket"; Santana—"Hold On"; Tommy Tutone—"867-5309/Jenny."

BILL DEAR

PACIFIC ARTS: Cheap Trick—"She's Tight," "If You Want My Love"; Juice Newton—"Love's Been a Little Bit Hard on Me"; Roseanne Cash —"I Wonder"; Clocks—"She Looks a Lot like You"; Mike Nesmith —"Rio," "Cruisin'."

PHIL SAVENICK AND DOUG DOWDLER

SAVENICK STUDIOS: Tom Petty—"You Got Lucky," "Change of Heart"; Rick Springfield—"Affair of the Heart," "Human Touch."

FRANCIS DELIA

WOLF CO.: Wall of Voodoo—"Mexican Radio"; Gary Numan—"Cars"; Bangles—"The Real World"; Plimsouls—"A Million Miles Away"; Ramones—"Psychotherapy."

MARTIN KAHAN

KAHAN PRODUCTIONS: Ian Hunter—"All of the Good Ones Are Taken"; Scandal—"Love's Got a Line on You"; the Breaks—"She Wants You"; Loverboy—"Working for the Weekend," "Only the Lucky Ones," "Queen of the Broken Hearts," "Hot Girls in Love"; Michael Bolton—"Fools Game"; Clarence Clemons—"Woman's Got the Power"; Kiss—"Lick It Up."

ARNOLD LEVINE

VCA TELETRONICS: Joan Jett—"I Love Rock & Roll"; Bruce Springsteen—"Atlantic City"; Billy Joel—"Goodnight Saigon"; Aerosmith—"Lightning Strikes."

DOUG AND STEVE MARTIN

MARTIN INDUSTRIES: Go-Gos—"Get Up and Go"; Blasters—"Barefoot Rock"; Violent Femmes—"Gone Daddy Gone"; Sparks—"I Predict."

SIMON MILNE

DIRECT PRODUCTIONS: Kajagoogoo—"Too Shy"; Naked Eyes—"Always Something There to Remind Me"; Missing Persons—"Destination Unknown"; Duran Duran—"Union of the Snake."

MIKE MANSFIELD

MANSFIELD ENTERTAINMENT, LTD.: Adam Ant—"Goody 2-Shoes," "Desperate but Not Serious," "Friend or Foe"; Electric Light Orchestra—"Hold on Tight to Your Dream."

CLIVE RICHARDSON

ISLAND PICTURES: Siouxsie and the Banshees—"Fireworks," "Slow Dive," "Spellbound"; Blancmange—"Living on the Ceiling," "Blind Vision," "Waves"; Howard DeVoto—"Rainy Season"; Depeche Mode—"Everything Counts"; Kid Creole and the Coconuts—"Annie, I'm Not Your Daddy"; Steve Winwood—"Still in the Game," "Valerie."

PETE SINCLAIR

LIMELIGHT: Dire Straits—"Twistin' by the Pool"; Gary Myrick—"Guitar Talk, Love and Drums"; Dave Edmunds—"Slippin' Away," "Information"; Culture Club—"Karma Chameleon."

LESTER BOOKBINDER

DIRECTORS GROUP: Dire Straits—"Tunnel of Love," "Romeo and Juliet," "Skateaway."

RICHARD CASEY

CASEY FILMS: Aldo Nova—"Fantasy"; Buck Dharma—"Born to Rock," "Your Loving Heart"; DFX 2—"Emotion."

STORM THORGESON

GREENBACK FILMS: Planet P—"Why Me?," "Static"; Robert Plant—"Burning Down One Side," "Big Log," "In the Mood"; Yes—"Owner of a Lonely Heart."

SOUND AND VISION: HOW ROCK VIDEOS ARE MADE

There's no one way to make a rock video. The creative problems and solutions vary from song to song, band to band, label to label, even director to director. The making of a rock video is a complex confluence of timing, promotion, and marketing strategy; style- and budget-consciousness; and in many cases, sheer frantic craziness.

Generally, things work something like this: At some point, the band, their management, and their label decide there should be a rock video. This may be agreed upon while the album is being recorded, after it's recorded but before it's released, or even after it's been released, so the label can watch radio play and chart action to see which song has the most potential to be exploited—which song to visualize. In one case, Billy Idol's "Dancin' with Myself," the video was produced almost two years after the song had been released. It is then decided what type of video to make: performance, concept, or some combination thereof. Prospective producers and directors are discussed, candidates are narrowed down and contacted, or, if the band and label have no concept of their own, they may contact a specific director because of his particular style and budget range. Budgets are roughly worked out, and the band, management, and label representative meet with the director and producer to finalize concepts and budgets. But before anyone considers the details of how a given video will be made, one should also consider why. The band's particular musical style and image determines not only what kind of clip they might make, but often whether they will make a clip in the first place.

"The multiformat hit potential of a song determines whether or not we make a clip," says independent producer Randy Hock. "It has to have AOR appeal, because that's MTV's base. But MTV's format is opening up regarding black acts, so things are always in flux. As more and more other outlets for rock videos proliferate, that makes things even more flexible. The number of prospective outlets for a video determines whether or not the video gets made. Radio also plays a part. If we don't make a video for a song, and radio picks up on it, we might then make a video."

But sometimes labels have little or no input at all. Perhaps as a result of the independent record-label explosion here and in England, many groups have taken to making their own videos before they have a contract. In this case, the video's primary objective is not necessarily to win the group exposure on MTV (although that might happen), but to interest record companies in signing the band. As MCA's Larry Solters notes, "More and more acts come to us with a video already made. Videos are becoming the new demo tapes, and they really work that way, too. You can see what a band looks like, how they move, as well as hear how they sound."

In fact, some bands have gotten signed as a result of independently produced videos. Pop band Scandal were signed by CBS on the basis of their video for "Goodbye to You" (straight in-studio lip-sync treated with op-art video effects). The song subsequently became a hit, thanks again in large part to MTV's rotation of the clip. Canadian group Saga were a hit at home and in Europe but could not land a U.S. recording deal as of early 1982. Their management financed a concept clip for "On the Loose," mixing onstage performance with a prison-escape scenario. The clip got onto MTV, and then the band landed an American deal with Epic. With more and more video production houses springing up, needing work to get more work, the "video demo" should figure greatly in rock's future.

The overall attitude of most labels these days seems to be that video, in an astoundingly short period of time, has become as important a promotional factor as touring or radio or advertising.

Despite all that, some labels and some artists are still somewhat suspicious of rock video. According to Perry Cooper, vice-president of artist relations and media development at Atlantic Records, "Sure you can do a video clip for a new act and get it shown all over the place and break the act that way, fine. But in a situation where you've got a Rolling Stones or a Genesis or an AC/DC, who are already very well-known to the public, they don't want their videos shown all over the place. Why not? Because they're all trying to sell concert tickets, and overexposure through video can kill an act quicker than anything."

However, with more and more bands making promo clips, the dangers of overexposure lessen. Still, as Cooper (whose protouring/anti-video-overexposure argument is dismissed by most other label execs) indicates, even superstar bands who don't seem to *need* rock video are thinking a lot harder about it.

Atlantic's Cooper goes on to make another interesting observation, though: "One way that rock video *does* work with superstar artists is when they're in a band and want to do solo projects. Video is the best way for them to establish a solo identity. We did that with Stevie Nicks of Fleetwood Mac, Pete Townshend of the Who, Phil Collins of Genesis, and Frida of ABBA. In most cases, a band member doing a solo project has a hard time touring, so video comes in very handy in those cases."

But regardless of why a video is made, one aspect seems consistent: most clips still are made in a hurry, often just days after a song begins inching up the charts.

Rock-video directors have mixed feelings about this arrangement, since common sense dictates that a project done in haste is not always done best. But most directors and labels blithely accept it as the way of the world.

Rock-video director Kevin Godley of Godley and Creme says: "Promo videos are part of the *pop* business, and as in pop music itself, things happen very quick. You don't have time to drag on and on analyzing the damn thing over and over. You go with gut instincts. It's comparable to making an album: if you take six months agonizing over it, it all gets very self-conscious and dragged out and bogged down. You're liable to lose the creative spark that made it seem worthwhile in the first place."

The rush scheduling of rock-video shoots adds to their cost. "It's funny," says producer Ken Walz, "but most labels end up throwing as much money away as they save by wanting the clips made so fast. You don't have time to plot things out so that they're as cost-efficient as they should be. You might have crews working overtime, and that alone could run your costs way up, especially if it's a union crew; you might have to get sets somewhere at a certain price when you could have gotten them a lot cheaper somewhere else, but you didn't have the time to find out."

Adds rock-video cameraman Daniel Pearl, "The rock videos I've worked on, and I've been on a lot, have all had totally nonunion crews. The people working on these crews are sort of Hollywood misfits, people like me from low-budget features who got sick of the hassle of that grind and find *this* grind a lot more fun and involving and satisfying.

"If we went by union rules, we couldn't shoot eighteen- or twenty-hour days like we do; we'd have to take ten-hour breaks between shoots, and that would mean a lot of rock videos could not be made. The shooting schedules are based on the nature of the music business, which is a very fast-breaking kind of thing. We shoot on weekends and holidays, we work overtime all the time. If we got paid union scale for overtime, that alone would end up breaking the record labels. If union rules were applied, we might get better paid and work in more comfortable conditions, but there would be a lot less work overall. The unions don't bother us in general, I guess because they can't be bothered to bother us, we're generally nonunion people, and the unions figure if we're nuts enough to want to work like this, good luck to us! In general, though, I'm just too busy to even think of how unionization might benefit us. It would be nice to have crew people organized the way labels have lists of studio session musicians, to exist on that sort of professional level—but then that might mean too much union restriction, which could kill the whole excitement of it."

The first important step in making a rock video is choosing the director. By this time, most labels have their own video departments, handling what promotion and marketing departments used to work overtime to do, and those video departments have compilation cassettes of the work of various directors, known as show reels. Sometimes bands come to the label after deciding to make a video and look at various show reels. Frequently label executives are present to offer advice. Len Epand of Polygram says, "The attitude of bands has changed drastically since MTV came along. Before that, most bands looked at videos as something they had to do to get out of the way, and they didn't think twice about it. That was always more true for the American bands than the British ones. But now you have bands coming in and saying, 'I want a video that'll look like "Beat It" ' or whatever.

"In a way, it's created a monster with the bands: now they come in with all these big ideas that are just not feasible with our budget ranges.

A section of a rock-video story board, mapping out each shot along with the song lyric to which it is set. This one is from the Hits' "Backstabber" (1983), directed by Joe Dea of Greg Kihn "Jeopardy" fame, who also drew this story board. Depending on the needs of the artist, director, and producer, story boards can be cruder and simpler than this one, or far more elaborate.

I mean, it's great that the bands are more conscious of video and all, but they still have a lot to learn about the vagaries of the production process itself."

One man who's trying to facilitate the band-director hookup process is Lenny Kalikow, a former singer who for several years has been publishing a music-industry tip sheet called *New on the Charts.* In early 1982 Kalikow, who'd been following both the European video outlets and the proliferation of club video in America, took the arrival of MTV as his cue and began a video tracking section in his publication. Within a year and a half, it had grown from a quarter of a page to at least two full pages, listing the latest promo clip productions by band, song, label, production house, and director.

Says Kalikow, "I knew that a lot of people who were seeing videos and wanted to find out more about them may not have known how to find out. So I called labels, who sent me to managers, who sent me to some postproduction studio where a director had been the week before, and so on."

In the summer of 1983, Kalikow solicited show reels from about two hundred producers and directors. He then set up cross-indexed card files with information on producers and directors and bands and songs. In his office at National Video Studios in New York, Kalikow runs a service where bands, managers, and labels can come for information on a director or a specific video and screen the videos. Essentially, Kalikow's Video Producers Clearinghouse is a multiple listing and library service. From the beginning, the Clearinghouse has received a lot of cooperation and support from the industry.

Kalikow's service (and there are bound to be more like it) will make things easier for record labels. But a few years ago, they had it pretty easy, too: there were only a handful of directors making clips; if a promo video was needed, one called Keefco or MGM, and that was that. Now, though, there is more competition between ever proliferating production houses as there are more clips to be made. Rock video has become a full-fledged industry. And, especially important, budgets have risen in tandem with the importance and recognition of the clips themselves. After the director, the most important decision is that regarding the budget. Everything about a rock video—the staff, equipment, film or video tape, effects, actors, extras, set, and countless other costs, from phone calls to costumes—costs someone money. Certainly a director's or an artist's creative vision is priceless, but only money makes it real. So although rock video has begun to come into its own as an art form, those who finance them—most often record companies —still view them primarily as promotional tools and judge their effectiveness by that standard.

Arnold Levine, a creative consultant to CBS Records who has also produced and directed videos for Billy Joel ("Goodnight Saigon"), Joan Jett ("I Love Rock 'n' Roll"), and Bruce Springsteen ("Atlantic City"), explains, "Budgets are always a big problem with music videos. Are they going up, down, or what? Nobody can ever really tell from case to case. Labels want to see more production values in a clip, but on the other hand, they have to know what it's going to cost them, and they have to consider what they're liable to get back in return. And you have to keep your overall promotional and marketing budgets for the year in mind: if you spend too much on a clip early in the year, it may hurt you later. The only exceptions are with really big artists: Michael Jackson, Billy Joel. In both cases, they've made very expensive videos, and in both cases they put some of their own money into it. Actually, Michael financed the 'Beat It' clip himself; he owns it outright. But those are exceptional artists; they can afford to do that."

Video budgets depend on several factors, but usually it's a simple matter of a given artist's stature (if they sell a lot of records, they'll get a bigger budget) or sales potential (if the label *thinks* they'll sell a lot of records, they'll get a bigger budget). Otherwise, unless the band and/or its management want to chip in their own money, they have to settle for between twenty-five thousand dollars and thirty-five thousand dollars, about average for a new band. Currently, thirty-five thousand dollars to fifty thousand dollars is the midrange. But more videos are being made for sixty-five thousand dollars to eighty thousand dollars. Many of the bigger rock-video production houses have set their own budgetary "floors"—they will not take on a job unless the budget is at least twenty thousand dollars to thirty thousand dollars. Even Ed Steinberg's Soft Focus, which in the past made clips with budgets under five thousand dollars for such New York new-wave artists as the Bush Tetras and Tom Verlaine, will now not make a clip for less than twenty thousand dollars.

Production values are the one aspect of rock video most affected by budget. Production values entail anything and everything from the amount and kinds of locations and/or sets as well as extras and/or dancers to be used, to the use of special effects (new high-tech digital video effects are especially expensive), to the decision whether to shoot the clip on video (cheaper) or film (expensive—thirty-five-millimeter being far more costly than sixteen-millimeter, which as of this writing, was the medium of choice for most rock videos). Why, if they're called "rock videos," are most clips actually shot on film? According to director Steve Barron, "Both film and video have their respective merits. For me personally, I like film better because it has a richer look, a nicer texture. Video looks too real, and at the same time too plastic; there's something very flat and harsh about it. It also tends to look cheaper than film, unless you're doing something very effects-oriented. And I think most record labels sense that difference—they believe, and rightly so in most cases, that seeing someone on film rather than video just makes them look more special. It's like advertising, the medium is the message—if you get a richer look with film, it sort of subconsciously reinforces the impression that there's something more special about this band."

Editing alone involves a series of complicated trade-offs. Most directors do shoot on sixteen-millimeter film, but some edit on film and then transfer the negative to video (at a "Tele-Cine" facility), while others first transfer the negative to video and then edit. Film editing is more time-consuming, but cheaper; video editing is quicker, but far more costly.

There are certain effects that can only be achieved with film editing,

and certain effects that can only be obtained with video. Michael Heldman, editor for the Los Angeles production house Pendulum Productions (he's worked on such clips as Quiet Riot's "Mental Health,"
Berlin's "The Metro," and Kansas's "Fight Fire with Fire"), explains
that "editing on film is much more *precise,* you actually physically
match up the sprocket holes on the celluloid. When you watch a video
and notice a jarring split-second of all-black screen, that's the result of
a sloppy video edit. It probably isn't even the editor's fault, it's just that
rock videos are made in such a hurry they didn't have time to get it just
right. On the other hand, there are certain things, especially most
special effects, that you can only get with video."

Now for the question everyone always asks: Who actually creates a
video clip? Is it all the director's ideas, or the band's, or a combination,
and if so, how much does each side put in? In most cases, directors
themselves come up with concepts. Artists like Devo, Toni Basil, and
Talking Heads who conceptualize and direct their own clips are the
exceptions to the rule, and bands who give any more than cursory input
into a concept are also unusual. Of course, this situation is in the
process of changing as bands become increasingly conscious of video.

Often look, style and visual content of the video are matched to the
graphics of the artist's logo, current album cover and advertising art;
rock-video examples of this are legion (i.e., Quiet Riot's "Metal Health"
and "Cum on Feel the Noize" both feature the silver mask on the cover
of *Metal Health*; Cyndi Lauper's "Girls Just Wanna Have Fun" has her
wearing the same fifties party dress she sports on the cover of *She's So
Unusual;* ZZ Top's "Gimme All Your Lovin' " and "Sharp-Dressed
Man" both feature the same cherry-red antique hot rod on the cover
of their *Eliminator* LP, and the band's double-Z logo appears in both
as a magical keychain). Sometimes the proclivities of rock-video directors for plundering popular culture are consciously exploited, and the
"look" of a particular popular film is aimed for. An RCA press release
on the making of a video for their band the Breaks in July 1983 noted
that "director Martin Kahan is going for a *Body Heat* 'look' in the
video." Another release a month later, though, reported that "the small
town of Piedmont, New York, was used as the location for the Breaks'
'She Wants You' video, because it was perfect for the small-town *Last
Picture Show* 'look' the band and director Martin Kahan had in mind."

Says director Russell Mulcahy, "The concepts have almost always
been my own for the clips I've done, except for more recently, when
we've hired storyboard artists and scriptwriters with whom I collabo-

Through the magic of special effects, the British Paul McCartney appears to shake hands with the German Paul McCartney in this scene from McCartney's "Pipes of Peace" video (1984), directed by Keith MacMillan of Keefco. The video is based on a historical World War I incident in which British and German troops in one particular battlefield declared a momentary, unofficial truce and exchanged pleasantries.

rate. But going back to my earliest clips, I wrote the concepts myself. Most of the time the bands couldn't care less, so long as they weren't made to look ridiculous. And in some cases, if the band looked *properly* ridiculous, that would be a bonus—it would make people stop and take a closer look at the video, which is the idea anyway. But I always had hassles from record labels to have to show the band performing somehow in the clip. That's an understandable consideration for a record label, but for me as a creative person, it tended to get in the way of really crafting a solid concept and working out a narrative. You always had to cut to the guitar solo or something, which would inevitably ruin any pretense to a real story line.

"Ultravox were the first band I'd ever worked with who really gave me input creatively, and it was great input. Prior to that, there was the occasional art-school band like XTC who took an interest and contributed an idea here or there, but that was nothing like Ultravox, who were full of ideas and really, really into it. I welcome that kind of input —after all, it's their song that you're conceptualizing. To me, the ideal relationship would be to marry the idea of the band, who are very close to the song, and an objective third party like a director, in an organic, workable relationship. That should produce ideal results. That happened with me and Ultravox and Duran Duran. For the Duran Sri Lanka shoots, me and my story-board artist, Marcello Anciano, rode around in a van with a few guys from the band, just hatching ideas and jotting them down, for a week."

Adds Keith Williams, a scriptwriter who's worked with Mulcahy on such videos as Billy Joel's "Pressure" and "Allentown" and Supertramp's "It's Raining Again," as well as with Brian Grant on Donna Summer's "She Works Hard for the Money," Asia's "Don't Cry" and "The Smile Has Left Your Eyes," and with Tobe Hooper on Billy Idol's "Dancin' with Myself": "The *last* thing I do is listen to the lyrics of a song for a concept. When I'm given the track, I first ask what the budget's going to be, and then if the band has anything in mind. Do they have to perform in it, and if so, do they just lip-sync, or do they play instruments, or just act, or what? After that, I sit down and listen to the music. The feel of it, the flow, the arrangement, the rhythm, the tempo. . . . Generally, I go with my first instinct and run with it. It's the *feeling* you get from the music, coupled with your image of the band, whatever you know about them or what they or their people have told you. If the hook feels right, it's easy to go on and develop it; it's getting the right hook to start with that's the hard part. Sometimes it comes to you in a flash; sometimes you can listen to a song all day and nothing comes. Basically, it's the most unobvious way of getting to the obvious. If it's too literal to the song, it's boring, because you're seeing what you're hearing. A good video is not boring because it takes the song and puts it into another context you hadn't thought of right away, yet it retains some sort of fidelity to what the song's about in general.

"It's really easiest," he concludes, "when you don't have to worry about contriving a way to fit the band performing into it. It's much easier to run with a good narrative idea and get a really nice piece out of it. The best example I can think of is Supertramp's 'It's Raining Again.' The band were very happy not to perform in it at all, they just appear in cameo roles, like the saxophonist plays a bus driver, and so on. But that's the exception to the rule, and in this business, you have to please your clients."

Says director Steve Barron: "I never go for a literal concept. A song is something abstract, people get different impressions of it in their own heads. I think the video should be somehow semiabstract or something, so it's sort of realistic and literal to the song but not too much, so people can interpret it in different ways. Sometimes it's just a certain sound effect or something in the song that sparks off an idea. Especially with the synthesizer bands, the sound effects they get can be very suggestive. A certain synthetic drum sound may sound like water splashing, so that kicks off the concept right there."

But what about going too far from the literal interpretation—when people accuse clips of having absolutely nothing to do with the song itself? "Well," says Barron, "believe it or not, a *lot* of the time when you ask an artist what the song is supposed to be about, they say, 'I don't know.' Or the old tried-and-true explanation, 'The song means whatever people take it to mean.' So you make a deliberately ambiguous video in the same sense. So what are you going to do? You just let your imagination run with it and come up with something everyone's happy with."

Barron cites Michael Jackson's "Billie Jean" as an exceptional case in his *oeuvre:* "With that one, and this only happens very occasionally, I had this concept lying around that I'd tried before with other bands, and it hadn't worked, so I was waiting for the right performer to use it on. It was a sort of man-with-the-Midas-touch idea, and for Michael Jackson, it just seemed perfect. Michael himself had no input on that. That clip was exceptional in another way: it's the only clip I've ever done, and I've been doing at least two a week for some time now, where I had a story board done for it. Usually I just do a one-page treatment of the concept, matching the shots with the lyrics. I had to do a story board for 'Billie Jean' because it was all happening *so* fast, they had to see exactly what they were getting, because Michael's very picky and all, which is the way it should be."

Barron has also gone through the agony of having what he thought were great concepts rejected and reworked. "With the Rod Stewart clip for 'Baby Jane,' " he recalls, "I wrote an original concept that I thought was one of the best I'd ever done: it was to be set on a pier by a bay, and Rod would be on the pier singing, and there'd be this big white yacht called 'Baby Jane' just pulling out from the pier. Then we'd cut to a dockside bar with all these old sea dogs in it, and Rod would be there having a drink but obviously thinking about this girl Baby Jane he'd been singing about—so it was like maybe he was hallucinating the yacht's name because of his obsession with her or something. And then he'd run back out to the pier and see the boat on the water and start singing to it, and you'd really think he was so crazy in love he was hallucinating. But Rod or his people didn't like that idea. I tried another, and they still didn't like it. By that time the bug had bitten me: I wanted to get the job done already. So I came up with this thing with Rod in this fancy bedroom and the lady's shoes and all. . . . People always ask me why the shoe fetish in that video, and I have no answer. I don't recall how it came up. I do recall that the opening cymbal crash in the song suggested the image of the chandelier falling. . . . I ended up using the original idea in Dolly Parton's 'Potential New Boyfriend.' "

In the same vein, director Brian Grant explains, "I did a clip for Stevie Nicks's 'Stand Back' that I was really proud of. It was this massive, sprawling Civil War production with zillions of extras and sets and cannons and horses and all. *Gone with the Wind* in three minutes, you know? We did this whole thing in, like, three days, worked our heads off, and then Stevie Nicks looks at the rough cut and rejects the whole thing because she thinks she looks too *fat* in a couple of shots!" Nicks, who could afford to be vain, threw about $80,000 out the window on that one; subsequently she went to Pendulum Productions in Los Angeles and had *Flashdance* choreographer Geoffrey Hornaday direct another, acceptable clip for "Stand Back" for a somewhat smaller sum.

On the other hand, director Julian Temple says, "I'm willing to work with a band on the concept if they have valid ideas. Someone like Ray Davies is exceptional in that regard; he always has good ideas. But once I come up with a concept I like, if the artist or his company don't like it, I'll either argue it out or drop the job—I won't change it for them.

By now I guess I'm known as the guy who has to do things his way."

A classic example of a band having no input whatsoever into a clip, and the director managing to complement them perfectly anyway, is ZZ Top's "Gimme All Your Lovin'" and "Sharp-Dressed Man," both directed by Tim Newman. "I'd done 'I Love L.A.' for my cousin Randy," says Newman, "and after that I sort of vowed that I'd only do clips for bands I liked. But then Jo Bergman at Warners called and offered the ZZ Top job. I wasn't a real fan of theirs, but I thought, 'Why not?'

"I came up with this whole concept myself. The only outside input was Warner Brothers telling me that the red hot rod on the cover of their album (*Eliminator*) had to be shown in the video, and the band had to be seen performing a little bit. So I worked up this concept: the red car contains these three beautiful, very sexy women who drive up to this gas station in the middle of nowhere and sort of make this grease monkey's day, if you know what I mean. And the idea of ZZ Top magically materializing at key moments was my idea. The band themselves had no idea whatsoever what was happening on the shoot—but then, shooting out of sequence and all, anyone outside filmmaking wouldn't understand it. What they *did* contribute, though, is that sort of Johnny Carson golf-swing motion they make whenever they materialize—that's something they were just doing off the set, fooling around waiting for their gear to be set up. So I worked that into it. And I thought ZZ Top themselves, looking like they did with those incredibly long beards, had actual visual potential: they looked like R. Crumb characters to me, real grizzled but cool.

"Basically, the theme of the video is just male-adolescent fantasy; the message of it is, these girls may come into *your* town next.

"So that video proved very successful, and then I got called to do another one for them, 'Sharp-Dressed Man.' And from remembering the 'they may come to *your* town' idea, I just thought, 'Aha! A sequel! We'll have the girls coming to another town.' So we did it. And I consciously made it totally different than the first one, but with the same elements: the first one was noon in the desert, the second one was nighttime in a big city disco. I kept the idea that the girls are dressed totally wrong for where they are: in the first one it's the desert but they're all dressed to the nines in stockings and dresses and jewelry; in the second they're in a fancy club but they're very casually dressed. And of course I kept those magical symbols from the first one: the car, the girls, the Z-shaped key, the band materializing. So it's like, wherever these girls and this car appear, some guy's fantasies are going to be unlocked. Now I understand that at their live shows, they're throwing a Z-shaped key out into the audience to end the show. I wonder if they have a red hot rod parked out in front of the concert hall. . . ."

"Sharp-Dressed Man" wasn't strictly the first rock-video sequel; Devo, for one, has always used recurrent hallmark imagery in their videos. Julian Temple has since done a similar job with the Kinks' "Come Dancing" and "Don't Forget to Dance," as has Mark Rezyka with Quiet Riot's "Metal Health" and "Cum on Feel the Noize." But Newman's ZZ Top clips were the first big-budget rock-video continuing series of the post-MTV age, and the idea was certainly brilliant. The two clips were remarkably effective in expanding ZZ Top's audience beyond its usual hard-rock contingent. When asked whether or not Newman's repeated use of key symbolic images in the two ZZ Top clips was merely the time-honored commercial technique of "product identification," he blushes and laughs, "Well, I don't like to think of it quite that coldly, but yeah, I guess you could say that. I *am* a commercial director by trade."

Newman did have it easy in one respect: when he went to work on them, ZZ Top had virtually no visual image whatsoever. On the opposite pole, Bill Parker's work with Shalamar on their "Dead Giveaway" video shows how a director can collaborate sympathetically with a band who already have an established image but who are consciously in the process of changing that image, and who use the promo video as the most convenient and immediate way of announcing that change to the consumer public. In between, there is the work of Bob Giraldi and Steve Barron with Michael Jackson, making brilliantly apposite use of Jackson's already well-known image as a mysterious, "magical" manchild with their own complementary concepts.

On the other hand, director Chris Gabrin of Limelight, who made Martin Briley's "Salt in My Tears" video, claims, "Martin came to me with the concept for that worked out already. I just fine-tuned it. He'd just gone through his second divorce, so the song was very personal for him. He already had the idea of this girl sort of cleaning him out of house and home and all that. I basically helped make it farcical, to take the sting out of it a bit, and he agreed that was a good idea. I always think humor is a secret weapon that's never used often enough in rock videos. And I shot a few videos for John Cougar Mellencamp in Indiana for his album *Uh-Huh*. He was amazing: he kept helping me set up scenes, he'd get behind the camera and look through it, the whole bit. He just wanted to know what it was going to look like. I don't mind that at all, so long as the artist knows what he's doing. John did. It was loads of fun."

Says Chuck Statler of working with a highly video-conscious band like Devo, "They have *all* the concepts worked out. I basically act as more or less a technical director. But they're the exception to the rule. I've worked with loads of other bands—Madness, Elvis Costello, Nick Lowe, the Michael Stanley Band, the J. Geils Band, the Cars, the Waitresses, Donnie Iris—and in nine times out of ten, the band has no real idea what they want to do. They look at you and say, 'You're the director.' And how can you blame them? They've never had to think about acting and direction, they've just had to think about songs and playing and stage moves. Stage moves are very different than acting on camera, and sometimes it's hard for someone to make that adjustment. You don't have to overplay to the camera the way you do onstage."

What happens when a director given to outlandish flights of fancy like Russell Mulcahy tells a band about his concepts? "It all depends on how drunk they are at the time," he laughs. "No, seriously. When I did my first clip for the Motels, 'Only the Lonely,' I was sent up to a suburb of San Francisco to see them play and meet with them after. So I saw them play, fine, they were good. Then I go to their hotel room. And it's the typical band-on-the-road-after-a-hard-gig thing, right? So I'm sitting in a corner waiting for a chance to tell these people my high concepts, right? So in walks [Motels lead singer] Martha Davis, and instantly the room quiets down. She's exhausted, plops into a chair, looks up at me and says, 'Okay, Russell, what are your ideas?' So the room's gone from peak noise level to dead quiet in a few seconds, right? And I go, 'Right, okay,' and for fifteen minutes I explain all these epic, sweeping concepts. And after all that, Martha looks up and says, 'I didn't understand a word you just said.' So I'm putting on a nice smile and thinking, *'Right.'* But see, it just goes to show you: when we met again, they were great, and on the shoot, Martha turned in one of the best performances I've ever gotten from a singer."

Indeed, Davis's forties vamp star turn combined with Mulcahy's sprawling grandeur (and some allusions to Stanley Kubrick's *The Shining*) to create one of the most eye-catching videos of 1982, one that immeasurably boosted the band's career as well as being nominated for some AVAs at the first American Video Awards.

Producers and directors cherish the creative freedom rock videos offer and worry that the creative process will become what it is in advertising, where decisions are made by committee, with various creative teams providing input and more "noncreative" parties holding approval power.

Siobhan Barron, Limelight video production chief, claims, "Re-

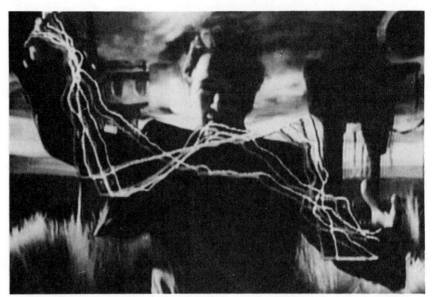

A special-effects scene from Heart's "How Can I Refuse?" (1983), directed by Mark Rezyka for Pendulum Productions: a mysterious magician prepares to conjure a floating crystal ball to bewitch Heart's Ann and Nancy Wilson.

cently, I've noticed that more and more often record companies send their own sort of unit producers or consultants to shoots to look over our shoulders. That bugs me. I mean, look, we owe our livings to record companies, they're the ones who pay us, and I don't want to seem ungrateful. But in the early days, we were always left to our own devices; sometimes the band or their management or the company demanded to approve what we had in mind, but often they just said, 'Here's the band, here's the song, now come up with something.' And we did, and we did good work that promoted those bands. Now it's like it's all become too big a deal for them to trust us or something, and all I'm saying is, *we're* the ones who really got this thing going so it could get to this level, so treat us with the respect we deserve."

Director Kevin Godley speaks for just about every rock-video director interviewed for this book when he says, "If and when rock videos get to the level of advertising, having to kowtow to all the product managers and all that decision-by-committee rot, that's when I hope I'll be out of this business." Naturally, commercial directors making rock videos, like Bob Giraldi and Tim Newman, concur. Newman says, "Sure, I can make a lot more money making one commercial than a

dozen rock videos. But making videos is so liberating and fun for me."
Giraldi is more of an exceptional case: he was a chief writer for some
blue-chip advertising firms before he directed commercials; he's used to
creative control. "I don't want to sound pompous," says Giraldi, "but
there's only *one* star on my sets, and that's me."

So why did he get into rock videos? "Basically, I wanted a change.
And they turned out to be a lot of fun, very challenging and rewarding
to me artistically. What's so great about rock videos is that it's all about
doing something *else* besides the same old commercials and movies.
These things are another world altogether. I hope rock videos don't go
the way of advertising. Rock videos have always been a way of people
saying, 'To *hell* with your advertising methods, I wanna do something
different.' "

But rock videos, being promotional items, can't help but go the way
of advertising. They already are going that way. More and more production houses have hired scriptwriters and story-board artists. (Story
boards are pictorial scene-by-scene depictions of the proposed video
scenario, either crudely drawn or painterly and sophisticated, with
appropriate lyrics running as captions under each "frame.")

And there are some like Steve Barron. "I think the form is suffering
from a lack of discipline in the creative process or something. I think
you see too many rock videos that don't really work. I'd like to see more
discipline go into them. I welcome the day when it gets like advertising;
it'll make directors work harder to do better work."

The majority of rock videos that are made seem to reflect a certain
aesthetic. However, it would be unfair to discuss only how videos are
made for pop, rock, and new-wave acts. In fact, some of the more
interesting videos have come from black-music artists. But given the
current music climate and America's longstanding preference for white
pop and its subgenres over black music, it has been the field of black
music that has been particularly sensitive to the various factors that
determine how a video may be made—often with unfortunate results.
The two most obvious examples of blacks in video are, of course,
Michael Jackson and Prince. These, however, are clearly the exceptions
to the rule. Although charges of racism in MTV's programming are not
without substance, care should be taken to remember that MTV's
programming is dictated by demographics. While this should not be
taken as an acceptable excuse, it is clear that music videos by black
artists are discovering their own outlets and that black groups are
beginning to look to MTV and similar rock-video outlets as a means
of receiving the same exposure, with the same positive results other

groups have enjoyed now for some time. Indeed, by late 1983 MTV had opened up its format considerably.

The classic example to date is Shalamar's "Dead Giveaway." Shalamar, a very popular mainstream black-pop vocal trio, was formed in the late seventies and quickly became one of the most successful acts in the hit-making stable of leading black-pop label Solar Records. In the late seventies, Shalamar made a few video clips, the best known being "Night to Remember" and "I Don't Want to Be the Last to Know." Both were in the then-typical black-pop video vein: gauzy, soft-focus, flatly shot romantic scenarios with male vocalists Howard Hewitt and Jeffrey Daniel in natty *GQ* mohair suits, and female vocalist Jody Watley in a frilly white lace gown. But in August 1983, Shalamar released a new album, *The Look,* and single, "Dead Giveaway," with a stunning video for "Dead Giveaway" that convincingly proved that this was a very new and different Shalamar: the tune snapped and crackled to an electropop beat; the band dressed in the height of British new-wave fashion (angular jump suits for Hewitt and Daniel; "Buffalo Gals" third-world thrift-shop togs for Watley) and moved with new-wave angularity.

There were very few black video directors working in rock video as of this writing: there are Limelight's Don Letts; filmmaker Michael Schultz (who worked with Paul Schrader on *Blue Collar* and himself directed the popular "Black *American Graffiti*" *Cooley High*), who has produced and directed many of Earth, Wind and Fire's effects-laden videos; Gary Keyes, whose most famous clip is probably the Weather Girls' campily surreal movie-musical takeoff "It's Raining Men"; and Alvin Hartley, whose "The Message" for Grandmaster Flash and "Magic's Wand" for Whodini are two of the best and most distinctive black-rap videos.

Hartley in particular points out the problems unique to making black-music videos: "I always talk to people at MTV to try to find out what I need to do to make a black video they'll accept, and they have an answer for everything; it's no use trying to talk to them. But I do respect them as pioneers and leaders in the field and all. I just feel that *blacks* should make videos for black artists, and so far that's a minority opinion, excuse the pun. I mean, who knows this music best? Who's it made by and for? So let *us* do the visuals for it, too. Meanwhile, the white rock videos are getting *down.* And the black artists who can get down that way—Michael Jackson, the Pointer Sisters, Eddy Grant— are the exceptions to the rule.

" 'The Message,' that was a classic case. Grandmaster Flash's label,

Sugar Hill, nearly threw me out when I told them I'd need at least eighty-five hundred dollars to do it right, and that's a microscopic sum compared to most white rock videos. The thing with a label like Sugar Hill is, they think—they *know*—they can spend ten thousand dollars on a twelve-inch rap single and make a hundred thousand dollars back on it. With a video, they don't know *what* they're going to get out of it, if anything. They aren't sure about outlets for black videos, although that is changing for the better right now, which is great. But, you know, black music always has more limited outlets and exposure than white music, that's the nature of the game. So you have limited financing, too —we keep getting short shrift. I made 'The Message' for five thousand dollars, and though a lot of people complement me on it, I can't stand to see it because I know how much better it could have been with a little more money. Same thing with Whodini's 'Magic Wand,' which I did for eight thousand dollars.

"Then again, even when you see a black artist get the full treatment from a big label, with a big-budget video and all that, it often falls into the same old show-biz trap that so many rock videos fall into. Take Gladys Knight's 'Save the Overtime for Me,' [directed by veteran Hollywood and Broadway choreographer Kenny Ortega] which had all this break dancing and stuff in it. Nice choreography, great to see break dancers and all—but it has *nothing* to do with the song. Now for one thing, Gladys Knight is someone a lot of black folks grew up on, she's *heavy.* She deserves better than that. If I could've made that video, I would've done something more in line with the lyrics. There's a serious message to that song; it's about a woman who has to make a whole day go by without her man. People *feel* that, it's part of life. So instead of putting her in the middle of all these *break dancers,* for God's sake, I would've had Gladys sitting at home, calling her girlfriends, playing solitaire like it says in the song—doing things real people do to pass the time waiting for their loved one. Things people can *relate* to. Maybe that's too literal for some people, but I think it could've worked. You can't have a video that's too showy and Hollywood and all that with someone like Gladys Knight—it overshadows her, and she's too great to be overshadowed by break dancers spinning around while she's singing a serious love song. Or am I being too idealistic?"

Adds director Don Letts, "First of all, me being black and over six feet and wearing dreadlocks like a Rastafarian, and usually wearing shades and combat fatigues—when I walk into a record company, they just bug out, man. I'm there trying to explain a concept to them and they can't believe I can speak English. In a way, that sort of attitude carries over to the way they do black artists' videos, even to the way they do all videos. They're going too Hollywood for me, it's let's flatter pop stars and make rock idols and heroes and all that again. I work with the Clash, I started with the punk scene, and now it's like that never happened. If this keeps up, I'm not long for this business. And the thing is, I'd really love to work with more black acts. With just about any black act, you just have to capture them *performing* and it'll be better than any white band's clip. Black performers are just better to watch in general than most white performers. What can I say? We've got rhythm, we're better dancers, you know? It's a terrible stereotype I know, but can you deny it? It happens to be true in most cases. But now they want to take black acts and do the same things to them as they do to white acts, so it's the same old story again. It's hopeless for a guy like me, I guess. I don't like all this contrived Hollywood nonsense. I don't mind some production values, but that shouldn't be the point, that's window dressing. The point is *content.* And that scares record companies, businessmen in general."

The "Hollywood aesthetic," as it applies to both white and black acts, is something to be discussed in greater depth later. At any rate, black artists *are* progressing rapidly, as far as equality in production values with that of white acts, though it seems the vital "street-music" acts will remain more on the "underground" fringe for the meantime.

And so it goes. There are as many ways of making a rock video as there are bands, songs, directors, and labels; while directors supply the concepts in nine cases out of ten, just as often they do receive some sort of input from the band, if only in discussing and perhaps modifying their own concepts for the band's approval.

The actual preproduction—lining up locations, sets, actors, extras, crews, scriptwriting or doing storyboards, etc.—is undertaken; the video itself is shot, often in a few days; then there is postproduction (editing, special effects, etc.); then the completed clip itself is finally delivered to the label, which then handles distribution and promotion.

Now, here's an up-close and personal look at the making of one rock video, from inception to completion.

ON LOCATION—DIARY OF A ROCK-VIDEO SHOOT

ARTIST: Cyndi Lauper, former lead singer with Blue Angel, a pop-rock band influenced by late fifties and early sixties sounds, who released two critically acclaimed albums in 1980 and 1981, but who never quite made it. Cyndi's powerful, distinctive nasal voice was often compared to Connie Francis, Brenda Lee, and Teresa Brewer; her petite, blond, all-American looks often evoked comparisons with Sandra Dee. Cyndi was, in the summer of 1983, ready to launch a solo career.

THE CLIP: For "Girls Just Wanna Have Fun," the first single from Cyndi's debut solo album, *She's So Unusual,* on Portrait Records, an affiliate of CBS subsidiary Epic.

PRODUCER-DIRECTOR: Ken Walz, who's overseen a host of fine rock videos, will produce; Ed Griles, who directed the two 1980 Blue Angel clips that Walz produced, "I Had a Love" and "Late," will direct. Aside from those, Griles has also directed rock videos for Rainbow and Dr. Hook with Walz. His other credits include scores of TV commercials, network-syndicated interstitial vignette programs like *Seventh Inning Stretch* (vintage footage of great moments in baseball history), the network-syndicated historical series *America's Heroes,* and several made-for-TV movies.

If such a thing as a "typical" rock-video shoot exists, this is not one of them. For one thing, the director is an experienced maker of promo clips, yet hasn't made one for two years. "I'm coming back," says Griles, "because Cyndi wanted me, and she's so great to work with that I didn't mind. There's no money in rock videos; I do them because they're fun, and creatively rewarding in the right circumstances. These are the right circumstances." For another thing, the logistics in this particular case mean that the video will not be shot in a week-long frenzy but will be plotted out over the comparatively leisurely course of about two months; this is partly due to advance planning and partly due to the release schedule for Cyndi's album.

Finally, there is the artist herself: Cyndi is not just a pretty face onstage, a pretty voice on record. She's an experienced actress as well, and remembers, "I began performing as a little girl growing up in Queens. I was always singing on the street for the old ladies next door; they'd give me quarters for lunch at school. By age eight, I was doing Barbra Streisand impressions for my parents. In school, I was always starring in plays and things." Besides all that, as will be seen, Cyndi plays an unusually large creative role in the conceptualizing and staging of the video itself, from start to finish. "I had a lot to say about the Blue Angel videos," says Cyndi, "and this time, I have even more to say, since I've already had experience with it, and since there's so much rock video around now. I know what I want and don't want—I don't want to be portrayed as just another sex symbol."

AUGUST 20, 1983: Recording of *She's So Unusual* is just about completed. All through the two-month recording process, Cyndi has been thinking about which song to make into a video, and how. Cyndi and her manager, Dave Wolff, decide with Portrait president Lenny Petze and Epic product manager Dan Beck that the first single, and the video, will be "Girls Just Wanna Have Fun," a bouncy, fun number with a strong singalong chorus. Today, with the album officially completed, Cyndi, Wolff, Petze, and Beck sit down at Epic's offices to discuss the video. Cyndi has a loose idea for the concept: "Just a logical thing suggested by the title and lyrics—you know, girls wanting to have fun, and maybe having a hard time doing it. But not heavy; keep it fun." Everyone likes the idea. Cyndi says she wants to work with Ken Walz and Ed Griles, for the reasons outlined above.

AUGUST 21: Dan Beck calls Walz about the Lauper video project. Walz instantly agrees to do it and calls Griles, who is in the midst of completing a TV movie. He, too, agrees instantly to do the job, but can't be ready for at least a couple of weeks. No problem, says Walz; the album isn't being released until at least early October. This day, an audio cassette of Cyndi's album and her cover photo are sent to Walz's office. He gives them to Griles, who immediately begins listening to the song and coming up with ideas.

AUGUST 24: Walz and Griles meet with Cyndi, Wolff, and Petze and Beck at Epic's offices. Concept and budget are discussed. Griles outlines a tentative scenario: "Cyndi's idea is perfect. I see it fleshed out like this: we open with an establishing shot of Cyndi in the dress on her album cover; she's dancing down a street. She comes up the street and starts singing the song, and enters her house. Her mother's up. It's early morning, and Mom's angry: where's she been all night? Cyndi sings to her mother, then dances down the hall to the chorus, 'Girls just wanna have fun.' Cyndi goes into her bedroom and calls some girlfriends on the phone to have a party. Then we see Cyndi on the street, rounding up outrageously dressed people into a chorus line that gets bigger and bigger as she leads them back to her house. She's having this wild party in her room, which is just packed with people. Her parents come down the hallway, obviously apprehensive at least, and pretty angry too. Then we can do a takeoff on that stateroom scene in that Marx Brothers movie, *A Night at the Opera.* As the parents are spying through the keyhole, the door bursts open and all these people spill out on top of them. And that's it."

Everyone likes the concept; it's an imaginative yet literal complement to the song's lyrics and spirit, and is obviously true to Cyndi's own original conception. The budget for such a shoot is discussed. Specific necessities are outlined—extras, locations, shooting days, etc. It is agreed that the next day, Walz will meet with Beck to finalize the budget.

AUGUST 25: Walz and Beck decide on a $35,000 budget, right in line with typical rock videos of the day. There will be one day of exterior shooting on location, somewhere in the metropolitan New York area, and one day of studio shooting. The clip will be shot on sixteen-millimeter film. There will be a crane shot. There will be one major postproduction expense: a digital-video special effect to be done with the latest piece of high-technology, a device known as the Mirage. New York's Broadway Video (run by *Saturday Night Live*'s former producer, Lorne Michaels) just got one; it costs over nine hundred dollars an hour to use. Cyndi's music lawyer, Eliot Hofman, is also legal adviser for Broadway Video; he is contacted, and aside from agreeing to facilitate use of the Mirage, he agrees to be an extra in the video. Dave Wolff will also appear, as will Dan Beck and Cyndi's record producer, Rick Chertoff.

AUGUST 26: Cyndi, Dave Wolff, and Ken Walz drive around New York City, scouting locations for the exteriors of the video shoot. In the car, Cyndi muses: "Let's go down to the West Village. That's such a beautiful part of New York, so old-world, with all those little side streets, a part of the city most people don't know. There ought to be lots of good locations there."

Driving through the West Village's tiny side streets, they happen upon Gay Street, a narrow, L-shaped drive connecting Christopher Street and Waverly Place that's lined with well-preserved old brownstone houses. With its curving shape and the façades of the old houses, viewed from street level, Gay Street looks more like a Hollywood back lot than an actual street. Everyone agrees it will be perfect. "And we can do some other shots around here," says Cyndi, "like on Christopher Street, in Sheridan Square. . . ." Walz also suggests other Manhattan locations to provide contrast to the homey West Village, to indicate that in the video Cyndi will be picking up her outrageous chorus line all over town. They agree to include the fountains of the Metropolitan Museum of Art uptown, and the Wall Street area downtown.

AUGUST 29: Walz alerts his twenty-two-person crew and Ed Griles that the shoot should be taking place during the first or second week of September. Production assistants Allison Mackie and Mark Wade contact appropriate city authorities to make sure the locations can be secured; city police will be on hand to make sure all goes well. Director of photography Francis Kenny (who manned one of the cameras at the

Shooting the opening scene of Cyndi Lauper's "Girls Just Wanna Have Fun" video (1983) in New York City's Greenwich Village: (left to right) production assistant Allison Mackie; Cyndi Lauper; producer Ken Walz (in white shirt); key grip Dan Mahoney; director Ed Griles (bending); and cameraman Francis Kenny

Who's simulcast "last concert," as well as having shot many of Walz's videos) is contacted. Cyndi asks that the choreographer for the video be Martha Graham cohort Mary Ellen Strom, who is contacted and agrees to do the job. She and Cyndi will get together several times over the next week to plot out choreography for both the street and studio scenes. Mother's Film Stage in the East Village, scene of several rock-video shoots as well as many commercials and fashion shoots, is secured for the studio shots on Sunday, September 11. Makeup will be done by Hollywood di Russo, who also happens to be curator of the P.S. 1 avant-garde/postmodern art museum in New York City.

During the week before the shoot, Cyndi not only works with choreographer Strom but contacts dozens of friends and business associates, as does Wolff, to appear as extras in the video. Within days, a passel of Epic secretaries, office workers at Wolff's management company, Hofman's legal firm, and friends and friends of friends, are lined up. Cyndi's mother will play the mother in the video, though she has no acting experience. Wolff, a longtime fan of professional wrestling, wants Captain Lou Albano to play the father. Albano had become manager of rock band NRBQ after his legendary wrestling career ended; Wolff calls NRBQ's label, Bearsville, who call Albano, who is more than willing to appear in the shoot. Wolff says, "I also wanted to get another famous pro wrestler, George 'the Animal' Steele, to get in drag to play the mother. But then I thought better of it. . . ." Arrangements for postproduction with Broadway Video are finalized.

SEPTEMBER 9: The first day of shooting starts at 7:00 A.M., with the crew setting up on the steps and fountains of the Metropolitan Museum. Cyndi arrives with Dave Wolff at 8:00 A.M. By 9:00 A.M. they're all set up. Ten or twelve extras are in thrift-shop punk costumes, and they run through their robot-like dance moves with Strom and Cyndi, while playback of the song blares over Fifth Avenue. By 10:30, shots of Cyndi leading the punk chorus line from the fountains and down the steps are completed, and the crowd of onlookers disperses as the crew packs up.

By 11:30, everyone's down on the corner of Water and Pine streets, in the shadow of the New York Stock Exchange, and the crew is again setting up. Onlookers gather. Cyndi suggests that a crowd of nearby hard-hats working on a construction site be integrated into the action. Griles agrees. Dozens of onlookers crack up as Cyndi mock-fights with some of the willing hard-hats, some of whom Cyndi bodily drags into the chorus line. Some business-suited stockbrokers join the action as well, chuckling and shaking their heads as Cyndi and Strom direct their moves. By half past noon, the shots are completed.

At 1:00 P.M., the crew is set up on Gay Street. Everyone takes an hour break for lunch. At 2:00 P.M., shooting begins in the Christopher Street subway station just off the busy Sheridan Square intersection. Again, a crowd gathers to watch. Some passers-by agree to take part and are brought by Strom to the wardrobe trailer after signing release forms, while Cyndi coaches the rest of the chorus line, which by now numbers about twenty people and includes Lenny Petze's four-year-old daughter. Cyndi, who appears to be doing as much directing as Griles or anyone else, runs them through their paces several times while waiting for the new chorus-line members to return to the location. Just as they do, a subway arrives at the station, and the disembarking passengers crowd the station exits, checking out the crew and crazily attired dancers. Ten minutes later, Strom and the rest have arrived, and Strom has finalized the choreography. Griles shouts "Action!" and a portable tape recorder blares the appropriate section of the song as the chorus line prances herky-jerkily up the steps and onto the street. Two more takes and they have it.

The crew moves across the street to Sheridan Square Park for more such shots. Passers-by gather: "What are they making? Oh, one of those MTV things. It's only one of those MTV things, Harry."

In these shots, Cyndi is to lead the punk parade down one of the sidewalks bordering the park. Francis Kenny will follow them, wearing a Steadicam—a camera in a specially built halter, gyroscopically rigged for just these kinds of moving shots. During the fourth take—this time without audio playback, as Cyndi merely shouts the song's chorus and the chorus line sings along—a car slams into the rear end of a taxi stopped at a red light on the side street adjacent to the shoot. The driver explains, "Sorry, man, I was watching them shoot." The taxi driver shouts back, "I oughta shoot *you*, man!" No serious damage is done, though, and with two uniformed policemen on hand, there will be no altercation. Shooting resumes.

After two more takes—during which production assistants Mark Wade and Mike Caffrey walk on either side of Kenny to make sure he doesn't bump into any trees or passing cars (Kenny's eyes must remain on his Steadicam's viewfinder)—they've got it, and adjourn to Gay Street.

By 4:00 P.M., the crew is set up. "We're waiting for the twilight," explains Walz, "because this is going to be for the opening shot of the video, when Cyndi's supposed to be coming home early in the morning. Twilight is perfect for simulating dawn." Here, Cyndi will prance up the street, dodging a newspaper delivery boy and man in a bathrobe walking his dog. The newspaper boy will be played by the son of the boyfriend of Walz's talent coordinator, Renee Geller; the man in the bathrobe will be Cyndi's record producer, Rick Chertoff; the dog will be Cyndi's own real-life pet, Sparkle, due on the set any minute with Cyndi's mother, Cathy Gallo.

While Griles confers with Kenny, and Cyndi gets made up in the wardrobe trailer, Walz orders production assistant Allison Mackie to water the street. "It makes it look prettier," explains Walz, "and it reflects light better." Mackie borrows a garden hose from Gay Street's most famous resident, radical lawyer William Kunstler, and waters the far end of the L-shaped side street. While Caffrey, Wade, and key grip

Dan Mahoney prepare a fifteen-foot crane for the crane shot, Cyndi rehearses this sequence with Griles.

Everything is set, and the light's just about right. But Cyndi's mom hasn't arrived yet with Sparkle. They're about to shoot without the dog when Cyndi's mom pulls up in a black fifties Cadillac complete with mammoth tail fins. Chertoff dons a bathrobe and takes the leash on Sparkle, a bouncing, bright-eyed mongrel collie. Griles does a couple of rehearsal takes, and everything is finally ready. But on the first take, the newspaper boy starts his run too early. "Wait till I say 'Action,'" shouts Kenny. Next take, audio man Dick Illy starts the music too late. After six takes, the shot is wrapped.

Now for the crane shot. The camera is affixed to the crane, there is more rehearsal and conferral between Griles and Cyndi. Overhead long shots with the crane will be intercut with Steadicam close-ups of Cyndi prancing up the street for the clip's opening sequence. After two rehearsal takes and four "live" takes, they have it. Then a tripod is set up at the far end of the street to get the actual first shot of the video, which will have Cyndi dancing in sped-up motion between two street-level apartment windows, in time to a rev-up synth-zap that opens the song. With the light fading fast, the shot is wrapped up in three takes. Shooting wraps for the day at 7:15 P.M., more or less on schedule. Again, a reminder of how different this shoot is from many rock-video productions, which take several sixteen- to twenty-hour shooting days and rarely run close to schedule.

SEPTEMBER 10: Production designer Power Boothe shops around for props for the interior scenes to be shot at Mother's Film Stage. Cyndi's "home" is to have a fifties camp retro look, so Boothe checks out some East Village and SoHo antique boutiques; one of them, Screaming Mimi's, was recommended to him by Cyndi, who used to work there. Boothe finds various kitschy African knickknacks, end tables, and ashtrays, as well as an ancient portable record player with polka-dotted plastic cover, and a multicolored pointillist-textured swag lamp. Other props come from various local prop shops. Furniture is on loan from the Salvation Army. The bedroom furniture—chests, dressers, and a bunk bed being constructed this afternoon—is painted turquoise by Boothe. Cyndi then spends a few hours decorating them with crimson and purple Jackson Pollock-like drips and splatters. By the end of the day, the furniture is resplendently cool camp. And the rest of the sets —the kitchen and hallway—are built. The crew finish the preproduction set work at about 8:00 P.M., some eleven or twelve hours after they started.

174

Sound and Vision:

SEPTEMBER 11: The final day of shooting, in which the home-set scenes of Cyndi orchestrating her party on the phone, the party itself, and the argument scenes with the parents in the kitchen, will be done. The crew arrive at Mother's Film Stage at 8:00 A.M. to start setting up. Mother's studio manager, Nick Smith, notes that the last rock videos shot here were for Carly Simon and Australian rockers INXS.

Shot lists are distributed to crew members and the gathering extras. The shot list contains the shooting schedule for the day, and it looks something like this (note that the numbers in parentheses following times are the numbers of shots in their sequence in the video itself; as one can see, the video, like most others and most movies, is shot out of sequence):

8:00 A.M.	Arrive
9:00 A.M. (11)	Girls on phone
10:00 A.M. (12)	Cyndi and all girls
10:45 A.M. (13)	Cyndi's room—TV
11:30 A.M. (13)	Telephone CU (close-up)
11:45 A.M. (5)	Mom/Cyndi—kitchen
12:30 P.M.	Lunch
1:30 P.M. (9)	Dad/Cyndi—full hallway
2:15 P.M. (10)	CU's—Dad/Cyndi
2:45 P.M. (7)	Cyndi full hallway
3:00 P.M. (21)	Party group full hallway
3:30 P.M. (20)	Mom/Dad group kitchen
4:00 P.M. (6)	Cyndi—half hallway
4:30 P.M. (24)	Mom/Dad—half hallway
5:30 P.M. (22)	Group fall out—half hallway
6:00 P.M. (23)	Cyndi—group party
6:30 P.M.	WRAP

As one can see, the video itself actually consists of at least twenty-four different shots, and this is the schedule for only one day of a two-day shoot. The distinctions between "half hallway" and "full hallway" are explained thus: full hallway means the actual hallway set remaining up, so that people walking down it can be filmed in long shot and with a camera tracking back from the action; half hallway means one side of the hallway set being taken down, so the camera can pan alongside people moving down it.

The first several scenes are shot smoothly, in two or three takes. Since

Lou Albano arrives early, at 10:30 A.M., and raring to go, it's decided to switch the shot sequence around and do his scenes earlier. Lou is a burly, outgoing fellow, and with his long, curly black hair and beard and mustache, he resembles a lovable Uncle Hell's Angel. The ear-piercingly loud Hawaiian shirt he wears, however, makes him look a lot more domesticated. On and off set, Lou is constantly huddling with and/or hugging and patting people on the back, making sure what he does is okay and generally raising everyone's already-high spirits. As a veteran professional wrestler, acting is nothing new to him, and indeed, he really makes his argument scenes with Cyndi and Cathy Gallo. Cyndi's mother, Cathy, is nervous at first—"I know this is nothing for Cyndi, but I've never acted, never been on a set before"—but with Lou's exuberant method-acting as the irate papa, she has no problem giving exactly the kind of wide-eyed reaction shots necessary. In one scene, Lou and Cathy march down the hallway towards the party in Cyndi's room, Lou fuming mad and Cathy the typical peace-making mother. Though he won't be heard in the video, Lou really acts out these scenes, shouting, "I don't know what that daughter of ours is up to in there, but I'm sure as hell gonna find out!" as he storms down the hallway. For a scene in which Lou argues with Cyndi, Walz comes up with the idea of having Cyndi throw a hammerlock on Lou as she lip-synchs the lines, "Oh Daddy, you know you're still number one/But girls just wanna have fun." Lou gives Cyndi a few tips; the scene is shot successfully in two takes, with Cyndi wearing a perfectly hilarious nervous, frozen grin as she holds the mammoth Lou against the hallway wall. Lou gets all his scenes perfectly in one or two takes. "Oh, Lou," says Cyndi, "you're such a natural." Lou smiles, hugs her, and coun-ters, "Hey kid, can I adopt you?"

Next comes the scene between Cyndi and her mother in the kitchen, picking up from the opening street scenes shot two days before—Cyndi is to dance into the kitchen, where Mom is cracking eggs into a bowl. Griles directs Cathy Gallo to stare aghast at Cyndi, mouth the lyric, "When you gonna live your life right?," roll her eyes heavenward, crack an egg onto her apron right over her heart, then bite her finger and hang her head. Cathy thinks she's got it. "Okay," shouts Griles, "rehearsal take." They run it through, and it looks okay. Now the camera is set up down the far end of the hallway leading out from the kitchen set; half the hallway has been taken down, so the camera will be able to pan along with Cyndi after she dances out of the kitchen and down the hall.

"Quiet on the set," yells Griles, "this is a keeper." The camera rolls, playback comes on, Cyndi dances in, Cathy Gallo goes through her

Cyndi Lauper with her real-life mother, Cathy Gallo, playing Cyndi's video mom in a scene from the "Girls Just Wanna Have Fun" video

paces more or less perfectly. Standing ovation from the crew. "Beautiful, Cathy, beautiful," cooes Griles, "but there was one problem." Power Boothe, standing outside the "kitchen" window, was to pull a string attached to a box of cornflakes on the kitchen counter, which was to fall in time to Cathy cracking the egg over her chest. But Power couldn't hear his cue over the din of playback. They run through it two more times and have it. Lou Albano gives Cathy a bear hug.

Next up is the "stateroom scene," in which Lou and Cathy peer into the keyhole of the door to Cyndi's room and the roomful of partiers spills out onto them. This will be the closing shot. Extras take their places behind a door built into the hallway wall set. They include Cyndi's lawyer, Eliot Hofman, a tall, distinguished, mustachioed Christopher Lee lookalike, in black tie and tails; Dave Wolff's lawyer, Joe

Zynczak, also in tux, as a butler with a tray of drinks; Bonnie Ross, R.N., an actual nurse in her uniform—also adorned with a feather boa —and an old friend of Cyndi's, and Rolling Stone Press's photographer, Laurie Palladino. After two takes in which a dozen people spill out the door on top of Lou Albano, the shot is wrapped. Says Lou, "I've been through Killer Kowalski and the rest, but never anything like that! . . . But seriously, how was I, okay?"

Lunch is taken at 3:15 P.M., but because of the rearrangement of the shooting schedule, they aren't really too far behind. Walz explains that a shot taken earlier of Cyndi and some girlfriends in Cyndi's bedroom will be "treated with the Mirage effect—a screenful of punkettes will turn into a bubble, which will float back into the screen to reveal other little Champagne and bubblegum-type bubbles rising and popping. We're also gonna put slow motion on the shot of people falling out the door onto Lou Albano."

Lunch over, the next shot takes place in the bedroom set: Cyndi sits in a chair watching TV, lip-synching the lines, "Some boys take a beautiful girl/And hide her away from the rest of the world." The TV screen shows a scene from *The Hunchback of Notre Dame,* with Charles Laughton's Quasimodo carrying Esmeralda up the cathedral steps, shaking his fist at the throngs outside. This was Griles's idea, but Cyndi adds the touch of sticking out her tongue at the screen between the two lines of the couplet. The TV itself, covered with a deco-modern white wood structure, is hooked up to an industrial video-cassette machine in a far corner of the room that plays back the *Hunchback* footage. It's manned by production manager X (yes, just X), who needs a clear line of sight to the TV through the assembled extras to cue playback properly; this results in the scene having to be taken three times.

Meanwhile, folk-pop singer Steve Forbert has arrived and gone into makeup; he will play Cyndi's boyfriend in the party scene. Dave Wolff and Rick Chertoff don firemen's suits for their roles in the party scene. As the bedroom set is prepared, Griles rehearses the "second wave" of revelers, who are to sashay into the room after the "first wave" has already filled it. In all, there will be some forty people crowded into the twelve-by-twelve-foot set. Griles to extras: "Don't just file neatly into the room—it's a *party,* right? You *mingle,* you recognize people and wave to them, and you never stop moving, doing the robot dancing, okay?" One of Joe Zynczak's legal partners arrives; he will don a Conehead for his part in the party scene. "Hey," he asks Griles, "can I smoke a cigar, too?" "Sure," replies Griles, "that'd be great." Forbert's out of makeup, in sharkskin suit and bow tie, and confers with Griles. Another extra who will play a pizza delivery boy arrives. Lenny Petze of Portrait arrives: "I just figured I'd drop by to see how much fun they were having."

They're ready for the party scene now, which, in the video, will come right before the closing shot of the revelers spilling out over Lou Albano. "Camera ready?" yells Griles. "Okay, gimme playback, and roll it. *Go* people, it's magic time!" The first wave of punkily dressed partiers flows into the room, and in seconds the set is crammed full of a frenzied mass of dancing, laughing, colliding people. Griles screams directions over the din of playback, and the second wave streams in. "Cut, cut, cut," shouts Griles, "that was good, but you people were too far back into the set. Let's take it again." After another take, two of the partiers have to retire: one with a bloody nose and another with a bruised eye; both received accidentally in the mad dancing fray. Nurse Ross checks them out. After two more takes they have it, but Griles now wants Francis Kenny to don a shoulder-camera and wade into the crowd to get close-ups of the party to be edited into the long shots. Playback comes on, the party starts again: Hofman slam dances with one punkette, while Zynczak twists through the fray with his tray aloft; Wolff and Chertoff brandish fire extinguishers; Dan Beck of Epic, in a nightshirt and nightcap and holding a candlestick, plays a sleepwalker who finds his way on top of the bunk bed to join in a pillow fight. Kenny is guided through the madness by Mike Caffrey and Mark Wade. After one take it looks perfect: "Thanks, everyone," shouts Griles, "that was great! Shooting is wrapped, you can all go home."

"Not yet!" comes a cry from key grip Dan Mahoney, who has discovered that halfway through the take the film ran out. "That hardly ever happens," says Walz as the revelers reassemble, "but this time, Francis couldn't hear the film run out in the camera because the playback was so loud. It's lucky we found out before anyone left." Griles waits for the film to be reloaded while giving directions to the partiers, as does Cyndi, who picks several extras to join her in dancing atop one of the dressers. Everything is set up. "Roll it!" yells Griles, "go crazy, everybody!" They do, and the shot is taken. "Okay, everyone," says Griles with authority, "*that's* a wrap!" Cheers and applause from the extras and crew, who take their time filing to wardrobe and taking down the sets. "If you could move out as quickly as possible, people," yells Griles, "they have another shoot in this studio tonight." The extras and crew grumble a bit, laugh, and go about their business. The typical postwrap atmosphere, elation mixed with exhaustion, takes hold of the room. The crew begin furiously breaking down sets while extras exchange phone numbers and make plans for postshoot drinking and *real* partying. Most of them do not go back to makeup and wardrobe, preferring to return to the streets looking the way they are. It's 7:30 P.M., the shoot complete, only ninety minutes behind schedule.

SEPTEMBER 13: "Daily rushes"—unedited, unsequenced raw footage from the shoot—are screened for Cyndi, Dave Wolff, Dan Beck, Lenny Petze, Ken Walz, and Ed Griles at the Maysles Brothers (of *Gimme Shelter* rockumentary fame) facility on Manhattan's West Side. So far, everything looks great. Cyndi takes a moment to reflect on this video, and rock video in general: "Oh I *loved* it, it was so great working with these people. What I loved most about working with Ken and Ed is that they made me feel so much a part of the team. From what I see and read and hear, it seems a lot of people sort of let themselves get into videos by people who are really making a jeans commercial in disguise, you know? Like using a woman's ass to sell a designer's name, or putting a pretty girl on the hood of a car. Naturally I'm very sensitive to that. But the great thing is that so was everyone else. They all wanted my input, to get things my way. Face it, if you make a video and do it wrong, once it's done you have to live with it from then on.

"I think what we've come up with is very close to the feeling I originally got from the song. I didn't write the song; Robert Hazard did, but I got a very definite feeling from it, and Ed's concept for the video matched it perfectly. It was a perfect mix of faith to the lyrics, drama bouncing off the lyrics.

"I can look at all the videos other people have done and see all the things I *don't* want to have done to me. I think *every* artist should have the right to express himself or herself visually—*and* to be able to do it sincerely and properly and not be made into something synthetic. If you can get all that, then video's great. And I got all of it, thanks to all these other people."

SEPTEMBER 15: Two days of preliminary film editing gets under way at Maysles Brothers, with Ken and Ed and some crew members present. Cyndi and Dave Wolff drop by to approve the rough cut.

SEPTEMBER 20: The rough-cut film is brought to Broadway Video, located in the famous Brill Building. The film stock is transferred onto one-inch broadcast-quality video tape using a "tele-cine." Ken and Ed preside over the three-day edit, with Cyndi, Dave Wolff, Dan Beck, Lenny Petze, and Eliot Hofman dropping in occasionally.

SEPTEMBER 22: With most of the editing done by Broadway Video's in-house editing team, the programming of the Mirage digital-effects machine begins. It will take a full twenty hours of real-time programming to set up the machine for sixteen seconds of actual on-screen footage.

SEPTEMBER 23: On the last day of editing, the Mirage is finally programmed. It now takes a full seven hours of real time to execute the sixteen-second "bubble" effect. The same hurry-up-and-wait atmosphere that pervaded the shooting holds here. Cyndi, Dave Wolff, and Dan Beck pop in and out to see how things are going. "It's Cyndi's video," says Walz, "and her career, so she has every right to be here to approve what's happening. Most artists don't do that, though; after the shoot that's usually it." With the bubble effect finally achieved to everyone's satisfaction, the entire finished video is run through from start to finish.

The clip follows the scenario outlined earlier, but there are far fewer scenes of Cyndi picking up partiers on the street than one might have expected. Still, the entire video is kinetic, innocent, irreverently exuberant—a perfect match for the song. And the Mirage "bubble" effect is exquisite: one shot of Cyndi amid a formation of party girls all singing the chorus is wrapped into a bubble shape, with the image of Cyndi and the girls revolving in and out of view around the bubble's surface; the bubble itself bounces around the screen like a pinball as other, smaller, computer-animated bubbles rise and pop around it. It's a startlingly apt visual analogue for the instrumental break it's set to, which features fizzy synthesizer pops. When it's over, the dozen or so people present applaud.

But Walz huddles with Cyndi and Dave Wolff for a minute. "We want to stretch the ending out," says Walz, "add some more party footage and keep repeating the chorus on the fade. Add another thirty seconds or so, because we have so much good party footage." An hour later, with the editors in the midst of stretching the end of the clip out, Dan Beck enters. After watching the entire clip, Beck queries, "Hmmm . . . there's so much energy in that party scene at the end, maybe we ought to stretch the song out in the video a few more seconds?" Walz and Cyndi, beaming and chuckling, answer in unison, "We beat you to it—we already did!" Beck smiles his approval. "Usually," says Walz, "you have to scramble just to fill three minutes. This is the first time we've ever actually added footage and lengthened the song." The edit is finally completed at 8:00 P.M. (it started at 9:00 A.M.). Champagne is uncorked, and everyone shakes hands. "Let's do this again real soon," says Cyndi, laughing on her way out with Wolff and Beck. "You bet," chorus Walz and Griles.

SEPTEMBER 26: The completed video for "Girls Just Wanna Have Fun" is delivered to Epic Records. Dan Beck and Lenny Petze screen it in a video-equipped conference room. They love it and call other execs and receptionists into the room to watch it. Everyone loves it. Meanwhile, another copy of the one-inch master tape is on its way to MTV.

SEPTEMBER 27: Ken Walz receives an ecstatic phone call from Eliot Hofman, who had just been called by Les Garland, MTV's programming chief. Garland had told Hofman, "This is one hell of a video. It looks like it'll really take off." Walz calls Garland immediately. "He says he can't promise how much rotation it'll get," says Walz, "but he thinks it's a real winner. This could be one of those cases where the video is so much fun it just gets the song off to a flying start."

OCTOBER 12: "Girls Just Wanna Have Fun" debuts on MTV, starting in "light" rotation (one or two plays a day). Quips MTV VJ Alan Hunter after playing the clip for the first time, "A 'fun' video indeed from Cyndi Lauper. . . ." With the single and album due for release within a week, it remained to be seen how much play both the video and the record would receive, and just how well Cyndi's video venture would go. All parties, however, from MTV executives to Walz, to Cyndi and her label people, were very hopeful.

Two months later, Cyndi would be one of the featured performers on MTV's third annual New Year's Eve Ball, which would be simulcast across the country. By this time, "Girls Just Wanna Have Fun" would be in heavy rotation on MTV, and seen frequently on most other rock-video shows. The song and video are genuine hits, and Cyndi appears to be on her way to stardom.

PROMO SELTZER AND HEAVY ROTATION: ROCK-VIDEO OUTLETS

There are five major outlets for rock video: television, which includes network, syndicated and local broadcasting, nationwide and local access cable, and UHF and low-power TV; clubs; satellite simulcasts, either to closed-circuit clubs and/or arenas, or to home television sets fitted with "addressible converters" to translate the satellite signal, supplied for a per-usage fee (thus satellite simulcasts are also known as pay-per-view programs); video jukeboxes; and home-video software, as in long-form video cassettes and video discs, and shorter-form packages like Sony's two-song Video 45s, and the three- to four-song Video EPs marketed in England by EMI-U.K.

So far, rock video on television has gotten the widest and highest degree of exposure, attention, and acclaim, which is only natural, since it's accessible to the greatest number of people and because television remains the most powerful and popular medium in the world. Furthermore, as Michael Boodro wrote in the August 1983 issue of the London arts monthly *ZX:* "MTV keeps the 'kids' (many of whom are now entering their thirties) hip and up to date, knowledgeable about all the latest bands from England and Germany, and provides them with up-close and seemingly intimate glimpses of their favorite rock stars—

all without necessitating their standing around in crowded rock clubs until one in the morning waiting for the show to go on, without forcing them to stand in line at stadiums or Ticketron outlets, and without having to put up with rowdy drunken teenagers puking on their shoes or shouting in their ears. The MTV audience can be hip and still get up early enough to go to their professional jobs.''

For the typical fan of the AOR bands populating MTV—or any other clips program playlist—almost any video, whether conceptual or straight performance, provides a better view of the artist and better sound than is possible in the typical live situation, where such bands perform in mammoth sports stadiums and most fans are hundreds of yards away from the onstage action. So there are trade-offs: the immediacy and human contact of a live show versus the distance and detachment of televised rock, with its concomitant and inherent passivity; the hassles of clubs or concerts versus the convenience of home viewing. Nobody is claiming that rock video will render actual live performance obsolete. In fact, most observers speculate that if there's enough (or too much) rock video around, there may be a reaction back towards smaller-scale, more intimate live shows. The future is contingent on so many elements it's difficult, if not impossible, to predict exactly where it may go. But we have already seen video infiltrate and change live performances—going back to the days when rock clubs installed video monitors and in-house cameras to simulcast onstage action, up to the Diamond Vision screens used to magnify arena-rock performances.

Meanwhile, here's a survey of rock-video outlets and what they have to offer:

TELEVISION

As of this writing, *all* of television—from tiny local low-power and UHF outlets to big national broadcast networks—seems to have gone video-clip crazy. On weekend evenings, especially in a cable-equipped home, there is no way to get away from rock video on the tube after, say, 11:00 P.M. And just about all of the literally hundreds of new rock shows around the country are showing promotional video clips. All except for one get most of the clips for free. This creates an intriguing paradox for record labels: they spend big money on the clips, but since they *are* promotional videos, labels must be satisfied to part with them for nothing in the hopes that if the video gets shown, monies will be indirectly recouped through record sales. Meanwhile, these shows turn free promotional material into *free programming.* No wonder that, starting in mid-1982, MTV made the tube go nuts for clips: they were hot, and they were dirt cheap.

MTV was a revolution in American television, not just rock on television: a twenty-four-hour, nationwide visual radio network. MTV was the brainchild of former radio programmer Robert Pittman. He describes MTV as "the natural medium for a generation that's grown up with their two favorite entertainment media—TV and rock music —on in their households all the time. But once that generation reaches adolescence, they tend to tune out TV in favor of rock music, which they see as something more their own. That twelve- to thirty-four-year-old age group has always been very elusive to TV programmers and advertisers. MTV is the first thing to come along that will draw those people back to watching their TVs—because MTV is a visual radio station playing their favorite music, on video and in stereo. MTV is meant to be viewed in an 'ambient' situation, the same way we listen to radio: you don't turn on the radio and sit there listening intently to it, you turn it on and leave it on in the background, and from time to time it draws your active attention. Same thing with MTV: it's radio with pictures. You're not supposed to watch it the way you watch regular TV."

But people did and do watch it like regular TV, for hours at a time —as well as watching it in the ambient way to which Pittman refers. Why do they watch it, transfixed, for hours at a time? Because of the very way in which Pittman describes what sets MTV apart from traditional TV: "We don't work along the lines of traditional TV. Rock video doesn't deal in conventions like narrative and plot and logical progression. It's like the music; it's about moods and emotions and energy and excitement. It's always changing. It's abstract; it's about *flow.*" And that flow, be it seductive or assaultive, is nonstop, twenty-four hours a day, every day.

But MTV's rotation of video clips isn't truly nonstop. There are the VJs, with chipper chatter and twice-hourly music news reports. MTV's VJs, incidentally, function the way DJs on most AOR stations do: they don't actually "play" or even select the videos themselves, they merely introduce them. Selection and frequency of play is decided by MTV's acquisitions committee, which views record-company videos each week, decides which to accept, and how heavily they are to be programmed. The actual sequence of the programming is worked out by computer, and that's why you'll probably never see the kind of clever, felicitous segues on MTV that radio uses. Rotation itself breaks down

Memphis, Tennessee's Dog Police in costume for their eponymous video clip, winner of the January 1984 edition of MTV's "Basement Tapes" for unsigned bands, and a good indicator of rising sophistication even among videos by unsigned, independent bands

thus: heavy rotation (which "is almost a guarantee of sales," according to one label executive), three or four plays per day; medium rotation, two or three plays per day; light rotation, one or two plays per day. Since degrees of rotation greatly affect record sales, in July 1983, MTV instituted a twenty-four-hour phone line, aimed mainly at record retailers, with prerecorded information on MTV's playlist, rotations, recent additions to the list, and upcoming world-première videos.

On weekends, there is a variety of special programming: big-name rock concerts, occasional cult films, and magazine-format shows like MTV's own in-house *Liner Notes* or IRS Records' *The Cutting Edge,* which happens to be the hippest, most daring exploratory rock-video show on TV. There is also the *Basement Tapes* competition every month, to which unsigned bands from around the country submit their independently produced videos to MTV's panel of rock stars and industry insiders. Five finalists are cablecast each month on a preannounced night, and viewers vote for their favorites by dialing the appropriate telephone number flashed on the screen. At the end of the year, the monthly winners are pitted in a big showdown, the grand prize being an EMI recording contract for a four-song EP and a video clip (the first big winners were Seattle's glitter-rock revivalists, Rail).

Finally, and most important, there are the channel's own promotional spots. Fittingly, for a station that uses promotional materials for its programming, MTV's promos are diabolically stylish. There are constant contests, like the "One Night Stands," in which lucky viewers and their pals are flown at MTV's expense to a free show and a night on the town with a superstar rock group (Fleetwood Mac and Journey were the first MTV "One Night Stands"; there have also been trips to Hawaii with Devo and Pat Benatar, a fully equipped "media-room" given away as "the ultimate electronic Christmas," and more), and which give rock stars further chances to "act" on camera.

Best of all, though, are MTV's ingenious in-house promos, mainly those featuring the animated MTV logo—the big *M,* the little *tv.* They were originally created by Fred Seibert and Alan Goodman, who have since moved on to the Playboy Channel's *Hot Rocks* show (about which more later). They are now done by various teams of producers and animators and feature such whimsical "characters" as a bewhiskered big *M* before a bathroom mirror, applying the little *tv* as shaving cream; a supersonic high-altitude zoom down on a quiet home that gets stamped with—and stamped out by—a blood-red MTV logo; an elephant in a jungle that metamorphoses into the MTV logo; and an *Altered States* logo, which bounces off the walls of a corridor, changing outline and hue just as William Hurt did in the climactic transformation scene of the movie.

"Traditionally," says Seibert, "corporate logos have been fixed, unchanging, very solid and recognizable. But with MTV, we were breaking all the rules anyway, so I figured why not break the rules for station logos as well?"

MTV's promotional style and attitude are all-important, for MTV is an extremely promotion-minded enterprise. Record companies are not the only ones benefiting from this promotional exposure. More recently, numerous films—*Flashdance, The Hunger, Stayin' Alive, Breathless, Dr. Detroit, Risky Business*—have either been cut down into three-minute montages keyed to soundtrack songs, or had crucial scenes excerpted (i.e. *The Hunger*'s opening montage featuring British new-wave band Bauhaus, *Risky Business*'s scene of star Tom Cruise dancing in his underwear to Bob Seger's "That Old Time Rock & Roll"), to be shown as video-clip trailers on MTV.

And yet, despite its high media profile and revolutionary status, as of late 1983, MTV was still in the red financially. How could this be, if it gets its programming free? For one, there's the enormous deficit left by MTV's twenty-million-dollar start-up costs. Then there are the costs of in-house production of promos, music news segments, *Liner Notes,* etc. Then there are the added costs of doctoring record-company master tapes, which still usually arrive at MTV with inferior soundtracks that must be reprocessed to be cablecast in stereo.

Above all, though, it's a matter of advertising dollars. If MTV was, in fact, drawing back that twelve- to thirty-four-year-old demographic, then why weren't advertisers jumping all over it from the beginning? Simple: they were waiting until MTV had the *numbers* to make big-budget advertising expenditures worthwhile. Not that MTV didn't have some big advertisers from the start: the usual youth-market purveyors of personal, health, and beauty products, clothes, cars, video games, movies, records, and candy bars. But it wasn't until the summer of 1983, when MTV's viewership hit the fifteen million mark and thus could be rated by the Nielsen Home Video Index ratings service, that advertisers took notice. The Nielsen ratings showed that:

- with fifteen percent penetration of American TV homes, MTV had the highest twenty-four-hour rating of any basic cable service ("basic" meaning that there is no additional per-month charge to receive it, as there is with, say, Home Box Office or Showtime);
- eighty-five percent of MTV's audience was aged twelve to thirty-four;
- eighty percent of that audience first encountered many recording artists on MTV;
- sixty-eight percent of that audience bought records after being influenced by MTV; and
- sixty percent of that audience listed MTV and/or rock video in general as a bigger influence in their record-buying habits than radio, retail advertising, concerts, or anything else on television.

These were things most record companies knew all along, although they never had any such real, tangible statistical evidence to prove it. As Jo Bergman of Warner Brothers puts it, "Yes, MTV reaches maybe fifteen million people, and in the TV-viewing universe that isn't really all that many. But MTV reaches the *right* fifteen million people, it really hits that demographic that goes out and buys records."

Some advertisers had suspected this, and some of them began cleverly adopting the style of MTV Videos in their commercials: there was the Miller beer ad with Southside Johnny and the Asbury Jukes rocking out the "Welcome to Miller Time" theme song to a partying bar full of folks, with an MTV-style Chyron-generated readout ("Southside Johnny, 'Welcome,' Miller Beer") in the bottom-left corner of the screen. Clairol's Summer Blondes spot went one better by including the Chyron readout at the beginning *and* end of their spot. A phone-order retail record store called Hot Rock assembled a stunning, rap-backed, two-minute montage of rock-video cliché images, replete with smoky, back-lit urban nightscapes and punk-chic models. The *real* commercials were becoming indistinguishable from the once-removed commercials that constituted MTV's programming—and that was the point.

With the MTV Nielsens out, Madison Avenue really picked up on what Andrew C. Brown had written in a December 1981 issue of *Fortune* magazine: "One of cable TV's charms is its ability to serve up specific audiences for advertisers, much as specialized magazines do. This is called 'narrow-casting,' and the purest example to date is Warner-Amex's MTV: Music Television."

"The beauty of MTV," says Thomas Sharbaugh, group marketing manager of Anheuser-Busch, who in the summer of 1983 ran a rock-video-styled Budweiser ad on MTV starring Karla DeVito, "is that there's nobody tuned in who doesn't understand it."

By the summer of 1983, MTV had more advertising in the first quarter of 1983 alone than in all of 1982, a trend that advertising chief Dominic Fioravanti says should have MTV in the black by early to mid-1984. Once that happens, the gray area of MTV's use of promos as free programming may get white-hot. But in the meantime, MTV will remain the standard by which all other forms of rock-video programming must be judged. It is revolutionary, the first and biggest in its brand-new field, and still synonymous with rock video in general in the eyes of many.

One result of MTV's prominence is its ability to influence the way video clips are made. Many rock-video producers and directors admit to making videos with MTV acceptance in mind. Some musicians think the same way. Says Midge Ure of British synth-rockers Ultravox, who directs his own and other bands' videos, "If a label gives you forty thousand dollars or whatever to make a promo, and you can't get it on the biggest outlet there is, then you've really blown it." Some labels have even taken to sending rough-cut videos to MTV's acquisitions committee to guarantee acceptance. "Sure that's done," says Jo Bergman of Warner Brothers, "of *course*—it's just sound business practice, protecting your own investment." Even a club-video maven like Rock-America's Ed Steinberg is not immune. His Soft Focus Productions has made dozens of clips, including EBN-OZN's highly produced "AEIOU (and Sometimes Y)," which was popular on MTV in the summer of 1983. "Whenever I sit down with a band to discuss shooting a clip," says Steinberg, "the first thing we say is: 'Yeah, it's great that Rock-America can get the tape out to all these clubs—but how do we get it on MTV?'"

Veteran music publicist Howard Bloom—whose clients have included established stars like Billy Joel and Simon and Garfunkel and new music acts like Billy Idol and Joan Jett—sheds further light on MTV's importance in the rock-video scheme of things: "We know that MTV can have a very powerful effect on record sales; that's been proven. If you look at the Top Ten records in the charts, you'll find that almost without exception, every single act in the Top Ten has heavy rotation on MTV. *Every single rock act.*

"MTV also shortens the time it takes for a band to achieve success," Bloom says. "It used to always take up to four years to achieve success at the gold or platinum record level. But look at some bands that got a lot of MTV play: Stray Cats, Missing Persons, and Culture Club all went gold with their first albums here; Men at Work of course went multiplatinum with theirs; Bryan Adams went gold after only two years in the U.S. market. Duran Duran is a story in itself.

"But there are different levels of success. Flock of Seagulls, for instance, and Haircut 100, both on Arista, both big MTV acts, both successful—but Flock of Seagulls sold literally twice as many records as Haircut 100. Beyond that, there are people spending thousands and thousands of dollars on videos and getting them on MTV and who are still not selling many records: Planet P, Chris Deburgh, and Sparks are good examples for mid-1983. They all did extremely well on MTV, yet didn't sell many records. Dexy's Midnight Runners had a number-one pop single with 'Come on Eileen,' and a wonderful video for it that got a lot of MTV play. But their album never went gold, and their tour here was a big disaster.

"The important thing to remember is that MTV can do a lot, but it won't necessarily do it all. It's just a *part* of the success formula that also includes radio, press, and touring."

While MTV has received the most exposure and acclaim, it has also been the subject of the most criticism. Mostly, MTV has been accused of racism in its format. But before we get to that issue, let's backtrack a bit and see how and why MTV operates the way it does. Remember that Bob Pittman and other top-line policy-making MTV executives like John Sykes and Les Garland come from backgrounds in record marketing and promotion, or the same kind of format-radio rock video was supposed to come along to supplant, or at least shake up. MTV was extensively researched while it was still on the drawing boards. Thousands of phone calls were made, and still are made, each week to potential viewers in the young rock audience. Like AOR radio, MTV follows the demographic pattern of "passive programming." Though it's the first omnipresent music-video network, and hence subject to the high expectations of observers who foresee the day when TV dials will be full of various genre-oriented music-video services, MTV programs the kind of music video its audience wants, and nothing else. And what MTV's audience wants, apparently, is white rock music, whether it be American hard rock or pomp-rock, or British new-wave synthesizer pop.

Pittman again: "Our research showed quite simply that the audience for rock music was larger, and that the mostly white rock audience was more excited about its music than the mostly black audience was about its music, rhythm & blues or disco or whatever you want to call it. The rock audience is more age-clustered, making it more attractive to advertisers. And there were just a lot more rock videos around than black-music videos to start with. So we logically went with a rock format."

MTV's programming is a perfect example of narrow-casting. True, both black and white music contribute at least equally to the spectrum of rock and pop music. True, MTV's policy ignores twenty-five years of cultural history that shows, time and time again, that without black music there could not *be* rock music. But things have changed since the naive fifties and the utopian sixties. In the seventies, AOR and other such formatted products demographically segmented the mass pop-music audience, mirroring other media trends towards cable narrow-casting and specialty magazines. To call MTV itself racist and leave it at that is too simple. It's perhaps best to see MTV as a product of its time and its medium, the offspring of tried-and-true conventional industry wisdom. Things are now at the point where one black man in the cable industry, Robert Johnson, president of the Black Entertainment Television cable network, is only being pragmatic when, in the summer of 1983, he says, "MTV is not racist. They may have made a mistake in selecting so narrow a musical format, but they have every right to provide specialized programming. In cable TV, that's the name of the game."

On the other hand, it seems a shame that MTV, as embodiment of the Next Big Thing, should only reinforce the preexisting status quo rather than break down barriers. And, one has to wonder how truly valid MTV's conventional wisdom is. Dennis D'Aquisto, who runs a video-equipped rock club in Racine, Wisconsin, says, "We show MTV for an hour or two when the club first opens, and people like it fine. Once the club fills up, our VJ goes to work—and we always mix black and white videos equally. And nobody in our audience complains, ever. Our audience is roughly three-quarters white and one-quarter black. I make my living from this club, and believe me, if my audience didn't like seeing black videos, I wouldn't show them. So to me, the MTV people are just being paranoid with all that 'it's gotta be rock' stuff about their format."

MTV is biased, and sensibly so, given its status as a big business venture. For his part, MTV's Bob Pittman says, "I'm tired of all this 'racist' stuff. Why doesn't anyone ever talk about the barriers we *have* broken down? Like between punk or new wave and mainstream rock?" True, MTV has given exposure to many new bands radio would not play initially, and most of them have been new wave, though certainly not punk. (The Clash, whose *Combat Rock* became their first platinum LP, thanks in large part to MTV exposure of their "Rock the Casbah" video, stand out as an exception to the rule.) New wave was, after all, the watering down of punk. New wave had been working its way into the mainstream, through fashion and advertising (who could forget Kraft's pre-MTV new-wave ad, with models in wraparound shades angularly spreading Miracle Whip on white bread and mustard on franks, to the tune of an electronic cop of Devo's "Whip It," while robotic voices intoned "Tune in to Kraft"?), before MTV came along. MTV only accelerated the process of domesticating new-wave's kitschy irony and essentially innocuous weirdness. Punk, like rock & roll in its inception, is far too dangerous to make it onto MTV. And beyond that, most viewers just don't want to see it.

Except, that is, on *The Cutting Edge.* As *Cutting Edge* producer Jay Boberg of IRS explains, "The show obviously benefits us and MTV, as well as, we think, giving a valuable service by educating people to things they'd otherwise probably never find out about, or run away from if they did. With *The Cutting Edge* on, MTV can tell all the people who accuse them of being too mainstream, 'Hey, look, for a whole hour each month we have all this *other* stuff.' People shouldn't come down on MTV and demand *more* of that, they should be grateful that what's there is there. MTV doesn't *have* to run *The Cutting Edge.*" But MTV's research shows that *Edge*—which has shown hard-core punk bands from the U.S. and U.K., hard-core reggae bands like Burning Spear, and hard-core black rap artists like Grandmaster Flash (demonstrating how to "break-mix" records) that MTV itself rarely, if ever, runs in its rotation—is by far its lowest-rated special program.

To be honest, though, MTV has never been without black faces. Most noticeable is that of VJ J. J. Jackson. What many people don't know about Jackson is that he, too, comes from a long AOR radio background; at Los Angeles's KLOS-FM in the mid-seventies, Jackson was one of Led Zeppelin's biggest American boosters. He sees no contradiction in being a black man and being the host of a mostly white rotation: "MTV is a rock & roll station. We play black artists like the Bus Boys, Phil Lynott, Pauline Black of the Selecter, because they're rock & rollers. On the other hand, I don't think you'd find a black-music station playing, say, Led Zeppelin, even though there's a mean, blues-based backbeat to that band. People never point out that we don't play someone like Christopher Cross. When we played Olivia Newton-John, there was a big backlash from the VJs and everyone else, because *that's* not rock & roll. You think Donna Summer, Prince, and Rick James are rock & roll? I don't. The difference had to do with lyrical content, presentation, and everything else. Because Prince puts on an outfit that might remind you of what Freddie Mercury [Queen's lead singer] wears doesn't mean he's rock & roll. Prince is very good at what he does, but it's rhythm & blues. I've never heard a long guitar run on any of his albums ever, and that's like the heartbeat of rock & roll. Take the guitar out of rock & roll and you've got no rock & roll. It's like taking the rhythm out of rhythm & blues. . . . What I'm saying is, if a TV channel or radio station wants to be rock & roll, or R&B, or country, or whatever, *fine.* But someone has to decide what the cutoff point is going to be. And people who don't agree with that particular cutoff point are going to be a little angry."

Never mind that MTV began playing Prince and Donna Summer shortly after Jackson spoke in the spring of 1983; his comment about rock being guitar music is more intriguing. True, MTV started out as, and still is, a great promoter of guitar-based hard rock. But most of the acts it's broken, the ones radio wouldn't play, the British new-wave acts, are *synthesizer*-based bands—Human League, Duran Duran,

Musical Youth create disorder in the court in their antic-fun-with-a-message clip for "Pass the Dutchie" (1983), directed with flair by rock-video seditionist Don Letts. In the wake of Michael Jackson's "Billie Jean" and "Beat It," this was one of the first black-music videos to receive substantial MTV play.

Thompson Twins, and Flock of Seagulls, to name a few. Jackson has no answer to this. Nor does anyone else at MTV—except, as in Pittman's case, to keep pointing to the demographic stats. These bands get on, and they "work." And that's the name of that tune.

Even in MTV's early days, though, there were some black acts in rotation—but only those whose music sounded white, such as all-black hard-rockers the Bus Boys, or mulatto street-poet Garland Jeffreys, or black-Irish hard-rocker Phil Lynott (there were also the two black members of now-defunct British "two-tone" band, the Specials). But MTV would not program two of the best rock videos around—the Tom Tom Club's "Genius of Love" and Chaz Jankel's "Questionnaire"—even though the clips were animated and showed no black faces (except for "Genius of Love," with its cartoon depiction of James Brown), and the artists in question were (except for a few ancillary Tom Tom Clubbers) white, because the music sounded too black. Was MTV just promo seltzer for an ailing white rock music industry, a grand capitalist minstrel show? Perhaps. Still, MTV did do more than just reinforce the prejudices of its mass audience, by playing the likes of Michael Jackson,

Prince, and Culture Club's Boy George—all of which may have left some of MTV's mass audience wanting more white heavy metal.

Still, some funny things would happen. Even while they wouldn't play the "Genius of Love" video, MTV in-house promos showed styrofoam puppet stereo speakers dancing to "Genius of Love." And in the summer of 1983, while MTV was refusing to air Grandmaster Flash's "The Message," Mark Goodman read a music-news item: Chris Difford and Glenn Tilbrook, who'd just folded their popular British rock band Squeeze, were writing new songs and sending them in the mail to Grandmaster Flash in the hopes that he'd record them. A fascinating item. Then Goodman tagged the story with: "Some of you may know that Grandmaster Flash's single 'The Message' was one of the most acclaimed songs of the past year." Really? Not if you watched MTV, you wouldn't. This left open the gaping question, Why wouldn't they play the clip?

Jeffrey Peisch, head writer for MTV's music-news department, explained, "That story was relevant to our audience because the members of Squeeze were involved; that was the hook. If Grandmaster Flash was working with a symphony orchestra or a black act like, say, the Spinners, we wouldn't have run that story."

At any rate, MTV came under criticism not only for alleged racism, but also for ignoring the past: MTV rarely, if ever, ran vintage rock videos (mainly, there was the odd old Doors clip), and never made connections between the past and present; MTV, as a promotional programming enterprise, is uncritical (though it is implicitly political).

Another Pittman pronouncement: "I don't think our audience is much interested in history." Indeed, they probably weren't either interested or aware of rock history. Back in 1981, the *Soho News* did a story on the crowds waiting in line for tickets to the Rolling Stones' U.S. tour concerts in New York City; most of those in line were aged twelve to fifteen; most of them, when asked, said things like, "Yeah, I like early Stones—you know, like *Sticky Fingers,*" seemingly unaware that *Sticky Fingers,* released in 1971, had been preceded by seven years' worth of Rolling Stones records. In line with this blissfully ignorant reality, MTV is an eternal *now* of the newest eye-and-ear candy. Imagine an MTV VJ saying, at the end of a Duran Duran or ABC clip, "Ever notice how much their music borrows from disco?" To be fair, it's true that vintage clips are much harder to come by than current ones. In late 1983, MTV finally did acknowledge rock history prior to 1981, with its "Closet Classics" segments, vintage "Beat Club" performance clips— which are obviously a lot easier to get than, say, vintage *concept* clips like the Kinks' "Dead End Street," or the Who's "Happy Jack," or the Beatles' "Strawberry Fields." Prior to MTV's acquisition of the "Beat Club" catalogue, the same vintage clips already had been shown to death on USA Network's *Night Flight* and *Radio 1990.*

All of this led some to be suspicious of MTV. The ultimate put-down came from veteran rock scribe Dave Marsh in *The Record,* when he noted MTV's apparent racism and ahistorical approach and concluded, "I don't want my MTV." Criticism came from other quarters as well, mainly from black-funk superstar Rick James, one of MTV's most consistently vociferous opponents. On the summer of 1983 ABC *Nightline* show that covered rock video, James asked, "Why should I, as a black artist in America today, spend good time and money on a video, when the biggest forum for music video in the world won't even play it? It's a real drag for me, man, and the only reason I keep complaining is that it's so important. But I know I have white fans as well as black fans—I see 'em at my shows. The thing is, they shouldn't call themselves 'MTV: Music Television.' They should call themselves 'White Rock TV' or something."

"It's a political thing, it isn't just MTV," says Arthur Baker, producer and cocomposer of Afrika Barmbaattaa's 1982 platinum rap hit "Planet Rock" and president of highly successful postrap, black-music label Streetwise Records. "It's the way popular music is run in this country: it's politics, who your label is, who's promoting you, what color your skin is. The only way MTV would ever play my music is if it was on a major label and if the faces were white. MTV gives me its standard answer: 'It's not our format, it's not rock.' Well, look at what they do play; Human League? That's not rock & roll; that's black music with white faces. ABC? That's white disco. Thompson Twins? That's white kids playing a mix of Latin, disco, and electronic beat music. They're all white groups playing black music. It's the same old story, racism. It's the same reason why, when *Time* magazine does a story about how pop music is heating up in the summer of 1983, they put David Bowie on the cover instead of Michael Jackson, who is easily the hottest performer in pop music today."

Still, some of Baker's acts did manage to get their videos onto MTV in the summer of 1983: Boston's all-black New Edition, with their Jackson Five-ish "Candy Girl," and British all-white new-wavers New Order, with "Confusion." Guess which one got played more?

But by that time, MTV had already had its color bar broken wide open by Michael Jackson. Beginning March 2, 1983, with Jackson's *Thriller* album and singles "Billie Jean" and "Beat It" selling millions, comfortably perched atop the black- and pop-music charts, the "Billie Jean" video (directed by Steve Barron for Limelight) was suddenly being seen on MTV. For his part, MTV's John Sykes says, "By the time we put that video into rotation, there was really no way for us to ignore 'Billie Jean.' It had moved beyond being a 'black-music' hit; it was an across-the-board smash, pop, black, dance charts, you name it. It was a *rock* song, a *pop* song. And as such, it fit our format."

One month later, Jackson broke the color bar open even further with his "Beat It" video. By that time, "Billie Jean" had become so hot on MTV that "Beat It" became an MTV World Première Video. And that was fitting: it was the first entree of a rich, experienced director of commercials into the field of rock video—in this case, Bob Giraldi, who did the innovative TV spots for Broadway shows like *Pippin, A Chorus Line,* and *Dreamgirls* as well as most of the legendary Miller Lite beer ads with sports stars; it was the first rock video to break the $150,000 budget mark; it was the first rock video to add sound effects extraneous to the content of the song but crucial to the clip's dramatic action (switch-blade knives flicking open, garage doors rising; Devo's 1980 "Whip It" was actually the first rock video to dub extramusical sounds, but in their case—the *thunk* of a beer can hit by a bullet—it was a single, rather incidental usage; "Beat It" made consistent and crucial use of dubbed-in "natural" sound throughout); and it happened to be one of the greatest rock videos ever made. Sure, it looked like one of Giraldi's all-singing, all-dancing Dr. Pepper ads, but it was also great entertainment, aesthetically appropriate to the song, and one of the all-too-rare incursions of genuine social comment into a widely seen rock video.

Instantly, "Beat It" became MTV's hottest, most talked about, most requested video. Entertainment critic Dennis Cunningham of WCBS-TV New York, in a summer of '83 report on rock video and MTV, aptly described it as *"the* drop-dead video of all time." The song's athletic guitar solo was played by heavy-metal hero Eddie Van Halen, and if the clip had *shown* Van Halen playing that solo, some speculated, that might have won over MTV's white rock hordes. The clip did not show Van Halen, but it won the hordes over anyway. The video and the song were simply too good to resist, once they got onto the medium all the kids were watching. Susan Blond of Epic, Jackson's label, reports, *"Thriller* had already sold about three million copies before any of the videos got on MTV. But *after* MTV, we were selling two hundred thousand copies of it a week, and we ended up selling six million more copies. It's a sad comment that it would take something like MTV to get an artist like Michael Jackson over to that audience, but so be it. And it did work."

In the wake of Jackson's success, more and more black acts got into MTV's rotation: Prince, Musical Youth, Eddy Grant, Peter Tosh. Now the questions became, Where did MTV draw the line, and how long before even Rick James would be seen on the channel? As John Sykes put it, "Hey, we're only one channel. There's only so much we can do. We think people like Prince and Eddy Grant are black-music artists who cross over to the rock audience, so we feel they fit our format. If Rick James gets to that level, we'll play him, too."

Still, as of this writing, Bob Giraldi himself called MTV "a bunch of racist bastards, pure and simple." Giraldi may be unduly frustrated with MTV because, while they played "Beat It" and his clip for Pat Benatar's "Love Is a Battlefield," MTV would not put Giraldi's clip for Diana Ross's "Pieces of Ice" into rotation, claiming that Ross lacked the requisite crossover appeal. But given that, and the typical reasoning of MTV executives like Pittman and Sykes, why, then, was MTV playing Lionel Richie's decidedly nonrock "All Night Long" video in the fall of 1983? And why, not long before that, did MTV finally format Tom Tom Club's "Genius of Love"? Why did MTV run VJ interviews with black reggae star Peter Tosh, and feature an in-depth tribute to blues giant Muddy Waters after his death on *Liner Notes*? These are in no way complaints, of course. Such moves are gratifying, even if they do make one wonder about MTV's attitude that "it's gotta be rock." Basically, as of this writing, all signs indicate that MTV is ready, willing, and able to adjust its programming to keep up with the onrushing competition of other rock-video shows (and, hopefully, to lay all accusations of racism to rest once and for all). And the competition is here.

Of course, there have been rock-concert shows since the early seventies. Even in the wake of Don Kirshner there were some good ones, and there still are—on, of all places, public for "educational" television. In 1973, one year after Kirshner's *Rock Concert* debuted, PBS unveiled what are now the two longest-running concert shows on television, the country-oriented *Austin City Limits* and the eclectic, Chicago-based pop-rock showcase *Soundstage*. They provide welcome, low-keyed, tasteful and entertaining as well as occasionally enlightening relief from all those video clips.

In the spring of 1983, two new rock-concert shows came on TV. There was the nationally syndicated *Rock & Roll Tonight*, presenting several bands prerecorded before a live audience at Perkins Palace in Pasadena, California, simulcast in stereo on local FM radio stations, and broadcast once a week, usually in the traditional late-night weekend time slots. Most of its acts were in the hard-rock and heavy-metal vein, but there have also been such "new music" acts as Culture Club and Psychedelic Furs, as well as occasional "superstar jams" (such as the opening show's, with venerable guitar wizard Les Paul dueling frets with rock guitar hero Jeff Beck and host Billy Squier). But as producer Bob Emmer noted, "Our shows are organized thematically—so you won't see, say, a Culture Club on the same show with, say, a Krokus." Smart move, in light of the marketing and genre segmentation that overtook the mass rock market in the seventies, and which has been mirrored in cable's concept of "narrow-casting" to specific, specialized audiences. But it didn't keep the show from being dropped in September 1983. A month later, along came the network-syndicated concert show *Rock TV.*

In August 1982, cable's USA Network introduced *Hot Spots,* taped live at rock clubs around the country, usually featuring one or two up-and-coming or unknown bands per show, and shown several times weekly on the cable network. *Hot Spots* is straightforwardly produced and has at times spotlit such deserving bands as Dream Syndicate, Bonnie Hayes and the Wild Combo, and NRBQ. To further illustrate the promotional power of rock on TV, Robert Hazard, featured in the first *Hot Spots* cablecast in August 1982, was signed by RCA Records within months of being seen on the show.

There has always been *American Bandstand.* Seemingly for almost as long, there has been *Soul Train,* the black-music answer to *Bandstand,* with its glitzier party atmosphere; it also does not use video clips. Since 1979, there has been *Solid Gold,* along with *Bandstand* the most successfully syndicated music show in the world, with its middle-of-the-road hits countdowns; it had never used video clips until late 1983, despite the claim by producer Brad Lachman in the summer of 1983 that it never would, since "the fact that we *don't* use them is what sets us apart from all those other shows."

All those other shows. There are literally hundreds of them around the country, many of them once-a-week half-hour weekend showcases, some of them on several times a week, some of them on for many hours a day. All of them showing video clips. Some with on-camera VJs, some with off-camera announcers, some with more creative alternatives. Most all of them owe their existence to the success of MTV.

MTV was certainly not the first rock show on TV. Nor was it even the first American TV show to regularly use video clips—that honor falls to Casey Casem's *America's Top Ten,* a video version of his famous, long-lived AM-radio hits countdown show, *America's Top 40. America's Top Ten* went into syndication in 1979; executive producer Syd Vinnedge says, "One of the main reasons for starting the show was as a way to get these video clips onto American TV." Casem and Vinnedge have maintained a commitment to rock video, strongly evidenced by their production of the first annual American Video Awards in mid-1983.

Nor was MTV the first cable service to show video clips in rotation. As early as 1979, *Video Jukebox* and Atlanta's Video Music Channel were syndicating their own prepackaged sequences of rock videos, with off-camera announcers instead of on-camera VJs, to such pay-cable networks as Home Box Office, which still runs *Video Jukebox* as occasional half-hour programming, and more often as filler between the movies that make up the bulk of its programming. And of course there was *Popclips.*

By early 1982, there were already enough rock-video shows on local broadcast and cable channels as well as on subscription-TV services (Wometco Home Television, ON-TV/Spectrum, L.A.'s Z-Channel, etc.) that a video-conscious label like Epic had a magazine-thick "video tracking sheet" prepared, listing them all by region. Back then, Epic's sheet listed about seventy-five such outlets. A year later, that number had nearly doubled. There are prime-time and late-night shows spun off of (and simulcast on) local radio stations, using the station's playlist format and DJs and VJs; independent video-clip shows, with or without on-camera VJs or off-camera announcers, in a variety of music-mix formats; afternoon new-wave *American Bandstand* clones like L.A.'s *MV3* (now syndicated around much of the country) and San Francisco's UHF *TV 20 Dance Party,* and more. Los Angeles, as of 1983, had about a half-dozen such shows; Detroit had four; Boston had three. Tulsa and Oklahoma City have them, as do Denver and Aspen, Seattle and San Diego, Phoenix and Tucson, Minneapolis and Wausau, Wisconsin, Tallahassee and Savannah and Charleston. Ft. Smith, Arkansas, has its own *Rock Image,* and in Mobile, Alabama, low-power-TV channel sixty-nine has its own *Video Music Box,* showing rock videos for twenty hours a day.

All across the nation, there were clips in heavy rotation. And while most of these local shows programmed AOR/new-music mixes in MTV's image, some of them were far more intriguing than MTV or any other nationally seen rock-video outlets. *Goodnight L.A.,* for instance, eschewed mainstream rock totally in favor of avant-garde and experimental music, much of it by unsigned local bands; it played lots of experimental video art as well as off-the-wall comedy pieces; the whole thing was stitched together not with VJs or off-camera announcers but by taking a Sony Portapak and video camera into L.A.'s streets after midnight to stop passing skateboarders or burger-flipping countermen and have them read intros for rock videos. Shows were often introduced by celebrity guests, anyone from lead Stray Cat Brian Setzer to the mayor of Los Angeles, to actor McLean Stevenson.

In California's Bay Area, there was *California Music Channel* (*CMC*), a one-man operation begun in 1981 by one-time radio DJ Rick Kurkjian as a low-power TV-clips showcase. As of this writing, it was being seen on four Bay Area cable channels and on a couple of local broadcast stations. Kurkjian sits alone at his control console with an unmanned camera trained on him, announcing clips as he fades them in and out on-camera, and doing on-camera ads for local retailers (shades of SCTV's Gerry Todd!) *CMC* has also managed to lure such big-bucks advertisers as Tower Records and the California Milk Advisory Board.

Big-time pay-cable networks were responding as well. Home Box Office, America's largest pay-cable network, with some 12.5 million subscribers, not only still had *Video Jukebox* but had stepped up its regular superstar pop concerts and taken them in a more rock-oriented direction, with the likes of Billy Joel, Neil Young, Donna Summer, Stevie Nicks, Hall and Oates, and David Bowie. Its sister service, Cinemax (2.5 million subscribers), expanded its just-movies format in September 1983 with *Album Flash,* a monthly, half-hour showcase for one pop-rock star and their just-released album, including interviews with and clips of the artist performing songs from that album (promotion as programming—a mini-MTV, as it were).

Also in 1983, Showtime absorbed Warner-Amex's foundering Movie Channel to get a total of 5.5 million viewers. Showtime also has run rock and pop concerts (US Festival highlights and Diana Ross live from Central Park in the summer of 1983). But in the autumn of 1983, Showtime unveiled *Rock of the 80s,* a new-wave concert showcase coproduced by L.A.'s KROQ new-music guru Rick Carroll; the first show featured such MTV stars as Stray Cats, Flock of Seagulls, Berlin, and Oingo Boingo. Showtime also announced that it would be running all of Duran Duran's long-form compilation of clips as a first-run feature program. The Showtime source reasoned, "It's one thing for MTV to show the clips one at a time in random rotation. But to show them all at the same time on one program, *that's* an event. Also, we know the Duran Duran cassette is available for home-video use, but we figure more people have Showtime and don't have home-video equipment than vice-versa, and even if they did, we still consider it viable programming."

In early 1983, Fred Seibert and Alan Goodman left Warner-Amex's Creative Services Department and MTV to create *Hot Rocks* for the Playboy Channel, another smaller-scale pay-cable service. *Hot Rocks* features the raciest, uncensored rock videos; its debut installment in July 1983 featured David Bowie's uncut "China Girl" (in which we see a closing shot of the nude Bowie making love to an Oriental model on a beach in a *From Here to Eternity* homage), Duran Duran's uncut "Girls on Film," and so on. So far, *Hot Rocks* has been restricted to weekly half-hour slots, probably because there isn't that much really racy rock video out there. But with a show like *Hot Rocks,* and the added possibilities of showing uncensored clips in clubs, it's a pretty safe bet that labels will increase the production of alternate-take clips to match the censorship, or lack thereof, of various outlets.

Black Entertainment TV, with three million viewers, had been programming *Video Soul* for ninety minutes on weekend evenings for a year or more before the actual rock-video explosion on TV. In September 1983, however, BET updated and refined *Video Soul,* recruiting two new smooth-talking VJs from Washington, D.C., music, radio, and news programs, integrating dancing, contests, hits-countdowns, etc., and slating the show for two-hour slots in prime-time on Mondays, Wednesdays, and Fridays.

One of the most ambitious cable music packages isn't even rock-oriented. The Nashville Network, an ad-supported basic-cable service, was launched by Group W Communications in March 1983 with over seven million subscribers. TNN programs eighteen hours a day, seven days a week, of country-music-oriented cultural programming: there are performance showcases for established and new artists, talent hunts, Nashville nostalgia and history, songwriting workshops. But there is also a country game show (*Fandango*), a country sitcom (*I-40 Paradise*), and *Country Sportsman* (duck-hunting with Merle Haggard, for example).

About the only thing on TV that comes close to being a rock version of the Nashville Network is basic-cable USA Network's *Night Flight,* which debuted in March 1981 and beams eight hours of highly eclectic, feature-length music video to over twenty million cable homes each weekend. Produced by ATI Video, *Night Flight's* commitment to range and depth of programming can be illustrated by a brief sampling of some of the programming it's shown: Neil Young's rockumentary *Rust Never Sleeps;* Devo's state-of-the-art, long-form conceptual video *The Men Who Make the Music* (before MTV showed it); the Residents' "One Minute Movies"; *Transes,* the critically acclaimed Moroccan rockumentary (which never got an American distribution deal); a Reggae Sunsplash concert special; and video art by such respected avant-gardists as John Sanborn and Kit Fitzgerald, Dan Reeves, and Ed Emschwiller. There are also experimental films by young filmmakers, VideoWest's music-news magazine *Take Off,* and various camp and cult films and vintage fifties TV shows. (One of *Night Flight's* most popular shows, the exuberantly *outré New Wave Theater,* won't be seen anymore because of the death of its host, Peter Ivers, in early 1983.) On the other hand, *Night Flight* has to constantly repeat a lot of its programming, simply because there isn't that much long-form rock video out there compared to the preponderance of one-song clips. And *Night Flight* has recently taken to running more and more clips anyway, something producer Cynthia Friedland swore the show would never do back in 1981. In fact, in the fall of 1983, *Night Flight* responded to the preponderance of clips shows on cable and broadcast TV by totally revamping its opening music-news segment *Take Off* and making it a series of thematic commentaries on rock-video clip motifs and trends (i.e., politics in rock videos, sex in rock videos, etc.), and inaugurated *Night Flight's Top 10 Video Picks.* Friedland explains, "When we started out, we thought people wanted longer-form programs, but in the wake of MTV and all the other shows like it, audiences seem to want more and more clips. Our audience has changed. Now the clips-oriented shows we run get the best response."

Night Flight had been the most daring and least condescending rock-video outlet, at least in terms of content, this side of *The Cutting Edge.* But with its growing accent on clips, clips, and more clips in late 1983, one had to wonder whether it could still fulfill Friedland's criteria: "*Night Flight* is cultural programming for people whose attention spans run longer than a three-minute video clip." As of this writing, at least, *Night Flight* was set to expand into coverage of ethnic music, with programs on Brazilian music and Nigerian juju (it had already run several salsa programs).

ATI also produces *Radio 1990,* a half-hour, Monday through Friday rock version of *Entertainment Tonight* that debuted in June 1983. *Radio 1990* mixes video clips with rock reportage by famed rock gossip columnist Lisa Robinson. The show is not a bad idea, but Robinson's "news" is no heavier in weight than MTV's music news, and the show could benefit greatly from half the slickness of *Entertainment Tonight.* Robinson *never* shows rock stars in on-camera interviews, instead prefacing her tidbits with a "Rod Stewart *tells* me . . ." or a "Mick Jagger *says.* . . ." Still, USA reports that *Radio 1990* is a big hit with audiences, and as of this writing was ready to expand it from thirty minutes to a full hour.

Night Flight always existed, and still does, as an antithetical alternative to MTV, not as competition. The first cable rock show to come along and blatantly challenge MTV was WTBS's *Night Tracks,* which debuted in June 1983 with six hours of remarkably wide-ranging music-video clips on late Friday and Saturday nights. Its broad eclecticism (belying the fact that its music mix is programmed by veteran AOR-format kings Burkhart-Abrams)—say, a Prince video followed by a Ronnie Milsap video, followed by New Edition, followed by Devo, followed by Barry Manilow—and use of low-keyed off-camera announcers in place of on-camera VJs mark it as a deliberate, direct response to MTV. *Night Tracks* executive producer Scott Sassa readily admits it: "Sure we counter-program against MTV. The one thing we hardly ever play is heavy metal, which is what they play the most. We go for a broad cross-section, because our audience is very broad and diverse. Some people think our format is *too* broad, but people have reacted very positively so far. And no, we won't go with on-camera VJs." *Night Tracks* regularly racks up two or three times the Nielsen ratings of MTV—TBS's audience, roughly twenty-two million, is larger than MTV's.

Also deserving of mention is another Warner-Amex cable service, Nickelodeon, ostensibly a children's programming network, though it happens to show some of the most interesting and rewarding rock on TV, not in the form of video clips, but in its *Livewire* show, for which new music acts turn up to chat candidly with teens and preteens. Nickelodeon also runs big-name rock concerts (i.e., Men at Work, Eddie Money) on its *Special Delivery* show.

In fact, youth-oriented shows actually account for a large chunk of a video tracking sheet like Epic's. Says Carter Merbreier, veteran host of Philadelphia's long-running kid's show *This Is It,* "We began including one rock-video clip in our show in 1982. It quickly became one of our most popular features. The thing is, girls always like to watch things about fashion and housekeeping and all; boys always like things about cars and sports; but the only thing both the girls and the boys like equally is music video."

On July 29, 1983, NBC (with access to over fifty million viewers) threw down the biggest gauntlet yet aimed MTV's way, with the première of its *Friday Night Videos* (*FNV*). With incredible irony, *FNV,* brainchild of *Saturday Night Live* producer Dick Ebersol, replaced *SCTV,* which long before had anticipated MTV with Rick Moranis's Gerry Todd (further irony: *SCTV* went to cable, with pay-service Cinemax). *FNV* goes for the biggest audiences by playing only the biggest-budget, most interesting conceptual clips by the biggest-name rock stars, black and white. If you already had MTV or a comparable cable or local rock video outlet, then *FNV* was old news dressed in the latest, fanciest colors. Indeed, at the precise moment that *FNV*'s announcer was declaring "Beat It," the show's first-ever video, "possibly the most popular video ever," it was being trounced by Def Leppard's "Photograph" on MTV's *Friday Night Video Fights.*

Laugh if you will, but note what NBC programming czar Brandon Tartikoff says: "You have to remember that MTV only has at most fifteen million viewers. We have nearly five times that amount. In a market like Chicago, one of the few major American cities without heavy cable penetration, they don't have any MTV. Now. We'd been losing two million dollars a year on *SCTV;* it was just too expensive to produce, and it wasn't drawing the twelve- to seventeen-year-old audience our advertisers wanted. At the same time, Dick Ebersol came to me with a typed proposal for a show that is basically what *Friday Night Videos* is now. We needed something to replace *SCTV,* and we were already thinking along musical lines; Dick's idea seemed perfect, because we knew MTV was getting hot, music video was an exciting new area, and the price for the programming was right. So, with *Friday Night Videos,* we were hoping for maybe a three rating and a sixteen audience share, which is what *SCTV*'s rating had always been, or something a little higher. For the first show, we got a five point six rating and a twenty-four share. In Chicago, we got a twelve point three rating and a fifty share. I'd call that good ratings. No, I'd call it phenomenal ratings."

FNV itself is slickly produced, all right, with sharp opening computer graphics by England's Cucumber Studios (who also made "Genius of Love," Chaz Jankel's "Questionnaire," and Donald Fagen's "New Frontier") and all those big-money, high-concept clips. The clips were broken up with the "Video Vote," in which viewers dialed phone numbers to pick their favorite of two competing videos; a "Hall of Fame" segment showing a vintage video; an on-the-road interview with a rock star; and a "Where Are They Now?" segment focusing on rock stars of yesteryear.

But the most interesting aspect of *Friday Night Videos* is that it's the first clips showcase to pay record labels for their clips. In fact, NBC has to pay for clips, as they are programming, and the network must fulfill its own network-programming administrative obligations, whereas cable is largely unregulated in this regard. NBC only pays about fifteen hundred dollars per clip (three thousand dollars counting repeat broadcasts; thirty-five hundred dollars for "Authorized Première Videos," *FNV*'s first première video, Elton John's "That's Why They Call It the Blues," had actually already been shown three weeks before on TBS's *Night Tracks*). That's a mere pittance to the network, and to the record labels spending up to ten times that amount to produce a single clip. Still, *FNV*'s administrative stipend may turn out to be some sort of precedent-setting gesture.

Even as *FNV* was premièring, some local shows around the country complained that some labels, mainly Warner Brothers (which had no comment on this), were charging them for clips. As David Kellog, producer of *Goodnight L.A.,* put it, "If labels begin charging low-budget shows like ours for the clips, we'll just have to close down. We can't afford it. The main reason we're on in the first place is that the clips are free programming. But if we had to close shop, the labels would be losing outlets, and losing promotional value, for their clips. They'd be cutting off their noses to spite their faces."

Perhaps. But on the other hand, Robin Williams, producer and host of Ft. Smith, Arkansas's *Rock Image,* says, "Every single record company has been totally cooperative with us. But that may be because, aside from NBC, we're the only rock-video outlet in our area. We don't have any MTV." Scott Sassa of *Night Tracks* might have put it best when he said, "With all these rock video shows proliferating, labels are going to have to start being more selective about giving out clips and/or charging certain places for them. Some sort of priority system is bound to develop." Some record label executives noncommittally echoed Sassa's suppositions, though nobody offered any definitive answers.

Todd Ralston, a DJ at San Diego's XTRA who also produces and hosts the *91X* weekend rock-video show, worries about just such a pecking order: "It's strange for me being both a DJ and a VJ. It struck me as very odd that MTV got the video for the Stray Cats' 'Sexy & 17' before we got the record." In fact, MTV got the video before *any* radio station got the record, simply because the video was released *before* the record to build anticipation for the disc's release. Ralston's worries, however, are still justified: such a move does indicate that video may be superseding radio as a promotional medium.

Meanwhile, with rock-video outlets proliferating, the counterprogramming scramble made for some interesting viewing. For instance, three weeks before *FNV*'s much-ballyhooed debut, MTV instituted its *Friday Night Video Fights* (note name) to compete with *FNV*'s "Video Vote." Def Leppard's "Photograph" took first place for twelve weeks running, over such stiff competition as "Beat It," Bowie's "China Girl," and Duran Duran's "Hungry like the Wolf." The idea of such a contest may seem meaningless, but it at least serves as a handy indicator of what sort of music lovers constitute MTV's core audience. As if the channel's rotation didn't already tell us, that audience (or at least that part of the audience willing and able to make a fifty-cent phone call) consisted of heavy-metal fans. In fact, it took AOR vets Journey, with "Separate Ways," to finally dethrone Def Leppard. MTV's *Basement Tapes* has fulfilled a similarly indicative function: grand prize winner of the first yearly contest was Seattle's Rail, a glitter-rock revival unit, replete with chest-length shag haircuts, form-fitting scooped-out jump suits, and platform boots.

Then again, maybe the *Friday Night Video Fights* and *Basement Tapes aren't* so indicative. Take the case of "Beat It" being trounced by Def Leppard. If Michael Jackson's MTV exposure helped triple sales of his *Thriller* album, that meant that a lot of people watching MTV liked his music and videos. So why did he still lose to Def Leppard? Probably because of the differences between the audience that likes Jackson's music and Def Leppard's fans. Jackson's fans are probably older, more sophisticated; they're more likely to be out somewhere at midnight on a Friday instead of watching TV. Whereas heavy-metal fans are generally younger adolescents who probably *are* home late Friday nights watching their MTV. Besides which, of all the different kinds of rock fans there are, heavy-metal fans are probably the most maniacally devoted, and the most likely to spend fifty cents or more to stuff the phone-in ballet boxes for their idols. Finally, there is the fact that the call-in totals for both the video fights (generally in the 100,000 range) and the *Basement Tapes* (highest total 81,000) represent only a small fraction of MTV's total potential viewers.

And still they kept coming: WABC-NY's *New York Hot Tracks,* a black-music video showcase broadcast live from metropolitan nightclubs and with popular local DJ Carlos de Jesus as host, debuted in June 1983, and by summer's end it had proved to be such a success that it was being syndicated around the country. In September, CBS added its own half-hour weekend *Music Magazine,* a VJs-with-clips show, and NBC brought out another syndicated concert show, *Rock TV.* With such a preponderance, a major shake-out seemed likely because of sheer overkill.

Among the rock shows slated for broadcast syndication in late 1983 and early 1984 were: MCA-TV's *The Pop 'n' Rocker Show,* a rock quiz show with host John "Bowser" Bauman of Sha Na Na; Dick Clark's *Salute,* with old-time rockers feted by current rock guest stars they'd influenced and walk-on celebs (the opening show had Jerry Lee Lewis with guest Keith Richards of the Rolling Stones and Ruth Buzzi); and *Music Guide,* rock's answer to *Sneak Previews,* with rock critics Robert Christgau (*Village Voice*), Steve Pond (*Rolling Stone*), and Mikal Gilmore (*L.A. Herald-Examiner*) to review both rock and pop records *and* rock videos, and with rock-star interviews by Robert Hilburn of the *Los Angeles Times.* And Atlanta's Video Music Channel (AVMC), which had withdrawn from national cable syndication in early 1982 to rework and expand its programming on its home turf, was planning to go back out into possible twenty-four-hour cable syndication. AVMC's playlist has always been as eclectic as that of *Night Tracks,* and if it does happen nationally, it should provide some very interesting competition for MTV.

Two much-anticipated nationwide cable systems in the offing are Apollo Entertainment Network (AEN) and Star Video Music. The former, originally slated to première in early 1983 and pushed back to mid-1984 because of a lack of prospective subscribers, would be the first national, heavy-duty black-oriented music-video network (as of now it plans to be on several hours a day, not twenty-four hours). AEN is owned by Inner City Broadcasting, whose roster of urban-contemporary (or modern black dance music) radio stations includes New York's WBLS, one of the few stations to regularly integrate black and white artists into its playlist. According to one AEN spokesman, AEN will operate the same way: "Like our radio stations, our television network will be a mirror of the contemporary black American musical experience. And that does *not* preclude white artists. So you'll see, say, Talking Heads, David Bowie, and the Rolling Stones as well as Michael Jackson, Rick James, and Grandmaster Flash." AEN also promises to show more than just clips: For three years now it's been renovating Harlem's legendary Apollo Theater as a production facility for original live and taped-live programming.

Star Video Music, produced by Solarvision, Inc., of Dallas, will be an ad-supported basic-cable service that was slated to go on the cable market in late 1983. Star's programming remains nebulous as of this writing, but it promises to range eclectically from rock concerts to

Hollywood musicals, from "the Beatles to Barbra Streisand, from Lionel Richie to Richie Havens . . . stars whose universal appeal crosses all boundaries of age, sex, race, occupation, or political persuasion," according to Star Video Music executive Alvin James, who adds, "we'll format adult contemporary artists, and we won't ignore jazz, reggae, and R&B music. But we will *not* play rock or country—we see ourselves filling the void between MTV and the Nashville Network." And there are sure to be more such narrow-casting music-video outlets in the future.

MTV does not see the preponderance of rock-video shows as competition, and with good reason. "They're *shows,*" says Bob Pittman of MTV, "they're only on once a week. We're a *network,* on twenty-four hours a day. There's really no comparison. If anything, these shows will *help* MTV, by exposing video music to more people, who will then want to see MTV." Scott Sassa of *Night Tracks* concurs: "NBC's show, for instance, will help us rather than hurt us, because it will bring more viewers to their sets to see video music. And in this instant-gratification generation, people will be channel-punching. We'll get seen by more people."

As to the pay-for-play issue regarding promotional clips as programming: for one thing, what with NBC's stipend and Sony selling video singles, the status of rock videos is in a state of flux, which may or may not work itself out. MTV, though, should be the last to come under the pay-for-play gun, because of the repetition factor of its twenty-four-hour rotation and its national-network status. As Robin Sloane of Elektra Records says, "MTV has the rotation, the repetition, it's always there. Repetition is what sells popular music. You can't put a price tag on that."

Or, as Cynthia Friedland of *Night Flight* puts it in succinctly summing up MTV's considerable influence: "MTV is like the Kleenex of music video. When people want a tissue, they ask for a Kleenex. When people discuss music video, they say MTV."

After the shake-out, there will still be much residue. What will it look like? More than likely, rock video will go the way of rock radio: big-time video showcases will get big-budget videos from big-name acts; newer music-video will be broken through an "underground" network of smaller-scale outlets. Video won't kill the radio stars; it will re-create them. Already, Polygram music video chief Len Epand says that the battles between NBC and MTV for rights to world première videos are "amazing, just like what FM stations used to do over a new Led Zeppelin album."

When asked about the future of rock video on TV, the response of EMI's Michelle Peacock typified that of all label executives: "Video's been such a great alternative to radio, I just pray that it doesn't follow in radio's footsteps with that same old rigid format. I hope we don't end up creating another monster." But how could such an attitude be any more than wishful thinking, given the fact that MTV's chief executives come from radio-format backgrounds, and the fact that we've already seen post-MTV rock on TV re-creating the segmented formats?

Now consider what Gerald Casale of Devo says: "It's so funny what happened to MTV. It's like, Einstein comes up with nuclear fission technology, so people sit around and think, 'Now what can we do with this? *Make a bomb.*' The possibility MTV represented in 1981 was incredible. And for its first year or so, we had it, we watched it, it was great—very open-ended, very unpredictable. Nothing like what it is now. What happened was that as soon as money started being the issue, as soon as MTV stopped being this revolutionary, experimental distribution arm for video music, as soon as it was attached to an AOR playlist and had a 'constituency' it was worried about, it became even more conservative than networks with arbitrary censorship. Within one year MTV was reduced to a parody of itself." Of course, Casale is extra bitter about this because when MTV first started with a limited library of clips, it was honored to be able to show many of Devo's groundbreaking videos. After a while, though, there were more than enough rock videos to fill MTV's rotation, and Devo became just another band to MTV.

But Casale's comments, while acerbic, provide substantial food for thought. As he concludes, "Hey, Devo's always had its theory of de-evolution, right? For rock video to go Hollywood the way it has should have been totally predictable, from our point of view. It's just that we as pioneers of music video thought we'd finally be vindicated by something like MTV. Instead, as proponents of de-evolutionary philosophy, we ended up being more right than we ever thought we'd be."

CLUBS

RockAmerica alone now services some 350 rock clubs, and there are several other video pools now competing with RockAmerica: one of them, New York-based Telegenics, specializes in "dance-music video" for postpunk rock discos; another, Sound and Vision, also based in New York, has proposed "ambient" or "mood" tapes for clubs, with sound and originally shot footage spliced together along such thematic lines as "Space," "Fashion," "Sports" (with three subgroups—general, summer, and winter), "Animals," etc. There are now video-only clubs like Revolver in Los Angeles, and Boston's 13UP, run by the Metro's Joe Verange. Any new club that opens these days has video and its own VJ (or VJs) as a matter of course. Some VJs only play the record-company tapes they get in compilation reels from RockAmerica or other such services. Some of them create their own montages of found footage to go with songs spun by club DJs. Back in 1980, for instance, Hurrah and the Ritz in New York were showing an uncredited found-montage video to go with Heaven 17's protest-funk song "We Don't Need This Fascist Groove Thing." The video mainly consisted of repeated shots of Ronald Reagan, Gerald Ford, and Jimmy Carter appearing to either hit themselves in the head or give a Nazi salute.

Some clubs, though, rarely show music videos at all. Mike Overington, VJ at New York's Studio 54, says, "Because we have an eighteen-by-twenty-four-foot screen, the things that work best for us are things that were shot for a big screen. That usually means movies. Things like clips from *Flashdance* are perfect for us. Of course, that was a movie that looked like a rock video; and on the other hand, more and more rock videos are shot on sixteen- or thirty-five-millimeter film and look like movies. So as they come along, we'll show more of them."

Dody Bowers, manager of Washington, D.C.'s preeminent rock venue, the 930 Club, says, "People can watch videos at home on TV, sure, but people also go out to clubs for a certain kind of experience. I don't think that with all the rock video happening on TV, club video should be overlooked or taken for granted. People see going out to a club as a sort of *event,* so everything that happens there is seen differently than when they're sitting at home watching TV. It's important to remember that clubs can play a lot of things that TV can't, and that includes cable TV."

Adds Chipper McKearnin, owner and manager and VJ of Club Maximus in New City, New York (which has over four thousand five hundred clips in its library and frequently takes audience requests for clips), "As far as people who think club video is a burn-out situation, that you can only see a video a few times before you get sick of it, remember that in a club, there are always other distractions as well: you can ignore the screens and get a drink, pick someone up, dance, go watch a band, play a video game, whatever."

Does club video promote records and artists the way MTV does? Definitely. Ed Steinberg of RockAmerica says, "With MTV getting such a high media profile, club video has definitely taken a sort of second-place spot now. But club video is seen by all the labels as a very important marketing tool, especially in early promotion, test marketing, laying a base to break an act, reinforcing MTV exposure, things like that. One company wanted to advertise with RockAmerica, and they commissioned some research that found that over nine million people see RockAmerica tapes each month. That's a lot of people. Record companies respect that."

Adds John Prentice, who runs the Park Avenue clubs in Milwaukee, Detroit, Buffalo, and Orlando, New York, "The biggest effect video's had on our clubs is to introduce our audiences to new music. We're in markets that have traditionally been more mainstream. We went from the big disco scene to a period of transition, and video has been crucial to that transition. When our clubs went with college nights and rock nights with video, we went from a polyester disco crowd to a teenaged rock audience. The college crowd is very wide open; there are people who are very hip to new, comparatively unknown acts, and a whole other segment who are into heavy metal. But with the crowds that obviously didn't listen to new-wave music, video definitely gave that music a new kind of acceptance by adding a visual aspect to it that made it fun. Prior to video, both the disco crowd and the heavy-metal crowd never wanted to know from a bunch of kids with purple hair playing synthesizers. But the videos of those kinds of acts entertain the kids."

Allen Cohen, who owns the 600 North club in Daytona Beach, Florida, has specialized in breaking new music acts in a traditionally staunch, mainstream market. "Down here," he explains, "people are very much into hard rock and heavy metal and Southern boogie rock, from the Allman Brothers right up to .38 Special. At 600 North, we don't even have a DJ, we just have a VJ, and our music always has videos to go with it. We start programming a strong mix of established acts and newer acts from 8:00 to 10:00 P.M., to prepare for our dance hours. Before the dance hours we can experiment, so we try to expose as many new music videos as we can. After we think we've exposed an act enough that way, we'll feature them in a special video night with reduced admission prices. And slowly but surely, we have broken new music acts like Bow Wow Wow, Flock of Seagulls, and Oingo Boingo. And remember that the radio stations here do not play those bands, and there isn't much cable here either, so people are exposed to those acts mainly through the club video. It's a struggle, but it can and does work."

So far, so good. But the pay-for-play specter looms over club video as well as TV. Says IRS Records' Jay Boberg, "If a club like the Ritz

David Bowie and friend paying tribute to *From Here to Eternity,* in one
of the closing scenes of Bowie's "China Girl" video (1983) that had to
be censored for MTV and other outlets—but not for video clubs

in New York has a video night and charges six dollars or eight dollars
admission and gets a thousand customers, which is about half its capacity, then it makes a lot of money. And it doesn't pay us for the clips.
But what am I going to do? Refuse to give it my clips, knowing that
some other label will give it theirs?"

Adds Chipper McKearnin, "I think it's very very wrong that the two
major record-label offenders—Warner Brothers and Capitol/EMI—
are now charging us for their clips. And that they don't supply their
videos to RockAmerica. I want these videos, and my audience wants
them. Once a couple of companies start doing that, the rest of them
might fall into line, and then where will we be?"

Ted Cohen of Warner Brothers' video department, who oversees
distribution of clips to clubs, answers, "The importance of videos is to

be shown. We aren't trying to obstruct that; that'd be a tremendous waste of time and money. But we're spending roughly $350,000 a month to produce and distribute rock videos. All we're trying to do is get a little something back out of it, to enable us to keep producing and distributing, and to maintain quality control of our videos."

Michelle Peacock of Capitol/EMI says, "We put our own video distribution and production department together because, no offense to Ed Steinberg and RockAmerica, we just figured why not do it ourselves and avoid the middleman? We only charge duplication costs, which are minor. And the response has been good from clubs so far."

Another specter looming over clubland is MTV, and televised rock video itself. Explains Steve Sukman of L.A.'s Revolver, "When we started four years ago, rock video was still a novelty. Now it's not. Everyone's feeling obligated to make videos, and they're being seen all over TV as well as in clubs. Now the thing to remember is that in the past, new music has always been broken first through *clubs.* That's not happening so much anymore on a lot of levels. What I see happening now is, MTV will get a video two or three weeks before it goes out to clubs. We have a reputation for showing the latest videos; if a video's already been shown on MTV for a few weeks, people aren't going to come to my club to see it. That hurts me, and it hurts the band as far as their video getting exposure at my club. Take the example of Flock of Seagulls's summer of '83 single, 'Wishing.' That was played more on MTV than in clubs, and it was played on MTV before it was played in clubs. It lost its 'play value' for me, so to speak, so I only used it as filler. It's really down to record companies working out their advance marketing strategies better. Sometimes I get videos for songs that have been in the *charts* for a month already. I feel cheated when that happens, and I know my customers feel the same way."

Ted Cohen of Warner Brothers responds, "It's a very complicated issue for us, especially regarding who gets what out of whatever is recouped from these videos. We're sort of feeling our way along in the dark, so to speak. Even though Warner Brothers formed a video department before most labels did, we're still as much in the dark as anyone else is right now. There are no rules. Nobody knows where it's all going to go."

Club video will surely not die, not soon, anyway, but—contingent upon factors like overall economy, legalities, and the amount of rock on TV—it will go through some interesting changes. At least, club video should become a vital aspect of the "underground" music-video network that will break newer acts—if things get to the point where televised rock video represents the establishment to be attacked and/or infiltrated. And we're already close to that stage.

Then again, this may be as good a place as any to remind you that America is actually behind most of the rest of the world as far as rock video goes. The importance of rock-video shows in places like Europe and Australia has already been mentioned. More recently, in the spring of 1983, RockAmerica sealed a deal with a Japanese firm to send compilations of rock videos on a monthly basis to over two hundred Japanese "music bars." "What they are," says Steinberg, "is not exactly rock clubs, they're a combination of bars, coffeehouses and record stores. They have tables and chairs, people sit around and watch music videos and drink. The Japanese are just nuts about anything American anyway, especially anything rock & roll. There are kids all over Japan dressing in rockabilly drag that puts American neorockabilly kids to shame. Japan just got its first music-video shows earlier in 1983: there's a rock show called *Music Tomato*—don't ask me about the names— and a black-music show called *Funky Tomato*. When they play a video, the next day, like clockwork, people go into the record stores and that record sells out. It happens even faster than in America. I mean it's really a next-day thing. Incredible. Just like in the music bars—the kids watch a music video, and then they buy the record right then and there. Actually, I don't even wonder anymore how long it'll take before America gets like that. It's already happening here at the Tower Records store in New York. They have all these monitors with MTV in there, and I've hung out and overheard kids watching a video and then deciding to buy that act's record."

SOFTWARE

True, there isn't nearly as much rock video available to the buying public on video cassette and video disc software as there are clips being shown on TV and in clubs. But a survey of what is available turns up more product than one might think. There's little use in quoting industry experts on the viability of music-video software: every one of them feels music-video is vital to the future of home-video programming, even though to date music video programs have been far outsold (and out-rented) by movies. But as audio quality on home-video hardware improves—Sony's 1983 introduction of Beta Hi-Fi, followed soon by announcements of comparable VHS improvements, was a major step in that direction—and as MTV and its ilk further promote consciousness of music video, things are likely to improve.

There are two formats for home-video software: video cassettes and video discs. Then there are Beta and VHS video tape formats, and LaserDisc (with shiny metal discs read by lasers that never touch the record, meaning greater durability and dirt-free operation) and CED (Capacitance Electronic Disc, read by a more conventional stylus-to-groove method, and hence cheaper than LaserDisc) video disc formats. Video discs are generally a better medium for music video: they have far superior sound and picture compared to all but the most high-tech and high-priced of VCRs; video discs are also much cheaper than video tapes. Still, VCR penetration in the U.S. has far outpaced that of video discs: there are approximately five million VCRs sold in the U.S., compared to about half a million video disc players.

There are well over a dozen different companies producing home-video music programming; most of them are conglomerates of record labels, film companies, and home-video licensers that create a dense, tangled thicket of associations far too complex to decipher here. Among the companies producing music-video software are: Thorn-EMI Video, Pioneer LaserVision (all but one of whose sixty LaserDiscs are music titles), RCA SelectaVision video discs, Warner Home Video, MGM/UA Home Video, RCA/Columbia Home Video, CBS/Fox Video, MCA Home Video, Media Home Entertainment, Embassy Home Entertainment, etc. The bulk of their music programs are Hollywood musicals and performances by middle-of-the-road pop stars. But there is some rock in there. The best way to survey all of it is either to check your local video store, or to get a comprehensive catalog, the best to date being *The Video Tape & Disc Guide to Home Entertainment* (available by mail order from the National Video Clearinghouse, 100 Lafayette Drive, Syosset, New York 11791). Among the best rock-video programs in long-form (either album-length, or about forty minutes, or an hour long, in general) are:

DevoVision: the Men Who Make the Music (1979): King of the long-form conceptual hill from rock video's ranking pioneers. This one mixes just about all of Devo's classic early-concept clips, live performances from Devo's eye-catching, athletic stage show, sardonic criticism-à-clef of the music business, and de-evolutionary propaganda. It's scabrously knowing and witty, very entertaining, and beautifully put together. The highlight comes early on, when Devo are called on the corporate carpet by Rod Rooter (brilliantly played by Michael Schwartz), Big Entertainment Records executive. Rooter to Devo: "Hiya boys. Locked parts with any female robots lately? . . . Hey, come on, are we not men?" Robert Mothersbaugh, father of Devo lead singer Mark and Devo guitarist Bob Mothersbaugh, also shines with a totally straight-faced performance as Devo, Inc., commandant General Boy. A must-have that is unmatched.

Devo: We're All Devo (1983): About the only thing that does match Devo's first compilation is this, their second, released as a Sony "Video LP," documenting more seminal unforgettables like "Whip It," "Freedom of Choice," "Beautiful World," and "Thru Being Cool." There's also more bizarre music-biz satire involving Rod Rooter, as well as guest appearances by onetime *Saturday Night Live* star Laraine Newman (girlfriend of Devo singer Mark Mothersbaugh) and Timothy Leary (it also includes a couple of clips from *The Men Who Make the Music*).

Grace Jones: a One-Man Show (1982): Jones started out as a fashion model, then became the darling androgyne of the disco era, then successfully crossed over to new-wave funk rock, thanks mostly to clever selections of cover songs and the magnificent musical backing of the Compass Point All Stars funk-rock reggae band, featuring the stellar rhythm team of Sly Dunbar and Robbie Shakespeare. Here, their music is hot as ever, while Jones's vocal delivery, by stark and effective contrast, is icy cool. To go with the great sounds, there's an overpowering visual feast: cryptically provocative vignettes, the expected eye-popping futuristic fashions, and stunning neoconstructivist sets and masks, most set within a beautifully choreographed stage show. Kudos to director —and Jones's packager—Jean-Paul Goude. If not the healthiest, then certainly the tastiest eye-and-ear-candy music video has yet produced.

Elton John: Visions (1982): Album-length concept video with remarkably tasteful and restrained direction by rock video's most over-the-top *auteur,* Russell Mulcahy. The high point is "Elton's Song," a poignantly muted drama of tentative schoolboy homoeroticism that provoked controversy in Britain.

Toni Basil: Word of Mouth (1981): Action-packed, all-singing, all-dancing rock video from the multitalented pioneer, featuring the classic cheerleader-rap "Mickey." Not much in the way of deep substance here, but it is an ebullient, well-crafted treat for the eyes.

Duran Duran (1983): Clips compilation of one of the ultimate rock-video bands. In fact, with Devo, Duran Duran established the two polarities of "ultimate rock-video bands": Devo, the serious, artistic, message-and-content-oriented side; Duran Duran, the vacuous, triumph-of-packaging-as-content side. All of the clips (except the softcore sensation "Girls on Film" by Godley and Creme and Ian Emes's Helmut Newtonesque "The Chauffeur") were directed by Russell Mulcahy, whose mastery of insolent sexuality, manipulative montage, and sheer image overload suits the fashion-plate band perfectly. Highlights include "Hungry like the Wolf," "Rio," and "Is There Something I Should Know?"

Michael Nesmith in Elephant Parts (1981): Equal parts *SNL* and *SCTV*-style mock-TV comedy, and very tasteful, whimsical, well-made music video from one of the pioneers in the field. It was also the first Grammy-winning music video. Full of the smart, friendly wit Nesmith managed to show on occasion in *The Monkees* TV show. The music is in his post-Monkees country-pop vein, though more highly produced. Music video highlights: "Rio" and "Cruisin'."

Olivia Physical (1982): Director Brian Grant demonstrates his incredible versatility in placing pure-pop superstar Olivia Newton-John in a multitude of settings, ranging from the shockingly (for her) hip hilarity of "Physical" to mistier, more domesticated pieces. First video disc to go gold, second Grammy-winning music-video program, first clips-compilation to be shown as a broadcast-syndicated TV special.

Rust Never Sleeps (1979): An exceptional concert rockumentary, not only for Neil Young's superb music (both solo acoustic and raw electric with Crazy Horse), but also for the conceptual touches Young added to the arena-rock context—hugely oversized amps and mikes, "road-eyes" (roadies scurrying about in capes and hoods, with glowing electric eyes reminiscent of characters in *Star Wars*)—which provide subtle evidence of Young's Devo connection. Aside from helping Devo get a record contract, Young also borrowed the title for this program from an advertising slogan Devo's Gerald Casale once wrote for an Akron, Ohio, rust-prevention company; Devo were also supposed to appear in this show, but instead they didn't get together with Young until the latter's antinuclear musical of 1983, *Human Highway.* Young directed under the pseudonym Bernard Shakey, and did a far better job here than on his earlier, obscurantist feature-length movie *Journey through the Past.*

The Tubes Video (1982): Mainly videos from the Tubes' *Completion Backwards Principle,* the album that finally brought them a big audience (thanks mainly to the AOR-styled "Talk to Ya Later"), directed by Russell Mulcahy, whose style here, though typically spectacular and sprawling, is more frenetic and gonzo than lushly cinematic. Also contains vintage performance footage of such early Tubes classics as "Mondo Bondage" and "White Punks on Dope," the only documentation we have of the band's pioneering multimedia stage shows. *Very* loosely conceptualized, but at least Mulcahy keeps the pace moving between production numbers, comedy, and horror-show set pieces. The Tubes are apt on-camera performers.

Making Michael Jackson's "Thriller" (1983): The ponderous, bombastic "Thriller" video itself—in which director John Landis throws Jackson's "Beat It" clip, his own *An American Werewolf in London,* and *Night of the Living Dead* against the wall and tries to make it all stick with big-bucks production values—does not, and probably never could, live up to its considerable ballyhoo. But this behind-the-scenes package is something else again: Jackson is as charismatic as ever, and watching him work out dance routines with choreographer Michael Peters is a treat; seeing how Rick Baker does his transformational makeup special effects is genuinely fascinating; and there's the unintended humor aspect, especially in the eerily smarmy on-set banter between Jackson and Landis, which after a bit begins to seem like a latent *SCTV* sketch—reminding us that, in essence, *Making . . .* is sort of the "Bob Hope Special" of rock video, a vanity production about a vanity production. Plus there are excerpts from "Beat It," Jackson's electrifying version of "Billie Jean" from Motown's twenty-fifth anniversary TV special, and the breathtaking computerized clip for the Jacksons' "Can You Feel It" by Robert Abel and Associates, all of which easily beat out "Thriller" for sheer musical-visual synergistic splendor.

Jethro Tull: Slipstream (1981): Surprise! One of British classical rock's most excessive seventies holdovers actually delivers a classy package, with concert performances of most of their fans' favorites linked by cryptic sci-fi conceptual footage, well-directed by veteran rock-video pioneer David Mallet. For fans of the band, a definite value for the money.

The Best of Blondie (1982): Mixing early and late performance and concept clips, mostly directed by David Mallet or Keefco's Keith MacMillan. Includes the 1981 "Rapture," but the earlier performance clips are just as exciting and have the added historical value of being largely responsible for breaking the band worldwide. Far easier to endure than the pioneering but tragically overdone *Eat to the Beat.*

Queen's Greatest Flix (1982): Performance and concept clips from the veteran hard-glitter-art-rock band. Certainly not to everyone's taste, and generally not a particularly wonderful music video either, but it does contain their vintage "Bohemian Rhapsody" clip.

Mantrap (1983): A fascinating failure, and a possible indicator of future directions. British fashion-band ABC's debut album *Lexicon of Love* serves as the basis for a heavily plotted, sub-feature-length (fifty minutes) extended-concept video. The Hitchcockian spy story has a Soviet lookalike for ABC singer Martin Fry working out a trading-places scheme; the ending is purposefully left ambiguous. Julian Temple, one of rock video's greatest directors, aptly matches the visuals to the mood rather than literal lyrical content of the songs, makes brilliant use of his "Poison Arrow" clip as a Fry nightmare sequence, and generally moves things along well. But his yeoman services are undone by the incredible stiffness of the actors—and that includes more than the band themselves. The fact that Temple had two weeks and a budget under three hundred thousand to shoot it didn't help, either.

New Video from Antarctica: Antarctica is a music-video label formed by now-parted video-art team John Sanborn and Kit Fitzgerald and New York avant-garde musician Peter Gordon. This compilation tape represents the most concentrated package of music-oriented video art available to the paying public as of this writing, and it's almost uniformly excellent as a document of why no less than *Cahiers du Cinéma* called Sanborn and Fitzgerald "unparalleled masters of the video form." They directed all the videos here for various underground artists, including Gordon's icily atmospheric "Antarctica," percussionist David Van Tieghem's delightful "Ear to the Ground" (in which he "plays" the streets of Manhattan), Jill Kroesen's sardonically satiric take on the politics of sexism, "Wilbur Mills Blues," and a short subtitled piece starring new-wave comic Eric Bogosian that Jim Capaldi later used as found visual material for his promo clip "That's Love." Maybe someday Sanborn's stupendous (albeit also stupendously *long*) visualization of New York avant-gardist Robert Ashley's postmodern opera *Perfect Lives (Private Parts)* will see a release to the software market.

As of this writing, other promising long-form conceptual music-video pieces were in the works, including a video album by the Kinks, *Return to Waterloo,* which will be directed by Julian Temple (who's done all the band's videos) and Kinks lead singer Ray Davies, or by Davies himself. Either way, Davies has already proved himself easily the best actor in rock, and his storytelling songs are naturals for video extrapolation.

There are also scads of concert videos around on both video cassette and video disc. Depending on your tastes, you can choose from: Rod Stewart, Stevie Nicks, the Kinks, Fleetwood Mac, Paul McCartney, Paul Simon (with and without Art Garfunkel), Bob Marley and the Wailers, Elton John, Joni Mitchell, the Grateful Dead, the Rolling Stones, the Who, ABBA, Rush, Todd Rundgren and Utopia, Stevie

Michael Jackson and members of the undead from his "Thriller" video (1983), directed by Hollywood filmmaker John Landis. *The Making of "Thriller"* is one of the best-selling pieces of music-video software ever.

Wonder, Edgar Winter, Jimi Hendrix, James Brown (from 1979), Pink Floyd (from the 1971 rockumentary flick *Live at Pompeii*), Earth, Wind and Fire, Ashford and Simpson, Dave Mason, Gary Numan, Alice Cooper, REO Speedwagon, Charlie Daniels, April Wine, the Go-Gos, Cream, Gladys Knight and the Pips with Ray Charles, and on and on. Among the stand-out concert rockumentaries are: *Olivia in Concert*, with dazzling Brian Grant direction; Tina Turner's aptly named *Nice 'n' Rough* with David Mallet's high-impact direction; and *The Who Rocks America: 1982 Tour* (mainly for historical value, as it captures their satellite-simulcast, supposed last concert ever).

There are also pure rockumentaries: historical footage and cultural overviews that go beyond just music into the sociology of style. Some are repackaged theatrical movies; some are original home-video productions. Among the best:

This Is Elvis: Possibly the finest rockumentary ever, giving a fast-moving, richly detailed overview of the history, fact, and myth that were Elvis Presley. Mostly unforgettable stuff, from clips of his 1956 TV appearances to his onstage nervous breakdown at his last-ever concert.

The Early Elvis: Complete versions of what may have been the first instances of rock video—Elvis Presley's smashing 1956 appearances on Dorsey Brothers, Steve Allen, and Ed Sullivan TV shows. Other video cassettes with some of the same classic footage include *Elvis in the 50s* and *Elvis: the Early Years.*

Elvis . . . '68 Comeback Special: In one of the high-water marks of rock performance on TV, Elvis, who had gone Hollywood long before, authoritatively reclaimed his King's crown with this stunning, red-hot performance, perfectly staged and directed by veteran TV-rock director Steve Binder.

Your Hit Parade: From a 1957 kinescope of the show mentioned earlier in this book, featuring the "Silhouettes" concept piece and other nuggets of naive prototypical music-video arcana.

Girl Groups: Based on Alan Betrock's book of the same title, mixing vintage TV clips and more recent interviews to fully live up to its subtitle, "The Story of a Sound." Featured are the Ronettes, Shirelles, Crystals, and more.

The Compleat Beatles: First rockumentary video cassette to go gold, and though it doesn't *quite* live up to its title, it's probably as close as we'll ever come to a comprehensive, digestible account of the all-time pop music phenomenon.

The Kids Are Alright: From Jeff Stein's loving rockumentary film tribute-history of the Who, with highlights including the vintage "Happy Jack" concept clip and a literally explosive performance on *The Smothers Brothers Show,* as well as too-brief glimpses of the band's earliest stage shows.

Jim Morrison: a Tribute to the Doors: Reverse the title and you've really got it. Not quite as comprehensive as the special *No One Here Gets Out Alive* that *Night Flight* has shown, but full of great vintage performance clips, including classics like "Light My Fire," "The End," and "Moonlight Drive." Connoisseurs of early TV rock camp will note that the Ed Sullivan show stage set for "Light My Fire" consisted of, what else, a bunch of doors.

Hullabaloo: A 1965 episode of the classic teen party TV show, featuring the Byrds, the Animals, Paul Revere and the Raiders, and—*gasp!* —Chad *without* Jeremy.

That Was Rock: A compilation of excerpts from *The T.A.M.I. Show* and its concurrent clone, *The Big TNT Show.* Basically marvelous and indispensable, but one *caveat:* For some unknown and inexcusable reason, they cut out James Brown's *T.A.M.I. Show*—stopping "Please Please Please"!

Ready Steady Go!: Fab-gear excerpts from the pioneering British sixties series. As they used to say at the start of this show, "The weekend starts here!"

The Beatles: Magical Mystery Tour: Poorly produced, exceedingly indulgent, difficult to sit through, but still semiseminal, and directed by the band themselves.

Then there are Sony's Video 45s, with two or three songs priced under twenty dollars (most long-form music-video programs are priced between thirty and sixty dollars). Long-form music videos have sold erratically; distributors hope for the inherent repeatability quotient of the music to change that eventually. The same goes for Video 45s. Sony won't quote sales figures, but software chief John O'Donnell claims they've sold better than expected. Reports from the field are contradictory: a Los Angeles dealer reports he's "very skeptical about the market for these . . . we haven't seen much demand yet, and consumers don't get too much for their money"; a St. Louis dealer claims, "Everyone who buys a Sony VCR buys at least one Video 45. Lots of other people do, too, and the market covers all ages, from teens to fifty-year-old men."

O'Donnell also reports that both record labels and superstar artists have been loath to commit to a format they aren't sure will work. As of this writing, Sony was set to release a David Bowie three-song Video 45, which, along with Duran Duran's two-song package, would be Sony's only big-name entry. "I'm dying to get Michael Jackson's 'Billie Jean' and 'Beat It,' " says O'Donnell, "I *know* that'd be an instant smash. But for now it doesn't look like it will happen."

Why are people unsure about Video 45s? For one, there is the usual wait-and-see attitude towards proper penetration of video hardware and affordable pricing of software. Mainly, though, industry insiders wonder whether consumers will want to pay roughly twenty dollars for ten or fifteen minutes' worth of rock video that they've probably already seen loads of times, and may even have taped off television themselves. Here again we can see how rock video merely repeats previous patterns of entertainment-industry give-and-take: When people re-create the "home taping" fears of the early eighties, they ignore some important facts. For one, just because people need to have a VCR to play a Video 45 does not necessarily mean they also have MTV. And, even if they do have MTV and a VCR, they never really know when the clip they may want to copy will come on; if it does come on, they have to be ready with the record and pause buttons on their VCRs, and they are still likely to miss the beginning and/or end of the clip because of MTV's own cuts and dissolves from clip to clip. Furthermore, home-taped clips can't match Sony's Beta Hi-Fi packages for sound quality. In our consumer society, people are conscious of quality. Just as kids outdo each other with higher- and higher-tech stereos and video game setups, they are more likely to be impressed, and hence to want, a complete and unexpurgated clips program that comes in its own handsome packaging. Once again, all of this is highly contingent on overall economic conditions, but if Sony can hold out long enough, and build up a network of cross-merchandising independent distributors, Video 45s just might make it.

Most record executives are guarded in their appraisals of the Video 45 future. But Randy Hock says, "Someone has to take the first step, and Sony's doing it—it's laying a base for what I'm sure is some sort of medium of the future. I can foresee video discs, album-long, selling for ten dollars. That'll wipe audio-only albums out totally. If people can afford music video that way, why should they buy just an old-fashioned audio album when they can have the option of the video at comparative cost?" IRS Records sales and marketing director Randy Freeman adds, "It's way too early to tell how it'll go, but it seems obvious that Sony's laying the groundwork for an entire new music-video industry." Indeed, in the late 1983 IRS started its own in-house home-video company, IRS Video.

The Sony Video 45s released to date are a mixed bag: some established artists, and, commendably, some completely unknown and rather adventurous talent as well. In the former camp: Mike Nesmith's "Rio" and "Cruisin' "; Duran Duran's "Hungry like the Wolf," and (the uncensored) "Girls on Film"; Elton John's "Breaking Down the Barrier," "Just like Belgium," and "Elton's Song"; Rolling Stones bassist Bill Wyman's "(Si, Si) Je Suis un Rock Star," "A New Fashion," and "Come Back Suzanne"; Todd Rundgren and Utopia's "Hammer in My Heart," "You Make Me Crazy," and "Feet Don't Fail Me Now"; Rundgren's own *Videosyncracy,* with "Hideaway," "Can We Still Be Friends," and "Time Heals"; and Rod Stewart's "Do Ya Think I'm Sexy," "Young Turks," and "Passion."

More exciting are Sony's more adventurous releases: Scottish video artist Jesse Rae's "Rusha" and "D.E.S.I.R.E."; New York State conceptual comedy band Blotto's hilarious "Lifeguard," "Metalhead," and

"I Quit"; and the *Danspak* tape, with four New York technopop artists aptly complemented with video by Merrill Aldighieri and Joe Tripician (whose backgrounds include PBS, *The Muppets,* and being VJs at Hurrah in the late seventies) that confidently straddles mainstream music-video and more avant-garde video art. Sony has also marketed some jazz "Video LPs" (actually not much longer than Video 45s; the generic name here merely reflects the fact that rock is still a singles medium, while jazz is not) by the big bands of Lionel Hampton, Bill Watrous, and Rob McConnell.

Finally, there are two other rock-video cassettes well worth mentioning:

Dire Straits: Making Movies (1981): A virtual prototype of Sony's Video 45s, as it contains only three songs (though they run a total of twenty-one minutes, whereas Sony's three-song Video 45s generally total less than fifteen minutes); however, it's priced more in line with long-form cassettes (that is, in the range of twenty-five to thirty dollars). At any rate, the videos are stunning: British commercials director Lester Bookbinder applies the high-contrast, superreal colors of European TV commercials to painterly compositions that are breathtakingly suspended somewhere between representational literalism and moody abstraction. Most impressive is the gorgeous "Skateaway," the only one of these three to get any MTV exposure.

Ralph Records Video Vol. 1 (1982): First off, this compendium of music video by America's strangest independent label includes the Residents' classic "Land of 1,000 Dancers," so it's indispensable. But it also includes more fine Residents videos: the otherworldly photo montage "Hello Skinny," and the "One Minute Movies," in beautiful living color, codirected with Graeme Whifler, still as bizarre and dreamlike as ever; plus Whifler's disturbingly madcap videos for Snakefinger, Tuxedomoon, and Renaldo and the Loaf. Something completely different, for just thirty dollars. Not sold in most stores, but available by mail from Ralph Records, 109 Minna, #391, San Francisco, California 94105.

SIMULCASTS

Simulcasts are made possible through satellite technology. On-location cameras beam the signal up to a satellite; the signal is beamed back to various "downlinks," or satellite receiving dishes at locations showing the simulcast, where the signal is transmitted back into a video image that can be seen thousands of miles away from the point of origin.

Locations able to receive satellite simulcasts are divided between public facilities—municipal auditoriums, sports stadiums, concert halls and large clubs, college campus gymnasiums or performance centers, etc.—and homes outfitted with "addressible converters" for translating the satellite signal. Between public and private locations, the total "universe" for satellite simulcast events—they have mostly been sports, especially boxing matches—is substantial. Satellite-simulcast events are known as "pay-per-view" events, since viewers pay a special one-time-only charge to receive the programs. This is to differentiate such events from satellite-delivered subscription-TV services.

The first pay-per-view satellite simulcast rock concerts took place in 1980. Japanese electropop band Yellow Magic Orchestra played a concert in Los Angeles in October 1980 that was simulcast live to Tokyo and New York. That same month, the Grateful Dead's concert at Radio City Music Hall in New York was simulcast to more than a dozen cities from the East Coast to the Midwest. The Dead simulcast was handled by John Scher's Monarch Productions, which booked acts into the Capitol Theater in Passaic, New Jersey, and which more recently was producing concert shows for the syndicated concert program *Rock TV* on MTV. For five years prior to the Dead simulcast, Monarch had been simulcasting Capitol stage shows on a large rear-projection screen to the back rows of the theater, and taping concerts that were then partially licensed to broadcast TV (e.g., a Capitol show by Bruce Springsteen that was widely shown in 1980, and that featured the memorable shot of one female front-row patron leaping onstage to give Springsteen a lingering soul kiss). The Dead simulcast was only partly successful because, as a Monarch staffer explained at the time, "there was confusion in the advertising since the simulcast was licensed out to individual promoters in each different city where it was sent. Even in New York it was hard to tell if the concert was *originating* in New York or just being received there. So most venues didn't sell out. But audience response was very favorable, very encouraging. Touring might get very very costly, to prohibitive levels, in the future, and simulcasts seem like a good alternative."

That's what a lot of people thought, but since that time, there have only been a handful more rock simulcasts. Basically, it simply seems to be a matter of the rest of the world—as in promoters, local distributors of addressible converters, etc.—catching up with the satellite technology. Touring costs *are* getting prohibitive, and more recent rock simulcasts have garnered gratifying audience response.

The first truly large-scale rock simulcast pay-per-view concert was by the Rolling Stones on December 18, 1981. The show, originating in Hampton, Virginia, was beamed out to some one hundred ninety-five thousand viewers in some fifty locations around the country. The Stones themselves produced it along with their parent label at the time, Atlantic Records; it was distributed and exhibited by the multi-faceted Oak Media, who also have the ON-TV satellite-subscription TV network (with half a million viewers, mainly in Los Angeles and Chicago), and who produce clips showcases, concert, and music-news shows for ON-TV and other broadcast and cable outlets. More recently, Oak participated in the simulcast to America and Europe of Diana Ross's summer 1983 concert in New York's Central Park, which was also simulcast on the pay-cable network Showtime.

In October 1982, the Campus Entertainment Network (now known as Campus Network), in conjunction with the Black Tie Network (a production company specializing in pay-per-view events), simulcast a Halloween Devo concert from Los Angeles to fifteen college campuses (total audience roughly six thousand) around America, in 3-D yet. Two months later, they joined forces again to simulcast the Who's alleged last concert ever from Toronto, which has since been released as a home-video cassette and disc. The Who simulcast went to thirty-seven public facilities, totalling fifty thousand viewers; thousands more picked it up at their homes. A spokesman for Campus Network (which now serves fifty campuses with a basic-cable entertainment channel featuring music video, and a pay-cable service for colleges with simulcast concerts, Broadway shows, and speakers, as well as movies and preproduced features) says, "Our research indicated that the Who simulcast got a tremendous response from the people who saw it. Seventy percent of the pay-per-view audience said they felt they were at a live show, not as if they were watching a concert on tape; and seventy-two percent thought seeing it simulcast was better than being at the show itself."

It is highly doubtful that "electronic touring" (as a Campus Network spokesman calls simulcast concerts) will replace extensive touring. It is, on the other hand, likely that as technology progresses, simulcast concerts will occur more and more as big-event adjuncts to tours by bands successful enough to merit a pay-per-view simulcast. Case in point: in September 1983, MTV announced that on December 6, 1983, it would present a live stereo worldwide simulcast of AOR heavyweights Asia from Tokyo's famed Budokan, in conjunction with Geffen Records (Asia's label) and Sun Artistes, Ltd. (Asia's management company). The program, titled "Asia in Asia," was to include a feature documentary on the band, the concert itself, and live backstage coverage before and after the show, with an MTV VJ on hand as host. Three different satellites were to transmit the show, potentially all over the world, and it would be simulcast in stereo to participating radio stations worldwide by Westwood One. Asia themselves did a special in-studio spot on MTV to announce the show. Brian Lane, Sun Artistes president, commented, "We chose MTV for this event because, until the advent of MTV, television was not a medium for rock & roll. MTV has changed all that, which in turn changed our attitude toward undertaking a project of this scope."

What Lane didn't say was that Asia—like such other megastar acts as David Bowie and the Police—had a hard time selling out their mammoth stadium dates on their American tour in the dog days of summer 1983, and that Asia actually canceled the last half of their U.S. tour to "prepare" for the simulcast, which was still over two months away. Undoubtedly, the band perceived such a mammoth "electronic tour" as the "Asia in Asia" simulcast as a quick and efficient way to reach the millions who may not have paid top dollar to see them live in a huge arena. If a band the stature of Asia must resort to such measures, then maybe electronic touring *will* phase out live concerts on some levels.

THE VIDEO JUKEBOX

Remember the Panoram Soundie and the Scopitone? Jack Millman does. Millman is president of Video Music International (VMI), a Los Angeles company that in 1982 introduced its Startime Video Muzzikboxx, the machine that brings the clunky Soundie/Scopitone concept sleekly into the space age. Standing six to seven feet high, with a twenty-six-inch TV screen enclosed in a high-tech-deco cabinet, this new video jukebox uses state-of-the-art computer-controlled video tape gadgetry to select from as many as forty to fifty different video clips, at fifty cents a clip. As of this writing, VMI had contracted virtually every major record label, as well as many vital independents, for software deals; there were some three thousand Startime Video Muzzikboxxes set up in bars, clubs, restaurants, laundromats, schools, bus and train stations, and airport lounges in the U.S., Britain, Canada, Australia, and the Philippines. Millman figures that "by 1985, the number of video jukeboxes around the world should roughly equal the number of jukeboxes there were at the height of the jukebox

That's Olivia Newton-John, as seen on the screen of Video Music International's Startime Muzzikboxx, a video jukebox you may be seeing a lot more of in the future.

era in the late fifties and early sixties—five hundred thousand units."

VMI compiles roughly a half-dozen different two-and-a-half-hour video-music-clip cassettes per month, distributed to on-site operators for two hundred dollars a month. Record labels supplying promo clips for use in the jukeboxes receive a ten percent royalty share of the per-month per-site operator fees. Jukebox rights have also been obtained from licensers ASCAP and BMI. The royalty is the kicker, though: In the eyes of record companies, that spells revenue, as in direct payback for promotional clips. "With increased penetration of the jukes," says Millman, "the multiples could be staggering, and could mean *great* potential revenue to the record labels."

If that isn't enough to spell near-guaranteed success, VMI's video jukeboxes will also have a second reel of taped commercials, to be played constantly while the juke is inactive, and while its random-access hardware is searching out selections between video clips. According to Millman, "we especially want to seek out advertisers in the two most restricted areas, liquor and tobacco, as well as soft-drink makers, movie and record companies, etc. I think the true power of this machine is as a service to the advertising industry. It represents the first-ever connection between Madison Avenue and the coin-operated world."

In the summer of 1983, New York-based Video Juke Box, Inc., unveiled prototypes of its own video jukebox in New York City and Ft. Lauderdale, Florida. This machine uses large-screen projection systems, and video *discs* instead of tapes, which means more trouble-free operation and the added advantage of no rewind time (laser discs have access to any selection anywhere on the disc instantly). The discs can hold up to ninety-six titles, though as of this writing, Video Juke Box President Joseph Reilly hadn't yet made any software deals with record labels. On the other hand, in line with more expensive video disc hardware (as opposed to cheaper video disc software), the machines cost a minimum eighteen thousand dollars apiece, whereas VMI's cost from seven thousand dollars to fifteen thousand dollars. Still, the disc-driven video juke, like VMI's, serves up clips at fifty cents a play. Reilly foresees his units in hotels, resorts, video-game arcades, airports, and especially in smaller-town bars and discos. A problem with the machine has been in convincing vending machine distributors to go with it. They're not willing to part with traditional music-only jukes, which are cheaper, and to try out something basically untested. Reilly believes music-only jukes are a thing of the past. His unit can also be hooked up to cable TV or closed-circuit simulcasts, and he can see the day when one club will have a show and it will be piped into other clubs everywhere via the juke.

Some of you may remember an old country song called "Hey Mister, That's Me Up There on the Jukebox." In the future, that will carry a somewhat different meaning—thanks to the rock-video explosion.

VIDEO KILLED THE RADIO STAR: MUSICIANS AND ROCK VIDEO

Rock videos promote record sales and give musicians instant exposure to potential audiences numbering in the millions. Interestingly, the range of reactions from musicians towards video is as wide as the range of musicians on video. There are some who could not care less either way. There are some who like the idea and take a passing interest in it, or who remain perplexed by it. There are those who resent it. There are others who make their own music and their own videos, and who see each as logical extensions of the other. There are those who see "acting" in rock videos as a welcome challenge, or a potential pain in the neck, or as no big deal at all, or as something they've all wanted to do. There are bands who work as equals with directors, those who just make sure their ideas are communicated to the director, and those who just show up for a shoot and let the director do all the work.

But how does rock video affect the *music*? Certainly, readers need not be reminded of the profound power of the television medium, nor that it's a "cool" medium, mandating passivity, while pop and rock music, for all their inherent abstraction, are "hot"—inspiring movement (is it really possible to dance while watching videos?). Another thing about rock videos on TV: Since TV's always had inferior sound until very recently, we've been trained to fix on the visuals before the audio; in a sense, rock videos can reduce a song to the level of a film's soundtrack, where it operates on a more subliminal level. Accordingly, rock video can short-circuit critical and analytical faculties, rendering them moot and powerless in all but the most doggedly skeptical cases. Too often, it seems the power of rock video is to sucker us in on mediocre music against our better judgment. To suspicious critics, MTV is the greatest such culprit. Of course, in the same regard, the music industry sees MTV as a snake-oil-selling savior. Certainly, MTV has already helped level mass tastes, and at least until something comes along to challenge its hegemony, we'll be largely at the mercy of MTV's lowest common denominator.

But there's much more to it than that. As Randy Newman puts it: "There are a lot of pretty women, pretty men on MTV. And yeah, I watch it, and it's pleasant to look at. But I mean, if the pretty people are the ones who are granted access to that powerful medium . . . You know, a picture is worth a thousand words, right?"

This leaves him, like many rock stars and rock performers who, like Newman, aren't conventionally considered "stars," at the mercy of the image-mongering *auteurs.* And some rock stars aren't so sure about all that. Take Rod Stewart—a genuine star. During the shooting of his "Baby Jane" video with Steve Barron, Stewart was heard (on ABC's *20/20*) grumbling, "These directors making these promos, it's like they're filming *Ben Hur* or *Gone with the Wind,* you know? I have no idea what's going on on the set, what they're doing has *nothing* to do with the song . . . but then we can't worry about that, now can we?"

Barron himself retorts, "I know what Rod said, but his comments were sort of taken out of context. Actually, he was being very straightforward—he didn't understand what was happening on the shoot, but it's hard for anyone without filmmaking experience to understand the logistics of a shoot. And he's right, the video had little or nothing to do with the song. What do close-ups of ladies' high-heeled shoes and smashing chandeliers have to do with a love song? Hell, *I* don't even know. That's just the way it went. But Rod wasn't really put off by it —just a little mystified, that's all. Which is normal."

Or as John Oates of superstar blue-eyed-soul duo Hall and Oates told *Newsday* in 1983, "We're very aware of the power of video, and it's a great medium and a great tool, but we're also very wary about the video *dictating* what the song should be about. It's one thing to enhance the emotion of the song. But the music itself should always come first."

Adds lead singer Sting (Gordon Sumner) of supergroup the Police (who's also acted in films *Brimstone and Treacle* and *Dune*), "I really don't like narrative in video, where you're given a very definite story line and told what to think. To me, that defeats the whole purpose of shooting a piece of music, because it robs the viewers of their imagination.

British new-music star Peter Godwin—whose seven-hundred-dollar video of "Images of Heaven" got heavy rotation on MTV in 1982, and whose song "Criminal World" was covered by David Bowie on *Let's Dance*—speaks the mind of a younger, more media-weaned generation when he explains, "Yes, a video *could* fix an abstract song to specific imagery, and that could make people angry or whatever. But it doesn't have to be like that. A video can just be a different experience. I enjoy 'China Girl' by David Bowie, I enjoy it by Iggy Pop, and I enjoy Bowie's video of it, all as separate experiences. I could be tired of the song but enjoy the video, or I could be tired of the video but enjoy the song. They're different experiences, so why not have more? Why have less? Why not have more choice? It's not limiting you to see a video, not really. I think if people say that, it's more a reflection on them than on the video."

On the other hand, August Darnell—the fashion-conscious leader of rap-funk-calypso-pop troupe Kid Creole and the Coconuts—wonders, "The attention that used to be devoted to the content and form of a song now seems to be given over to the visual presentation on the whole, and the video in particular. I mean, I know I've always been into dressing sharp, so I'm one to talk, right? But I think if songwriters compose with the video in mind, that could downgrade the quality of the song itself —if a certain phrase or image in a lyric doesn't quite fit, people might let it go and say, 'It's okay, we'll fix it in the video.' Before you know it, you might be writing a song, thinking, 'How can I get this on MTV?' Instead of thinking, 'How can I please myself as an artist with this?' "

Counters Michael Cotten, keyboardist with the Tubes—who were greatly aided by MTV exposure of their "Talk to Ya Later" and "She's a Beauty" clips but who had been experimenting with video in stage shows long before there was MTV: "It seems as if the idea of doing a video as a matter of course now with a record has to do with what happened when talking movies came in to replace silents. Maybe rock videos are the 'lookies' of today. A lot of people say how certain silent film stars died out because they had squeaky voices. But look at all that was gained with talking pictures. Now people say that if artists can't get over visually, they might be left by the wayside. It *is* a tragedy to lose artists like that to a new movement, but I think you have to look at what's *gained* with the new movement. That's the payoff. We're going to see a new kind of artist."

Some artists have held back longer than most from making a rock video. Veteran hard-rocking street-poet Bob Seger is one. As he puts it in an interview in *Musician,* "I want to do something special when I finally make the video move, something on a good-sized scale. I've watched MTV, and it's interesting, but the thing I hate about it is that there's no black music or R&B on it unless it's syrupy stuff. Where are Marvin Gaye and the rappers?" Seger finally did make his move into rock video in September 1983 with "Makin' Thunderbirds." While hardly an exceptional rock video, it was nicely understated and carried a strong-but-subtle sociopolitical message with its dissolves to Detroit automobile assembly lines (actually an echo of the naively surreal clip that Martha and the Vandellas did for "Dancing in the Streets" in 1965).

Others, like Shalamar, have changed their attitude towards video and have been rewarded with a hit. In this case, "Dead Giveaway." As Shalamar's Howard Hewitt explains, "Back when we made the 'Night to Remember' video, making a video was no big deal, just something you had to do. We shot that video and the 'I Don't Want to Be the Last to Know' video in the same day for something like twenty-five thousand dollars, total. And they were real static and shot on video tape; they looked like TV soap operas. But between then and 'Dead Giveaway,' we went through some changes, which the 'Dead Giveaway' video and *The Look* reflect. For one thing, we were *huge* in England, a much bigger deal than here. And from touring there a lot, Jeffrey [Daniel] and Jody [Watley] especially really got into the whole music and fashion thing happening there. It was a natural evolution for us. With *The Look,* we decided to make the move in that direction, with the music and the look of the band. The 'Dead Giveaway' video was shot in London over two or three days, and it cost about thirty-five thousand dollars. That alone shows how much things changed in a few years.

"The 'Dead Giveaway' video was directed by Bill Parker, who more or less came up with the concept. He and I were in this room backstage one night before a show, with a tape of 'Dead Giveaway' playing, and we were plotting the video scene by scene on index cards. Now, the lyrics of the song have this line, 'How long you gonna keep up this one-on-one charade?' We were trying to think up a concept for the video, and Bill just said, 'What about a "Madame X" espionage kind of thing?' And it just clicked. It was my idea to have the shot at the end where the woman drops her mask, and you see it shatter, and then you see that it was just Jody all along."

Shalamar had indeed effected a smashing crossover—though in this case, more through organic evolution than contrivance—and with strong MTV rotation, and with the video's being played on black-music-video outlets and as well as in dance clubs, "Dead Giveaway" and *The Look* both zoomed into the Top Twenties of both the black and pop album and singles charts, giving Shalamar their first crossover hit.

Brian Eno is a different fish in another kettle. Not a rock star, really, but an influential fringe figure, Eno started in rock with British fashion-forward band Roxy Music, then made such memorable avant-rock solo albums as *Taking Tiger Mountain by Strategy* and *Another Green World*. In the late seventies, he became an auxiliary member of influential new-wave band Talking Heads, and produced a series of "ambient" background-music albums. At that time he also showed a series of "ambient" music-video tapes at the Kitchen, a New York artists' space devoted to avant-garde video and to performance and conceptual art. The tapes consisted of static shots of an apartment building, the camera never moving, with subtle colorization effects injected every hour or so, all to the "tune" of the looming, distanced, celestial sighs of Eno's synthesized "discreet music." It was interesting, yes, but also much like watching paint dry.

"All you get in rock videos today," Eno told *The Face,* "are these amateur filmmakers, and all they know is how to do everything to a technically high standard and use all the latest tricks and effects. I hate rock videos. They're despicable. The good thing about them may be that the new video technology is being exorcised in this rush of gratuitous imagery. Maybe if people get all that crap out of their systems, something good will eventually come of it."

Even a more or less middle-of-the-road rock star who's benefited from MTV exposure can be suspicious of the typical aesthetics of big-budget rock videos. Take Huey Lewis, leader of the successful pop-rock band the News and whose 1982 Top Ten hit "Do You Believe in Love?" was helped along by a limpidly comical video in which Lewis and the News crooned to a woman sleeping obliviously in her bed.

"That video was basically my idea," says Lewis, "and it was supposed to be funny, you know, we're there singing to her and she doesn't know it, she's ignoring us, and when she finally does get up she goes

Randy Newman and friend cruising the city they adore in "I Love L.A."
(1983), directed by Randy's cousin, Tim Newman, the commercial
director who also did ZZ Top's most successful videos. Randy remains
suspicious of rock video—perhaps because this clip, though popular,
still failed to boost his record sales in a big way.

and makes coffee and keeps ignoring us. So then we had some Hollywood director there to express these ideas to. He was supposed to get
it translated properly onto the video, but I think he blew it. The point
of that video was that I was trying to wake the girl out of a dream, and
she never really wakes up out of it. But everyone I talk to missed that.
Somehow we didn't get it right. So I consider that a failure that I'm not
proud of, even though it did get on MTV and it did help sell more copies
of the record and all that.

"The thing is, I really hate the way that was produced. All that
rouge-on-the-cheeks, glossy pastel production crap, real Hollywood—
to me that stuff is totally cringe-worthy. I see myself as a real, street-
level rock & roller, not some pretty boy in makeup posing for the
camera. But with MTV and all, it's a real double-edged sword. I mean
it *is* a very powerful and important medium. Video's a whole other
thing. It's always a challenge just to make a record, and now we have
to deal with video. It's another creative challenge, which is cool. But
now everyone's making videos; there are so many out there that it's
harder and harder to get something that'll look distinctive."

Lewis adds, however, that on his next album, *Sports* (1983), he wrote at least one song with the video in mind. That song is "I Want a New Drug." "When I was writing it, I kept visualizing all these things . . . the song is antidrug, it's saying the new drug I need is *love*. So I kept imagining things drugs do to you that are lousy and writing lines to describe these visuals I was flashing on: there's a line, 'I need a new drug, one that won't make me crash my car.' And there's a line, 'one that won't make me feel three feet thick'—that's the Alka-Seltzer guy on TV, when they make the people with indigestion get all round and fat and bloated out? So in that case, a lyric to a song came from a TV image. That happened to work out fine. But I don't know about making it a practice to write every song with video in mind. . . ."

On the other hand, Bono Vox, lead singer of U2, asserts, "I always have visual images in mind when I write lyrics. Most of our songs have very cinematic imagery. I think *most* bands probably write songs with visuals in mind. In lyrics, you're usually describing things, mental pictures. It's not a very great leap to actually visualize them."

And then there are the bands who seem tailor-made for rock video: visual-conscious bands with a message, like Devo; image-conscious pretty boys, like Duran Duran; compulsive character actors, like David Bowie; inveterate storytellers like Ray Davies of the Kinks; media children like Thomas Dolby, who sees music and video as equal halves of a dynamic whole; and many more. What do they think of the brave new video wave?

"It always bothers me when I'm listed somewhere as an 'EMI recording artist,'" says Dolby. "That's only part of it. To me, involvement with video is only natural. When I write music I always have images in my head, so the songs are really soundtracks to my internal movies. Now I have the opportunity to externalize those movies. I think visuals are very important and that more artists will emerge who will stimulate their audiences in a visual and dramatic way rather than just with music. I think there are probably plenty of other 'recording artists' out there who'd love to make their own videos as well, but maybe they're intimidated by the technology of filmmaking or something. Gaining hands-on familiarity *is* important, but that still shouldn't stop bands from getting more visually oriented. Aside from continuing to make my own music and videos, I'm going to start making videos for other bands, too. I'd also like to get into multimedia musical theater."

Dolby's first efforts were impressive: "She Blinded Me with Science," with its slapstick twitting of British academic types and silent-movie title cards, was a big MTV hit; his self-directed, long-form home-video rockumentary *Live Wireless* is one of the better entries in the field; his early 1984 clip for "Hyperactive!" was a quantum leap beyond both.

Simon LeBon, Duran Duran's lead singer: "We're obviously very highly conscious of the visuals; it's as much a part of what we're about as the music, our clothes, the way we move. . . . It's all part of the whole."

One new kind of music-video artist is Toni Basil. Her parents were in vaudeville and big bands; she was a cheerleader at Las Vegas High. She assisted David Winter in choreographing *Shindig!* and *The T.A.M.I. Show;* she did choreography on Elvis Presley's movie *Viva Las Vegas;* she appeared in *Easy Rider* and avant-garde filmmaker Bruce Conner's *A Movie;* she choreographed David Bowie's *Diamond Dogs* stage extravaganza in 1974; she discovered pioneering L.A. street dancers the Lockers and with them made protean dance-rock videos for *Saturday Night Live;* she was the first music-video artist to sign a recording contract as such, in 1979.

Basil's long show-biz history, her work within the proscenium arch of staged performance, surface tellingly in her videos. There's no "puzzling evidence" here—just all-singing, all-dancing, bubbling, high-energy fun in a *That's Entertainment* tradition. Basil's avoidance of stilted image-mongering flash in favor of healthy, kinetic vitality marks her as a refreshing and important exception to the rock-video rule. Her classic "Mickey" is the penultimate example of her capacity to delight the eye and ear without ever getting too heavy.

Her work on "Once in a Lifetime" for Talking Heads, though, is classic in a different vein: choreographed, yes, but full of David Byrne's own enigmatically personal imagery and movement, while never gratuitously cryptic. "Those were all David's ideas," says Basil, "I was just there to help him translate them onto tape as best as possible."

For Basil, "My videos represent the culmination of an eighteen-year career. They are all-consuming for me, like monsters that create themselves; I get very compulsive with them. Most of the *Word of Mouth* videos were shot two or three in a day. The total budget for that was ninety thousand dollars. Though everyone says my videos are all about fun, and they basically, sort of are, I still see them as art pieces. They also happen to fulfill a promotional function. I take my work very seriously, although that doesn't necessarily show in the finished product. To me, taking your work seriously means you aren't afraid to be humorous or fun; some people think if they do that in a video, people might see them as clowns or something. I don't think that's true."

As of this writing, Basil was hard at work on more music and more videos. Her big idea was "to do an all-girl version of 'Beat It.' That'd be a real kick."

Even a merely image-conscious rock star of the ostensibly "old generation" like British rocker Billy Idol has more to say about his input into his videos than one might suspect. "I don't know if I'd call videos art," says Idol, "but I do see them as much more than just promotion. They're statements about me. And as such, they're very important to me. I don't just look at them as 'Oh right, I show up here at this time and they point me at the camera.' I work very closely with the directors —David Mallet for 'White Wedding,' Tobe Hooper for 'Dancing with Myself'—and they work closely with me to make sure that the video projects something that satisfies me. I wrote 'White Wedding' after my sister got pregnant and got married, thinking marriage would make it all okay. So the song was a direct and sarcastic reaction to that, a nasty put-down of the idea of marriages for convenience, that then got extended to a black-humored vision of weddings in general. The point of the song and the video is that people can be so *cruel* to each other. A lot of people missed the point of that video. They think I'm the instigator of all this cruelty to the girl, but actually I'm always commenting from the sidelines in it, I'm never the focus of the action and the cruelty. That misinterpreting, though—it can happen with songs as well as with videos. You can't be too bothered by it. You just try to do the best you can. . . . The way I do that is to maintain as much artistic control over the video as I can, which means either *I* come up with the concepts or *I* approve what the director comes up with. In 'White Wedding' and 'Dancing with Myself,' me and Mallet and me and Tobe had equal input. The main message to 'Dancing with Myself' is in that big red banner with Oktobriana on it. She's this Russian comic-book character, sort of a Soviet Wonder Woman, who represents all that was good, and all that was lost, about the October Revolution. I specifically wanted to have her in there, to promote awareness of what she's about. And there was one shot where I walked through a door and there was a red neon sign above it. Well, I made sure it wasn't just *any* red neon squiggle, but a Russian constructivist graphic design, to maintain that continuity with Oktobriana. Aside from that, the thing with the zombie kids climbing up the building, well, to me that's about a positive life force coming out of me and my music that liberates people, again in the Oktobriana spirit of things. My energy rejuvenates these mutant kids in this sort of postapocalypse world of theirs. And you notice that after they get blown off the roof once by my energy bolts, they climb up and *don't* get blown off again. That's part of the positive aspect of it.

"Basically, there *is* some pretty deep symbolism in there, and it's private symbolism, but I just have to go with my own instincts on what I want the video to be, and it should complement the song, not be something totally unrelated to the song that just looks pretty. Those clips do relate to the songs, I think. And hopefully people out there can see them and put it together themselves. Aside from that, what worries me about something like MTV is that when a clip of yours gets on there, people see it for a while, and they tend to identify you just by that, 'cause the medium *is* so powerful. So for the longest time everyone seemed to think that Billy Idol was 'Mr. White Wedding.' Well, I'm not—that's just one part of me. That to me is the real danger of rock video, that you have one image that people see over and over."

Midge Ure, singer and guitarist with British electropop band Ultravox, also seems to embody the "new artist." Like Thomas Dolby, Ure now directs his own videos for Ultravox, and has made clips for other artists like Fun Boy Three, Bananarama, Phil Lynott, Visage, and Monsoon.

"We've always had a great interest in visuals, me and our bassist, Chris Cross," explains Ure. "We've always been into photography, graphics, designs, and we've always designed our own album covers, our own stage sets, and all that. Writing songs, we've always had visuals in mind, so in effect, we were composing soundtracks for films that we weren't able to make just yet. We made our first videos with Russell Mulcahy, who's brilliant, and from whom we learned an awful lot. On the first one, 'Vienna,' we gave him ideas and he translated them. On the next few, 'The Voice' and 'The Thin Wall,' we gradually took a stronger and stronger hand in the direction, until Russell just said, 'Look, you guys don't really need me anymore, do you?' And though we were a bit scared at first, he was right. And we made our next clip, 'Reap the Wild Wind,' ourselves. It was a natural progression for us.

"It gets very disturbing and weird to find bands who are in control of their music but who don't care to control any other aspect of themselves. I mean, Fun Boy Three came to us and just said, 'Right, make us a video.' They left it all down to me! For *their* music! It makes me wonder . . . maybe it has to do with the fact that the production process of films and videos is still sort of mystified and kept behind closed doors. It used to be that way with record production as well, but more and more bands have gone in the booth and seen that it's not that hard once

In a direct homage to Roman Polanski's *Repulsion,* threatening arms emerge from the walls of a hallway to grapple for the hero of Ultravox's "The Thin Wall" (1981), directed by Russell Mulcahy. Ultravox's Midge Ure, who's gone on to direct several videos for his own band as well as other artists, readily cites Mulcahy's influence.

you get your hands on the machinery, and they've produced their own records. The next step is for them to do the same with video."

And yet, for someone so shocked by the cavalier attitudes of bands towards making videos, Ure himself does not go in for analyzing the imagistic content of videos too deeply: "I think they've been way too overanalyzed. They're basically just advertisements. You can either make it crass and vulgar like 'Ring around the collar,' or you can do it tastefully and with a certain standard of quality that remains true to your artistic expression. You don't have to overanalyze a pop promo to see that it's well done and effective, and that's all that matters."

So far, Kevin Godley and Lol Creme are the only prolific rock-video *auteurs* who initially made their names as musicians, with British pop-rock band 10cc. Adept at luridly provocative videos like "Girls on Film" and "Kiss the Bride," they are now more noted for the classy dignity they achieved with the Police's enhanced-performance clip "Every Breath You Take," something they had done years before, and just as effectively, in a more conceptual framework with Visage's "We Fade to Gray" and "Mind of a Toy." And then in mid-1983, using Jim

Whiting's kinetic sculptures, they crafted Herbie Hancock's "Rockit," a dazzlingly witty perpetual-motion extravaganza with ingenious edits timed to the stop-start rhythms of Hancock's post-rap electrofunk tune.

"No doubt," says Godley, "our backgrounds as musicians must help us somehow in relating to the musicians we work with, and in correlating our visuals with their sounds and lyric images. But even before we became directors, we always thought visually, imagistically, cinematically."

Our philosophy is to approach each video individually, not as a career overview kind of thing, but clip by clip, artist by artist, song by song. We'll only do a film for a song that we think will result in a good film. Which doesn't necessarily mean that we have to *like* the song or the artist. Anything can inspire the concept; it could be us, it could be something the artist says, whatever. Then, the thing is to make the best *quality* film we can. We're more concerned with making the finished product *look good* than with the small amount of money lining our pockets.

"We don't have any conscious influences, in fact we usually try to go against the grain of whatever's out there. 'Every Breath You Take' was a conscious attempt to move away from all the quick-cutting and brilliant colors, so we used slow dissolves and moody lighting and deep perspective and black-and-white to get a mood, an atmosphere, that matched the tone of the song. And we'd just seen Gjon Mile's forties jazz short, *Jammin' the Blues,* which influenced us. At this point, rock video seems to be heading for overkill. They'd better watch out or it'll become unendurable. MTV is great for a while, but after an hour or so it becomes so much visual wallpaper. Mostly me and Lol sit around picking holes in it.

"I don't think rock videos should be analyzed very deeply. Yeah, there is an 'art' to it, just like there's an 'art' to making a commercial, I suppose. It's just that either they work or they don't, and if you want to, you can see why. I'll give you an example of someone analyzing a rock video to death. This artist saw 'Wrapped around Your Finger' and loved it, and wanted us to do his video. He called us, and on the phone, he asked to be sent a script or a storyboard, or some sort of document of the meaning behind the concept to that video. We usually do scripts and storyboards, but in that case, we had a set with all these rows of candles, and that's what inspired us; we just went and shot it out of our heads. Anyway, this guy could not believe there wasn't a piece of paper the Police received that read, 'The circle of candles represents Sting trapped within his own life, and the lines of candles represent the straight line of love from one heart to another.' Now *that's* analyzing a video."

Like other rock-video *auteurs,* Godley and Creme would like to make a feature film. Godley says, "If making videos becomes this boring old big-business thing, then hopefully we'll be out of it by then. Hopefully we'll be making features. Or we could always go back to making music—though 'just music' isn't too appealing after you've been behind the camera awhile."

Gerald Casale of Devo is the one musician making his own videos (with the technical direction of Chuck Statler) with a profound and highly developed perspective on the content of rock videos and what their often-ambiguous imagery really means. As he puts it, "The fact that Devo was making rock videos before just about anyone else, and that we've since been overtaken in the public eye by all these other slicked-up videos, was just so totally predictable. We *never* approached video as a promotional afterthought. It was *always* an integral part of our artistic whole. We had messages and information to communicate, imagery to show people, and we documented it and showed it to people. But strong imagery like that, and messages that run any deeper than 'I'm pretty—buy me' scare the power brokers of the entertainment industry, so it's a no-no. Devo is a bunch of very bad boys in their eyes. So naturally, with their power structure and conventional wisdom, they just turned music video into the same old self-fulfilling prophecy. All that stuff about '*will* video kill the radio stars?' was just such a load of deceptive crap. All along they knew they couldn't afford to have that happen. They'd just use video, remake it in their own image, to remake and perpetuate the radio stars. So MTV breaks acts that AOR radio won't play. Is there really any difference between Duran Duran and Foreigner? They're just two different flavors of ear candy, that's all. Everyone can ramble on and on and on all they want about what a great new artistic and promotional opportunity music-video is, but we should all know that it's just going to update the same old song, refashion the status quo. Come on—do you think the industry that distributed rock & roll and produced rock product would ever have let rock & roll be really and truly subversive and revolutionary? Of course not. They'd be fools to let that happen. So everyone goes along deceiving himself. Now they're just doing it visually as well as sonically and lyrically. They aren't about to let rock video become a truly revolutionary medium

for imparting valuable new information and potentially subversive attitudes. Forget it, it's all over.

"And the tragedy of it is that people who do have something unique
and stimulating to say will be the exceptions to the rule, they'll be the
underlings, the serfs of the new corporate-feudal state, struggling on the
fringes while the mainstream of music-video just goes along being
record company baby pictures and puzzling evidence and chimps on
parade . . . the same old escapist nonsense. To me it's an anthropological
phenomenon to watch it happening. It's that same old de-evolutionary
American myth of false innocence. Now people are applying it to the
latest weapon in the corporate mind-control arsenal, which happens to
be rock video. Rock video won't really change anything at all. Duran
Duran is a successful video band precisely because they are so vacuous
—there's no threatening content or information to get in the way of that
chic hedonism. So they become part of the self-fulfilling prophecy, and
if anyone complains about it and says he wants to use the medium for
more content and information like it should be used, the power brokers
all ask, 'Are you saying we're making this happen? Are you saying that
people don't want this? It sold, didn't it?' To them you're sour grapes,
you're uptight, you're defensive. . . . The thing everyone pretends to be
innocent about is that while the power brokers may not actually tell
bands what music to compose and how to compose it, they do control
who gets access to the media and what happens overall. It's a more
subtle sort of control. There's no real mystery to it, but people don't
ever want to face up to that fact. I mean, rock & roll ceased being vitally
anarchistic a long time ago, but you try to explain that to kids today,
and they don't wanna hear it; to them it's boring and quaint. They just
want what they've been conditioned to want, which is big entertainment
in all its rich variety. . . . So now they want the eye-catching video that's
gonna make them go 'oh . . . *wow.*'

"Now, the only practical way to combat that is to somehow be real
clever and slip in there and subvert things however you can. So that'll
happen only occasionally, with the odd low-budget video or whatever.
. . . But I won't hold my breath waiting for them. Meanwhile, maybe
Devo should meet all this puzzling evidence—these new-wave rock &
roll women in department-store chic with shiny lips and hostile looks,
dangling earrings like dangling participles to just fill tape time—maybe
we should meet it head-on and shoot a video on a forty-foot sloop in
the Caribbean and make it look like a Max Factor ad or something. I
don't know. . . . Actually, our big subversive plan is to try to make the
Devo feature-film version of Orwell's *Animal Farm.* I can't believe

they'll ever let us get away with it, though. It'd be like an object-lesson of everything I've been talking about here—how the darker tendencies in human nature always win out, idealism inevitably gives in to the hideous side of human nature, and everyone laughs all the way to the last tragic scene. . . ."

PROPHETS AND PROFITS: THE FUTURE OF ROCK VIDEO

Rock video has already come so far, so fast, it seems almost impossible to predict accurately the course of its future.

By the autumn of 1983, consciousness of rock video had grown into self-consciousness, even among nationwide televised rock-video outlets: USA Network's *Night Flight* responded to the popularity of MTV by running not only more video clips in its previously all-long-format programs, but also revamping its opening "Take Off" segment into a thematic weekly examination of rock-video trends and motifs. Concurrently, NBC's *Friday Night Videos* undertook "Special Edition" shows not only citing prevalent rock-video trends, but also featuring comments from rock stars on their videos.

Further evidence of rock-video self-consciousness, as well as a reaffirmation that rock video's roots had long been taking hold outside of America, again came on *Night Flight* in the autumn of 1983, in the form of Andrew C. Rowsome, Michael Korican, and Almerinda Travassos's 1983 low-budget independent feature film *Recorded Live*—the first film about rock video (in this case, the *Candide*-like odyssey of a woman running a rock-video bootleg operation). *Recorded Live* was produced in Toronto, which, back in the mid-seventies, had brought us that innovative radical feminist rock-video cabaret troupe, the Hummer Sisters. As of this writing, Toronto's music-video scene was thriving on many levels—from home-grown video-clip shows like *The New Music, Video Singles,* and *Rockline,* to the stunning low-budget independent Devo-meets-Toni Basil *Boob Tube* clip by underground phenom Eva Everything, to the slick, ready-for-MTV clips of Rob Quartley (Blue Peter's "Don't Walk Past," Helix's "Heavy Metal Love"), Don Allen (Orphan's "Lonely at Night," the Tenants' "Sheriff"), and Bob Feresco (Parachute Club's "Rise Up," which bests Bob Rafelson's clip for Lionel Richie's "All Night Long" for colorful, dancing-in-the-streets *joie de vivre*), to Vancouver bar band Doug and the Slugs' hilarious self-produced clips for "Too Bad" and "Makin' It Work."

Long-form rock-video programming had also grown: As of this writing, major home-video software companies like RCA/Columbia and MCA Home Video were making intensive commitments to music-video software at affordable prices; dozens of rock stars were at work on full-length original rock-video projects for the home-video market, like proven rock-video talent Ray Davies of the Kinks, with the planned RCA video disc *Return to Waterloo,* to include new videos set to older Kinks hits.

Rock-video clips were attempting the transition from promotional to consumer items via Sony's Video 45s in America and EMI's Video EPs in the U.K. Pioneer LaserVision had upped the ante by lowering prices of its laser-disc video singles to audio-LP levels, and EMI Picture Music had launched K-Tel-style rock-video-clip compilation packages at bargain video-cassette prices.

Whether rock-video clips actually would complete the transition from promotional item to consumer product was an open question. As of this writing, video was not a proven sales medium for music programming, nor was music a proven home-video software seller. Home-video software makers and rock-video mavens all seemed to *believe* the market would develop, but nobody knew exactly when. It all depended on the penetration of home-video hardware, which in turn depended on the overall state of the economy, and on the overall degree of rock-video exposure on television. If people could see all the rock video they could stand at home *and* tape it off the air (which in itself depended on the controversial Betamax legislation still pending before Congress as of this writing), why should they buy it?

Sony's Video 45s may make rock videos attractive to the buying public. They are relatively inexpensive, their programming is focused and easily digested, and they are handsomely packaged. Most important, they come in Beta Hi-Fi, which is superior in audio fidelity to any other existing stereo system's or twenty-four-track studio's sound, and in fact is matched only by digital sound. Now consider our high-tech, conspicuous-consumption society. Then ponder this: Who will seem hipper to his friends, the kid who sits around all day watching MTV with his finger on his VCR's pause and record buttons, waiting for a clip he wants to record but isn't sure when he will see, and who is likely to miss the beginning and end of the clip and, in any event, to record it with subpar audio; or the kid who goes out and buys a Sony Video 45, with its slick packaging, superb sound, and complete, uncensored video clips? The answer is obvious and makes consumer rock video seem all the more viable.

But even if that does become the case, there are other issues complicating rock video's development: the legal rights of and compensation due the people who make or work on rock videos. If and when rock-video clips move beyond promotional (i.e., free to the user) status and become consumer items, they certainly will begin to generate tremendous amounts of money, perhaps millions of dollars. Myriad legal and bureaucratic procedures and standards will have to be worked out among musicians, actors, dancers, extras, producers, set designers, and crew people, all of whom will want to collect some percentage of the royalties earned from the sale and/or licensing of rock videos. Since these are *rock* videos, musicians who play on the audio track but do not necessarily appear in the video, as well as arrangers, songwriters, music publishers, record producers, and others, will also be eligible for a cut. By the time the royalty fee is divided, each person's percentage may be so small that it may not seem worth it. In addition to splitting the fees, each participant will also have to hire someone to see that his interests are protected. Add to that the cost of administering the process. Clearly, it could become so expensive a proposition that retail prices would have to be raised, perhaps to the point of actually killing the market altogether and putting the industry back at square one.

Veteran music-industry lawyer Martin Machat speaks for the many legal authorities contacted on this matter when he throws up his hands and sighs, "*Nobody* knows where it's all going legally. Everything has happened so fast that the record labels haven't really gotten around to all the legal wrangles rock video presents. It's all still very speculative, and everyone knows that if and when it does happen, it'll involve long and protracted legal battles between a lot of different parties."

The fact remains that administering any standard policies regarding the making of rock videos could be complicated and protracted enough to slow production. About the only concrete legal action taken so far is an agreement ratified in the autumn of 1983 by the American Federation of Musicians (AFM) covering performances by its contract players in rock videos. The agreement, running through 1985, would have contract players on a given video splitting a one-percent royalty share of all revenues from sale or licensing fees of a video, once fifty thousand dollars has been deducted for label-production expenses. Performers in videos would be paid a flat fee of one hundred fifteen dollars for on-camera appearances; if they aren't seen playing an instrument or lip-synching, as in many concept videos, they would receive no fee. If the AFM agreement becomes a factor, it could alter the course of typical rock-video productions and shift the trend back towards straight performance videos.

But whether the AFM agreement will really mean anything is still in doubt. Compare the one-percent video royalty with the standard six-percent royalty bands receive per sale of a standard $6.98 list price album; compare the $115 fee for an on-camera video appearance with the $340 standard fee for a session player performing on an audio album; and consider that the AFM itself admits its fifty-thousand-dollar cutoff figure is nebulous, since no fixed price has been set for the sale of rock-video clips; and one can see why most AFM members have termed the agreement "basically worthless" (as reported in the *Hollywood Reporter*, August 23, 1983). In fact, the one-percent royalty would seem workable *only* if rock-video software carried a higher-than-usual price tag.

Meanwhile, the record industry must face these issues. Already, music lawyers regularly negotiate video considerations into their clients' contracts, and as any record-label executive will tell you, there isn't a band being signed these days that doesn't demand a certain number of videos be made per year, or per album. Lawyers as well as band managers try to prevent labels from cross-collateralizing video-derived income or video expenses against an artist's record royalties; they negotiate fifty-fifty splits in revenue from commercial rock-video usage; they try to split the cost of a video equitably between the artist and the label, and so on. The legal questions *are* being raised, but nobody can predict the results yet, except to suggest that rock-video pacts might closely follow record deals in terms of basic content.

On the other hand, the economics of rock video alone could spark a major realignment of the industry. As Jeff Abelson, coproducer of Billy Idol's "Dancing with Myself" video, says, "I think promo clips are the forerunner of longer-form music productions that will ultimately be developed by major film studios, or, paralleling that, record labels will move beyond 'just music' and become total entertainment companies, not just labels with music-video wings. We're already seeing that start to happen with something like EMI Picture Music. Record labels just won't be able to keep spending hundreds of thousands of dollars promoting records with video afterthoughts. They'll have to start making specialized music-video or music-film programming that sells itself. The Billy Idol video was actually produced more like a film than like a typical rock-video promo—it was planned out over a period of several months among a few different parties. Same thing with the Sheena Easton 'Telefone' video I coproduced with Simon Fields of Limelight. And both of those videos had budgets under one hundred thousand dollars. I don't see how labels can resist that kind of forethought and cost-effectiveness."

Music-video has another kind of software potential, and it's already being developed: instructional programs. Baltimore's Axis Video has already successfully marketed instructional drumming video cassettes featuring jazz giant Max Roach and acclaimed percussionist Bill Bruford. New York's Drummer's Collective began a home video wing in 1983 that has marketed over a dozen instructional video cassettes, featuring not only top-flight drummers like Steve Gadd, Yogi Horton, and Bernard Purdie, but guitarists, keyboardists, bassists, and horn players as well.

And what about the TV medium, where it all began? By the time you read this, there will surely have been a shakeout of rock-video programs on TV, followed by a leveling off. We can hope that out of it will come a wider variety of local and national music-video outlets for all kinds of music, from the mainstream to the avant-garde. Already, the Star Video Music channel promises to start delivering "adult contemporary" middle-of-the-road music twenty-four hours a day on ad-supported basic cable, starting in January 1984. As Star Video Music executive Alvin James says, "We plan to fill the void between MTV and the Nashville Network. We'll program mainstream stars, and some R&B, reggae, and jazz—but we won't go for the hard-core inner-city dance-music audience, because that audience just hasn't been wired for cable yet."

Probably—and especially once inner-city areas do get wired for cable —the proliferation of broadcast and cable rock-video outlets will mirror previous radio-format and record-distribution patterns: The rock audience will have rock videos, the black audience will have black videos, the mainstream audience will have mainstream videos, the jazz audience will have jazz videos, the country audience will have country videos—and rarely, if ever, shall any of them cross paths.

The most interesting things to watch for are back-and-forth reactionary trends arising from the counterprogramming of rock-video outlets and shifts in audience tastes as a result of overexposure to certain kinds of rock videos. Already, we've seen parody videos—Weird Al Yankovic's "Ricky," a takeoff on Toni Basil's "Mickey" via "I Love Lucy"; Dean Martin's "Since I Met You, Baby," described by Jo Bergman as "a parody of MTV video clichés"; and, as this book is going to press, director Erik Nelson described his video clip for British folk rocker Richard Thompson's "Wrong Heartbeat," as a "parody of rock-video clichés." We undoubtedly will see more of them.

Indeed, the movement towards parody videos only further illustrates the growing awareness of rock-video clichés that most rock-video directors mentioned in the *Auteurs* chapter. As Brian Grant indicated, "The whole thing seems to have reached a plateau; everyone's ripping everyone else off. . . ." One clever way of dealing with this is to come right out and make an honest joke of one's borrowings and references—as in the Motels' late-1983 clip "Remember the Night" (directed by Val Garay), which at one point fades from color to black-and-white to show someone throwing a bowl of white rice up in the air, just like in David Bowie's "China Girl" video, and then shows a blond man in a black overcoat (again, just like Bowie in "China Girl") holding a cue card that reads, "Refer to David Bowie's 'China Girl' video." At any rate, if, in fact, rock video's first golden age is over, there will surely be more to come. Rock video is here to stay, all right; too much time and money have been invested. How it grows and evolves, nobody can guess. Who would have ever predicted the Sony Walkman or home computers?

Beyond that, performers' attitudes towards videos will, of course, continue to change as well. Some new band is sure to come along and establish its integrity by claiming something like MTV to be too commercial, too establishment (but then, that's already happened, as demonstrated earlier by a quote from the Violent Femmes about having "sold out to MTV"). On the other hand, some bands may become so keyed to video exposure that they'll add to their mystiques by refusing to do live shows. And maybe, as Robert Hilburn ingeniously predicted in the *Los Angeles Times* in August 1983, "David Bowie, the godfather of pop video, will decry that the video movement has cost pop music its soul. He will then announce his retirement (Bowie's agonized press conference will, of course, be carried live over MTV. It will also be released in stereo on video cassette and video disc)."

And, of course, certain megastars will outdo one another with higher and higher budgets and longer and more involved concept clips. Michael Jackson's "Thriller" is surely the most extravagant "vanity production" to date—a "clip" of fourteen-minute duration, with a budget of one million dollars, in which the song itself is decidedly in the background of the action most of the time.

Then again, there was the fall 1983 announcement that John Cougar Mellencamp would begin directing clips for other performers. This is not exactly a first (in fact, it's a parallel to artists acting as record producers for other artists, as Mellencamp did with Mitch Ryder in 1983)—Toni Basil, for instance, is one performer who's directed other people's videos, but then again, she has a long history of audio-visual experience, which Mellencamp does not have. If more and more relatively inexperienced rock performers start grabbing the directorial reins, who knows how rock videos could evolve? Look what such musicians-turned-*auteurs* as Devo and Godley and Creme have done already.

TV sets themselves are going through some changes as well, and many of them could easily be keyed to rock video. There are already "component TV" systems (like Sony's Profeel) and as of this writing it appeared that actual stereo broadcasts were an imminent reality. There are a variety of front- and rear-projection large-screen TVs. In the not-too-distant future, we'll have 3-D holographics as well, which will not only give the illusion of three dimensions (as some rock videos, like Lynn "Will Powers" Goldsmith's "Adventures in Success," have already attempted with partial success) but will add to that enhanced "presence" by making it seem as if performers are *actually in the room with you.* Imagine "Beat It" in large-screen holographic stereo, with Michael Jackson prancing down *your* stairs to turn imminent gang-war into celebratory dance, or Def Leppard lead singer Joe Elliott leaping right out of the screen into your lap at the end of "Photograph." Such technoentertainment wonders could definitively bury memories of the days when rock and TV didn't go together.

At the other end of the spectrum, the subversive, oppositional, and/or alternative underground rock-video network to which Gerry Casale alluded in the last chapter will almost certainly grow, as music-video consciousness and cheap, accessible production equipment proliferate. The only question will be where we'll be able to see the products of this rock-video underground. More than likely, it will be in rock-video clubs. With MTV and its ilk weaning millions on big-budget Hollywood-style productions, rock video on TV is fast going the way of image

While Devo and assorted cowboys and cowgirls look on, Devo's Mark Mothersbaugh prepares to "Whip It," in the classic 1980 video by the band who foresaw the future of rock video before most did.

massage. Video clubs, on the other hand, are still a more wide-open and experimental environment for video programming—more often than not, an image *barrage.*

But clubs have also established themselves as the testing grounds for video trends that resurface later in more established, mainstream outlets like broadcast and cable-network TV. As Candace Brown, a VJ at L.A. "videotheque" Revolver puts it, "We get all sorts of bigwigs jamming the club every night to pick up everything they can from what we do here—cable execs, hotel-chain reps, foreign club owners. . . . You'd die if you saw our guest list." Indeed, Ed Steinberg's Rock-America video pool now services not only clubs but Holiday Inns, roller-skating and ice-hockey rinks, and drive-in theaters.

Meanwhile, the course of club video itself will evolve. For now, there are two alternative club-video routes: the large-screen centrally located, as in New York's the Ritz; or the more intimate "video lounge," like the one pioneered at New York's Danceteria by video artist Kit Fitzgerald, where a dozen small TV sets play in a living-room environment. There are hundreds of variations in between. As to the importance of club video, there is no denying it: a club cannot afford to open these days without installing some sort of video system (RockAmerica's Steinberg also consults with clubs on what kinds of systems to install). And keep in mind what VJ Chris Holland of Toronto club Larry's Hideaway says, in summing up the importance of video in a club: "My function is to excite people with energizing video. I set the whole mood for the evening. Club video has become a social lubricant."

Devo's Gerry Casale, naturally, envisions a darker scenario: "I can just see the day coming—and it may already have started happening—when the creative mercenary idea will expand to all phases of music-video productions. There'll be guys hired out by labels to write music, guys to arrange it, session men to play it; there'll be directors and producers hired out to make videos, and actors or models used to lip-sync the lyrics. The bands themselves, effectively, will no longer exist. It'd be just like Tin Pan Alley or disco, or the girl-group era—stamp-out time; the faces are interchangeable as long as the right creative mercenaries are behind the scenes crafting the product." That may seem unduly extreme, but on the other hand, the fact that video is already once-removed from the spontaneous reality rock & roll was supposed to uphold makes it seem more likely—the logical and ultimate fulfillment of what began when someone thought up the idea of lip-synching.

More encouraging, or so it seems for now, is the spread of home computers. British electropopper Pete Shelley released a British single, "Telephone Operator," in mid-1983 that contained computer-encoded information that, when a turntable was connected with a Timex-Sinclair home computer, would display computer-animated imagery and a readout of the song's lyrics on the computer's display terminal. Unfortunately, Shelley's U.S. deal with Arista expired before the experiment could be attempted in the U.S.

But hot on the heels of that fascinating development, former Public Image Ltd. guitarist Keith Levene—the man who helped foment the world's first rock-video riot—was working on some concepts along the same lines. Public Image, as its name implied, had been formed not so much as a band but as a "communications corporation." In the wake of its demise, Levene not only went solo but formed another, similar concern, Multi-Image Corp. With MIC, Levene was hard at work programming interactive music-video instructional programs for children to use in their home computers. "I'm more concerned," says Levene, "with the generations that are *growing up* with MTV, and the ones that will be born *after* MTV. They're the ones who have the most to gain from an intelligent alternative to all that rot, and the most to lose by being subjected to the same old thing. My programs would allow kids to create their own visuals for the music, or their own music for the visuals. Ultimately, they'd hopefully be able to learn to create their own music *and* visuals. If I can get these programs to kids *before* they get infected with the MTV syndrome . . ."

Whether Levene manages that or not, interactive home-computer video could be the *real* video revolution of the future.

Meanwhile, some rock videos—Michael Jackson's "Beat It," Donald Fagen's "New Frontier," and Kansas' "Fight Fire with Fire" among them—have been blown up to thirty-five-millimeter film and been shown as feature-film trailers in movie houses. It seems inevitable that theaters will begin devoting entire evenings, or week-long screening schedules, to rock videos. There will follow a shift in rock-video production and aesthetics, with the big public screen, rather than the small home screen, in mind.

Some record labels have taken steps in the promotion-as-programming direction. Epic, for instance, has already produced a series of "video profiles" of their new music acts, with three-minute tapes of interviews and clips excerpts sent to hundreds of local rock-video shows around the country. These could give the locals—if they're still out there—a way of competing with something like MTV, but not much of a way. Epic's profiles, after all, are preproduced press kits on video, whereas MTV's walk-on interviews are more spontaneous and are keyed to constant music-news updates.

Then, of course, there will be video jukeboxes everywhere we turn, showing us still more video clips. With all these clips on display all over the place, other art forms are sure to be more strongly affected—you'll see more movies that look and function like video clips, for instance. Who knows where it will all end? In the meantime, with everyone making videos, performers' attitudes towards videos are sure to evolve as well. We've already heard of performers writing songs "with the video in mind." Even a major band like Journey has been affected; the *New York Times Magazine* of May 8, 1983, concluded its coverage of the shooting of Journey's first elaborate concept video, "Separate

Ways," with this: "Although [Journey lead singer] Steve Perry seems fairly pleased with the experiment, he is not yet a total video convert. 'I still hope the music comes first,' he says. However, guitarist Neil Schon seems to have seen the wave of the future for rock music, and decided it works. 'Next time,' he says, putting his arm around director Tom Buckholz, 'you're going to write the songs with me. That way, we'll definitely get it right.' "

In fact, Schon and Buckholz had been beaten to the punch as far as altering the creative music-video process. MGMM director Brian Grant and scriptwriter Keith Williams were already at work on a ground-breaking project for Olivia Newton-John. As Grant explains it, "Keith and I will work out the concept and scenario for a whole video album, and *then* Olivia and her people will write songs to fit the video. This, I believe, is a first." Indeed, it appears so—and is also a genuine case of the video tail wagging the musical dog.

Of course, as more and more people both inside and outside the burgeoning music-video industry become more conscious of rock-video style and content, the aesthetics of the medium will change in kind with evolving sophistication and competition. We've already seen such videos as Michael Jackson's "Beat It," Pat Benatar's "Love Is a Battlefield," and ZZ Top's "Sharp-Dressed Man" innovate by introducing dialogue and sound effects extraneous to the clips' musical tracks but integral to the videos' plot lines. Perhaps in the future, more performers will revert to straight performance clips. Questions will have to deal with: Does rock video rob the listener of his or her ability to imagine imagery for an abstract song? And, more important, does "acting" in a concept video demystify the performer too much? And if so, will that affect the perception of that performer by his or her audience, and will the effect be good or bad?

In the future, we may also see more and more performers making videos of their older songs. Billy Idol's already done it with "Dancing with Myself," which was three years old when its video was finally made. In this vein, a perfect candidate appears to be Ray Davies of the Kinks, who for years has been writing wonderful songs as sharply *observed* stories and vignettes that would be naturals for visualization.

Another alternative route, aside from the aforementioned instructional music video cassettes, has already been anticipated by producer Mark Mawrence's "ambient" music videos for his Earth Sky-Open Sky Productions. His first project, "The Evolutionary Spiral," released in mid-1983, uses free-associative streams of abstract and representational imagery, flowing edits, and electronic mood music in what Mawrence terms a "fourteen-minute multimedia montage, with no dialogue but with universal appeal. Music video need not be so manipulative and one-dimensional in its attention-grabbing. The more people see *those* kinds of videos, the more they'll want to see *our* videos, which let their attention spans 'breathe' and hold up better to repeated viewings."

But will the idea of "repeated viewings" even be relevant in the future? Jo Bergman of Warner Brothers notes, "The only people who ever mention the word *repeatability* in rock videos are those over twenty or thirty. Kids never even worry about it." Indeed, the generations growing up with MTV, with home computers and video games and video clubs and video jukeboxes, *are* post-literate. Their attention spans, and the ways they'll satisfy them, will necessarily be different than the older, literate-based generation's.

Finally, there is Sony's CD—the Compact Digital Audio Disc, possibly Sony's biggest future-shock wavemaker ever. CDs look like 45-sized versions of mirror-bright album-sized laser video discs. They are read by laser beams, so the "needle" never touches the disc; therefore, CDs could conceivably last forever without wearing out. Since CDs have no "grooves" and are read by laser light, they have a clear protective coating and are impervious to scratches and dirt. You can literally throw dirt on a CD and then play it. CDs, for the moment, can fit just over one hour of music on one side, and digital sound is superior, in specifications anyway, to any other kind of audio fidelity recording. CD players are somewhere between the size of an average audio cassette deck and a Walkman portable cassette player. They will eventually phase out record turntables, cassette decks, Walkmen, and car stereos and tape decks. They are *the* medium of the future: priced competitively with conventional records and players, with the added bonus of being programmable to make random tracks accessible and to repeat portions of songs as many times as the user likes.

According to Sony's Mark Finer, "For the moment, CDs can only accommodate still-frame visuals, frozen images held onscreen for a few seconds, the duration of a song, whatever. Mainly, visuals are used for televised readouts of the information you're used to seeing on the backs of album jackets—personnel and producers on the album, song lists, song lengths, etc. Getting *moving* pictures onto CDs should happen sometime in the future, given laser video discs, which aren't that far from CDs anyway, and the explosion of rock video. It's all contingent on the refinement of the manufacturing process and the proliferation of the hardware, but some sort of fusion of the CD and the laser video disc seems likely in the not-too-distant future. If CDs take off at all, and we're sure they will, that'll have to happen. For now, maximum playing time on a CD is about seventy-four minutes, and having moving images on a CD would mean sacrificing most of that playing time to accommodate the encoding of the visuals. Maybe the next thing you'll see will be CD Video 45s."

Just imagine what an admittedly pictorialist rock-video *auteur* like Russell Mulcahy, or an ex-album-cover-artist like Storm Thorgeson, could do, even within the confines of still-frame CD visuals. And you thought rock videos *already* looked like *Vogue* fashion ads!

Speaking of which, *Rolling Stone* magazine published a cover story on MTV in late 1983 by Steven Levy. Headlined "The Selling Out of Rock," the article concluded that MTV and its promotional video clips were turning rock music into commercial jingles. Though even such a hard-line rock critic as *The Village Voice*'s Robert Christgau found such a proposition "somewhat tendentious," Levy's point was proven within a few months with the February 1984 debut of a Pepsi commercial featuring Michael Jackson and the Jacksons, and directed by Bob Giraldi of "Beat It" fame. The commercial featured the Jacksons performing Michael's smash hit "Billie Jean"—but with the lyrics altered to extol Pepsi. If that isn't turning rock music into commercial jingles, then what is? Though rock and pop songs have always had things in common with commercial jingles—mainly, the express aim of getting under your skin—this provided some serious new food for thought.

Then again, we'd already seen many rock songs used and/or altered to sell products in TV commercials: Buddy Holly's "It's So Easy" for Fantastik spray cleaner, the Human Beinz's garage-rock classic "Nobody but Me" for Philadelphia cream cheese. Rock video mirrors such phenomena as much as it precipitates them.

At any rate, rock video is definitely here to stay, and we'll definitely be watching it. And the anthem of the rock-video future, rather than "Video Killed the Radio Star," might well be the hermetic scenario, daubed in cathode-ray blue, painted back in 1977 by David Bowie. The song, prophetically, was entitled "Sound and Vision," and its forecast of an age when we'll all be sitting home absorbing information overload from our zillion-channel wraparound-screen electronic hearths goes like this:

> Don't you wonder sometimes about sound and vision?
> Blue, blue, electric blue, that's the color of my room,
> Where I shall live . . . waiting for the gift of sound and vision.

ROCK VIDEO'S HOT 100

Keith Richards of the Rolling Stones says it best: "Rock videos are no different than music, or movies, or anything else—eighty-five percent of it is crap, and if it weren't, then you'd never know about the fifteen percent that's good."

Here, we salute the rock videos that are not crap. How does a video make it into our Hot 100? Quality in craftsmanship and production values help, but most videos these days have those. Rather, a Hot 100 video is one that transcends the genre's inherent limitations, through ideas or ingenuity or some such stroke of inspiration, to become either something akin to art, or to at least become an artful piece of promotional entertainment. Above all else, a Hot 100 video has to have some sort of content rather than contrivance, genuine ideas rather than gratuitous images. Of course, there are some cases where the latter are used in such a way that they epitomize certain rock-video tendencies and, in their own way, transcend them; these videos will be cited, too.

Before getting to the Hot 100 proper, it should be noted that our initial tabulation of prospective Hot 100 rock-video candidates totaled well over one hundred. Therefore, we will here dispense with those pioneering efforts that have either already been described in great detail in this book, or which were important and innovative in their day but which are now simply too crude to hold up to today's production standards. These videos make up the Rock-Video Hall of Fame (like our Hot 100 videos, they are listed according to band, song title, album from which the song came, year, director, and producer):

The Kinks, "Dead End Street" (from the Warner-Reprise album *Kinks Kronikles*), 1966, director and producer unknown.

The Who, "Happy Jack" (from the MCA-Decca album *Happy Jack*), 1966, director and producer unknown.

The Beatles, "Strawberry Fields Forever" and "Penny Lane" (from the Capitol-EMI album *Magical Mystery Tour*), 1967, produced and directed by the Beatles. Classics of avant-garde, surreal, post-Richard Lester psychedelia. "Penny Lane" is especially memorable for its final sequence: the band sit at a huge banquet table set up in a field; butlers place their instruments on the table; and then, *the table is overturned* —anticipating by over a decade one of director Russell Mulcahy's favorite, most overdone cliché images, as seen in Duran Duran's "Hungry like the Wolf " and the Motels's "Only the Lonely," as well as many others.

Captain Beefheart, "Lick My Decals Off, Baby" (TV commercial for album of same name), 1970, directed by Don Van Vliet (Captain Beefheart), produced by Warner Brothers Records. A TV commercial, yes, but also a pioneering example of rock-related surrealist visual expression of unparalleled originality. And it *is* on video. See it at the Museum of Modern Art in New York.

Queen, "Bohemian Rhapsody" (from the Elektra Records album *A Night at the Opera*), 1975, directed by Bruce Gowers, produced by Lexi Godfrey for Jon Roseman Productions. Primitive by today's standards, yes, but also the first case of a video being primarily responsible for making a song a hit, as well as anticipating rock-video techniques to come, using special effects to enhance an already bombastic performance and make viewers go, "Oh, *wow!*"

The Residents, "Land of 1,000 Dances" (from the Ralph Records album *Third Reich & Roll*), 1975, produced and directed by the Residents for the Cryptic Corp. The most utterly, exuberantly original and bizarre performance video ever. After a delightfully dreamlike pixilated opening, in which the Residents, as always in creepy costume, wheel shopping carts with pointy telephone-wire conductor-like structures affixed to their fronts before a stylized backdrop, we cut to the Residents performing their mutant-tribal trash-masher perversion of the sixties dance-rock classic. It was all shot with sixteen-millimeter color film, but everything in it is black and white! The viewer will notice that at the start of the performance, there are three Residents cavorting onscreen; after a few seconds, the fourth jumps in from off-camera, stage left. This is because the band had no cameraman—the fourth Resident got the camera rolling, then joined the action. It ends abruptly with a sci-fi storm trooper in a prototype of a Devo jump suit entering and zapping the Residents with a ray gun (anticipating Devo's "Thru Being Cool"). Once you see it, you'll never forget it.

Devo, "Jocko Homo" and "Secret Agent Man" (originally released in 1976 as *In the Beginning Was the End: the Truth about De-evolution* from the Warner Brothers Records album *Q: Are We Not Men? A: We Are Devo!*), directed by Chuck Statler with Devo, produced by Statler and Devo. "Jocko Homo" has already been described at great length. "Secret Agent Man" (note: *not* the version on Devo's debut LP; this one's woozier, more distorted) bears further comment. Simply by combining the music's ominous atmosphere, an after-hours factory setting, see-through plastic masks worn by the band (and Mark Mothersbaugh's Booji Boy mask), their Caligari-somnambulist movements, and cuts to perverse imagery (best of which is a prototype of Miss Piggy being spanked by two men in monkey masks) with Statler's already concrete flat, static, basic-industrial *mise-en-scène,* Devo created one of the most otherworldly and haunting enhanced performance videos (as well as one of the first) ever.

Elvis Costello, "Accidents Will Happen" (from the Columbia Records album *Armed Forces*), 1978, directed by Annabelle Jankel and Rocky Morton, produced by Andy Morahan for Cucumber Studios. Important merely as the first rock video by animation kings Cucumber, and a lovely little piece that stands on its own. Cucumber took actual Costello performance footage and "traced" it via computer graphics, then programmed in random collapses and re-formations of the imagery into horizontal color bars and the like (the "accidents" that "will happen").

Mike Nesmith, "Rio" (from the Pacific Arts video album *Elephant Parts*), 1977, directed by Bill Dear, produced by Nesmith.

Suicide, "Frankie Teardrop" (from the Red Star Records album *Suicide*), 1978, directed by Paul Dougherty and Michael Robinson, produced by Dougherty and Edit deAk. About as atypical as rock video gets: a ten-minute-plus film, made apart from the band, using footage shot by two different parties (Robinson and deAk) over two years (plus some found footage), rarely if ever shown as a promotional video . . . and it's *art*. Robinson and deAk, both New York underground independent filmmakers, took footage they'd shot in Europe, then played it back on two projectors and refilmed the two source reels, applying various filters and other effects to the overlapped imagery; Dougherty then transferred the result to video and played with it some more, using a CMX computer-assisted editing system (now standard in the industry, though, in 1978, this was probably the first time it was used on a rock video). The result is breathtaking: every bit as terrifying as Suicide's epic tale of urban dissolution and psychotic violence, with deliberate dissolve edits that make the uncompromising images even more hauntingly poetic. A typical image: a bird pecking at food, superimposed over what appears to be a cadaver in a concentration camp.

The Boomtown Rats, "I Don't Like Mondays" (from the Columbia Records album *A Tonic for the Troops*), 1979, directed by David Mallet, produced by Lexi Godfrey for MGM Productions. Again, primitive by today's standards, but perhaps the first successful rock-video attempt at delineating a cogent narrative through multiple sets and substantial characterizations. Also an unusually restrained example of Mallet's directorial style.

The Buggles, "Video Killed the Radio Star" (from the Island Records album *The Golden Age of Plastic*), 1979, directed by Russell Mulcahy, produced by Lexi Godfrey for MGM Productions. As Mulcahy himself says, "Technically, this video was pretty ropey. . . . But the ideas and the energy were there—after this video, record labels came to me for my 'look' and pretty much gave me a free conceptual rein." Indeed, stylistically, its excessive use of quick cuts, zooms, and garishly bleeding superimpositions is much closer to David Mallet's style than Mulcahy's own. There is a silver-suited space woman traveling about in a gravity-defying clear capsule (symbol of the new freedom of video?), and a lost little girl wandering through the surreal proceedings, watching and/or causing technomischief. Both motifs have recurred in Mulcahy's more recent work (the ultra-cheap flying-on-wires effect of the space woman is seen with the "bright-eyed" choir boy in Bonnie Tyler's "Total Eclipse of the Heart," and the wandering child is seen in Duran Duran's "Is There Something I Should Know?"). And there is the memorable image of a pile of TV sets erupting through a floor to displace a mountain of old thirties-style radio sets, which combined with the song's title to make this *the* signifying video clip of the pre-MTV rock-video age.

Nick Lowe, "Cruel to Be Kind" (from the Stiff-Columbia Records album *Labour of Lust*), 1979, directed by Chuck Statler, produced by Dave Robinson for Stiff Records. It could have been Elvis Costello's "Oliver's Army" or Madness's "One Step Beyond," but this is arguably the best example of Statler's early work outside of Devo: as straightforward and unostentatious as an industrial training film, as antically humorous as a Richard Lester Beatles movie. Here, Lowe and Rockpile perform by poolside; Dave Edmunds does a hilarious turn as Lowe's chauffeur, driving Nick to his real-life wedding to Carlene Carter. Though there is indeed footage of the wedding itself, the minister in the video was a neighbor of Carter's—who was a last-minute replacement for an elderly gent Statler found the day of the shoot at the Okie Dog fast-food joint down the road from Carter's house in L.A. He backed out at the last minute.

Commander Cody, "Two Triple Cheese, Side Order of Fries," 1979, directed by Joe Dea, produced by VideoWest. Ingenious use of chromakey as Cody is made to appear to be driving his car on a burger-joint tabletop, dodging giant fries, shakes, and burgers; there are also quick cuts to burgers and fries whose preparation is choreographed, various other high jinks in the burger joint, and the classic shot of french fries dancing in formation (they did it with strings). Fast-paced, funny, ingenious—and on a budget of just two hundred fifty dollars!

And now the Rock Video Hot 100.

ABC, "The Look of Love" (from the Polygram album *Lexicon of Love*), 1982, directed by Brian Grant, produced by Scott Millaney for MGMM. Grant claims the inspiration for this clip's cartoon-park setting came from a sequence in the forties movie musical *An American in Paris*. But Grant's own extensive background in British TV comes to the fore, and the video ends up looking more like a Benny Hill take on New Romantics. That's not necessarily bad, and the clip is certainly funny, cute, and well made. But viewers have always been sharply divided on it: the song is *so* grandly serious and sincere; is the video inappropriately farcical, or a necessary deflation of singer Martin Fry's bard-of-love pretentions, or just a fascinating case of cognitive dissonance that falls somewhere in between? ABC themselves wanted a light, mocking approach. Grant certainly gave it to them, and in colorful, kinetic, vaudeville-video fashion to boot. By the way, the balding, bearded, bespectacled old gent seen shoveling spaghetti into his face in this clip has also made cameos in just about every other MGMM video (the schoolmaster in Bonnie Tyler's "Total Eclipse of the Heart," a party guest in Billy Joel's "Pressure," and in Ultravox's "Vienna," and elsewhere). He is MGMM wardrobe supervisor Michael Baldwin, the most-often-seen extra so far in rock-video history.

ABC, "Poison Arrow" (from *Lexicon of Love*), 1982, directed by Julian Temple, produced by Siobhan Barron for Limelight. A richly textured romantic nightmare, befitting the song's elegant depiction of the fatality of desire. ABC's Martin Fry plays four roles: a performer in *A Midsummer Night's Dream*-style production in an opera house; an opera house patron watching himself onstage; an usher backstage at the opera house, trying and failing to seduce the starlet; and a singer in a band at a tacky nightclub. The pinnacle of Temple's visualization of Fry's grandiloquent fear and longing comes in a fantastic dream sequence in which, in Temple's own words, "the girl literally cuts Martin down to size"—she blows powder from her makeup case in his face, he shrinks to the size of an ant and scurries around her table between twenty-foot-tall cocktail glasses. Her dropping a pill into one of the glasses coincides with a resounding tympani downbeat. In the finale, Fry, in the opera house audience, watches the starlet, as a Diana/Cupid, embrace another Fry; abruptly, she turns towards the camera (i.e., towards the Fry in the audience) and shoots that poison arrow. Just about the only one of Temple's clips to approach the flashy surrealism of the MGMM school, though it still retains potent vestiges of Temple's own characteristic narrative focus.

Adam Ant, "Goody Two-Shoes" (from the Epic Records album *Friend or Foe*), 1982, directed by Mike Mansfield with Adam Ant, produced by Mansfield. Adam finally lives up to his self-proclaimed status as Prince Charming, with a completely captivating, high-energy performance as himself: mainly, Adam Ant attacked by the press and attacking them back. But there's this one female reporter—it's the old riff of skeptical businesswoman seduced by the rock star. She trails Ant to his boudoir, all the while letting her hair down, removing her jacket, finally doffing her glasses and tossing her luxuriant mane to execute a hot-and-sexy pas de deux and embrace with Adam. Meanwhile, fine comic touches are added to the sleekly choreographed tale of seduction in the form of a prying butler sneaking peaks through the bedroom keyhole. Also note Adam's quick tribute to Elvis Presley's *Jailhouse Rock* production number.

Bryan Adams, "Cuts like a Knife" (from the A&M Records album *Cuts like a Knife*), 1983, directed by Steve Barron, produced by Simon Fields for Limelight. Perhaps the all-time example of rock video's deliberate, provocative ambiguity. Adams and band perform the ringing, singalong power-pop tune in an empty swimming pool, while nearby a lovely girl changes into a bathing suit. Barron keeps cutting from Adams to the girl, from his switch-blade knife to her gold heart-shaped locket. The insistence of the editing forces us to make some sort of ominous connection among all the elements. Things come to a head when the girl ascends the diving board over the empty pool. Then: cut to the knife, cut to the locket, cut to Adams performing in the pool, looking up towards the diving board; cut to the girl diving into the empty pool; cut to the locket falling off its hook in the dressing room; cut to the knife, flung into a wood-paneled wall; cut to the girl, rising from the pool healthy and *wet;* cut to her putting her locket back on; cut to the knife being folded back up; cut to the girl looking blankly satiated; cut to Adams gazing at her with muted longing. The end. The rug has been pulled out from under the expectations that Barron's suggestive imagistic and editorial counterpoint have engendered.

Philip Bailey, "I Know" (from the Columbia Records album *Continuation*), 1983, directed by Jack Cole, produced by Paul Flattery for Flattery, Halperin and Cole. Perhaps the most stunning black-music clip since "Beat It," the clip is a full-fledged minimovie in which Earth, Wind and Fire singer Bailey is cast as a former high-school track star, now driving a cab, who picks up a former flame (her picture's on his dashboard) now a big star. While he casts meaningful glances at her in the rear-view mirror, and her manager and publicity flack bombard her with advice, she ignores all in some sort of soured-on-success funk. As she and her entourage leave the cab at an airport, she finally sees and recognizes Bailey—but alas, too late, as she is dragged away, casting longing glances over her shoulder. And then the happy ending: Bailey gets back in his cab, slamming his door with disappointed finality; then, in his rear-view mirror, he sees her, standing alone by a gate, holding her luggage; he gets out of the cab, they exchange more meaningful glances; she shrugs and sighs, "Guess I missed my flight," then, her voice fairly a-tremble, asks, "Philip Bailey, do you still love me?" Bailey replies, "You know it," and they embrace and drive off, happily ever after. Believe it or not, it's emotional and compelling and romantic, and the use of dialogue and "natural" sound effects over the music track is in no way contrived—in fact, the clip would've seemed more contrived without them.

Toni Basil, "Mickey" (from the Chrysalis/Radial Choice Records album *Word of Mouth*), 1981, produced and directed by Toni Basil. In addition to having choreographed *Shindig!* and *The T.A.M.I. Show*, and tours for David Bowie and Bette Midler, among others, as well as having directed Talking Heads' classic "Once in a Lifetime" clip, Basil was also a high-school cheerleader. Here, she combines a lovingly choreographed salute to those bygone days with a charmingly direct and murderously catchy song of sassy adolescent desire. It's a perfect fusion of music and visuals, and is as serious and as fun as teenage romance can be, with cheerleader formations (featuring the Carson High crew from California) and human pyramids choreographed in an unpretentiously exuberant colloquial ballet. Basil's all-singing all-dancing, *That's Entertainment* aesthetic is a welcome relief from the oppressively chic, ambiguous image-mongering of most rock videos, and "Mickey" is the best example of how and why. It also (like most of the *Word of Mouth* video album) pioneered a technique now used by many rock-video directors, especially David Mallet in Def Leppard's 1983 clips: cutting to a freeze-frame image and holding it a few seconds before starting the new sequence. It's in the Museum of Modern Art's video collection, was one of MTV's first giant video hits, and remains a classic case of a song reaching number one on the charts almost entirely because of video exposure.

Adrian Belew, "Big Electric Cat" (from the Island Records album *Lone Rhino*), 1982, produced and directed by John Sanborn, Kit Fitzgerald, and Dean Winkler. State-of-the-art high-tech psychedelia, a dazzling display of digital-video-effects tricks, a freewheeling yet disciplined play on perspectives and geometry in zero-gravity negative space: a mix of live action (with a striking cat-eyed mystery girl turning all the boys' heads) and digital animation, with frame-stored images dancing and zooming in and out of formation as if M. C. Escher were orchestrating a game of fifty-two-pickup.

Blotto, "Metalhead" (from the Blotto Records EP *Combo Akimbo*), 1982, directed by Tom Gliserman and Gary Glinski with Blotto, produced by Blotto. America's funniest independent band (they hail from Albany, New York) also make hilarious, ingenious videos on thousand-dollar budgets. "I Wanna Be a Lifeguard" and "I Quit" (included with "Metalhead" on a Sony Video 45) are also fine, but

Sergeant Blotto (*sic*) is taken by surprise by some Señor Wences-style hands "lip-synching" the chorus of Blotto's "Metalhead" (1982), a hilarious heavy-metal parody produced by Blotto themselves for roughly $1,000. The clip got substantial MTV play and is now available on Blotto's Sony Video 45.

"Metalhead" is easily their best video. It's a devastating satire of heavy-metal mania in which Sergeant Blotto (other band members include Bowtie Blotto, Broadway Blotto, Cheese Blotto, and Lee Harvey Blotto) is transformed from a normal kinda guy into a raving, maniacal heavy-metalhead. The clip includes an allusion to Señor Wences, a drummer playing his kit with baseball bats, guitars played with hatchets, a horde of Hell's Angels, an appearance by heavy-metal guitar hero Buck Dharma, and the now-famous shot of Sarge Blotto in bed wearing smoking headphones, which MTV uses in many of its in-house promos (the smoke effect was obtained by having two off-camera Blotto members blow cigar smoke through tubes into the headphones). One of the first parody videos ever.

David Bowie, "Look Back in Anger" (from the RCA Records album *Lodger*), 1979, produced and directed by Bowie and David Mallet. Among all of Bowie's first big batch of concept clips—the flip, hip, casually ominous pop-surrealism of "DJ"; the burlesque-drag enhanced performance of "Boys Keep Swinging" (with its signature coda, in which Bowie, in drag as Marlene Dietrich, Tallulah Bankhead, and Margaret Thatcher-types, arrogantly smears his lipstick, a trick repeated at the end of his "China Girl" video)—"Look Back in Anger" is the one that's most influenced, or most anticipated, much of the subsequent course of rock video. It's a cockeyed, humorous, mock-Dorian Gray scenario, with a hysterical Bowie gradually trading places with his decaying painted portrait. Or something like that. The theme of ego-identity loss became one of rock video's most popular motifs, and many of this video's signifying hallmarks were paid homage in Brian Grant's 1983 clip for the Fixx's "Saved by Zero."

David Bowie, "Fashion" (from the RCA Records album *Scary Monsters*), 1980, produced and directed by Bowie and David Mallet. Bowie should have titled the song "Fascion." It's among his most blatant and acidic musical messages. The video is a more profound comment on pernicious trendiness than the song itself. Mallet's camera deliberately lingers in key scenes, capturing the unglamorous, everyday signs of commonality behind the star's façade, as when Bowie is seen absentmindedly wiping his nose onstage. Even more pointed is the equation of the ticket line with a new-depression soup line; the poor unfortunates queueing up are actually more strikingly dressed than the performers they're trying to get in to see (in fact, their outfits anticipate Vivienne Westwood's early eighties Dickensian ragamuffin, technosavage costumes). The high point comes when Bowie sings "Listen to me/Don't listen to me . . ." to his counterpart in the audience—a concise evocation of missed signals and failed communication in the pop arena. Along the way, Mallet gets to parody the style of his own British TV commercials with scenes of exuberant, banal people cheerily miming the "beep-beep" refrain. Watch for MTV VJ Alan Hunter making a few cameos as one of the people in the soup line.

David Bowie "Ashes to Ashes" (from the RCA Records album *Scary Monsters*), 1980, produced and directed by Bowie and David Mallet. Bowie's best, most ambitious and disturbing video. He appears in several guises—as a Pagliacci clown, a high-tech junkie (Major Tom stranded in a different kind of outer space), an asylum inmate—in this cautionary anti-addiction tale of psychic dissolution. Bowie's imagery is powerfully cryptic and evocative: flamboyantly surreal costumes; an exploding kitchen (actually an old Kenny Everett show set, reused by Mallet in Billy Idol's "White Wedding" video); the vaguely Slavic figures in procession before an approaching bulldozer; the clown sinking into a vibrant blue lake as Bowie croons, "I never did anything out of the blue"; the clown walking away down a beach, being lectured by his granny. But most impressive are Mallet's deliberately overloaded direction—demented, horror-movie camera angles, heavy solarizations, neurotic cuts from supersaturated color to black and white—and the stunningly elegant self-referential video-within-video motif, wherein each new sequence is introduced by Bowie holding a post-card-sized video screen displaying the first shot of the next scene.

David Bowie, "Let's Dance" (from the Capitol Records album *Let's Dance*), 1983, directed by Bowie and David Mallet, produced by Ross Cameron for Sierra Productions. Fine use of symbolism and surrealist evocations (i.e., the homage to Buñuel's *Un Chien Andalou,* when the aborigine boy suddenly drags an industrial machine through the streets of Sydney, Australia) enhance a genuine "message" video—the message in this case being that we should all think twice about colonialism, imperialism, and racist assimilation. The aborigines represent the assimilated; the red shoes they are initially fascinated by and eventually reject (stomping all over them atop a hill by Sydney's harbor) represent the assimilators. Bowie alleges that his "China Girl" clip carries similar allegorical weight, but it's done better here.

Bow Wow Wow, "Do You Wanna Hold Me" (from the RCA Records album *When the Going Gets Tough the Tough Get Going*), 1982, directed by Tim Pope, produced by Gordon Lewis for GLO Productions. A good example of Pope's early, rough-hewn, high-energy style. This clip actually mixes film and video in a nonnarrative stream of imagistic consciousness and multi-textural overload revolving loosely around the song's lyrics, a cockeyed tribute to California, "where Mickey Mouse is as big as a house." The lovely Annabella appears in several varieties of Disney costumes. The song's implicit critique of consumer culture is reflected in the gross-me-out closeups of band members stuffing their faces with junk food (echoing Devo's "Freedom of Choice"). Best image: the step-framed (every other frame is held for a second, giving a herky-jerky, silent-movie look) guitar solo in which guitarist Matthew Ashman wears a Ronald Reagan mask and is gradually engulfed by reels of celluloid. And if you watch closely, you'll see the image of former Bow Wow Wow mentor Malcolm McLaren flash by like a duck in a shooting gallery.

Martin Briley "The Salt in My Tears" (from the Polygram Records album *One Night with a Stranger*), 1983, directed by Chris Gabrin, produced by Siobhan Barron for Limelight. Briley, who based the song on a true experience, plays the about-to-be-divorced man whose soon-to-be-ex literally cleans him out of house and home. He is impassive and never moves from his couch (actually, he had food poisoning the day of the shoot and *couldn't* move from the couch). Any possibilities of mean-spirited sexism in the song's title chorus are completely defused by Gabrin's deft comedic *mise-en-scène,* and by the bravura performance of *Octopussy* star Marie Elise Gretner, who brilliantly turns her avenging Queen Bitch character into a wonderfully self-parodying caricature. One of the best uses of humor in rock video.

Jon Butcher Axis, "Life Takes a Life" (from the Polygram Records album *Jon Butcher Axis*), 1983, directed by Joe Dea, produced by Ken Walz for Ken Walz Productions. Joe Dea puts his strong narrative skill to tear-jerking effect in a cautionary social-comment tale that starts with the band performing the moody ballad in an apartment; Dea then pans to reveal police on the street outside the building and a crazed sniper holed up a few rooms away from the band. A black cop tries to talk the white sniper into surrender, then enters the building for the big showdown. Meanwhile, flashback cut-ins show a young white boy and a young black boy playing army with a toy gun and a guitar, respectively. As the cop prepares to burst into the sniper's room, Dea cuts back to the two kids mock-shooting each other and falling "dead" in slow motion; they laugh as they get back up, then Dea cuts to the aftermath of the cop-sniper confrontation—two bodies being carried out to a waiting ambulance. Were the cop and sniper those two little boys with two little toys, or did Dea merely posit a heavy-handed, though effective, analogue for the way we learn violence? Decide for yourself, but Dea's treatment of the theme is remarkably concise and really rather moving.

Captain Beefheart and the Magic Band, "Ice Cream for Crow" (from the Epic Records album *Ice Cream for Crow*), 1982, directed by Don Van Vliet, produced by Ken Schreiber. For just ten thousand dollars, the most wayward, self-determined, and idiosyncratic artist in modern American electric music made one of the best enhanced-performance videos ever. It's rarely been shown outside the Museum of Modern Art's video installation, probably because Beefheart's music is just too strong and eccentric, even for clubs: a tragedy. The video is well produced without being overbearingly slick, is beautifully photographed by

Daniel Pearl, and is imbued with Beefheart's unique spirit without ever resorting to obvious, cloying surrealistic contrivance. It opens with Beefheart wiping his brow with a tissue as he sings the rollicking blues romp's opening line, "It's so hot!" (and it was—the clip was shot in the Mojave Desert, not far from Beefheart's mobile home); we see the Magic Band performing in color by day, in black and white by night; we see a crow flying between two mesas; a rolling tumbleweed, like some natural ecology officer, picks up bits of tissue strewn over the desert scrub; Beefheart and his band members stand solemnly before cacti and beneath power lines, displaying the Captain's stunning abstract expressionist canvases; and when guitarist Gary Lucas breaks into a Hawaiian slide-guitar riff, Beefheart executes a neo-hula dance as Lucas literally flips his lid (his fedora flies off his head). Throughout, Beefheart mugs it up for the camera. It's delightful to see a renegade like Beefheart presented so well; that the clip works on so many other levels makes it even better.

The Cars, "Since You're Gone" (from the Elektra Records album *Shake It Up*), 1981, produced and directed by Paul Justman. A haunting, limpidly paced, subtly black-humored portrait of the aftershock of lost love: singer Ric Ocasek's girl has left him, and now literally nothing is the same. He sees her but she doesn't see him, then she disappears; his household appliances activate themselves; her shoes march right out of the house. The same motif was used by Venezuelan filmmaker Luis Arias for Ocasek's solo video, "Something to Grab For," but this is much better at etching an atmosphere of lingering, bittersweet melancholia.

The Cars, "You Might Think" (from the Elektra Records album *Heartbeat City*), 1984, directed by Charlex and Jeff Stein, produced by Stein, Charlex, and Cathy Dougherty. This hysterical gem is an ebullient catalog of video sight gags, embellishing the tale of Car Ric Ocasek chasing down the girl he loves. Many of the visual puns are affectionately lifted from lowbrow pop culture: a giant hand reaching through a window to pluck the girl from her bed (from the Grade Z camp classic *Attack of the 50-Foot Woman*); next a shot of Ocasek hanging off the Empire State Building in King Kong fashion, girl in hand. But then there are such original bits as the girl at her makeup table, opening her lipstick, and Ocasek spinning out of the tube; Ocasek's head on a fly's body buzzing the girl in her bed, and then a car with Ocasek at the wheel (get it?) zooming at the girl under the covers of her bed after she's swatted the fly away. As in Thomas Dolby's "Hyperactive!," the

Rolling Stones' "She Was Hot," and Devo's "Dr. Detroit," playful humor combines with great command of special effects in a marvelously irreverent and energetic video. And while this video has the occasional possibly malevolent touch, as when Ocasek-as-Kong drops the girl from the Empire State Building, all sins are atoned for by take-it-past-the-limit absurdity and a winning spirit—no matter what Ocasek does, the girl just keeps coming back, intact and smiling bemusedly. This is a surprising piece of work coming from Jeff Stein, who directed the admittedly fine Who documentary *The Kids Are Alright;* but then co-directors/producers Charlex are the same folks responsible for those oh-so-delightfully tacky *National Enquirer* TV spots, the ones with the similarly cartoonish special effects.

George Clinton, "Atomic Dog" (from the Capitol Records album *Computer Games*), 1983, directed by Peter Conn, produced by Coco Conn for Homer and Associates. Homer and Associates is a leading innovator in state-of-the-art digital computer-graphic effects. But with a performer like Clinton and a song like "Atomic Dog," it proves that high tech needn't be all sterile network sports show, digital image flips and the like. The clip starts off showing Clinton, Dr. Funkenstein himself, seriocomically observing the goings-on in a video-game arcade; it then pans into one of the money-hungry games itself, which becomes a moving, high-tech allegory for the human follies and foibles Clinton has always satirized. There is a jiving battle of the sexes, delightful animation (apparently based on Pedro Bell's cartoons for Parliament-Funkadelic album sleeves) of human-animal mutations (put to much better use here than in Bob Giraldi's stilted "Pieces of Ice" clip for Diana Ross), streetwise choreography of live and animated characters, and a stunning multilevel neo-Donkey Kong set through which the live and cartoon characters execute their strange pursuits, and over which the camera slowly pans, giving the clip the feel of a sort of modern *Metropolis*. Most important, "Atomic Dog"—as beautifully executed as it is—retains a crucial fidelity to Clinton and his notorious *modus operandi.* That is, somehow the clip is *funky,* too.

Culture Club, "Do You Really Want to Hurt Me?" (from the Epic Records album *Kissing to Be Clever*), 1982, directed by Julian Temple, produced by Siobhan Barron for Limelight. Julian Temple once again uses onscreen titles to travel through history (as in the Kinks' "Predictable"), this time to construct a seamless demidocudrama detailing the timelessness of Boy George's ability to outrage people. Here Temple works the same sort of contextualizing magic with a performer's persona that Steve Barron and Bob Giraldi executed with Michael Jackson in "Billie Jean" and "Beat It." The use of impassive blackface minstrels as the courtroom gallery adds a fine ironic touch to this only semifictional story of *the* New Age blue-eyed soul star.

Devo, "Satisfaction" (from *Q: Are We Not Men? A: We Are Devo!*), 1978, directed by Chuck Statler and Gerald Casale, produced by Chuck Statler. Arguably the first great enhanced-performance rock video: dramatic low-angle shots of the band performing their diabolical remake of the Rolling Stones classic against almost black-lit minimalist backdrops, capturing the robotic stage moves and yellow reactor-attendant jump suits that set the pop world on its eyes and ears in the late seventies; intercut with Devoesque images of frustration (singer Mark Mothersbaugh trying to make out with a girl in the backseat of a car and being foiled by driver General Boy, played by his father) and perversity (Mark Mothersbaugh as Booji Boy, sticking his fork into a toaster and pulling the smoking appliance into his playpen as the current makes his body convulse). This was also the first appearance in a rock video of L.A. punk dancer Spazz Attack, seen here executing somersaults from a standing position; he later appeared in many of Toni Basil's videos. This chip also pioneered the now-standard technique of quick-cutting previously seen imagery as the song and clip near conclusion.

Devo, "The Day My Baby Gave Me a Surprize" (from the Warner Brothers album *Duty Now for the Future*), 1979, directed by Chuck Statler and Gerald Casale, produced by Statler. Because of its ambitious use of multiple matte effects, this clip tripled Devo's five-thousand-dollar budget range. For instance, the band perform matted against a background of abstract video geometrics, and a baby is matted against a sky background so he appears to fly with the greatest of ease from one suburban back yard to another. There is also a high-tech reactor-room set, some charming animation, more stunning evidence of Devo's fashion savvy (i.e., the neo-Foreign Legion headgear, and the opaque wrap-around shades worn during most of the performance scenes), and Devo's typically self-possessed performance. This and "Come Back Jonee" are Devo's most light-hearted clips to date.

Devo, "Whip It" (from the Warner Brothers Records album *Freedom of Choice*), 1980, directed by Gerald Casale, produced by Chuck Statler for DevoVision. Probably Devo's most pointedly perverse and vicious satire of all-American kitsch: S&M comes home on the range as a new form of down-home fun. While the rest of Devo urgently perform the irresistible tune in a minicorral, singer Mark Mothers-baugh executes a crackling "whip-tease," snapping the clothes right off a trembling Latin spitfire; Mom whips up pies and cream ("Come and get it," reads a subtitle) while Mothersbaugh whips down the Latin girl, and a hunky cowpoke rolls in the hay with a cross-eyed Oriental girl who's just managed to shoot a beer can with a pre-"Beat It" *bonk* ("Ride 'em cowboy," reads the subtitle as we see her clothes fly out the window and the Latin girl's whipped-off clothes fly *in* the window). Casale overlit an old Paramount Western set to achieve the Technicolor look. Note that in keeping with Chuck Statler's neo-industrial style, Casale's camera never actually moves (except in the closing shot to follow drummer Alan Meyers, stalking purposefully off the set as Mom cries in a classic subtitle tag, "Oh that Alan!"); the editing, on the other hand, is as sharp as the crack of a whip.

Devo, "Freedom of Choice" (from *Freedom of Choice*), 1980, directed by Chuck Statler and Gerald Casale, produced by Devo, Inc.

Skateboarders shot from low angles zoom out over the viewer. Devo's Mark Mothersbaugh, in toga and shiny black nose, plays the subject of lyrics that go, "In ancient Rome there was a poem/ About a dog who had two bones/ He took one and took the other/ He ran in circles and he dropped dead." Devo, wearing extraterrestrial light-bulb-head masks, appear at key moments: popping out of a pixilated assemblage of doughnuts just as the hand of Roman centurion Casale reaches down from off-camera to pluck the one unoccupied doughnut (an unsettling close-up shows another alien lip-synching while munching the doughnut with his mouth open); or watching uniformed faddists zap nonconformists back into uniform. From age-old fabled folly to modern-day faddism, the point is the same—our ideals of "freedom" in a consumer society are a naive joke. Technically (with multiple mattes, special effects, and pixilation) the satirical message is driven home with overpowering élan; "Freedom of Choice" is imagistically powerful as well, especially in its stunningly appropriate casting of Devo themselves as *Outer Limits* aliens, which is exactly how most people perceived them.

Devo "Beautiful World" (from the Warner Brothers album *New Traditionalists*), 1981, directed by Gerald Casale, produced by Chuck Statler for DevoVision. This and "Freedom of Choice" are Devo's most openly and pithily message-oriented videos, and this one is arguably the greatest video ever by the world's greatest rock-video band. It opens on a gorgeously stylized set where Mark Mothersbaugh's Booji Boy, stage left, plays at a control panel and activates a large projection screen, stage right (an early instance of the Pirandellian video-within-the-video motif now so common), which shows Gerald Casale in a mock-JFK "Devo-Do" hairpiece, singing a devastatingly sardonic greeting-card verse to a world Devo obviously thinks is anything but beautiful. Booji Boy has actually tuned in to a classically Devoesque parade of fifties Americana, presented in a quick-cut montage of found images from black-and-white newsreels and TV footage: it starts innocently, then gets more perverse as we see female dancers brutally contorting themselves; as Booji Boy dances to the campy parade of subtly strange images, more unsettling scenes are cut in—street riots, WWI trench battles, the Ku Klux Klan carrying a burning cross. . . . As Booji Boy oohs and aahs in delight and disgust, and Casale sings, "It's a beautiful world for you . . . But not for me," we see a slow-motion close-up of a grotesquely undernourished black baby, a mushroom cloud, a fifties civil defense film about atomic radiation, and a closing shot of an Ann Miller-type majorette in salute against an American flag background, obviously taken from a forties or fifties propaganda film. "Beautiful World" just may be the most powerful sociopolitical use of sustained, concentrated montage since the legendary "Odessa Steps" sequence of Eisenstein's *The Battleship Potemkin.* At the very least, it's a Bruce Conner treatment of *Atomic Cafe* and does everything the acclaimed antinuke pseudodocumentary did in one-thirtieth the time and with thirty times the power. Kudos to editor Dale Cooper as well as to Casale.

Devo, "Thru Being Cool" (from *New Traditionalists*), 1981, directed by Gerald Casale, produced by Chuck Statler for DevoVision. More or less a recruitment film for the Devo Wants You! campaign to "eliminate the ninnies and the twits"—those who cannot or will not comprehend and act on Devo's philosophy of the world. Like "Whip It," this is a piece of mean, seriocomic entertainment with a message. As in "The Day My Baby Gave Me a Surprize," multiple mattes and special effects are used effectively, never obviously or gratuitously. The closing scene, for instance, in which some jogging health freaks are zapped by the converted, racially and sexually integrated pack of spudettes, uses four or five different mattes to give the illusion that the joggers are being chased down a road full of traveling cars, and are hit by the ray guns of the spudettes. The mutant homunculus-baboons from "Secret Agent Man" make a welcome comeback appearance in one scene, and in a lovely comic touch, some victims' faces are gunned into abstract, distorted wipes to the lines, "Put the tape on erase/ Rearrange your face/ We always liked Picasso anyway." Also, this is the first rock video to show kids break dancing (along with Toni Basil's concurrent "Cross-eyed and Painless" for Talking Heads).

The chicken-people lovers in Devo's "Love Without Anger" (1982)

Devo, "Love Without Anger" (from *New Traditionalists*), 1981, directed by Gerald Casale, produced by Chuck Statler for DevoVision. Devo's acid critique of human romantic relationships adroitly mixes shots of the band as choirboys reading from the book of love, shadow-animation of human-chicken mutants chasing each other with killer scissors, comical static-shot inserts of the mutant homunculi in frustrated lust, a hysterical, pixilated sequence of a perverse, violent though bloodless tryst between Barbie and Ken dolls (the pixilation was done by the Church of the SubGenius, a mock-Moral Majority new-wave cult that's Devoesque, though not actually affiliated with Devo, Inc.), and the perverse romantic activities of the chicken-people (at one point, he gives her a valentine candy box—full of worms).

Devo, "Theme from *Dr. Detroit*" (from the Backstreet Records album *Dr. Detroit*), 1983, directed by Gerald Casale, produced by Robert Weiss for Universal Pictures. "Time Out for Fun" (with its memorable opening shot of the spud boys' heads atop rotating potato bodies) and "Peek-a-Boo" (with its sinister, "interactive" computer-graphic media-mix) are tempting latter-day Devo citations, but as of this writing, *Dr. Detroit* was the most exceptional piece: the most creative movie-trailer-as-promo-clip yet (and infinitely better than the movie it promotes); and Devo's most good-humored video to date. Yet for all the winning comic touches, this rollicking vignette of high-tech identity-transference between Devo's Mark Mothersbaugh and *Dr. Detroit*'s Dan Aykroyd carries the subtle sting of trademark Devo motifs: interactivity between people and media and the good old lab-bred Frankenstein's monster riff. Casale's use of special effects has never been more playful or adept.

Dire Straits, "Skateaway" (from the Warner Brothers Records album *Making Movies*), 1981, directed by Lester Bookbinder, produced by Mervin Lloyd for Director's Project. The ultimate example of European postmodern commercial techniques in rock video: lushly photographed superreal colors and textures you can practically taste and feel; overwhelmingly sensual without being blatantly sexual. Bookbinder (who is in fact a British commercial director) also proves himself a master pictorial composer on a par with Russell Mulcahy (as in Duran Duran's "Is There Something I Should Know?") or Steve Barron (Fleetwood Mac's "Hold Me") at their mock-Magritte best. The "story," if you can call it that, has something to do with the ways in which an untamable, free-spirited, roller-skating girl bops through gray modern life, turning heads and ruffling feathers. But the star of this show is the stunning art direction and photography, exemplified in the magnificent overhead shot of the girl roller-skating in a curlicue pattern through a steeplechase of opened umbrellas. Pure visual pleasure, and the song's pretty nice, too.

Thomas Dolby, "Hyperactive!" (from the Capitol Records album *The Flat Earth*), 1984, directed by Dolby with Danny Kleinman, produced by Siobhan Barron for Limelight. Dolby's 1982 surreal slapstick farce for "She Blinded Me with Science" was a funny, well-done video and an auspicious debut for Dolby as a musician who also directs his own videos. With its use of silent-movie title-card inserts, it also cleverly pointed up the seldom-observed fact that the "action" in rock videos invariably falls in line with silent movie acting. But "Hyperactive!" is something else again, with stunning and witty use of special digital effects completely at the service of the song. Mostly, it's Dolby on a couch being interviewed by a psychiatrist (a *real* shrink, too, just as genuine eccentric scientist Dr. Magnus Pyke played the Eccentric Scientist in "She Blinded Me with Science"); both wear boxes over their heads, which digitally flash various facial expressions (recalling similar gambits by the Swiss mime troupe Mummenschanz), and so on. Dolby's performance, especially when he digitally turns his own head into his own ventriloquist's dummy, is perfectly played and delightfully comic.

Duran Duran, "Hungry like the Wolf" (from the Capitol-EMI Records album *Rio*), 1981, directed by Russell Mulcahy, produced by Eric Fellmer for MGMM.

A minimovie, epic in sweep, befitting its blatant allusions to *Raiders of the Lost Ark* (there's also a touch of *Apocalypse Now,* when singer Simon LeBon's head rises out of a river in slow motion as rain pours down). Simon LeBon chases a wild beauty through Sri Lanka's exotic jungles, casbahs, watering-holes and open-air markets; in the process, he overturns the now-legendary barroom table (the locals weren't expecting it, and several were injured by flying glass) and has his brow mopped by a young Indian. When he and the woman-cum-beast finally do meet in a very close encounter, Mulcahy's ravenously tracking and panning camera, insinuating erotic ambiguity, and editing wizardry (frames sliding in from the left or right, double and triple split-screen edits on and around the beat, etc.), which have been the real stars of the show all along, come into full play: either she jumps him, or he jumps her; either love is made, or murder committed. We're not sure, but LeBon does sport telltale scratch marks on his cheek. No matter: we've been dazzled, seduced, and abandoned. The premier example of the made-in-heaven marriage of a band and a director.

Duran Duran, "Is There Something I Should Know?" (from the Capitol-EMI Records album *Carnival*), 1982, directed by Russell Mulcahy, produced by Jackie Adams for MGMM. A blue-lit interior with a constructivist staircase. A red ball bounces *up* the stairs in slow motion. Simon LeBon shakes his fist at a shaft of light as he lip-synchs. A fogbound forest. The steps of a civic edifice. Cryptic, bowler-hatted surveyors. A naked baby crawling about before giant video screens (playing scenes from other Duran Duran videos, like "Save a Prayer" and "Lonely in Your Nightmare"). A little boy in a floppy hat chases the bouncing red ball through the forest. The little boy sits at a dusty table in a forgotten chamber; the table is strewn with compasses and slide rules; an old man, either dead or asleep, is collapsed at the table; wind blows the dust off the table. And so on. None of it makes any kind of logical sense. And that doesn't matter: this is the epitome of Mulcahy's "photographic" style, and as such is pure, pictorial-geometric viewing pleasure, with constructivist sequential split-screen edits, homages to Magritte (the scenes with the bowler-hatted men), the rhythmic superimposition of frames within frames, and one amazing scene in which LeBon appears to zoom backwards into the forest while standing still (a trick used by John Landis in Michael Jackson's "Thriller").

Duran Duran, "Girls on Film" (from the Capitol Records album *Rio*), 1981, directed by Kevin Godley and Lol Creme, produced by Lexi Godfrey. Kevin Godley recalls: "Lol and I were told by Duran's management simply to make a very provocative, sexy video that had some sort of tenuous connection to the band and would be seen in clubs and cause people to talk." And they did. In fact, Duran Duran themselves are barely visible in the clip. What we do see are a bevy of gorgeous, scantily clad (or in some cases nude in the uncensored version) ladies pillow-fighting on a whipped-cream-covered phallic pole; lady wrestlers riding piggyback on black men wearing *Equus*-style horse heads; a woman who flips a sumo wrestler and then massages him into further submission; one model-wrestler who kisses a male lifeguard so intensely she appears to drown him in a child's plastic wading pool. All of it takes place in a combination fashion-show runway and wrestling ring; all of it is shot like classic soft-focus, soft-core porn. The first and, to date, last word in sexist rock video.

Eurythmics, "Sweet Dreams (Are Made of This)" (from the RCA Records album *Sweet Dreams*), 1983, directed by Dave Stewart and Annie Lennox, produced by Jon Roseman. With her blazing blue eyes, carrot-colored crew cut, and impeccably tailored men's suits, mannish girl Lennox is certainly a presence onscreen, but she's nearly upstaged by all the *très outré* symbolism: Lennox prone on a conference table in an RCA board room while a cow saunters by from out of nowhere; Lennox singing and Stewart working a computer console in a misty meadow full of more contented cows; masked cellists in rowboats, and so on. Stewart claims it all has to do with the permanence of nature versus the artifice of modernity, adding that when he told Lennox his left-field concepts, "she agreed they were nice surrealistic images to go with the song." Indeed, the use of cows as visual non sequiturs harks back to Luis Buñuel's *L'Age d'Or* (1930), in which a cow lounges on a plush canopy bed in a bourgeois mansion for no apparent reason. Eurythmics, however, lack Buñuel's revolutionary guts: at the end of "Sweet Dreams," all the preceding irrationality is rationalized as we see Lennox awaking in bed—the "it was all just a dream" coda so many rock videos end up using.

Eva Everything, "Boob Tube" (from the Great Shakes Records album *Boob Tube*), 1983, produced and directed by Eva Everything. A charming, catchy little electropop ditty, which with its exceptionally ambitious and contents-packed video, examines and questions the ways in which children of the global village are suckled on the electronic breast: "What do you want most out of life? . . . What do you need to see you through? . . . I catch the rhythm of the airwaves . . . Boob tube bliss will do. . . ." Eva's camera choreography is perfect, rhythmically kinetic and sharply controlled, bouncing back and forth between the prim, bespectacled Eva watching the boob tube and the hipper, saucier Eva *on* the tube; there are smoothly edited sequences of a succession of hands wiping diagonally across a TV-tit onscreen; in the end, the viewing Eva is literally sucked right into the set, merging with the onscreen Eva. There's more: The song and video keep being "interrupted" by "Boob Tube" "programming"—a phone-in talk show whose number is 555-BLAB; and most hilarious of all, a guy in a Superman suit and a batwing headdress known as "Record Breaker," who, yes, stands there smashing records handed to him from off-camera (the voice-over announcer urgently asks, "Is there a record he can't break?"). And there's plenty more besides. There's enough wit, insight, humor, information, ideas, and energy here to make Eva Everything some sort of Canadian Toni Basil-meets-Devo (Evo?). But the fact that "Boob Tube" *looks* so good, and that Eva made the whole thing herself for just eight hundred dollars (earlier, she made another fine video, "Polyester Passion," for even less), makes her something else again.

Donald Fagen, "New Frontier" (from the Warner Brothers Records album *The Nightfly*), 1983, directed by Annabelle Jankel and Rocky Morton, produced by Andy Morahan for Cucumber Studios. Sweet, subtly ironic nostalgia for the Cold War years to which the song title refers. A teen-age couple—he nervous and nerdy in horn-rims, she blond and beautiful, intelligent and assured, "Wearing Ambush and a French twist"—party and tryst in a fallout shelter, embarrassed and tentative at first. The transition from their own interpersonal romantic

Cold War to something, er, hotter, is signaled by a lovely homage to *E.T.*'s homage to Michelangelo's Sistine Chapel creation fresco. Meanwhile, animated figures out of Picasso, Miró, Tanguy, and/or Klee canvases dance about them like abstract cherubim (Klee animation?), fluttering in time to Fagen's vocal vibrato on the line "We're going to a wingding"; a Picassoesque cubist portrait of a woman rearranges itself into the album-cover graphic of Dave Brubeck's *Take Five* as Fagen croons, "I hear you're mad about Brubeck. . . ." Classic fifties art-and-commerce graphics and designs are exploited to the hilt, but they never overshadow the sensitively told, beautifully acted tale of the two lovers. Warm, witty, and stunningly crafted, "New Frontier" is a treat for the eyes and ears, *and* emotionally penetrating and uplifting. Easily the most awesome of Cucumber's consistently great accomplishments, and possibly the greatest rock video ever. Fagen himself, by the way, never makes an appearance, aside from a brief glance at the *Nightfly* LP cover as a poster on the fallout shelter wall.

Fleetwood Mac, "Gypsy" (from the Warner Brothers Records album *Mirage*), 1982, directed by Russell Mulcahy, produced by Simon Fields for Gowers, Fields and Flattery. Mulcahy cannily makes the most of Stevie Nicks's annoyingly overbearing white-witch fancies in this stunningly produced, sweeping mini-epic, which moves effortlessly from Nicks's own lace-adorned boudoir to an elegant nightclub, from sepia-toned Depression-era black-and-white sequences to a florid Technicolor fantasy forest. And Nicks herself turns in a fine performance, especially in the scene in which she runs out of the nightclub into the rain and strikes a theatrically anguished pose. Of course it all has nothing to do with the song, but then the song has nothing to do with anything, anyway.

Fleetwood Mac, "Hold Me" (from *Mirage*), 1982, directed by Steve Barron, produced by Simon Fields for Gowers, Fields and Flattery. Here Steve Barron pioneered the now much-abused rock-video technique of setting a band in a desert. Barron's use of it works better than most subsequent attempts (Captain Beefheart's "Ice Cream for Crow" excepted). Beyond that, Barron here proved himself as adept a post-surreal pictorial composer as Russell Mulcahy. "Hold Me" virtually overflows with homages to surrealist painter René Magritte, and not even the gratuitous cuts to Stevie Nicks acting her usual space-cadet self get in the way of the pure visual feast. What really makes it all connect and stick in the memory is Barron's strikingly poetic analogue for the song's sentiment of romantic longing: two human hands reaching out to touch each other, reflected in a free-form arcade of jagged mirror shards stuck in a sand dune.

Peter Gabriel, "Shock the Monkey" (from the Geffen Records album *Security*), 1982, directed by Brian Grant, produced by Chryssie Smith for MGMM. A dizzying, blue-lit, *noir*-like schizoid psychodrama, sort of Bowie's "Ashes to Ashes" meets *Altered States*. Gabriel, who, like Bowie has a history of infusing live performance with mime and character acting (mainly with Genesis), here plays a three-piece-suited businessman on the brink and a shamanistic, Kabuki-masked alter ego. The video is about the battle between the two halves of Gabriel's self for total control. The businessman tries to go about his work even as his office is going haywire (not unlike the exploding kitchen in "Ashes to Ashes"); then he's spinning on a carousel; then he's neck-deep in swampy muck; then the shaman is sitting in the office while a monkey cavorts about the desk. Grant's pacing perfectly matches the song's psychotic, stop-start arrangement. "What sparked the idea," says Grant, "was the line 'Don't monkey with the monkey.' It's just about a guy trying to stay in touch with primal instincts, or those instincts taking him over, or . . . I just pictured someone in a normal, sterile environment suddenly taken into a primeval nightmare." And that's just what Grant worked up here. Storyboard artist Marcello Anciano probably had a lot to do with it, too—his own clip for Gabriel's "I Don't Remember" is more or less a full-color Xerox of "Shock the Monkey" but nowhere near as powerfully dislocated and disturbed.

Golden Earring, "Twilight Zone" (from the Polygram Records album *Cut*), 1982, produced and directed by Dick Mass for Red Bullet Productions. A kinky, paranoid minimovie classic: the singer is pursued by cloak-and-dagger mystery men and nearly done in by a seductive Mata Hari; he's bound and drugged by dancing girls in Nazi leather regalia; in an homage to Luis Buñuel's *The Discreet Charm of the Bourgeoisie*, the red curtains in a parlor suddenly part to reveal the singer at center stage before a full-house theater audience; in one of the aisles, a little girl flashes a look as blankly suggestive as any typical rock-video model's; onstage, the singer lip-syncs the song's chorus as his pursuers sing backup while doing a soft-shoe shuffle; finally, the protagonist is seen tied to a chair and blindfolded, about to be executed. Throughout, the image of a bullet slicing through a playing card in superslow motion is cut in whenever we hear the refrain "You are all alone when the bullet hits the bone." Dick Mass produced this beautiful exploitation of James Bond-style male-adolescent fantasies on the remarkably low budget of sixteen thousand dollars; it made the song Golden Earring's first big hit in a decade and kept the band from breaking up. The camera work and set design are picture perfect.

Eddy Grant, "Electric Avenue" (from the Epic Records album *Killer on the Rampage*), 1982, directed by Steve Barron, produced by Siobhan Barron for Limelight. A classic example of Steve Barron's latter-day semiabstract and seminarrative surrealism: the charismatic Grant lip-syncs while sitting in a living-room chair watching a shark on TV; he gets up and steps right into—*water! Deep* water (the living room set was built on a ten-foot-high scaffold in a pool on Grant's home island of Barbados, where the clip was shot). Cut to Grant washing up on a beach. There's also some perplexing business with a bespectacled little schoolgirl, and there are constant cuts to a close-up of a hand turning a motorcycle throttle, precisely timed to the crunching electrofunk tune's synthesized rev-up effects. The entire clip is treated with posterization, an effect not unlike solarization, which adds to the dreamy atmosphere.

Herbie Hancock, "Rockit" (from the Columbia Records album *Future Shock*), 1983, directed by Kevin Godley and Lol Creme, produced by Lexi Godfrey and Fiona Fitzherbert for Media Lab. Ballet Mécanique, rock-video style: Jim Whiting's ingeniously designed computer-controlled robot-mannequins and Godley and Creme's witty "scratch" editing immeasurably magnified the impact of Hancock's admittedly fine supersyncopated electrofunk étude. It's all bizarre kineticism, and at times approaches some sort of malevolent black humor, as when some of the robots are seen convulsing spastically in bed, or when one robot keeps bashing another's head into a kitchen table. The only other thing that needs to be noted about this legendary clip is that Hancock (who happens to be black) appears only on a small video monitor set within the motorized mayhem. Hancock wanted it this way, knowing that it would increase his chances of getting the clip into MTV rotation. The gambit worked, of course, and MTV rotation helped "Rockit" become one of the surprise smash hits of 1983. Godley and Creme's subsequent clip for Hancock's "Autodrive" was another inventive winner—the second great modern-era instrumental clip.

The Human League, "Don't You Want Me" (from the A&M Records album *Dare*), 1981, directed by Steve Barron, produced by Siobhan Barron for Limelight. A simple song of aching romantic longing and frustration, given an elaborate visual complement in Steve Barron's first big breakthrough concept clip. We are privy to a bittersweet love-lost scenario involving singers Phil Oakey, Susan Sulley, and Joanne Catherall that takes place on and off the set of a movie being made. Thus, "Don't You Want Me" seems to be an homage to Truffaut's *Day for Night,* and in fact, Barron admits it is: "If you look closely, there's one shot where someone's holding a clapper board up to the camera, and on it is written 'Le League Humain,' which was our little in-joke reference to Truffaut." There are also breathtaking tracking shots redolent of Marcel Ophuls. The lighting and cinematography are relentlessly beautiful, and the editing is as powerful and irresistible as heartsickness welling up in your throat. There is also the greatest rack-focus shot (that is, when focus and perspective shift from one side of the frame to the other within a single shot) in the history of rock video, from Oakey to Catherall and back again in the screening room. Finally, "Don't You Want Me" is the apotheosis of the hallowed rock-video tendency to show people staring down the camera with intense, meaningful looks and soulful puppy-dog eyes; it's not just expediently exploiting those looks, it's all *about* those looks.

Joe Jackson, "Steppin' Out" (from the A&M Records album *Night and Day*), 1982, directed by Steve Barron, produced by Simon Fields and Siobhan Barron for Limelight. Now here's a perfect idea for a concept video: a classic escapist fantasy story within a genre generally devoted to escapist fantasy. A maid cleans a ritzy apartment as her dressed-to-the-nines male and female employers leave for a night on the town; the maid strikes the classic pose—grabbing a black-and-gold lamé gown and falling back on the plush bed with a dreamy smile—and fancies *herself* dancing it up with the man who's just left. Jackson then appears, playing the living-room grand. In keeping with the fantasy motif, the maid wakes from her revery just as her employers, looking perturbed with each other, return. Jackson splits as well, dropping the carnation we'd seen on his piano on the sidewalk in front of the hotel in which the final shot reveals it's all been taking place. Just before the fade, we see the man rub his chin thoughtfully and move towards the piano—is he about to replay Jackson's role and start the maid's fantasy off for real? Barron's handling of the concept, shot purposefully in misty soft-focus, is elegantly economical, full of diffused light and sweeping camera moves.

The Jacksons, "Can You Feel It (The Triumph)" (from the Epic Records album *Triumph*), 1981, produced and directed by Robert Abel, for Abel and Associates.

One of the earliest examples of a black-music video with a big-budget "look" that could compete with anyone else's—in fact, this eight-minute clip, produced for the Jacksons' 1981 tour, was way ahead of most of its contemporaries in terms of production values alone. Sumptuous computer animation depicts the Jacksons as huge, luminous, God-like figures reaching down from the heavens to spangle earthlings of all colors with magical stardust, bringing everyone together in peaceful, joyous harmony. Beautifully executed, and aesthetically apt to boot —the original concept of music as a force of racial unity was written by Michael Jackson himself. Sections of this video are included in the *Making Michael Jackson's "Thriller"* home-video cassette.

Michael Jackson, "Beat It" (from *Thriller*), 1983, directed by Bob Giraldi, produced by Antony Payne for Gotham Entertainment. By general consensus, the greatest, or at least the most popular, rock video of all time. And why not? Here you have another riveting performance by Jackson, starting out in classic teen-wimp position, face-down on his bed in his room, head buried in the pillow his hands clutch desperately (not unlike Sal Mineo's Plato in *Rebel without a Cause*), then metamorphosing into a sweet black angel who prances into a ghetto garage just in time to turn an imminent gang war into a celebratory communal dance. Here you have a great antimacho rock-disco song given a perfectly appropriate visualization, and in the process you have an all-too-rare case of genuine social comment in a rock video. Here you have the stupendously overpowering final sequence, in which twenty dancers mimic Jackson's fluid high-stepping. You also have cinematic allusions to *West Side Story, The Warriors,* and even *Escape from New York* (with gang members leaping out of manholes), as well as the innovative use of key dramatically vital soundtrack noises (switch-blades flicking open, garage doors rising and falling with an ominous *clank*) dubbed onto the music track. As Giraldi's first rock video, this has to rank as the most auspicious entree in the field—so auspicious, in fact, that his subsequent rock videos (Diana Ross's "Pieces of Ice," Pat Benatar's "Love Is a Battlefield," Paul McCartney and Jackson's "Say Say Say") haven't come close to matching this one's enormous impact.

Michael Jackson, "Billie Jean" (from the Epic Records album *Thriller*), 1982, directed by Steve Barron, produced by Simon Fields for Limelight. Michael Jackson plays a magical, mystical protagonist in a Technicolor-*noir* cat-and-mouse spy story: everything Jackson touches glows, and the trench-coated tail who pursues Jackson can never capture him, either in the flesh or on film. The clip starts with Jackson strutting down a street-scene set somewhere between Skid Row and *The Wiz*'s Yellow Brick Road, with the street lighting up wherever Jackson steps. The closing shot, after Jackson has once again eluded his nemesis, shows the street lighting up by itself, suggesting that Jackson is there, but now invisible. Steve Barron was able to identify a performer like Jackson with a ready-made concept that was perfectly tailored to the situation at hand. "Billie Jean" is far from being a literal analogue to the song's lyrics about paternity-suit paranoia, but it *is* a wonderfully felicitous once-removed complement, feeding off of the song's shadowy arrangement and slinky beat as well as Jackson's well-known aura of manchild androgyny, and transposing them via atmospheric sets and lighting and a properly suggestive yet open-ended scenario. "Beat It" gets most of the glory when discussing Michael Jackson's videos, but "Billie Jean," in its own way, is just as good.

Chaz Jankel, "Questionnaire" (from the A&M Records album *Questionnaire*), 1981, directed by Annabelle Jankel and Rocky Morton, produced by Andy Morahan for Cucumber Studios. Yes, Chaz and Annabelle Jankel are related (they're brother and sister). Here, one-time Ian Dury Blockhead Chaz has a superslick disco-salsa tune, for which Annabelle and company have produced a semiabstract neon graphic extravaganza. Whereas Tom Tom Club's "Genius of Love" is all innocent, sunny, childlike perpetual motion against a white void, "Questionnaire" is all sexy, continental perpetual motion against a black void: wheels spinning within wheels, angular constructivist shapes, miniature traffic lights and neon bar signs, flying lips that emit light when they part to sing (and this was *before* Laurie Anderson used the same technique in her "O Superman"); the only break comes when a Carmen Miranda-type dances a samba against a blinding white light background. True "visual music," a smoldering sound- and vision-track for a plush tropical cruise.

Joan Jett, "Bad Reputation" (from the Boardwalk Records album *Bad Reputation*), 1982, directed by David Mallet, produced by Jackie Adams for MGMM. Simply by being her own tough, uncompromising, gum-chewing self, Joan Jett has been able to maintain one of the most consistent, and consistently appealing, video personae in all of rock. The stark, grungy black-and-white barroom-chant performance of "I Love Rock & Roll" (produced and directed by Arnold Levine) is tempting to cite as Jett's best video, but "Bad Reputation" tops it. It is simply the most devastatingly funny attack on the record business this side of the between-clips scenes in Devo's *The Men Who Make the*

Music. The camera, taking Jett's point of view, shows us a succession of label executives turning thumbs down on Jett's demo tapes; then, following Jett's own true-life surprise success story, she and her band form their own label and, as a silent movie-style title card tells us, "The record's a hit." The rest of the video consists of those same label execs all-too-happily welcoming Jett into their corporate dens. The finale has Jett performing atop a table in a nightclub while the assembled execs dance around her. Mallet used a similar before-and-after approach in Jett's 1983 "Fake Friends" video.

J. Geils Band, "Centerfold" (from the Capitol-EMI Records album *Freeze-Frame*), 1981, produced and directed by Paul Justman. Again displaying his unique, blunt-yet-refined American surrealism, Justman brings this ode to homeroom horniness to life by bringing the wet-dream fantasies themselves to realer-than-real (as in dreamlike) life, as a bevy of schoolgirls gyrate around the jiving Peter Wolf, first in letter sweaters and saddle shoes, then in flimsy, though not too revealing, camisoles and nighties. As in the Cars' "Since You're Gone," Justman's fluid editing and judicious use of slow motion heighten the dream-within-a-dream aura. It doesn't match the sis-boom-bah singalong pace of the song itself, but it still works just fine.

Billy Joel, "Allentown" (from the Columbia Records album *The Nylon Curtain*), 1982, directed by Russell Mulcahy, produced by Jackie Adams for MGMM. One of Mulcahy's few truly narrative and truly sweet videos: a poignant, beautifully choreographed (by Kenny Ortega) tale of steelworkers and Vietnam vets (the obvious allusion to *The Deer Hunter* is, for once, *not* exploited heavy-handedly), of the work ethic and patriotism, of failed dreams and broken promises, and strong bodies and stronger faith. In the style of forties movie musicals, the new-depression barroom, in which Joel is perfectly cast as a hobo minstrel playing on the sidelines, opens onto a flag-waving production number, only to close back into its former run-down intimacy. There are some ridiculous moments that almost ruin it all, as when Mulcahy casts a bunch of lean, handsome hunks as showering steel-millers. But such lapses are overshadowed by the emotional connections, which are especially strong in the heart-rending scene where one steelworker sees his Viet-vet brother (or is it friend?) in a wheelchair, is taken aback for a second, then hugs him. In scope and dramatic momentum, this is another epic minimovie for Mulcahy, and another incredible break for Joel, a performer with zero visual appeal who just happens to have had some of the most eye-catching videos of all time crafted around him.

Billy Joel, "Goodnight Saigon" (from the Columbia Records album, *The Nylon Curtain*), 1982, directed by Jay Dubin and Arnold Levine, produced by Levine. Basically an enhanced-performance clip that manages, through subject matter and tone, to connect to the high political-emotional concept of "Allentown." Here, Joel performs his Vietnam War hymnal accompanied by a choir of Viet vets; intercut are actual slides and photos taken by American soldiers during the war. Levine also used geographically pertinent still photos to similar atmospheric and sentimental effect in Bruce Springsteen's "Atlantic City," which never once shows Springsteen performing and instead focuses on still shots and filmed snippets in moody black and white of the decaying boardwalk.

Billy Joel, "Pressure" (from the Columbia Records album *The Nylon Curtain*), 1982, directed by Russell Mulcahy, produced by Jackie Adams for MGMM. A tense Joel is strapped into a chair on a bottom-lit metal grid, blitzed by an onslaught of mind-controlling imagery flashing in constant quick-cut on a huge screen before him (an allusion to *A Clockwork Orange*). Joel's shoes are splashed with puddle water by a passing car; Great Danes snap at his soaked cuffs. Joel is sucked into a shag carpet at an elegant party where coffee cups erupt like little volcanoes, and another man is sucked right into a water-splashing wall —all the while, everyone else pretends not to notice. A schoolboy walks down a sterile, overlit hallway, only to be sucked, *Poltergeist*-fashion, into a TV set. The same schoolboy is seen in class, his desk tottering and then overflowing with water. . . . There's little or no conventional narrative meaning here, but there *is* an awesome amount of free-associative apocalyptic water and technology imagery, enhanced by some remarkably creative special effects, and it all manages to cohere into a powerfully disturbing video—purposefully and appropriately over the top.

Billy Joel, "Tell Her about It" (from the Columbia Records album *An Innocent Man*), 1983, directed by Jay Dubin, produced by Jon Small for Parallel Communications. A slick, rollicking bit of fun. BJ and the Affordables perform the neo-Motown tune on "The Ed Sullivan Show," *circa* 1963 (as an opening title card indicates); noted Sullivan impersonator Will Jordan is on hand to introduce them. Simultaneously, Joel—in the same rockabilly pompadour and wrap-around shades he sports onstage—travels around as an invisible Greek chorus, dropping in on various locales where people are watching him on *Sullivan* and dispensing advice to the lovelorn. There's a Mom and Pop

Performance-within-a-performance: *The Ed Sullivan Show* recreated (note vintage CBS cameras) for the smash appearance of "BJ and the Affordables" in Billy Joel's hugely popular clip "Tell Her About It" (1983), directed by commercial maker Jay Dubin. The clip also features Sullivan impersonator Will Jordan and a cameo by comic Rodney Dangerfield.

at home; a barroom; a sorority pajama party. Even a Russian cosmonaut circling the globe tunes in and claps and sings along. In the finale, comedian Rodney Dangerfield, who's been making a cameo appearance in the wings alongside Jordan the whole time, thanks Joel for warming his crowd up, only to have Jordan/Sullivan introduce Petrushka the dancing bear instead. Rodney still don't get no respect; unfortunately, Dubin missed a golden opportunity by forgetting to have Dangerfield actually *say* his catch phrase. Still, in all, a thoroughly warm and winning video.

Elton John, "I'm Still Standing" (from the Geffen Records album *Too Low for Zero*), 1983, directed by Russell Mulcahy, produced by Jacqui Byford for MGMM. This is pure pop video. Total choreography, of beautiful male and female bodies, and of cameras and editing techniques. As such, it's a dazzling piece of pure visual kineticism that not even someone like Toni Basil has been able to match yet. Shot on the French Riviera, with choreography by Arlene Phillips (who used to choreograph the saucy Hot Gossip dancers on the Kenny Everett show and who has choreographed most MGMM videos, including Donna Summer's "She Works Hard for the Money"), it's the most extravagant display this side of Duran Duran's "Rio" of Mulcahy's trademark use of brightly colored inks on bodies. And Mulcahy's usual gift for insolent sexuality perfectly matches the song's subtle hints of arrogance.

Greg Kihn, "Happy Man" (from the Beserkely Records album *Rockihnroll*), 1981, directed by Joe Dea, produced by Erik Nelson for VideoWest. Following the off-the-wall hilarity of Dea's low-budget classic "Two Triple Cheese" for Commander Cody, this black-and-white video was the first instance of Dea's mastery of narrative within the three-minute clip. It's the usual boss versus the workers assembly-line drama, set in a guitar factory, natch, with Kihn as our hero. Dea's pacing never flags, and he gets vivid performances from just about all of the supporting players. In the most memorable scene, the frustrated Kihn literally punches the clock and smashes it to pieces (echoing a similar shot in Peter Yates's film *Breaking Away* involving Jackie Earl Haley).

Greg Kihn, "Jeopardy" (from the Beserkely Records album *Kihnspiracy*), 1983, directed by Joe Dea, produced by Tawn Mastrey and Rebecca Vermeul for L.I.P.S., Inc. Joe Dea does it again, orchestrating traditional male fear of the institution of marriage into a macabre, seriocomic *Grand Guignol* classic. Clean-cut Kihn winningly plays an average-Joe reluctant groom getting cold feet on his wedding day, who then dreams that the entire bridal party has turned into hideous decayed ghouls right out of *Dawn of the Dead.* And, throughout the ceremony of unholy matrimony, they want him to become one of them. Kihn's fantasy starts after he endures the smug well-wishing of his future in-laws: he imagines his friends mocking him on his way to the altar, he thinks he sees his future in-laws shackled with handcuffs and then linked at the gut by a grotesquely pulsating piece of mutant flesh. When he places the ring on his bride's finger (he's so distracted that the minister reminds him about the ring—using a graphic finger-in-the-circle sign—three times) and lifts her veil for a kiss, she is a decaying corpse; her skull's jaw drops open in time to a dubbed-in scream. A tinfoil monster (a sort of low-budget version of John Carpenter's *The Thing*) explodes from the floor of the ghoul-infested church; Kihn kills it with an oblong piece of pew that he had grabbed while being dragged back to the altar by the monster. Kihn then "plays" the piece of wood during the song's guitar solo (a hilariously ironic way to make an obligatory connection to performance). His escape dissolves into Super-8 footage of the "real" bride and groom leaving the church; but then we pan back and see that the film is being watched by the decayed corpses of the bride and groom. We finally cut back to Kihn, still looking in the mirror and flashing A-OK signs to his in-laws—the tip-off that what's come before has been a fantasy. Kihn then grabs a bottle of champagne and high-tails it out the back door to his sports car. A similarly perturbed bride-to-be exits from another church across the street, throws her bouquet to the ground, looks at Kihn, looks back at the bouquet, smiles suggestively, and then Kihn swings his car round to pick her up. As they drive off, we hear the champagne bottle's cork pop.

This was one of the first rock videos to dub in extramusical sound effects (the bride's scream, the wood rending when the monster explodes from the floor, the champagne cork popping). It's also one of the most ambitious and entertaining rock videos ever, especially considering that Dea shot it all in two days on a budget of roughly twenty thousand dollars.

King Crimson, "Heartbeat" (from the Warner Brothers Records album *Beat*), 1982, produced and directed by John Sanborn and Kit Fitzgerald. New York avant-garde video artists Sanborn and Fitzgerald (whose partnership has since dissolved) made an auspicious debut in promo video with this low-budget job, which offsets the song's slow ballad tempo with a steady stream of swiftly flowing dissolves, image overload in the classic Sanborn vein. The clip balances shots of a solitary Adrian Belew writing a letter to his love with time-lapse scenes of dinner and party crowds gradually melting down to keep focusing on the obscure object of Belew's desire, played by New York avant-garde performance artist Jill Kroesen. Sanborn deliberately packs the imagery in, so you have to see it several times to digest it all. This is ultimately a unique and satisfying video translation of aching, obsessive long-distance desire, all the better because it never once resorts to what would only be static shots of the band performing.

The Kinks, "Predictable" (from the Arista Records album *Give the People What They Want*), 1981, directed by Julian Temple, produced by Siobhan Barron for Limelight. We time-travel from the fifties to the present with Ray Davies via subtitles ("Meanwhile, in Swinging London . . .") and costume changes that cast the ever-adept Davies as a rockabilly greaser, a mid-sixties mod, a late sixties hookah-puffing hippie (and Frank Zappa look-alike!), and a seventies punk—as well as a frumpy housewife, vacuum cleaner in hand—watching the times change on TV. Ray's telly broadcasts the early Kinks, Kinks-derived punks the Jam, and rockabilly revivalists Stray Cats, as the lip-synching Davies nods sagely and pronounces each trend "Predictable . . ." The message that there's nothing new under the sun is delivered with a delightful, subtly satirical humor.

The Kinks, "Come Dancing" (from the Arista Records album *State of Confusion*), 1983, directed by Julian Temple, produced by Siobhan Barron for Limelight. The song is classic Ray Davies: the razing of a dance hall in the name of progress sparks a bittersweet rumination on the value and permanence of emotion and memory in the face of an ever-changing exterior landscape. The video, too, is classic Davies: Ray plays both "himself" (the "grown-up singer in a band") and an aging, mustachioed lounge lizard brilliantly; the latter turns out to be the former boyfriend of the singer's elder sister, who used to patronize the dance hall. Flashbacks show the lounge lizard's troubled romance with the singer's sister, and the singer-as-child is played by a wonderful little boy who at one point mimics Dave Davies's hard-rock guitar solo on a tennis racket while dressed in a British schoolboy's shorts and cap (the same image appears in Madness' "Our House"). It all culminates in the invitation to acknowledge our feelings, to "come dancing." Like any great Kinks song, Julian Temple's video is impressive and touching in both its sweep and its compactness, its scope and its intimacy, its humor and its pathos. One of the truly sweetest rock videos ever made, and one of the tiny handful to look back at the past not with campy derision but with fond nostalgia, a sentiment totally befitting Davies's music. The story continues in "Don't Forget to Dance," a less coherent story, again starring Ray Davies as the aging spiv.

Krokus, "Screaming in the Night" (from the Arista Records album *Head Hunter*), 1983, directed by Joe Dea, produced by Leslie Rabb. Another purposefully and appropriately overdone macabre concept clip by Joe Dea, here fully exploiting heavy metal's innate leanings towards the Gothic and macho. Dea says the clip is a land-based version of the old Charlton Heston epic *The Vikings*. A band of pagans trek across the desert to their king's throne room with a captive in tow; the captive, Krokus's vocalist, is chained and imprisoned; he sees a guard murder his loved one with a knife (Dea wanted to show the guard licking the knife clean of blood, but knew it would be censored by MTV); through some special-effects magic involving a pyramidlike chamber, our hero escapes—into a modern-day luncheonette, where he sees himself in the clip's fantasy on a TV. Obsessed, he strides right over the lunch coutner, stepping in people's plates, right up to the TV set, trying to figure out how to get inside the screen. Given the perfect felicity of such spectacular pulp fantasy, the frequent complaints one hears that this video is tasteless are rendered moot. Of *course* it's tasteless—that's the point.

M, "Pop Muzik" (from the Sire-Warner Brothers Records album *New York London Paris Munich*), 1980, directed by Brian Grant, produced by Scott Millaney for Millaney-Grant. Not unlike Toni Basil's "Mickey," Brian Grant's rock-video bow makes up for its studio-bound shots against the same white-void background with verve, smarts, a variety of camera angles and kinetic editing; all it lacks is choreography as stunning as Basil's. The song, with its elastic twang guitar, fatback horns, Andrews Sisters-on-helium "shoo-be-do-be-do-wop" harmonies, and stop-start computer beat, is easily as wonderful a piece of ephemeral pop fodder as "Mickey," and that helps make this video as much a classic as "Mickey." Grant just keeps cutting, between M (né Robin Scott) pounding out the rhythm on a bass drum or wreaking havoc on a turntable (set up on a huge album-shaped table), and a pair of new-wave dollies. In a memorable final sequence, the dollies flank M at the turntable, forming a comical *dis*assembly line that disposes of 45s with slap-happy robotic movements.

Madness, "Our House" (from the Geffen Records album *Madness*), 1983, produced and directed by Dave Robinson. Madness videos are essentially interchangeable: they're all madcap-funny, full of Lesterian antics and music-hall slapstick; there's always group-formation movement, whether eccentric dancing or, as here, the band members' shifting their heads from side to side while watching TV; inevitably there is someone dropping in via parachute or swinging on wires up above the earth bound band. From their very first clip, the Chuck Statler-directed "Madness," little has changed; and no wonder, for as Statler himself says, "A band like Madness didn't know or care much about making videos, but then again, you can't say they had nothing to do with the clips—with a band like them, you just let them behave, point the camera, and you have a great clip." "Our House" stands out from the rest in that here Madness refine their nutty personae with hearty doses of sentimentality, while Robinson's ever-active camera provides a panorama of the shenanigans in their house (which contains squash courts, swimming-pool-sized baths, etc., and in which the band play tick-tack-toe on sleepy Mom's forehead and the like).

John Cougar Mellencamp, "Crumblin' Down" (from the Polygram Records album *Uh-Huh*), 1983, directed by Chris Gabrin, produced by Simon Fields for Limelight. We are in what appears to be a sparsely furnished warehouse. A giant ladder, a row of parking meters, and a single light bulb burning atop a tall pole comprise a starkly geometric set, atmospherically lit in deep reds and blues glowing from the shadows. Gabrin, using some of the sharpest art direction in the history of rock video, then simply sets Mellencamp here and has him let loose with an absolutely riveting performance: when Mellencamp lip-syncs the line "I know I'm a real cool dancer," he proves it by leaping the parking meters and gyrating, almost out-of-control, right out of the picture. Towards the end, Gabrin makes exceptionally tasteful use of special effects, spinning multi-image trails of Mellencamp's dancing form as the star pirouettes, dips, and sways. Easily one of the classiest and most effective performance videos ever.

Men at Work, "It's a Mistake" (from the Columbia Records album *Cargo*), 1983, produced and directed by Tony Stevens for Kali Productions. Men at Work, one of rock video's great success stories, have always gone for an ultraliteral, Beatles/Madness madcap-antics approach, as in "Who Can It Be Now" and "Down Under"; their literalness is best epitomized in "Overkill," when Colin Hay sings "Time to hit the streets and smell the desperation" and actually sniffs his nostrils. Hay called this video their best clip to date after its summer 1983 release, perhaps because it was Men at Work's first video to add social comment to their trademark approach. The theme here is simple and obvious: it's a mistake to push the button and end the world; war is folly. So what else is new? And the clip may be called into question by some for leavening such a message with the band's usual clowning, both as soldiers on maneuvers and as military brass in the missile control room. But in its own way—and especially in the classic shot of Hay's face wearing an embarrassed "oops" expression after he's "pushed" the button by accidentally stubbing out his cigar in what he thought was an ashtray—it manages to be a sort of offhanded rock-video analogue to *Dr. Strangelove*. It's not Devo's "Beautiful World" by a long shot, but it *is* something. It's also worth noting that this video came out right in the midst of the fervor over the smash hit film *WarGames*.

Men Without Hats, "Safety Dance" (from the Backstreet Record album *Rhythm of Youth*), 1983, directed by Tim Pope, produced by Gordon Lewis for GLO Productions. A far cry from Tim Pope's earlier high-impact video style, "Safety Dance" is shot on lush film stock and plays off the song's madrigallike cadences to evoke a medieval country fair set in the lovely Old English countryside. Pope's assured, wide-screen camera work follows singer Ivan Doroschuk over hill and dale, accompanied by a dwarf jester, a girl, and a bounding little terrier, till he gathers all the people in the town square, where all and sundry take part in the safety dance. Safety from what? Quick cut-ins at the close tell you: Doroschuk shades his eyes and looks up at the skies to see war planes and rockets in black-and-white found-footage. Hmm . . . this could've been a Kinks video, eh? At any rate, it's distinctively warm, very well produced, and makes wonderful use of color, especially the reds everyone seems to wear and the lush forest greens.

The Motels, "Only the Lonely" (from the Capitol Records album *All Four One*), 1982, directed by Russell Mulcahy, produced by Jackie Adams for MGMM. Yet another classically extravagant high-concept job from Mulcahy, overflowing with such stylistic hallmarks and trademark motifs as *femmes fatales,* glamorous nightclubs, old-world decadence, overturned tables, spilling liquids, windblown, back-lit diaphanous curtains and women's garments, and all sorts of meaningful looks and portentous occurrences that finally add up to nothing. And there is the usual Mulcahy spot-the-reference film tribute, this time to the hallucinatory barroom scenes in Stanley Kubrick's *The Shining.* As in the old star-vehicle days of Hollywood, Mulcahy constructs everything around lead singer Martha Davis. She struts through the now empty, now full bar with a desperate look; elegantly dressed gigolos either ignore her or cast her strange glances; during the sax break, a string quartet plays while wind blows their sheet music away; finally, Davis is left prone on a table in the deserted bar, a luxurious leftover from an endless evening of revelry. Or something like that.

The Motels, "Take the 'L' Out of Lover" (from *All Four One*), 1982, directed by Russell Mulcahy, produced by Jackie Adams for MGMM. Really not all that different in mood and feeling from "Only the Lonely," but vastly different in technique. Here, Mulcahy places the video proceedings within a "True Lover" comic book—scenes open with pages turned, etc. Mulcahy's water fetish surfaces again, with lovers on the beach splashed by a wave and Martha Davis diving into a pool in s-l-o-w motion. You can also play spot-the-film-quote again; this time something has been lifted from Francis Ford Coppola's *One from the Heart.* Overall, however, as with most Mulcahy videos, you are swept away by the dazzling combination of high production values, overpowering technique, and provocatively ambiguous image-mongering.

Musical Youth, "Pass the Dutchie" (from the MCA Records album *Youth of Today*), 1982, directed by Don Letts, produced by Siobhan Barron for Limelight. "I always like to throw a spanner in the works," says the politically committed Letts, and here he does it in style. Just as the song itself disguises hard-bitten social protest ("How does it feel when you got no food?") with lilting pop-reggae, Letts leavens his courtroom prosecution/persecution scenario with dollops of slapstick humor and Mack Sennett/Richard Lester antic mischief. Musical Youth themselves enliven the proceedings considerably with their fresh-faced energy, and finally come off as both adorable and potentially unlawful.

Olivia Newton-John, "Physical" (from the MCA Records album *Physical*), 1981, directed by Brian Grant, produced by Scott Millaney for MGMM. A slapstick health-spa-workout analogue for the song's celebration of carnality, built Mallet-style from electric video colors and constant quick cuts from medium-wide angle setups to close-ups, finally enlivened by Olivia's own forthright performance. The best scene is the last one, making a hilarious seriocomic connection between body-consciousness and homosexuality, as two now hunky, former fatties spurn Olivia's wide-eyed advances only to walk hand in hand to the showers. Somehow the video—not unlike the song—manages to be both provocative and innocent.

The Police, "Every Breath You Take" (from the IRS/A&M Records album *Synchronicity*), 1983, directed by Kevin Godley and Lol Creme, produced by Lexi Godfrey and Fiona Fitzherbert for Media Lab. Maybe the most outstanding enhanced-performance video ever, perfectly complementing the mood and pace of a classic song with immaculate video-sculpture setups, atmospheric lighting, slow-dissolve edits, and lingering superimpositions. According to Godley, "We made this one as a direct reaction to all the constant quick-cutting we kept seeing in videos on MTV." Godley also cites the influence of Gjon Mile's classic forties jazz short *Jammin' the Blues;* another possible influence may have been David Bowie's similarly subdued black-and-white performance videos for "Wild Is the Wind" or "Heroes." "Every Breath You Take" was made in four different versions: straight black and white, and black and white tinted with red, blue, or yellow. Any way you slice it, it's an exceptional piece.

Olivia Newton-John, appropriately framed by a muscleman's bicep in "Physical" (1982), directed by Brian Grant, and as responsible as anything for successfully crossing ONJ over to a sassier, punkier image

The Pretenders, "Brass in Pocket" (from the Sire-Warner Brothers Records album *The Pretenders*), 1980, produced and directed by Mark Robinson for Modern Productions. Pretenders singer-songwriter Chryssie Hynde proves she has as much presence on screen as on record, playing a waitress in a working-class café that's visited by her carefree band mates and their chic girlfriends. Hynde and the band members make tentative eye contact, the girlfriends get mad, and band and girls split, leaving Hynde behind. The drama is handled a bit clumsily, but it's still affecting, managing to turn the cocky self-assertion of the "I'm special" chorus into Hynde's last-resort defense of her self-esteem.

The Ramones, "Psychotherapy" (from the Sire Records album *Subterranean Jungle*), 1983, produced and directed by Francis Delia for Wolfe Company. Along with Wall of Voodoo's "Mexican Radio," Delia's best work yet. Here, rock video's clichéd asylum-inmate motifs (going all the way back to Russell Mulcahy's 1979 "Making Plans for Nigel" with XTC, at least) come home to roost—with a vengeance. Delia's refusal to use any it's-only-a-joke safety valve heightens the brutal tension of his savvy creep-show touches and some very convincing performances. Highlights: a stunning *Alien* homage during an attempted lobotomy—a sequence graphic enough to keep this video off the air- and cable-waves—and the closing shot of the hero-inmate unlocking his fellow-crazies (who, of course, include the Ramones themselves).

Prince, "Little Red Corvette" (from the Warner Brothers Records album *1999*), 1983, directed by Bryan Greenberg, produced by Beth Broday for Broday-Greenberg Productions. Nearly every director and performer interviewed for this book mentioned Prince's "1999" and "Little Red Corvette" as classic performance clips and as welcome relief from overdone concept clips. What's so special about them? Mainly Prince himself: he can stare down the camera like nobody's business, and that's all he has to do to make the screen smolder. Both clips look virtually identical—set on the same stylized smoke-filled stage with venetian-blind backdrops, with the same quick cutting and garish video pinks and purples—which, despite the fact that Greenberg directed this one and Bruce Gowers the "1999" clip, reinforces the contention of Warner Brothers' Jo Bergman that "Prince pretty much directs his own videos himself." So why pick this over "1999"? Hard to say, exactly, but Prince's performance here seems just a tad more personal and camerawise.

Quiet Riot, "Cum on Feel the Noize" (from the Pasha/CBS Records album *Metal Health*), 1983, directed by Mark Rezyka, produced by Mary Guida for Pendulum Productions. Another great rock-video sequel: here Rezyka takes off from his equally fine "Metal Health," which also keyed in on the metallic goalie mask from Quiet Riot's album cover. In fact, the kid who stars in this one is the same kid to whom Quiet Riot's lead singer tossed the mask from the stage in "Metal Health" (the sequence is briefly replayed here). Otherwise, another classic heavy-metal scenario: the kid turns on his stereo, and his entire room cums on and feels the noize—the bed and walls and floor shake, the stereo grows humongous, smoke fills the room. When the kid finally manages to pull the plug on his stereo (the plug, too, having grown to mammoth proportions), there is an explosion, and in an exquisite shot that Rezyka could and should have held a few seconds longer, the kid's bedroom opens up into a stage on which Quiet Riot are playing. From then on it's straight performance, until the fade, when we cut back to the kid's room: as the song fades, the smoke clears, and the stereo shrinks back to normal size, *but* there are now eyes in the metal mask hanging on his wall. This story may continue. . . .

The Residents, "One-Minute Movies" ("Moisture," "Act of Being Polite," "Perfect Love," and "Simple Song," from the Ralph Records album *Residents Commercial Album*), 1980, directed by Graeme Whifler with the Residents, produced by the Residents for the Cryptic Corp. Petite pinnacles of haunting, dreamlike symbolism, each clip evoking serious otherworldly ritual. The Residents' giant bloodshot-eyeball masks are recurrent motifs; the imagery itself gains power because Whifler and the Residents never try to rationalize or gratuitously contextualize it. The best of these four minimasterpieces are "Act of Being Polite" (a seated girl holding a package, wearing the eyeball mask and a Raggedy Ann wig; lovely Wes Takahashi animation of a heart being squeezed by a steel pile driver and then, as a grimacing face appears on the valentine, bursting) and "Perfect Love" (middle-aged Ralph stock-video player Bill Owen is watching TV while lying on his bed; eyeball-masked Residents hand puppets appear on screen "lip-synching" the lyrics; the TV emits smoke, and in about a dozen shifting-perspective quick cuts, Owen and his bed fly up to the ceiling; it ends with an "impossible" static shot of Owen, defying gravity, sitting on a wall perplexedly regarding a painted portrait of a woman). But all four videos are stunning, because of the Residents' incredible imagery and Whifler's equally awesome use of camera angles and movement, cutting and color. Also worth noting are Whifler's constantly zooming found-footage montage and collage for the Residents' "Hello Skinny," and his terrifying "Songs for Swinging Larvae" for Renaldo and the Loaf (the clip is based on an actual California child-abduction case). Rock video doesn't come much better than this. Once seen, the "One-Minute Movies" cannot be forgotten.

The Rolling Stones, "Undercover of the Night" (from the Rolling Stones/Atco Records album *Undercover*), 1983, directed by Julian Temple, produced by Michael Hamlin for Midnight Films. The Stones had always made rather shabby, we-couldn't-care-less clips—until this one, a dense extravaganza of some of Temple's favorite motifs (narrative structure and momentum, multi-allusive comments on media and their relation to reality, the idea of a rock star playing multiple roles—here Mick Jagger plays three parts) shot on location in Mexico City. The song is a paranoiac look at the repressiveness and terrorism of coup-riddled Central America—and so is the video, in its remarkably sweeping yet brutally direct style. Jagger's white-suited, mustachioed journalist alter ego (which, along with the breathtaking opening pan, recalls Orson Welles's *Touch of Evil,* also shot south of the border, as well as the more obvious comparisons to *Missing* and *Under Fire*) watches the Stones perform on TV, surveys the carnage of a burning city in revolt against martial law, finds a terrified native girl quivering under her bed covers (get it?), and tries to flee the scene with her; the "real" Jagger watches the Stones perform on TV along with the same native girl in bed (is this a flashback?) before they're raided by the authorities; as guerrilla Keith Richards prowls the scene wearing a skull mask, the "real" Jagger is marched out onto a bridge, a bag over his head, and shot several times in full view of Temple's unflinching camera (thus the clip was banned by the BBC for excessive violence); white-suited Jagger is shot to death in his car at the end while making his getaway. Periodic cut-ins reveal that we're seeing it all through the eyes of a young American boy and girl, watching it all at home on MTV; a black-comedy ending has a military figure rushing into their room to "fire" a remote control at the TV in a futile effort to turn it off—and the last thing the recalcitrant set flashes is the MTV logo! Easily one of the most ambitious and provocative rock videos ever. Hats off to Temple, and to the Stones for going with him.

The Rolling Stones, "She Was Hot" (from *Undercover*), 1984, directed by Julian Temple, produced by Michael Hamlin for Midnight Films. As in Thomas Dolby's "Hyperactive!" and all too few other rock videos, a delightfully playful use of special effects dominates proceedings as Anita Morris, from the hit Broadway show *Nine,* portrays the title character visiting her incendiary sexuality upon the various Stones: the seams of her stockings ignite, she smokes Keith Richards' cigarette right down to the filter in a split second, she burns Mick Jagger right into the floor (literally), she turns Ron Wood's guitar to floppy rubber, she causes amplifiers and TV sets to explode and the very earth to shake. Perhaps Temple's most remarkable directorial feat here, though, is in the closing scene, with Stones drummer Charlie Watts portraying a sleazoid type, winking as he shows us a photo of Morris ("Linda Lava" says the copy on the photo) and picking up the several phones ringing off the hook in his office (ostensibly, worldwide demand for Morris's heated talents): Temple actually gets Watts to do more than crack his trademark smirk! This closing sequence also features a few nice touches quite typical of Temple's style: the film-within-the-film motif (a TV screen in Watts's office showing first Morris, then Mick Jagger), and the musical "tag" of playing the early Stones classic "Off the Hook" as the clip fades out.

The Raybeats, "Jack the Ripper" (from the Shanachie Records album *It's Only a Movie!*), 1984, produced and directed by Pierce Rafferty and Margie Crimmins. The greatest use of found-footage montage in rock video since Devo's "Beautiful World"—and fittingly, since the latter was a sort of mini-*Atomic Cafe,* this one's from the makers of *Atomic Cafe.* It's also the best instrumental video ever, after Godley and Creme's Herbie Hancock clips. Here, to charging, twanging neo-surf rock, Rafferty and Crimmins set more cold war-vintage archival footage: news reels of Red Chinese appearing to gird up for chemical warfare, counterpointed by lovely, naïvely futurist fifties American techno-propaganda animation (somewhat reminiscent of "New Frontier"), and snippets of mild suburban perversity (a cigar-chomping dad sashays about his rec room to his new hi-fi, implying the decadence of consumerism; a clean-cut school kid freaks out in class and gleefully rips his textbooks apart). Thanks to magnificent editing (by Rafferty and Crimmins), the Mongols end up blowing away the asleep-at-the-switch, dreaming-of-tomorrow, high-living Yanks. Cautionary parable as barbed revisionist social critique, just as *Atomic Cafe* was, but sharper. And little short of awesome as a piece of visual-music synergy.

Siouxsie and the Banshees, "Spellbound" (from the Polydor Records album *Greatest Hits*), 1981, directed by Clive Richardson, produced by Polydor Records UK. Richardson's best video ever by far has nothing to do with the Hitchcock film of the same name—except that it's far more grippingly suspenseful than Hitch's weakest well-known feature. Matching the song's taut dissonances and urgent rush of tribal rhythm, Richardson uses handheld cameras and Max Ophuls-on-amphetamines tracks and dollies, the camera lens hugging the ground as it races hungrily for the kill through polarized color fields and forests. Intercut are shots of Siouxsie herself performing in Kabuki-like clothing and movements, and shots of shogun-assassin bandits moving in for a kung fu kill. More than merely atmospheric, the clip captures and superbly intensifies the visceral rush of fear and flight, hunger and pursuit, and leaves the viewer breathless.

Bruce Springsteen, "Atlantic City" (from the CBS Records album *Nebraska*), 1982, produced and directed by Arnold Levine for Teletronics. This video made some waves initially because Springsteen was nowhere to be seen in it. Hopefully, this did not cause people to miss the video's elegantly made point about the passing of a way of life along the now-deserted Boardwalk. Shooting entirely in luminous, near-dreamy black and white (as in Bryan Adams's "This Time," directed by Steve Barron, which was shot by famed movie cinematographer Laszlo Kovacs), Levine paints an ominously elegiac picture of the Boardwalk, the once-magnificent/now-deserted hotels, and cuts it with shots of the new casinos that have taken over Atlantic City. Emotionally evocative without being sentimental, Levine's "Atlantic City" is also perfectly apposite to Springsteen's song, and even manages to rise to the level of subtle social criticism.

Stray Cats, "Stray Cat Strut" (from the Capitol-EMI Records album *Built for Speed*), 1981, directed by Julian Temple, produced by Siobhan Barron and Simon Fields for Limelight. Obviously just playing on the idea of the band's name and letting his imagination run wild, Temple applied strict directorial discipline and made use of ingenious art direction—as in the brilliant use of color and purposely stagy sets—to craft what may be the finest, truest visualization of rockabilly since Elvis Presley's big-production dance number in *Jailhouse Rock*. There's a cartoonishness to the look of the video that perfectly complements the band's stature as pomp-adore revivalists, and Temple's camera prowls like, well, like a stray cat, befitting the tune's confident swagger. The band perform in a back alley set replete with street lights and neon signs, trash cans overflowing with fish skeletons, clothes hanging out to dry from the tenement windows above, real cats, cartoon cats, bopping ponytailed rockabilly dollies, and the classic irate old neighbor lady who throws buckets of water and garbage out her window to shoo the stray cats away. When the rockabilly dollies finally come dancing out to flank Stray Cat Brian Setzer, it's no less than a minor epiphany.

Stray Cats, "Sexy & 17" (from the Capitol-EMI Records album *Rant 'n' Rave with the Stray Cats*), 1983, directed by Ian Leech, produced by John Diaz for Cinerock and T'boo Dalton for EMI. Commercial director Leach, shooting in beautiful thirty-five-millimeter film, starts things off with a nod to *Blackboard Jungle* and the general collective unconscious of antsy teens who are stuck in school (rock myth meets cinema myth): a mean, dowdy Miss Crabtree-style teacher addresses her class; Stray Cat Brian Setzer, seated behind a bespectacled nerd, declares as the tune's guitar riff kicks in that he can't deal with school.

The classroom erupts as the rhythm section comes in, and from there it's colorful, insouciantly sexy and funny action all the way. Leach builds and maintains a strong visual rhythm, cutting from the band cavorting to Setzer's sweetheart getting dressed and made up, dancing and winking at the camera; but the best, most winning sequences are those in which teachers and students take turns slamming each other against hallway lockers while lip-synching the chorus.

Donna Summer, "She Works Hard for the Money" (from the Geffen Records album *She Works Hard for the Money*), 1983, directed by Brian Grant, produced by Chryssie Smith for MGMM. Grant wisely avoided focusing on the wooden Summer, instead depicting a lousy day in the lousy life of a typical working mother—a waitress and sweatshop worker who dreams of being a dancer—played marvelously by Cindy Devore. If only for finally positing a viable feminist alternative to the typical rock-video portrayals of women, "She Works Hard for the Money" is a great, important video. Beyond that, it's very well put together, thanks to Grant's assured, objective-subjective *mise-en-scène* and Devore's penetrating performance. Grant elected to feature a white actress simply to guarantee MTV acceptance; the song and video still manage to carry a more or less universal impact. Grant says he partially intended the clip as "an answer to *Flashdance*—it's all about what might happen to the working woman-dancer ten years down the line. Beyond that, it's just a statement of how bloody horrible it can be to be a woman in today's society."

Supertramp, "It's Raining Again" (from the A&M Records album *Famous Last Words*), 1982, directed by Russell Mulcahy, produced by Jackie Adams for MGMM. Mulcahy's trademark grand sweep rhapso- dizes a touching little tale of love and/or friendship found, lost, and doggedly sought, with the male protagonist (the band themselves are visible only in quick cameos; for instance, sax man John Anthony Helliwell plays a bus driver) enduring humiliation and worse (a brutal back alley beating) in his quixotic quest. Miraculously, Mulcahy does not overdo the rain motif, and his unusual (for him, anyway) restraint makes his use of water symbolism all the more poignantly poetic. As usual, Mulcahy uses multiple locations and showy camera moves a- plenty, but the song's sweet, wistful sentimentality is the star, making this one of Mulcahy's more emotionally affecting clips.

Talking Heads, "Once in a Lifetime" (from the Warner Brothers Records album *Remain in Light*), 1980, produced and directed by Toni Basil and David Byrne. The music merges Afro-polyrhythmic funk with Philip Glass's steady-state trance-music tintinnabulations; the lyrics hint enigmatically at some sort of spiritual epiphany amid the everyday. In the video, David Byrne combines his own penguin-on-LSD spastic dancing with the strangely evocative body language of possessed preachers and shamans that he's seen in film footage. We see Byrne, in suit and horn-rims, doing an Egyptian chicken dance in the foreground while multiple Byrnes execute the same moves in the background. We see Byrne "swimming" against a bubbly blue *moiré* matte background. Only at the end do we see the "real" Byrne placidly chanting the chorus's contrapuntal underlay, "Letting the days go by. . . ." A great song, a great video, each full of life's bittersweet mysteries, concealing as they reveal, tantalizing with hidden meanings that are just on the tips of our visual tongues. The concepts were all Byrne's; Basil acted as technical director. On the new-wave club scene, this video justifiably caused the biggest sensation since Devo's and Bowie's videos; also fittingly, it was among the first clips inducted into the Museum of Modern Art's permanent rock-video installation.

Talking Heads, "Burning Down the House" (from the Warner Brothers Records album *Speaking in Tongues*), 1983, produced and directed by David Byrne. As David Bowie himself put it, "For my personal taste, this is exactly what I think videos should be. There are rough edges, some amateurism, and it's all so appealing. Mistakes are often more appealing, and it's full of great ideas. Ideas cost nothing. . . ." Well, "Burning Down the House" is *not* high-concept slick, but it could hardly be called amateurish, either. The key, though, is the word *ideas*. Back in 1980, with "Once in a Lifetime," David Byrne demonstrated that along with Devo and the Residents, he is one of the very few rock performers with a strong sense of original imagery and ideas with integrity. This video is surreal and non-narrative and full of enigmatically evocative images that stay with you, though you can't explain why: Byrne's face, and then flames projected against the side of a house; the faces of other people—a young boy, an old woman—projected onto the faces of the lip-synching Talking Heads; those other people literally hanging all over the Heads while they play in a low-ceilinged ballroom; Byrne and his young-boy alter ego with their backs to the camera, matted against a screen full of static. The theme seems to be psychic and physical possession, transference of persona; the "house" burning down may be our own sense of self. Projections were courtesy of New York avant-garde performance and video artist Julia Hayward.

Tommy Tutone, "867-5309/Jenny" (from the Columbia Records album *Tommy Tutone II*), 1981, produced and directed by Mark Robinson for Modern Productions. Along with Rick Springfield's "Don't Talk to Strangers" (which actually preceded this), this is the classic example of a seldom-seen manifestation of a hard-rock lover's paranoia: the guy who is made a cuckold by his girl and ends up a pitiful voyeur, watching her get it on with another guy. In this case, "867-5309" serves as both hot blond Jenny's phone number and as Tutone's prisoner's number after he gets arrested for being a Peeping Tom. Tutone's likable, realistic performance adds to the sting of this clip.

Tom Tom Club, "Genius of Love" (from the Sire-Warner Brothers album *Tom Tom Club*), 1981, directed by Annabelle Jankel and Rocky Morton, produced by Andy Morahan for Cucumber Studios. Animated figures—based on the cartoon graphics of New York artist James Rizzi that were used on Tom Tom Club's album cover—constantly metamorphose, in time to the slinkily syncopated eighties funk beat. The naive psychedelic primitivism of Rizzi's drawings combines with the nonstop kinetic pace to form a festive, slap-happy animated dance for a winsome dance classic. This is the ultimate rock video for little kids of all ages.

Pat Travers, "I'd Rather See You Dead" (from the Polydor Records album *Black Pearl*), 1980, produced and directed by Ken Walz. As in ZZ Top's "Gimme All Your Lovin'," Martin Briley's "Salt in My Tears," and Krokus's "Screaming in the Night," hard-rock macho sexism and violence are neutralized through sheer comical excess. Here, Pat keeps trying and failing to kill his spunky little girlfriend: he sticks her with a knife that turns out to be made of rubber; he slips her a Mickey in a drink, and she downs it smilingly to no apparent ill effect; he even fails at blowing up her Jaguar. Pat should've known things weren't going to work out right at the start of the clip, when he looks at her body in a coffin and she suddenly wakes with a start to lip-sync a lyric. Very black humor, yes, but humor nonetheless—and it cannot be overemphasized that humor is the secret weapon in rock video that's used all too little. Otherwise, this is a characteristically well-produced Ken Walz clip, and like the others Walz produced in 1980—Travers's "I La La Love You," Blue Angel's "Late," and "I Had a Love"—it's not only smoothly paced and nice-looking, but it daringly, for its time, eschews performance altogether (the Blue Angel clips used only minimal performance, which was still daring for the times).

Twisted Sister, "You Can't Stop Rock 'n' Roll" (from the Atlantic Records album *You Can't Stop Rock 'n' Roll*), 1983, directed by Arthur Ellis, produced by Simon Fields for Limelight. Yet another classic heavy-metal pulp scenario: Twisted Sister's tune is not only powerful enough to blow out the protective earphones of the stodgy "Taste Squad" officers tailing the band, it's also enough to turn all the Taste Squad operatives who hear it (including those back at the office listening in via remote transmission from the Taste Squad car) into raving, long-haired, denim-clad, mascaraed heavy-metal maniacs—just like the title says. And Arthur Ellis demonstrates an exceptional control of narrative momentum: everything moves right along, there's nothing forced or extraneous, and Twisted Sister deliver a characteristically apt heavy-metal video performance.

Ultravox, "The Thin Wall" (from the Chrysalis Records album *Vienna*), 1981, directed by Russell Mulcahy, produced by Lexi Godfrey for MGM. Mulcahy's made several eye-catching videos for Ultravox: "Vienna," with its oppressive old-world decadence and perversion (also the first rock video with the image bordered in black at the top and bottom to give the illusion of a Cinemascope screen), and "The Voice" (arranged in history book chapters, with written titles zooming out at the viewer for each new sequence—a technique Marcello Anciano later used in Peter Gabriel's "I Don't Remember"). But "The Thin Wall" may be the most striking example of controlled hysteria in exploiting the typical rock-video concept-clip themes of anxiety, paranoia, and related symptoms of psychic dissolution. Most memorable sequences: a car that suddenly, inexplicably fills up with water; the hallucinatory image of a line of swimmers stroking through desert sand; and two more classic Mulcahy spot-the-reference film quotes—the giant elasticized checkerboard floor (a Fellini reference not unlike the one Mulcahy used in the set for Kim Carnes's "Bette Davis Eyes" or Kansas's "Play the Game") and the maniacal arms and hands reaching out from the "thin walls" of a corridor (directly from Roman Polanski's *Repulsion*).

Visage, "Mind of a Toy" (from the Polydor Records album *Fade to Grey*), 1981, directed by Kevin Godley and Lol Creme, produced by Lexi Godfrey. Godley and Creme gave New Romantic fashion band Visage the lushest video treatment anyone had ever received: this was one of the first rock videos shot on film (it predates Duran Duran's "Hungry like the Wolf" by several months) and makes ravishing use of muted, filtered colors, diaphanous lighting, sumptuous sets, fluid dissolves, and slow motion. Consciously or unconsciously, Russell Mulcahy alluded to it in Duran Duran's "Is There Something I Should Know?" when he showed a ball bouncing along a staircase. Along with Godley and Creme's "Fade to Grey" for Visage, this clip is every bit as striking and beautiful (if not more so) as Visage's Steve Strange always seemed to think *he* was. Siobhan Barron of Limelight echoes the sentiments of many others when she says, "I always despised Steve Strange until I saw Godley and Creme's Visage videos."

Wall of Voodoo, "Mexican Radio" (from the IRS Records album *Call of the West*), 1983, produced and directed by Francis Delia for Wolfe Company. A stylized studio set with a deco-moderne TV monitor before which the band performs, a door standing freely in the desert, a roasting iguana, a man's face emerging from a bowl of beans, cheap, grainy footage of the hubbub of everyday Mexican street life, and vocalist Stan Ridgeway's fine line in facial tics (not to mention the old self-referential trick of shooting the band being shot in the studio set) all somehow coalesce into a seductively bizarre little off-the-wall gem, easily the best work to date by the wildly erratic Delia. MTV exposure of this video was instrumental in giving Wall of Voodoo their only hit record.

Weird Al Yankovic, "Ricky" (from the Columbia/Scotti Brothers Records album *Weird Al Yankovic*), 1982, directed by Janet Greek, produced by George Cook. Weird Al, the man who brought you such classic pop parodies as "My Bologna" (based on the Knack's "My Sharona") and "Another One Rides the Bus" (Queen's "Another One Bites the Dust"), here lovingly sends up Toni Basil's "Mickey" by way of "I Love Lucy." Al himself plays Ricky Ricardo, Tress MacNeille plays Lucy, and they're both fine. The clip is of course in black and white—until the fiesta finale, when Weird Al is finally revealed, playing his accordion. The classic shot here comes, during a typical "Lucy" domestic squabble, when her iron burns a hole through both Ricky's shirt *and* the ironing board. In a marvelous comic take-off on rock video's typical use of geometric framing and meaningful looks, Ricky and Lucy gaze portentously through the triangular hole the iron has burned through the board. Subsequently, Weird Al parodied Joan Jett's "I Love Rock & Roll" with "I Love Rocky Road" (directed by Dror Soref): whereas Joan got a barroom full of rowdies to raise their fists in unison, Al gets an ice-cream parlor full of folks to lift their sugar cones as one. But "Ricky" is funnier and better executed, and perhaps not coincidentally, got a lot more exposure. Late-breaking honorable mention to Weird Al's amazing take-off on "Beat It"—"Eat It."

Wet Picnic, "He Believes" (from the Unicorn Records EP *Wet Picnic*), 1982, directed by Marcello Epstein, produced by Alexis Olmchenko

A man's head, lip-synching the lyric "Radio," suddenly appears in a bowl full of beans—one of many arrestingly bizarre images in Wall of Voodoo's highly successful clip for "Mexican Radio" (1983), directed by Francis Delia

---

for Pendulum Productions. The song itself is a limp washout of a ballad, but the video! Ah, the video: now *this* is a minimovie. Breathtakingly shot, with superior production values and all sorts of painstakingly achieved special effects, a luminously dreamy, multilevel play on a man's fantasies of sexual wish fulfillment and frustration, liberally sprinkled with both hot soft-core sex (the subject watching a porn flick in which a stunning blond nurse strips for her patient and humps the bedposts) and mordant black humor (the subject spies the object of his ardor reclining in an alley, but when he moves to embrace her, she's only a cardboard cutout poster; he picks it up and carries it away regardless). Perhaps the most impressive example to date of a totally awesome video rescuing a thoroughly mediocre song—though unfortunately the video is too sexy to have been played anywhere but on Playboy Channel's *Hot Rocks.*

Whodini, "Magic's Wand" (from an Arista/Jive Records single), 1983, produced and directed by Alvin Hartley. I'm tempted to cite

Hartley's clip for Grandmaster Flash and the Furious Five's "The Message," but this one actually does a better job of enhancing both the song and the performers. It's a rap tribute to New York funk DJ "Mr. Magic," who himself makes a guest appearance, surrounded by Whodini members and other dancers who are flipped from one side of the screen to the other via digital effects. The best sequence, though, is the opening, wherein one Whodini raps an explanation of rap to another Whodini acting as a curious bystander. Hartley's clips are very low budget, and they do look it, but there's something here that all the money in the world can't buy: a forthright, streetwise energy and endearing charm. Besides, come to think of it, even though this clip cost well under ten thousand dollars, it doesn't look *that* low budget at all.

Yello, "I Love You" (from the Elektra Records album *You Gotta Say Yes to Another Excess*), 1983, produced and directed by Dieter Meier for This Heat Films. A three-piece synthesizer band from Switzerland, once on the Residents' Ralph Records label, Yello's leader Dieter Meier is also an experienced experimental filmmaker with some other striking Yello videos under his belt, including "Pinball Cha Cha" and "The Evening's Young." "I Love You" avoids Meier's trademark pixilations in favor of lush, cinematic sweep. Yello's Boris Blank makes hilarious use of facial tics as a blasé macho man, the highly suspicious object of his girlfriend's outright adoration; the girl is played by Blank's real-life paramour, and she's perfect—a cross between Lina Wertmuller and Andrea Martin's Edith Prickley of *SCTV*. The clip equates the macho man's fear of romantic commitment with the dangerous way the girl drives their car. There is some wonderful car-mounted photography and some enigmatically evocative shoe fetishism, culminating in the lovely shot of Blank making the girl's shoes dance while superimposed fireworks go off around his head.

Neil Young, "Cry Cry Cry" (from the Geffen Records album *Everybody's Rockin'*), 1983, directed by Tim Pope, produced by Gordon Lewis for GLO Productions. A sustained, surreal non sequitur: Neil Young stands by a desert highway, flagging down cars and trains that never stop for him. There's no real narrative and no logical conclusion, but there is one of the funniest shots in rock-video history: after a life-size freight train whizzes by, the camera pulls back to reveal Young standing with legs apart as a toy train puffs along between his parted feet. The video is a classic for that alone. Also worth mentioning is Pope's clip for Young's "Wonderin'," wherein half-speed and double-speed camera recording and playback are expertly used to give the impression, as Pope puts it, "that Neil is living his life out of time with everyone else around him." Like "Cry Cry Cry," "Wonderin' " possesses a curious comic melancholy, as much due to Young's own cockeyed deadpan performance (he's the Jack Nicholson of rock) as to Pope's subtle directorial hand.

ZZ Top, "Gimme All Your Lovin' " (from the Warner Brothers Records album *Eliminator*), 1983, directed by Tim Newman, produced by Gary Buonanno for Dancing Buffalo Productions. Already described at some length earlier in this book, this is an absolute masterpiece of product identification as ritual symbolism: three strutting femmes who are cosmopolitan counterparts to the magically materializing band members who appear at key moments to execute their Johnny Carson golf-swing motion and move a grease monkey's fantasy along; the cherry-red hot rod from the album cover; and the double-Z key chain. It also has the classic, ambiguous "resolution": was it all a dream? It seems that way, but then the grease monkey sees the key chain, and then the hot rod zooms by. . . . Many people accuse this clip of typical rock-video sexism, but it's so obviously and perfectly realized a piece of male-adolescent wish fulfillment that such complaints seem a bit unfair. Along with the subsequent "Sharp-Dressed Man," it is the first, and possibly best-ever, rock-video sequel treatment. Still, "Gimme All Your Lovin' " works better on its own.

INDEX

ABOUT THE AUTHOR

Michael Shore, a former editor of *The Soho News* and *Home Video,* has written about music, video, and related matters for *The Village Voice, Omni, ArtNews, Musician, Music-Sound Output, The Record, Video Review, Billboard,* and *Rolling Stone.* He contributed to *The Rolling Stone Encyclopedia of Rock and Roll* and *The Rolling Stone Rock Almanac.* He was also a featured speaker at the Canadian Independent Record Producers Association's October 1983 "Video Visions" seminar in Toronto, and was a judge and presenter at *Billboard*'s first annual Video Music Awards in Pasadena, California, in December 1983.